Employment Discrimination Law: Selected Statutes and Regulations

Employment Discrimination Law: Selected Statutes and Regulations

EIGHTH EDITION

Arthur B. Smith, Jr.
SHAREHOLDER
OGLETREE, DEAKINS, NASH, SMOAK & STEWART, P.C.
CHICAGO, ILLINOIS

Charles B. Craver
FREDA H. ALVERSON PROFESSOR OF LAW
GEORGE WASHINGTON UNIVERSITY

Ronald Turner
ALUMNAE LAW CENTER PROFESSOR OF LAW
UNIVERSITY OF HOUSTON

CAROLINA ACADEMIC PRESS
Durham, North Carolina

Print ISBN 978-1-5310-0017-2
Ebook ISBN 978-1-5310-0018-9

Carolina Academic Press, LLC
700 Kent Street
Durham, NC 27701
Telephone (919) 489-7486
Fax (919) 493-5668
www.caplaw.com

Printed in the United States of America

Contents

Employment Discrimination Law: Selected Statutes and Regulations

U.S. Constitution: 5th, 13th & 14th Amendments

FIFTH AMENDMENT

No person shall be ... deprived of life, liberty, or property, without due process of law....

THIRTEENTH AMENDMENT

SEC. 1. Neither slavery nor involuntary servitude, except as a punishment for crime whereof the party shall have been duly convicted, shall exist within the United States, or any place subject to their jurisdiction.

SEC. 2. Congress shall have power to enforce this article by appropriate legislation.

FOURTEENTH AMENDMENT

SEC. 1. All persons born or naturalized in the United States, and subject to the jurisdiction thereof, are citizens of the United States and of the State wherein they reside. No State shall abridge the privileges or immunities of citizens of the United States; nor shall any State deprive any person of life, liberty, or property, without due process of law; nor deny to any person within its jurisdiction the equal protection of the laws.

....

SEC. 5. The Congress shall have power to enforce, by appropriate legislation, the provisions of this article.

The Surviving Remnants of Post-Civil War Civil Rights Legislation

Civil Provisions

42 U.S.C. § 1981.[1] *Equal rights under the law.*

(a) All persons within the jurisdiction of the United States shall have the same right in every State and Territory to make and enforce contracts, to sue, be parties, give evidence, and to the full and equal benefit of all laws and proceedings for the security of persons and property as is enjoyed by white citizens, and shall be subject to like punishment, pains, penalties, taxes, licenses, and exactions of every kind, and to no other.

(b) For purposes of this section, the term "make and enforce contracts" includes the making, performance, modification, and termination of contracts, and the enjoyment of all benefits, privileges, terms and conditions of the contractual relationship.

(c) The rights protected by this section are protected against impairment by nongovernmental discrimination and impairment under color of State law.

42 U.S.C. § 1981A.[2] *Damages in Cases of Intentional Discrimination in Employment.*

(a) Right of Recovery.

(1) Civil rights. In an action brought by a complaining party under section 706 or 717 of the Civil Rights Act of 1964 (42 U.S.C. 2000e-5) against a respondent who engaged in unlawful intentional discrimination (not an employment practice that is unlawful because of its disparate impact) prohibited under section 703, 704, or 717 of the Act (42 U.S.C. 2000e-2 or 2000e-3), and provided that the complaining party cannot recover under section 1977 of the Revised Statutes (42 U.S.C. 1981), the complaining party may recover compensatory and punitive damages as allowed in subsection (b), in addition to any relief authorized by section 706(g) of the Civil Rights Act of 1964, from the respondent.

(2) Disability. In action brought by a complaining party under the powers, remedies, and procedures set forth in section 706 or 717 of the Civil Rights Act of 1964 (as provided in section 107(a) of the Americans with Disabilities Act of 1990 (42 U.S.C. 12117(a)), and section 505(a)(1) of the Rehabilitation Act of 1973 (29 U.S.C. 794a(a)(1)), respectively) against a respondent who engaged in unlawful intentional discrimination (not an employment practice that is unlawful because of its disparate impact) under section 501 of the Rehabilitation Act of 1973 (29 U.S.C. 791) and the regulations implementing section 501, or who violated the requirements of section 501 of the Act or the regulations implementing section 501 concerning the provisions of a reasonable accommodation, or section 102 of the Americans with Disabilities Act of 1990 (42 U.S.C. 12112), or committed a violation of section 102(b)(5) of the Act, against an individual, the complaining party may recover compensatory and punitive damages as allowed in subsection (b), in addition to any relief authorized by section 706(g) of the Civil Rights Act of 1964, from the respondent.

(3) Reasonable accommodation and good faith effort. In cases where a discriminatory practice involves the provision of a reasonable accommodation pursuant to section

---

1. Derived from § 1 of the Civil Rights Act of 1866 and §§ 16 and 18 of the Civil Rights Act of 1870. 14 Stat. 27; 16 Stat. 144. In the 1874 revision of the United States Code, it was codified as § 1977. 18 Stat. 348. Amended by the Civil Rights Act of 1991. 105 Stat. 1071 (1991).

2. Added by the Civil Rights Act of 1991. 105 Stat. 1071 (1991).

102(b)(5) of the Americans with Disabilities act of 1990 or regulations implementing section 501 of the Rehabilitation Act of 1973, damages may not be awarded under this section where the covered entity demonstrates good faith efforts, in consultation with the person with the disability who has informed the covered entity that accommodation is needed, to identify and make a reasonable accommodation that would provide such individual with an equally effective opportunity and would not cause an undue hardship on the operation of the business.

(b) Compensatory and Punitive Damages.

(1) Determination of punitive damages. A complaining party may recover punitive damages under this section against a respondent (other than a government, government agency or political subdivision) if the complaining party demonstrates that the respondent engaged in a discriminatory practice or discriminatory practices with malice or with reckless indifference to the federally protected rights of an aggrieved individual.

(2) Exclusions from compensatory damages. Compensatory damages awarded under this section shall not include backpay, interest on backpay, or any other type of relief authorized under section 706(g) of the Civil Rights Act of 1964.

(3) Limitations. The sum of the amount of compensatory damages awarded under this section for future pecuniary losses, emotional pain, suffering, inconvenience, mental anguish, loss of enjoyment of life, and other nonpecuniary losses, and the amount of punitive damages awarded under this section, shall not exceed, for each complaining party.

(A) in the case of a respondent who has more than 14 and fewer than 101 employees in each of 20 or more calendar weeks in the current or preceding calendar year, $50,000;

(B) in the case of a respondent who has more than 100 and fewer than 201 employees in each of 20 or more calendar weeks in the current or preceding calendar year, $100,000; and

(C) in the case of a respondent who has more than 200 and fewer than 501 employees in each of 20 or more calendar weeks in the current or preceding calendar year, $200,000; and

(D) in the case of a respondent who has more than 500 employees in each of 20 or more calendar weeks in the current or preceding calendar year, $300,000.

(4) Construction. Nothing in this section shall be construed to limit the scope of, or the relief available under, section 1977 of the Revised Statutes (42 U.S.C. 1981).

(c) Jury Trial. If a complaining party seeks compensatory or punitive damages under this section

(1) any party may demand a trial by jury; and

(2) the court shall not inform the jury of the limitations described in subsection (b)(3).

(d) Definitions. As used in this section:

(1) Complaining party. The term "complaining party" means

(A) in the case of a person seeking to bring an action under subsection (a)(l), the Equal Employment Opportunity Commission, the Attorney General, or a person who may bring an action or proceeding under title VII of the Civil Rights Act of 1964 (42 U.S.C. 2000e *et seq.*); or

(B) in the case of a person seeking to bring an action under subsection (a)(2), the Equal Employment Opportunity Commission, the Attorney General, a person who may bring an action or proceeding under section 505(a)(l) of the Rehabilitation Act of 1973 (29 U.S.C. 794a(a)(l), or a person who may bring an action or proceeding under title I of the Americans with Disabilities Act of 1990 (42 U.S.C. 12101 et seq.).

(2) Discriminatory practice. The term "discriminatory practice" means the discrimination described in paragraph (1), or the discrimination or the violation described in paragraph (2), of subsection (a).

42 U.S.C. § 1982.[3] *Property rights of citizens.* All citizens of the United States shall have the same right, in every State and Territory, as is enjoyed by white citizens thereof to inherit, purchase, lease, sell, hold, and convey real and personal property.

42 U.S.C. § 1983.[4] *Civil action for deprivation of rights.* Every person who, under color of any statute, ordinance, regulation, custom, or usage, of any State or Territory or the District of Columbia, subjects, or causes to be subjected, any citizen of the United States or other persons within the jurisdiction thereof to the deprivation of any rights, privileges or immunities secured by the Constitution and laws, shall be liable to the person injured in an action of law, suit in equity, or other proper proceedings for redress. For purposes of this section, any Act of Congress applicable exclusively to the District of Columbia shall be considered to be a statute of the District of Columbia.

42 U.S.C. § 1985(c).[5] *Conspiracy to interfere with civil rights....* If two or more persons in any State or Territory conspire or go in disguise on the highway or on the premises of another, for the purpose of depriving, either directly or indirectly, any person or class of persons of the equal protection of the laws, or of equal privileges and immunities under the laws; ... the party so injured or deprived may have an action for the recovery of damages, occasioned by such injury or deprivation, against any one or more of the conspirators.

42 U.S.C. § 1986.[6] *Same: action for neglect to prevent.* Every person who, having knowledge that any of the wrongs conspired to be done, and mentioned in section 1985 of this title, are about to be committed, and having power to prevent or aid in preventing the commission of the same, neglects or refuses so to do, if such wrongful act be committed, shall be liable to the party injured, or his legal representatives, for all damages caused by such wrongful act, which such person by reasonable diligence could have prevented; and such damages may be recovered in an action on the case; and any number of persons guilty of such wrongful neglect or refusal may be joined as defendants in the action; and if the death of any party be caused by any such wrongful act and neglect, the legal representatives of the deceased shall have such action therefor, and may recover not exceeding $5,000 damages therein, for the benefit of the widow of the deceased, if there be one, and if there be no widow, then for the benefit of the next of kin of the deceased. But no action under the provisions of this section shall be sustained which is not commenced within one year after the cause of action has accrued.

42 U.S.C. § 1988.[7] *Proceedings in vindication of civil rights.*

---

3. Derived from § 1 of the Civil Rights Act of 1866. Codified as § 1978 of the Revised Statutes. 18 Stat. 348.

4. Derived from § 1 of the Civil Rights Act of 1871. 17 Stat. 13. *See also* § 2 of the 1866 Act and § 17 of the 1870 Act (criminal penalties imposed for similar behavior).Codified as § 1979 of the Revised Statutes. 18 Stat. 348. Coverage of the District of Columbia was added by Pub. L. No. 96-170, § 1, Dec. 29, 1979, 93 Stat. 1284.

5. Derived from § 2 of the 1871 Act. *See also* § 6 of the 1870 Act. Codified as § 1980 of the Revised Statutes. 18 Stat. 348.

6. Derived from § 6 of the 1871 Act. Codified as § 1981 of the Revised Statutes. 18 Stat. 349.

7. Derived from § 3 of the 1866 Act and § 18 of the 1870 Act. The last sentence of § 1988 was added by Pub. L. No. 94-559, § 2, Oct. 19, 1976, 90 Stat. 2641. The portion of § 3 of the 1866 Act that is

(a) The jurisdiction in civil and criminal matters conferred on the district courts by the provisions of this chapter and Title 18, for the protection of all persons in the United States in their civil rights, and for their vindication, shall be exercised and enforced in conformity with the laws of the United States, so far as such laws are suitable to carry the same into effect; but in all cases where they are not adapted to the object, or are deficient in the provisions necessary to furnish suitable remedies and punish offenses against law, the common law, as modified and changed by the constitution and statutes of the State wherein the court having jurisdiction of such civil or criminal cause is held, so far as the same is not inconsistent with the Constitution and laws of the United States, shall be extended to and govern the said courts in the trial and disposition of the cause, and, if it is of a criminal nature, in the infliction of punishment on the party found guilty.

(b) In any action or proceeding to enforce a provision of sections 1981, 1981A, 1982, 1983, 1985, and 1986 of this title, title IX of Public Law 92-318, or in any civil action or proceeding, by or on behalf of the United States of America, to enforce, or charging a violation of, a provision of the United States Internal Revenue Code, or title VI of the Civil Rights Act of 1964, the court, in its discretion, may allow the prevailing party, other than the United States, a reasonable attorney's fee as part of the costs.

(c) In awarding an attorney's fee under subsection (b) in any action or proceeding to enforce a provision of sections 1981 or 1981A of this title, the court, in its discretion, may include expert fees as part of the attorney's fee.

Criminal Provisions

18 U.S.C. § 241.[8] *Conspiracy against rights.* If two or more persons conspire to injure, oppress, threaten, or intimidate any inhabitant of any State, Territory, or District in the free exercise or enjoyment of any right or privilege secured to him by the Constitution or laws of the United States, or because of his having so exercised the same; or

"If two or more persons go in disguise on the highway, or on the premises of another, with intent to prevent or hinder his free exercise or enjoyment of any right or privilege so secured—

"They shall be fined not more than $10,000 or imprisoned not more then ten years, or both; and if death results, they shall be subject to imprisonment for any term of years or for life."

18 U.S.C. § 242.[9] *Deprivation of rights under color of law.* Whoever, under color of any law, statute, ordinance, regulation, or custom, willfully subjects any inhabitant of any State, Territory, or District to the deprivation of any rights, privileges, or immunities secured or protected by the Constitution or laws of the United States, or to different punishments, pains, or penalties, on account of such inhabitant being an alien, or by reason of his color, or race, than are prescribed for the punishment of citizens, shall be fined not more than $1,000 or imprisoned not more than one year, or both; and if bodily injury results shall be fined under this title or imprisoned not more than ten years, or both; and if death results shall be subject to imprisonment for any term of years or for life.

---

now contained in § 1988 was codified as § 722 of the Revised Statutes. 18 Stat. 137. Amended by the Civil Rights Act of 1991. 105 Stat. 1071.

8. Derived from § 6 of the 1870 Act. Codified as § 5508 of the Revised Statutes. 18 Stat. 1073. The penalty provisions were modified by the Civil Rights Act of 1968.

9. Derived from § 2 of the 1866 Act and § 17 of the 1870 Act. Codified as § 5510 of the Revised Statutes. 18 Stat. 1074.

Civil Rights Act of 1964, as Amended

78 Stat. 253 (1964), as amended 86 Stat. 103 (1972),
92 Stat. 2076 (1978), 105 Stat. 1071 (1991), 123 Stat. 5 (2009)

Title VII. Equal Employment Opportunity[10]

DEFINITIONS

SEC. 701 [42 U.S.C. § 2000e]. For the purposes of this title—

(a) The term "person" includes one or more individuals, governments, governmental agencies, political subdivisions, labor unions, partnerships, associations, corporations, legal representatives, mutual companies, joint-stock companies, trusts, unincorporated organizations, trustees, trustees in bankruptcy, or receivers.

(b) The term "employer" means a person engaged in an industry affecting commerce who has fifteen or more employees for each working day in each of twenty or more calendar weeks in the current or preceding calendar year, and any agent of such a person, but such term does not include (1) the United States, a corporation wholly owned by the Government of the United States, an Indian tribe, or any department or agency of the District of Columbia subject by statute to procedures of the competitive service (as defined in section 2102 of title 5 of the United States Code), or (2) a bona fide private membership club (other than a labor organization) which is exempt from taxation under section 501 (c) of the Internal Revenue Code of *1954*, except that during the first year after the date of enactment of the Equal Employment Opportunity Act of 1972, persons having fewer than twenty-five employees (and their agents) shall not be considered employers.

(c) The term "employment agency" means any person regularly undertaking with or without compensation to procure employees for an employer or to procure for employees opportunities to work for an employer and includes an agent of such a person.

(d) The term "labor organization" means a labor organization engaged in an industry affecting commerce, and any agent of such an organization, and includes any organization of any kind, any agency, or employee representation committee, group, association, or plan so engaged in which employees participate and which exists for the purpose, in whole or in part, of dealing with employers concerning grievances, labor disputes, wages, rates of pay, hours, or other terms. or conditions of employment, and any conference, general committee, joint or system board, or joint council so engaged which is subordinate to a national or international labor organization.

(e) A labor organization shall be deemed to be engaged in an industry affecting commerce if (1) it maintains or operates a hiring hall or hiring office which procures employees for an employer or procures for employees opportunities to work for an employer, or (2) the number of its members (or, where it is a labor organization composed of other labor organizations or their representatives, if the aggregate number of the members of such other labor organization) is (A) twenty-five or more during the first year after the date of enactment of the Equal Employment Opportunity Act of 1972, or (B) fifteen or more thereafter, and such labor organization

10. Includes 1972 amendments made by P.L. 92-261 underlined; 1978 amendments made by P.L. No. 95-555 printed in italics; 1991 amendments made by P.L. 102-166 printed in bold; and 2009 amendment made by P.L. 111-2 printed in bold italics.

(1) is the certified representative of employees under the provisions of the National Labor Relations Act, as amended, or the Railway Labor Act, as amended;

(2) although not certified, is a national or international labor organization or a local labor organization recognized or acting as the representative of employees of an employer or employers engaged in an industry affecting commerce; or

(3) has chartered a local labor organization or subsidiary body which is representing or actively seeking to represent employees of employers within the meaning of paragraph (1) or (2); or

(4) has been chartered by a labor organization representing or actively seeking to represent employees within the meaning of paragraph (1) or (2) as the local or subordinate body through which such employees may enjoy membership or become affiliated with such labor organization; or

(5) is a conference, general committee, joint or system board, or joint council subordinate to a national or international labor organization, which includes a labor organization engaged in an industry affecting commerce within the meaning of any of the preceding paragraphs of this subsection.

(f) The term "employee" means an individual employed by an employer, except that the term "employee" shall not include any person elected to public office in any State or political subdivision of any State by the qualified voters thereof, or any person chosen by such officer to be on such officer's personal staff, or an appointee on the policymaking level or an immediate adviser with respect to the exercise of the constitutional or legal powers of the office. The exemption set forth in the preceding sentence shall not include employees subject to the civil service laws of a State government, governmental agency or political subdivision. **With respect to employment in a foreign country, such term includes an individual who is a citizen of the United States.**[11]

(g) The term "commerce" means trade, traffic, commerce, transportation, transmission, or communication among the several States; or between a State and any place outside thereof; or within the District of Columbia, or a possession of the United States; or between points in the same State but through a point outside thereof.

(h) The term "industry affecting commerce" means any activity, business, or industry in commerce or in which a labor dispute would hinder or obstruct commerce or the free flow of commerce and includes any activity or industry "affecting commerce" within the meaning of the Labor-Management Reporting and Disclosure Act of 1959, and further includes any governmental industry, business, or activity.

(i) The term "State" includes a State of the United States, the District of Columbia, Puerto Rico, the Virgin Islands, American Samoa, Guam, Wake Island, the Canal Zone, and Outer Continental Shelf lands defined in the Outer Continental Shelf Lands Act.

(j) The term "religion" includes all aspects of religious observance and practice, as well as belief, unless an employer demonstrates that he is unable to reasonably accommodate to an employee's or prospective employee's, religious observance or practice without undue hardship on the conduct of the employer's business.

(k) The terms "because of sex" or "on the basis of sex" include, but are not limited to, because of or on the basis of pregnancy, childbirth, or related medical conditions; and women affected by pregnancy, childbirth, or related medical conditions shall be treated

11. The last sentence of (f) shall not apply with respect to conduct occurring before November 21,1991. *See* P.L. 102-166, Section 109(c) (November 21, 1991).

the same for all employment-related purposes, including receipt of benefits under fringe benefit programs, as other persons not so affected but similar in their ability or inability to work, and nothing in section 703(h) of this title shall be interpreted to permit otherwise. This subsection shall not require an employer to pay for health insurance benefits for abortion, except where the life of the mother would be endangered if the fetus were carried to term, or except where medical complications have arisen from an abortion: *Provided*, That nothing herein shall preclude an employer from providing abortion benefits or otherwise affect bargaining agreements in regard to abortion.

(l) The term "complaining party" means the Commission, the Attorney General, or a person who may bring an action or proceeding under this title.

(m) The term "demonstrates" means meets the burden of production and persuasion.

(n) The term "respondent" means an employer, employment agency, labor organization, joint labor-management committee controlling apprenticeship or other training or retraining program, including an on-the-job training program, or Federal entity subject to section 717.

EXEMPTION

SEC. 702 [42 U.S.C. §2000e-1].

(a) This title shall not apply to an employer with respect to the employment of aliens outside any State, or to a religious corporation, association, educational institution, or society with respect to the employment of individuals of a particular religion to perform work connected with the carrying on by such corporation, association, educational institution, or society of its activities.

(b) It shall not be unlawful under section 703 or 704 for an employer (or a corporation controlled by an employer), labor organization, employment agency, or joint labor-management committee controlling apprenticeship or other training or retraining (including on-the-job training programs) to take any action otherwise prohibited by such section, with respect to an employee in a workplace in a foreign country if compliance with such section would cause such employer (or such corporation), such organization, such agency, or such committee to violate the law of the foreign country in which such workplace is located. [12]

(c) (1) If an employer controls a corporation whose place of incorporation is a foreign country, any practice prohibited by section 703 or 704 engaged in by such corporation shall be presumed to be engaged in by such employer.

(2) Sections 703 and 704 shall not apply with respect to the foreign operations of an employer that is a foreign person not controlled by an American employer.

(3) For purposes of this subsection, the determination of whether an employer controls a corporation shall be based on

(A) the interrelation of operations;

(B) the common management;

(C) the centralized control of labor relations; and

---

12. Subsection (b) shall not apply to conduct occurring before November 21, 1991. *See* P.L. 102-166, Section 109(c) (November 21, 1991).

(D) the common ownership or financial control of the employer and the corporation.

DISCRIMINATION BECAUSE OF RACE, COLOR, RELIGION, SEX, OR NATIONAL ORIGIN

SEC. 703 [42 U.S.C. §2000e-2].

(a) It shall be an unlawful employment practice for an employer—

(1) to fail or refuse to hire or to discharge any individual, or otherwise to discriminate against any individual with respect to his compensation, terms, conditions, or privileges of employment, because of such individual's race, color, religion, sex, or national origin; or

(2) to limit, segregate, or classify his employees or applicants for employment in any way which would deprive or tend to deprive any individual of employment opportunities or otherwise adversely affect his status as an employee, because of such individual's race, color, religion, sex, or national origin.

(b) It shall be an unlawful employment practice for an employment agency to fail or refuse to refer for employment, or otherwise to discriminate against, any individual because of his race, color, religion, sex or national origin, or to classify or refer for employment any individual on the basis of his race, color, religion, sex, or national origin.

(c) It shall be an unlawful employment practice for a labor organization

(1) to exclude or to expel from its membership, or otherwise to discriminate against, any individual because of his race, color, religion, sex, or national origin;

(2) to limit, segregate, or classify its membership, or applicants for membership or to classify or fail or refuse to refer for employment any individual, in any way which would deprive or tend to deprive any individual of employment opportunities, or would limit such employment opportunities or otherwise adversely affect his status as an employee or as an applicant for employment, because of such individual's race, color, religion, sex, or national origin; or

(3) to cause or attempt to cause an employer to discriminate against an individual in violation of this section.

(d) It shall be an unlawful employment practice for any employer, labor organization, or joint labor-management committee controlling apprenticeship or other training or retraining, including on-the-job training programs to discriminate against any individual because of his race, color, religion, sex, or national origin in admission to, or employment in, any program established to provide apprenticeship or other training.

(e) Notwithstanding any other provision of this title, (1) it shall not be an unlawful employment practice for an employer to hire and employ employees, for an employment agency to classify, or refer for employment any individual, for a labor organization to classify its membership or to classify or refer for employment any individual, or for an employer, labor organization, or joint labor-management committee controlling apprenticeship or other training or retraining programs to admit or employ any individual in any such program, on the basis of his religion, sex, or national origin in those certain instances where religion, sex, or national origin is a bona fide occupational qualification reasonably necessary to the normal operation of that particular business or enterprise, and (2) it shall not be an unlawful employment practice for a school, college, university, or other educational institution or institution of learning to hire and employ employees of a particular religion if such school, college, university, or other educational institution or institution of learning is, in whole or in substantial part, owned, supported, controlled, or managed by a particular religion or by a particular religious corporation, association, or society, or if the curriculum of such school, college, university, or other educational institution or institution of learning is directed toward the propagation of a particular religion.

(f) As used in this title, the phrase "unlawful employment practice" shall not be deemed to include any action or measure taken by an employer, labor organization, joint labor-management committee, or employment agency with respect to an individual who is a member of the Communist Party of the United States or of any other organization required to register as a Communist-action or Communist-front organization by final order of the Subversive Activities Control Board pursuant to the Subversive Activities Control Act of 1950.

(g) Notwithstanding any other provision of this title, it shall not be an unlawful employment practice for an employer to fail or refuse to hire and employ any individual for any position, for an employer to discharge any individual from any position, or for an employment agency to fail or refuse to refer any individual for employment in any position, or for a labor organization to fail or refuse to refer any individual for employment in any position, if—

(1) the occupancy of such position, or access to the premises in or upon which any part of the duties of such position is performed or is to be performed, is subject to any requirement imposed in the interest of the national security of the United States under any security program in effect pursuant to or administered under any statute of the United States or any Executive order of the President; and

(2) such individual has not fulfilled or has ceased to fulfill that requirement.

(h) Notwithstanding any other provision of this title, it shall not be an unlawful employment practice for an employer to apply different standards of compensation, or different terms, conditions, or privileges of employment pursuant to a bona fide seniority or merit system, or a system which measures earnings by quantity or quality of production or to employees who work in different locations, provided that such differences are not the result of an intention to discriminate because of race, color, religion, sex, or national origin, nor shall it be an unlawful employment practice for an employer to give and to act upon the results of any professionally developed ability test provided that such test, its administration or action upon the results is not designed, intended or used to discriminate because of race, color, religion, sex or national origin. It shall not be an unlawful employment practice under this title for any employer to differentiate upon the basis of sex in determining the amount of the wages or compensation paid or to be paid to employees of such employer if such differentiation is authorized by the provisions of section 6(d) of the Fair Labor Standards Act of 1938, as amended (29 U.S.C. 206 (d)).

(i) Nothing contained in this title shall apply to any business or enterprise on or near an Indian reservation with respect to any publicly announced employment practice of such business or enterprise under which a preferential treatment is given to any individual because he is an Indian living on or near a reservation.

(j) Nothing contained in this title shall be interpreted to require any employer, employment agency, labor organization, or joint labor-management committee subject to this title to grant preferential treatment to any individual or to any group because of the race, color, religion, sex, or national origin of such individual or group on account of an imbalance which may exist with respect to the total number or percentage of persons of any race, color, religion, sex, or national origin employed by any employer, referred or classified for employment by any employment agency or labor organization, admitted to membership or classified by any labor organization, or admitted to, or employed in, any apprenticeship or other training program, in comparison with the total number or percentage of persons of such race, color, religion, sex, or national origin in any community, State, section, or other area, or in the available work force in any community, State, section, or other area.

(k)(1)(A) An unlawful employment practice based on disparate impact is established under this title only if—

(i) a complaining party demonstrates that a respondent uses a particular employment practice that causes a disparate impact on the basis of race, color, religion, sex, or national origin and the respondent fails to demonstrate that the challenged practice is job related for the position in question and consistent with business necessity; or

(ii) the complaining party makes the demonstration described in subparagraph (C) with respect to an alternative employment practice and the respondent refuses to adopt such alternative employment practice.

(B)(i) With respect to demonstrating that a particular employment practice causes a disparate impact as described in subparagraph (A)(i), the complaining party shall demonstrate that each particular challenged employment practice causes a disparate impact, except that if the complaining party can demonstrate to the court that the elements of a respondent's decision making process are not capable of separation for analysis, the decision making process may be analyzed as one employment practice.

(ii) If the respondent demonstrates that a specific employment practice does not cause the disparate impact, the respondent shall not be required to demonstrate that such practice is required by business necessity.

(C) The demonstration referred to by subparagraph (A)(ii) shall be in accordance with law as it existed on June 4, 1989, with respect to the concept of "alternative employment practice".

(2) A demonstration that an employment practice is required by business necessity may not be used as a defense against a claim of intentional discrimination under this title.

(3) Notwithstanding any other provision of this title, a rule barring the employment of an individual who currently and knowingly uses or possesses a controlled substance, as defined in schedules I and II of section 102(6) of the Controlled Substances Act (21 U.S.C. 802(6)), other than the use or possession of a drug taken under the supervision of a licensed health care professional, or any other use or possession authorized by the Controlled Substances Act or any other provision of Federal law, shall be considered an unlawful employment practice under this title only if such rule is adopted or applied with an intent to discriminate because of race, color, religion, sex, or national origin.[13]

13. Section 105(b) of P.L. 102-166 (November 21, 1991) provides:

(b) No statements other than the interpretive memorandum appearing at Vol. 137 Congressional Record S 15276 (daily ed. Oct. 25, 1991) shall be considered legislative history of, or relied upon in any way as legislative history in construing or applying, any provision of this Act that relates to Wards Cove—Business necessity/cumulation/alternative business practice.

Section 402(b) of P.L. 102-166 (November 21, 1991) provides:

(b) Certain Disparate Impact Cases.-Notwithstanding any other provisions of this Act, nothing in this Act shall apply to any disparate impact cases for which a complaint was

(l) It shall be an unlawful employment practice for a respondent, in connection with the selection or referral of applicants or candidates for employment or promotion, to adjust the scores of, use different cutoff scores for, or otherwise alter the results of, employment related tests on the basis of race, color, religion, sex, or national origin.

(m) Except as otherwise provided in this title, an unlawful employment practice is established when the complaining party demonstrates that race, color, religion, sex, or national origin was a motivating factor for any employment practice, even though other factors also motivated the practice.

(n)(1)(A) Notwithstanding any other provision of law, and except as provided in paragraph (2), an employment practice that implements and is within the scope of a litigated or consent judgment or order that resolves a claim of employment discrimination under the Constitution or Federal civil rights laws may not be challenged under the circumstances described in subparagraph (B).

(B) A practice described in subparagraph (A) may not be challenged in a claim under the Constitution or Federal civil rights laws—

(i) by a person who, prior to the entry of the judgment or order described in subparagraph (A), had—

(I) actual notice of the proposed judgement or order sufficient to apprise such person that such judgement or order might adversely affect the interests and legal rights of such person and that an opportunity was available to present objections to such judgment or order by a future date certain; and

(II) a reasonable opportunity to present objections to such judgment or order; or

(ii) by a person whose interests were adequately represented by another person who had previously challenged the judgment or order on the same legal grounds and with a similar factual situation, unless there has been an intervening change in law or fact.

(2) Nothing in this subsection shall be construed to—

(A) alter the standards for intervention under rule 24 of the Federal Rules of Civil Procedure or apply to the rights of parties who have successfully intervened pursuant to such rule in the proceeding in which the parties intervened;

(B) apply to the rights of parties to the action in which a litigated or consent judgment or order was entered, or of members of a class represented or sought to be represented in such action, or of members of a group on whose behalf relief was sought in such action by the Federal Government;

(C) prevent challenges to a litigated or consent judgment or order on the ground that such judgment or order was obtained through collusion or fraud, or is transparently invalid or was entered by a court lacking subject matter jurisdiction; or

(D) authorize or permit the denial to any person of the due process of law required by the Constitution.

(3) Any action not precluded under this subsection that challenges an employment consent judgment or order described in paragraph (1) shall be brought in the court, and if possible before the judge, that entered such judgment or order. Nothing in this

---

filed before March 1, 1975 and for which an initial decision was rendered after October 30, 1983.

subsection shall preclude a transfer of such action pursuant to section 1404 of title 28, United States Code.

OTHER UNLAWFUL EMPLOYMENT PRACTICES

SEC. 704 [42 U.S.C. §2000e-3].

(a) It shall be an unlawful employment practice for an employer to discriminate against any of his employees or applicants for employment, for an employment agency, or joint labor-management committee controlling apprenticeship or other training or retraining, including on-the-job training programs, to discriminate against any individual, or for a labor organization to discriminate against any member thereof or applicant for membership, because he has opposed any practice made an unlawful employment practice by this title, or because he has made a charge, testified, assisted, or participated in any manner in an investigation, proceeding, or hearing under this title.

(b) It shall be an unlawful employment practice for an employer, labor organization, employment agency, or joint labor-management committee controlling apprenticeship or other training or retraining including on-the-job training programs, to print or publish or cause to be printed or published any notice or advertisement relating to employment by such an employer or membership in or any classification or referral for employment by such a labor organization, or relating to any classification or referral for employment by such an employment agency, or relating to admission to, or employment in, any program established to provide apprenticeship or other training by such a joint labor-management committee indicating any preference, limitation, specification, or discrimination, based on race, color, religion, sex, or national origin, except that such a notice or advertisement may indicate a preference, limitation, specification, or discrimination based on religion, sex, or national origin when religion, sex, or national origin is a bona fide occupational qualification for employment.

EQUAL EMPLOYMENT OPPORTUNITY COMMISSION

SEC. 705 [42 U.S.C. §2000e-4].

(a) There is hereby created a Commission to be known as the Equal Employment Opportunity Commission, which shall be composed of five members, not more than three of whom shall be members of the same political party. Members of the Commission shall be appointed by the President by and with the advice and consent of the Senate for a term of five years. Any individual chosen to fill a vacancy shall be appointed only for the unexpired term of the member whom he shall succeed, and all members of the Commission shall continue to serve until their successors are appointed and qualified, except that no such member of the Commission shall continue to serve (1) for more than sixty days when the Congress is in session unless a nomination to fill such vacancy shall have been submitted to the Senate or (2) after the adjournment sine die of the session of the Senate in which such nomination was submitted. The President shall designate one member to serve as Chairman of the Commission, and one member to serve as Vice Chairman. The Chairman shall be responsible on behalf of the Commission for the administrative operations of the Commission, and except as provided in subsection (b), shall appoint, in accordance with the provisions of title 5 United States Code governing appointments in the competitive service, such officers, agents, attorneys, administrative law judges, and employees as he deems necessary to assist it in the performance of its functions and to fix their compensation in accordance with the provisions of chapter 51 and subchapter III of chapter 53 of title 5, relating to classification and General Schedule pay rates:

Provided, That assignment, removal, and compensation of hearing examiners shall be in accordance with sections 3105, 3344, 5362, and 7521 of title 5.

(b)(1) There shall be a General Counsel of the Commission appointed by the President, by and with the advice and consent of the Senate, for a term of four years. The General Counsel shall have responsibility for the conduct of litigation as provided in sections 706 and 707 of this title. The General Counsel shall have such other duties as the Commission may prescribe or as may be provided by law and shall concur with the Chairman of the Commission on the appointment and supervision of regional attorneys. The General Counsel of the Commission on the effective date of this Act shall continue in such position and perform the functions specified in this subsection until a successor is appointed and qualified.

(2) Attorneys appointed under this section may, at the direction of the Commission, appear for and represent the Commission in any case in court. provided that the Attorney General shall conduct all litigation to which the Commission is a party in the Supreme Court pursuant to this title.

(c) A vacancy in the Commission shall not impair the right of the remaining members to exercise all the powers of the Commission and three members thereof shall constitute a quorum.

(d) The Commission shall have an official seal which shall be judicially noticed.

(e) The Commission shall at the close of each fiscal year report to the Congress and to the President concerning the action it has taken and the moneys it has disbursed. It shall make such further reports on the cause of and means of eliminating discrimination and such recommendations for further legislation as may appear desirable.

(f) The principal office of the Commission shall be in or near the District of Columbia, but it may meet or exercise any or all its powers at any other place. The Commission may establish such regional or State Offices as it deems necessary to accomplish the purpose of this title.

(g) The Commission shall have power—

(1) to cooperate with and, with their consent, utilize regional, State, local, and other agencies, both public and private, and individuals;

(2) to pay to witnesses whose depositions are taken or who are summoned before the Commission or any of its agents the same witness and mileage fees as are paid to witnesses in the courts of the United States;

(3) to furnish to persons subject to this title such technical assistance as they may request to further their compliance with this title or an order issued thereunder;

(4) upon the request of (i) any employer, whose employees or some of them, or (ii) any labor organization, whose members or some of them, refuse or threaten to refuse to cooperate in effectuating the provisions of this title, to assist in such effectuation by conciliation or such other remedial action as is provided by this title;

(5) to make such technical studies as are appropriate to effectuate the purposes and policies of this title and to make the results of such studies available to the public;

(6) to intervene in a civil action brought under section 706 by an aggrieved party against a respondent other than a government, governmental agency, or political subdivision.

(h)(1) The Commission shall, in any of its educational or promotional activities, cooperate with other departments and agencies in the performance of such educational and promotional activities.

(2) In exercising its powers under this title, the Commission shall carry out educational and outreach activities (including dissemination of information in languages other than English) targeted to—

(A) individuals who historically have been victims of employment discrimination and have not been equitably served by the Commission; and

(B) individuals on whose behalf the Commission has authority enforce any other law prohibiting employment discrimination, concerning rights and obligations under this title or such law, as the case may be.

(i) All officers, agents, attorneys, and employees of the Commission shall be subject to the provisions of section 9 of the Act of August 2, 1939, as amended (the Hatch Act), notwithstanding any exemption contained in such section.

(j)(1) The Commission shall establish a Technical Assistance Training Institute, through which the Commission shall provide technical assistance and training regarding the laws and regulations enforced by the Commission.

(2) An employer or other entity covered under this title shall not be excused from compliance with the requirements of this title because of any failure to receive technical assistance under this subsection.

(3) There are authorized to be appropriated to carry out this subsection such sums as may be necessary for fiscal year 1992.

(k)(1) There is hereby established in the Treasury of the United States a revolving fund to be known as the "EEOC Education, Technical Assistance, and Training Revolving Fund" (hereinafter in this subsection referred to as the "Fund") and to pay the cost (including administrative and personnel expenses) of providing education, technical assistance, and training relating to laws administered by the Commission. Monies in the Fund shall be available without fiscal year limitation to the Commission for such purposes.

(2)(A) The Commission shall charge fees in accordance with the provisions of this paragraph to offset the costs of education, technical assistance, and training provided with monies in the Fund. Such fees for any education, technical assistance, or training-

(i) shall be imposed on a uniform basis on persons and entities receiving such education, assistance, or training,

(ii) shall not exceed the cost of providing such education, assistance, and training, and

(iii) with respect to each person or entity receiving such education, assistance, or training, shall bear a reasonable relationship to the cost of providing such education, assistance, or training to such person or entity.

(B) Fees received under subparagraph (A) shall be deposited in the Fund by the Commission.

(C) The Commission shall include in each report made under subsection (e) of this section information with respect to the operation of the Fund, including information, presented in the aggregate, relating to-

(i) the number of persons and entities to which the Commission provided education, technical assistance, or training with monies in the Fund, in the fiscal year for which such report is prepared,

(ii) the cost to the Commission to provide such education, technical assistance, or training to such persons and entities, and

(iii) the amount of any fees received by the Commission from such persons and entities for such education, technical assistance, or training.

(3) The Secretary of the Treasury shall invest the portion of the Fund not required to satisfy current expenditures from the Fund, as determined by the Commission, in obligations of the United States or obligations guaranteed as to principal by the United States. Investment proceeds shall be deposited in the Fund.

(4) There is hereby transferred to the Fund $1,000,000 from the Salaries and Expenses appropriation of the Commission.

+[(**14**) Added by Pub. L. 102-411, §2, 106 Stat. 2101 (October 14, 1992).]+

PREVENTION OF UNLAWFUL EMPLOYMENT PRACTICES

SEC. 706 [42 U.S.C. §2000e-5].

(a) The Commission is empowered, as hereinafter provided, to prevent any person from engaging in any unlawful employment practice as set forth in section 703 or 704 of this title.

(b) Whenever a charge is filed by or on behalf of a person claiming to be aggrieved, or by a member of the Commission, alleging that an employer, employment agency, labor organization, or joint labor-management committee controlling apprenticeship or other training or retraining, including on-the-job training programs, has engaged in an unlawful employment practice, the Commission shall serve a notice of the charge (including the date, place and circumstances of the alleged unlawful employment practice) on such employer, employment agency, labor organization, or joint labor-management committee (hereinafter referred to as the "respondent") within ten days, and shall make an investigation thereof. Charges shall be in writing under oath or affirmation and shall contain such information and be in such form as the Commission requires. Charges shall not be made public by the Commission. If the Commission determines after such investigation that there is not reasonable cause to believe that the charge is true, it shall dismiss the charge and promptly notify the person claiming to be aggrieved and the respondent of its action. In determining whether reasonable cause exists, the Commission shall accord substantial weight to final findings and orders made by State or local authorities in proceedings commenced under State or local law pursuant to the requirements of subsections (c) and (d). If the Commission determines after such investigation that there is reasonable cause to believe that the charge is true, the Commission shall endeavor to eliminate any such alleged unlawful employment practice by informal methods of conference, conciliation, and persuasion. Nothing said or done during and as a part of such informal endeavors may be made public by the Commission, its officers or employees, or used as evidence in a subsequent proceeding without the written consent of the persons concerned. Any person who makes public information in violation of this subsection shall be fined not more than $1,000 or imprisoned for not more than one year, or both. The Commission shall make its determination on reasonable cause as promptly as possible and, so far as practicable, not later than one hundred and twenty days from the filing of the charge or, where applicable under subsection (c) or (d), from the date upon which the Commission is authorized to take action with respect to the charge.

(c) In the case of an alleged unlawful employment practice occurring in a State, or political subdivision of a State, which has a State or local law prohibiting the unlawful employment practice alleged and establishing or authorizing a State or local authority to grant or seek relief from such practice or to institute criminal proceedings with respect thereto upon receiving notice thereof, no charge may be filed under subsection (a) by the person aggrieved before the expiration of sixty days after proceedings have been commenced under the State or local law, unless such proceedings have been earlier terminated, provided that such sixty-day period shall be extended to one hundred and twenty days during the first year after the effective date of such State or local law. If any requirement for the commencement of such proceedings is imposed by a State or local authority other than a requirement of the filing of a written and signed statement of the facts upon which the proceeding is based, the proceeding shall be deemed to have been commenced for the purposes of this subsection at the time such statement is sent by registered mail to the appropriate State or local authority.

(d) In the case of any charge filed by a member of the Commission alleging an unlawful employment practice occurring in a State or political subdivision of a State which has a State or local law prohibiting the practice alleged and establishing or authorizing a State or local authority to grant or seek relief from such practice or to institute criminal proceedings with respect thereto upon receiving notice thereof, the Commission shall, before taking any action with respect to such charge, notify the appropriate State or local officials and, upon request, afford them a reasonable time, but not less than sixty days (provided that such sixty-day period shall be extended to one hundred and twenty days during the first year after the effective date of such State or local law), unless a shorter period is requested, to act under such State or local law to remedy the practice alleged.

(e) (1) A charge under this section shall be filed within one hundred and eighty days after the alleged unlawful employment practice occurred and notice of the charge (including the date, place and circumstances of the alleged unlawful employment practice) shall be served upon the person against whom such charge is made within ten days thereafter, except that in a case of an unlawful employment practice with respect to which the person aggrieved has initially instituted proceedings with a State or local agency with authority to grant or seek relief from such practice or to institute criminal proceedings with respect thereto upon receiving notice thereof, such charge shall be filed by or on behalf of the person aggrieved within three hundred days after the alleged unlawful employment practice occurred, or within thirty days after receiving notice that the State or local agency has terminated the proceedings under the State or local law, whichever is earlier, and a copy of such charge shall be filed by the Commission with the State or local agency.

(2) For purposes of this section, an unlawful employment practice occurs, with respect to a seniority system that has been adopted for an intentionally discriminatory purpose in violation of this title (whether or not that discriminatory purpose is apparent on the face of the seniority provision), when the seniority system is adopted, when an individual becomes subject to the seniority system, or when a person aggrieved is injured by the application of the seniority system or provision of the system.

(3)(A) For purposes of this section, an unlawful employment practice occurs, with respect to discrimination in compensation in violation of this subchapter, when a discriminatory compensation decision or other practice is adopted, when an individual becomes subject to a discriminatory compensation decision or other practice, or when an individual is affected by application of a discriminatory decision or other practice, including each time wages, benefits, or other compensation is paid, resulting in whole or in part from such a decision or other practice.

(B) In addition to any relief authorized by section 1981a of this title, liability may accrue and an aggrieved person may obtain relief as provided in subsection (g)(1), including recovery of back pay for up to two years preceding the filing of the charge, where the

unlawful employment practices that have occurred during the charge filing period are similar or related to unlawful employment practices with regard to discrimination in compensation that occurred outside the time for filing a charge.

(f) (1) If within thirty days after a charge is filed with the Commission or within thirty days after expiration of any period of reference under subsection (c) or (d), the Commission has been unable to secure from the respondent a conciliation agreement acceptable to the Commission. The Commission may bring a civil action against any respondent not a government, governmental agency, or political subdivision named in the charge. In the case of a respondent which is a government, governmental agency, or political subdivision, if the Commission has been unable to secure from the respondent a conciliation agreement acceptable to the Commission, the Commission shall take no further action and shall refer the case to the Attorney General who may bring a civil action against such respondent in the appropriate United States district court. The person or persons aggrieved shall have the right to intervene in a civil action brought by the Commission or the Attorney General in a case involving a government, governmental agency, or political subdivision. If a charge filed with the Commission pursuant to subsection (b) is dismissed by the Commission, or if within one hundred and eighty days from the filing of such charge or the expiration of any period of reference under subsection (c) or (d), whichever is later, the Commission has not filed a civil action under this section or the Attorney General has not filed a civil action in a case involving a government, governmental agency, or political subdivision or the Commission has not entered into a conciliation agreement to which the person aggrieved is a party, the Commission, or the Attorney General in a case involving a government, governmental agency, or political subdivision, shall so notify the person aggrieved and within ninety days after the giving of such notice a civil action may be brought against the respondent named in the charge (A) by the person claiming to be aggrieved, or (B) if such charge was filed by a member of the Commission, by any person whom the charge alleges was aggrieved by the alleged unlawful employment practice. Upon application by the complainant and in such circumstances as the court may deem just, the court may appoint an attorney for such complainant and may authorize the commencement of the action without the payment of fees, costs, or security. Upon timely application, the court may, in its discretion, permit the Commission, or the Attorney General in a case involving a government, governmental agency, or political subdivision, to intervene in such civil action upon certification that the case is of general public importance. Upon request, the court may, in its discretion, stay further proceedings for not more than sixty days pending the termination of State or local proceedings described in subsections (c) or (d) of this section or further efforts of the Commission to obtain voluntary compliance.

(2) Whenever a charge is filed with the Commission and the Commission concludes on the basis of a preliminary investigation that prompt judicial action is necessary to carry out the purposes of this Act, the Commission. or the Attorney General in a case involving a government, governmental agency, or political subdivision may bring an action for appropriate temporary or preliminary relief pending final disposition of such charge. Any temporary restraining order or other order granting preliminary or temporary relief shall be issued in accordance with rule 65 of the Federal Rules of Civil Procedure. It shall be the duty of a court having jurisdiction over proceedings under this section to assign cases for hearing at the earliest practicable date and to cause such cases to be in every way expedited.

(3) Each United States district court and each United States court of a place subject to the jurisdiction of the United States shall have jurisdiction of actions brought under

this title. Such an action may be brought in any judicial district in the State in which the unlawful employment practice is alleged to have been committed, in the judicial district in which the employment records relevant to such practice are maintained and administered, or in the judicial district in which the aggrieved person would have worked but for the alleged unlawful employment practice, but if the respondent is not found within any such district, such an action may be brought within the judicial district in which the respondent has his principal office. For purposes of sections 1404 and 1406 of title 28 of the United States Code, the judicial district in which the respondent has his principal office shall in all cases be considered a district in which the action might have been brought.

(4) It shall be the duty of the chief judge of the district (or in his absence, the acting chief judge) in which the case is pending immediately to designate a judge in such district to hear and determine the case. In the event that no judge in the district is available to hear and determine the case, the chief judge of the district, or the acting chief judge, as the case may be, shall certify this fact to the chief judge of the circuit (or in his absence, the acting chief judge) who shall then designate a district or circuit judge of the circuit to hear and determine the case.

(5) It shall be the duty of the judge designated pursuant to this subsection to assign the case for hearing at the earliest practicable date and to cause the case to be in every way expedited. If such judge has not scheduled the case for trial within one hundred and twenty days after issue has been joined, that judge may appoint a master pursuant to rule 53 of the Federal Rules of Civil Procedure.

(g)(1) If the court finds that the respondent has intentionally engaged in or is intentionally engaging in an unlawful employment practice charged in the complaint, the court may enjoin the respondent from engaging in such unlawful employment practice, and order such affirmative action as may be appropriate, which may include, but is not limited to, reinstatement or hiring of employees, with or without back pay (payable by the employer, employment agency, or labor organization, as the case may be, responsible for the unlawful employment practice), or any other equitable relief as the court deems appropriate. Back pay liability shall not accrue from a date more than two years prior to the filing of a charge with the Commission. Interim earnings or amounts earnable with reasonable diligence by the person or persons discriminated against shall operate to reduce the back pay otherwise allowable.

(2) (A) No order of the court shall require the admission or reinstatement of an individual as a member of a union, or the hiring, reinstatement, or promotion of an individual as an employee, or the payment to him of any back pay, if such individual was refused admission, suspended, or expelled, or was refused employment or advancement or was suspended or discharged for any reason other than discrimination on account of race, color, religion, sex, or national origin or in violation of section 704(a).

(B) On a claim in which an individual proves a violation under section 703(m) and a respondent demonstrates that the respondent would have taken the same action in the absence of the impermissible motivating factor, the court—

(i) may grant declaratory relief, injunctive relief (except as provided in clause (ii)), and attorney's fees and costs demonstrated to be directly attributable only to the pursuit of a claim under section 703(m); and

(ii) shall not award damages or issue an order requiring any admission, reinstatement, hiring, promotion, or payment, described in subparagraph (A).

(h) The provisions of the Act entitled "An Act to amend the Judicial Code and to define and limit the jurisdiction of courts sitting in equity, and for other purposes," approved March 23, 1932 (29 U.S.C. 101-115), shall not apply with respect to civil actions brought under this section.

(i) In any case in which an employer, employment agency, or labor organization fails to comply with an order of a court issued in a civil action brought under this section, the Commission may commence proceedings to compel compliance with such order.

(j) Any civil action brought under this section and any proceedings brought under subsection (i) shall be subject to appeal as provided in sections 1291 and 1292, title 28, United States Code.

(k) In any action or proceeding under this title the court, in its discretion, may allow the prevailing party, other than the Commission or the United States, a reasonable attorney's fee (**including expert fees**) as part of the costs, and the Commission and the United States shall be liable for costs the same as a private person.

CIVIL ACTIONS BY ATTORNEY GENERAL

SEC. 707 [42 U.S.C. § 2000e-6].

(a) Whenever the Attorney General has reasonable cause to believe that any person or group of persons is engaged in a pattern or practice of resistance to the full enjoyment of any of the rights secured by this title, and that the pattern or practice is of such a nature and is intended to deny the full exercise of the rights herein described, the Attorney General may bring a civil action in the appropriate district court of the United States by filing with it a complaint (1) signed by him (or in his absence the Acting Attorney General), (2) setting forth facts pertaining to such pattern or practice, and (3) requesting such relief, including an application for a permanent or temporary injunction, restraining order or other order against the person or persons responsible for such pattern or practice, as he deems necessary to insure the full enjoyment of the rights herein described.

(b) The district courts of the United States shall have and shall exercise jurisdiction of proceedings instituted pursuant to this section, and in any such proceeding the Attorney General may file with the clerk of such court a request that a court of three judges be convened to hear and determine the case. Such request by the Attorney General shall be accompanied by a certificate that, in his opinion, the case is of general public importance. A copy of the certificate and request for a three-judge court shall be immediately furnished by such clerk to the chief judge of the circuit (or in his absence, the presiding circuit judge of the circuit) in which the case is pending. Upon receipt of such request it shall be the duty of the chief judge of the circuit or the presiding circuit judge, as the case may be, to designate immediately three judges in such circuit, of whom at least one shall be a circuit judge and another of whom shall be a district judge of the court in which the proceeding was instituted, to hear and determine such case, and it shall be the duty of the judges so designated to assign the case for hearing at the earliest practicable date, to participate in the hearing and determination thereof, and to cause the case to be in every way expedited. An appeal from the final judgment of such court will lie to the Supreme Court.

In the event the Attorney General fails to file such a request in any such proceeding, it shall be the duty of the chief judge of the district (or in his absence, the acting chief judge) in which the case is pending immediately to designate a judge in such district to hear and determine the case. In the event that no judge in the district is available to hear and determine the case, the chief judge of the district, or the acting chief judge, as the case may be, shall certify this fact to the chief judge of the circuit (or in his absence, the acting chief judge) who shall then designate a district or circuit judge of the circuit to hear and determine the case.

It shall be the duty of the judge designated pursuant to this section to assign the case for hearing at the earliest practicable date and to cause the case to be in every way expedited.

(c) Effective two years after the date of enactment of the Equal Employment Opportunity Act of 1972, the functions of the Attorney General under this section shall be transferred to the Commission, together with such personnel, property, records, and unexpended balances of appropriations, allocations, and other funds employed, used, held, available, or to be made available in connection with such functions unless the President submits, and neither House of Congress vetoes, a reorganization plan pursuant to chapter 9, of title 5, inconsistent with the provisions of this subsection. The Commission shall carry out such functions in accordance with subsections (d) and (e) of this section.

(d) Upon the transfer of functions provided for in subsection (c) of this section, in all suits commenced pursuant to this section prior to the date of such transfer, proceedings shall continue without abatement, all court orders and decrees shall remain in effect, and the Commission shall be substituted as a party for the United States of America, the Attorney General, or the Acting Attorney General, as appropriate.

(e) Subsequent to the date of enactment of the Equal Employment Opportunity Act of 1972, the Commission shall have authority to investigate and act on a charge of a pattern or practice of discrimination, whether filed by or on behalf of a person claiming to be aggrieved or by a member of the Commission. All such actions shall be conducted in accordance with the procedures set forth in section 706 of this Act.

EFFECT ON STATE LAWS

SEC. 708 [42 U.S.C. §2000e-7].

Nothing in this title shall be deemed to exempt or relieve any person from any liability, duty, penalty, or punishment provided by any present or future law of any State or political subdivision of a State, other than any such law which purports to require or permit the doing of any act which would be an unlawful employment practice under this title.

INVESTIGATIONS, INSPECTIONS, RECORDS, STATE AGENCIES

SEC. 709 [42 U.S.C. §2000e-8].

(a) In connection with any investigation of a charge filed under section 706, the Commission or its designated representative shall at all reasonable times have access to, for the purposes of examination, and the right to copy any evidence of any person being investigated or proceeded against that relates to unlawful employment practices covered by this title and is relevant to the charge under investigation.

(b) The Commission may cooperate with State and local agencies charged with the administration of State fair employment practices laws and, with the consent of such agencies, may, for the purpose of carrying out its functions and duties under this title and within the limitation of funds appropriated specifically for such purpose, engage in and contribute to the cost of research and other projects of mutual interest undertaken by such agencies, and utilize the services of such agencies and their employees, and, notwithstanding any other provision of law, pay by advance or reimbursement such agencies and their employees for services rendered to assist the Commission in carrying out this title. In furtherance of such cooperative efforts, the Commission may enter into written agreements with such State or local agencies and such agreements may include provisions under which the Commission shall refrain from processing a charge in any cases or class of cases specified in such agreements or under which the Commission shall relieve any person or class of persons in such State or locality from requirements imposed under this section. The Commission shall rescind any such agreement whenever it determines that the agreement no longer serves the interest of effective enforcement of this title.

(c) Every employer, employment agency, and labor organization subject to this title shall (1) make and keep such records relevant to the determinations of whether unlawful employment practices have been or are being committed, (2) preserve such records for such periods, and (3) make such reports therefrom, as the Commission shall prescribe by regulation or order, after public hearing, as reasonable, necessary, or appropriate for the enforcement of this title or the regulations or orders thereunder. The Commission shall, by regulation, require each employer, labor organization, and joint labor-management committee subject to this title which controls an apprenticeship or other training program to maintain such records as are reasonably necessary to carry out the purpose of this title, including, but not limited to, a list of applicants who wish to participate in such program, including the chronological order in which applications were received, and to furnish to the Commission upon request, a detailed description of the manner in which persons are selected to participate in the apprenticeship or other training program. Any employer, employment agency, labor organization, or joint labor-management committee which believes that the application to it of any regulation or order issued under this section would result in undue hardship may apply to the Commission for an exemption from the application of such regulation or order, and, if such application for an exemption is denied, bring a civil action in the United States district court for the district where such records are kept. If the Commission or the court, as the case may be, finds that the application of the regulation or order to the employer, employment agency, or labor organization in question would impose an undue hardship, the Commission or the court, as the case may be, may grant appropriate relief. If any person required to comply with the provisions of this subsection fails or refuses to do so, the United States district court for the district in which such person is found, resides, or transacts business, shall, upon application of the Commission, or the Attorney General in a case involving a government, governmental agency or political subdivision, have jurisdiction to issue to such person an order requiring him to comply.

(d) In prescribing requirements pursuant to subsection (c) of this section, the Commission shall consult with other interested State and Federal agencies and shall endeavor to coordinate its requirements with those adopted by such agencies. The Commission shall furnish upon request and without cost to any State or local agency charged with the administration of a fair employment practice law information obtained pursuant to subsection (c) of this section from any employer, employment agency, labor organization or joint labor-management committee subject to the jurisdiction of such agency. Such information shall be furnished on condition that it not be made public by the recipient agency prior to the institution of a proceeding under State or local law involving such information. If this condition is violated by a recipient agency, the Commission may decline to honor subsequent requests pursuant to this subsection.

(e) It shall be unlawful for any officer or employee of the Commission to make public in any manner whatever any information obtained by the Commission pursuant to its authority under this section prior to the institution of any proceeding under this title involving such information. Any officer or employee of the Commission who shall make public in any manner whatever any information in violation of this subsection shall be guilty of a misdemeanor and upon conviction thereof, shall be fined not more than $1,000, or imprisoned not more than one year.

INVESTIGATORY POWERS

SEC. 710 [42 U.S.C. § 2000e-9].

For the purpose of all hearings and investigations conducted by the Commission or its duly authorized agents or agencies, section 11 of the National Labor Relations Act (49 Stat. 455; 29 U.S.C. 161) shall apply.

NOTICES TO BE POSTED

SEC. 711 [42 U.S.C. § 2000e-l0].

(a) Every employer, employment agency, and labor organization, as the case may be, shall post and keep posted in conspicuous places upon its premises where notices to employees, applicants for employment, and members are customarily posted a notice to be prepared or approved by the Commission setting forth excerpts from, or summaries of, the pertinent provisions of this title and information pertinent to the filing of a complaint.

(b) A willful violation of this section shall be punishable by a fine of not more than $100 for each separate offense.

VETERANS' PREFERENCE

SEC. 712 [42 U.S.C. § 2000e-11].

Nothing contained in this title shall be construed to repeal or modify any Federal, State, territorial, or local law creating special rights or preference for veterans.

RULES AND REGULATIONS

SEC. 713 [42 U.S.C. 2000e-12].

(a) The Commission shall have authority from time to time to issue, amend, or rescind suitable procedural regulations to carry out the provisions of this title. Regulations issued under the section shall be in conformity with the standards and limitations of the Administrative Procedure Act.

(b) In any action or proceeding based on any alleged unlawful employment practice, no person shall be subject to any liability or punishment for or on account of (1) the commission by such person of an unlawful employment practice if he pleads and proves that the act or omission complained of was in good faith, in conformity with, and in reliance on any written interpretation or opinion of the Commission, or (2) the failure of such person to publish and file any information required by any provision of this title if he pleads and proves that he failed to publish and file such information in good faith, in conformity with the instructions of the Commission issued under this title regarding the filing of such information. Such a defense, if established, shall be a bar to the action or proceeding, notwithstanding that (A) after such act or omission, such interpretation or opinion is modified or rescinded or is determined by judicial authority to be invalid or of no legal effect, or (B) after publishing or filing the description and annual reports, such publication or filing is determined by judicial authority not to be in conformity with the requirements of this title.

FORCIBLY RESISTING THE COMMISSION OR ITS REPRESENTATIVES

SEC. 714 [42 U.S.C. § 2000e-13].

The provisions of sections 111 and 114, title 18, United States Code, shall apply to officers, agents, and employees of the Commission in the performance of their official duties. Notwithstanding the provisions of sections 111 and 114 of title 18, whoever in violation of the provisions of section 114 of such title kills a person while engaged in or on account of the performance of his official functions under this Act shall be punished by imprisonment for any term of years or for life.

EQUAL EMPLOYMENT OPPORTUNITY COORDINATING COUNCIL

SEC. 715 [42 U.S.C. §2000e-14].

The Equal Employment Opportunity Commission shall have the responsibility for developing and implementing agreements, policies and practices designed to maximize effort, promote efficiency, and eliminate conflict, competition, duplication and inconsistency among the operations, functions and jurisdictions of the various departments, agencies and branches of the Federal government responsible for the implementation and enforcement of equal employment opportunity legislation, orders, and policies. On or before October 1 of each year, the Council shall transmit to the President and to the Congress a report of its activities, together with such recommendations for legislative or administrative changes as it concludes are desirable to further promote the purposes of this section.[14]

EFFECTIVE DATE

SEC. 716 [42 U.S.C. §2000e-15].

(a) This title shall become effective one year after the date of its enactment.

(b) Notwithstanding subsection (a), sections of this title other than sections 703, 704, 706, and 707 shall become effective immediately.

(c) The President shall, as soon as feasible after the enactment of this title, convene one or more conferences for the purpose of enabling the leaders of groups whose members will be affected by this title to become familiar with the rights afforded and obligations imposed by its provisions, and for the purpose of making plans which will result in the fair and effective administration of this title when all of its provisions become effective. The President shall invite the participation in such conference or conferences of (1) the members of the President's Committee on Equal Employment Opportunity, (2) the members of the Commission on Civil Rights, (3) representatives of State and local agencies engaged in furthering equal employment opportunity, (4) representatives of private agencies engaged in furthering equal employment opportunity, and (5) representatives of employers, labor organizations, and employment agencies who will be subject to this title.

NONDISCRIMINATION IN FEDERAL GOVERNMENT EMPLOYMENT

SEC. 717 [42 U.S.C. §2000e-16].

(a) All personnel actions affecting employees or applicants for employment (except with regard to aliens employed outside the limits of the United States) in military departments as defined in section 102 of title 5, in executive agencies as defined in section 105 of title 5 (including employees and applicants for employment who are paid from nonappropriated funds), in the United States Postal Service and the Postal Rate Commission, in those units of the Government of the District of Columbia having positions in the competitive service, and in those units of the legislative and judicial branches of the Federal Government having positions in the competitive service and in the Library of Congress shall be made free from any discrimination based on race, color, religion, sex, or national origin.

(b) Except as otherwise provided in this subsection, the Equal Employment Opportunity Commission shall have authority to enforce the provisions of subsection (a) through ap-

14. Reads as Amended by Reorganization Plan No. 1 of 1978, 43 Fed. Reg. 19807 and Executive Order 12067. 43 Fed. Reg. 28967 (June 30. 1978).

propriate remedies, including reinstatement or hiring of employees with or without back pay, as will effectuate the policies of this section, and shall issue such rules, regulations, orders, and instructions as it deems necessary and appropriate to carry out its responsibilities under this section. The Equal Employment Opportunity Commission shall—

(1) be responsible for the annual review and approval of a national and regional equal employment opportunity plan which each department and agency and each appropriate unit referred to in subsection (a) of this section shall submit in order to maintain an affirmative program of equal employment opportunity for all such employees and applicants for employment;

(2) be responsible for the review and evaluation of the operation of all agency equal employment opportunity programs, periodically obtaining and publishing (on at least a semiannual basis) progress reports from each such department, agency, or unit; and

(3) consult with and solicit the recommendations of interested individuals, groups, and organizations relating to equal employment opportunity.

The head of each such department, agency, or unit shall comply with such rules, regulations, orders, and instructions which shall include a provision that an employee or applicant for employment shall be notified of any final action taken on any complaint of discrimination filed by him thereunder. The plan submitted by each department, agency, and unit shall include, but not be limited to—

(1) provision for the establishment of training and education programs designed to provide a maximum opportunity for employees to advance so as to perform at their highest potential; and

(2) a description of the qualifications in terms of training and experience relating to equal employment opportunity for the principal and operating officials of each such department, agency, or unit responsible for carrying out the equal employment opportunity program and of the allocation of personnel and resources proposed by such department, agency, or unit to carry out its equal employment opportunity program.

With respect to employment in the Library of Congress, authorities granted in this subsection to the Civil Service Commission shall be exercised by the Librarian of Congress.

(c) Within ninety days of receipt of notice of final action taken by a department, agency, or unit referred to in subsection (a), or by the Civil Service Commission upon an appeal from a decision or order of such department, agency, or unit on a complaint of discrimination based on race, color, religion, sex, or national origin, brought pursuant to subsection (a) of this section, Executive Order 11478 or any succeeding Executive orders, or after one hundred and eighty days from the filing of the initial charge with the department, agency, or unit or with the Civil Service Commission on appeal from a decision or order of such department, agency, or unit until such time as final action may be taken by a department, agency, or unit, an employee or applicant for employment, if aggrieved by the final disposition of his complaint, or by the failure to take final action on his complaint, may file a civil action as provided in section 706, in which civil action the head of the department, agency, or unit, as appropriate, shall be the defendant.

(d) The provisions of section 706(f) through (k), as applicable, shall govern civil actions brought hereunder, **and the same interest to compensate for delay in payment shall be available as in cases involving nonpublic parties.**

(e) Nothing contained in this Act shall relieve any Government agency or official of its or his primary responsibility to assure nondiscrimination in employment as required by the Constitution and statutes or of its or his responsibilities under Executive Order 11478 relating to equal employment opportunity in the Federal Government.

[42 U.S.C. §2000e-16a].

(a) Sections 2000e-16a to 2000e-16c of this title may be cited as the "Government Employee Rights Act of 1991."

(b) The purpose of sections 2000e-16a to 2000e-16c of this title is to provide procedures to protect the rights of certain government employees, with respect to their public employment, to be free of discrimination on the basis of race, color, religion, sex, national origin, age, or disability.

(c) For purposes of sections 2000e-16a to 2000e-16c of this title, the term "violation" means a practice that violates section 2000e-16b(a) of this title.

[Sec. 2000e-16b].

(a) All personnel actions affecting the Presidential appointees described in section 1219[15] of title 2 or the State employees described in section 2000e-16c of this title shall be made free from any discrimination based on-

(1) race, color, religion, sex, or national origin, within the meaning of section 2000e-16 of this title;

(2) age, within the meaning of section 633a of title 29; or

(3) disability, within the meaning of section 791 of title 29 and sections 12112 to 12114 of this title.

(b) The remedies referred to in sections 1219(a)(1)[16] of title 2 and 2000e-16c(a) of this title-

(1) may include, in the case of a determination that a violation of subsection (a)(1) or (a)(3) of this section has occurred, such remedies as would be appropriate if awarded under sections 2000e-5(g), 2000e-5(k), and 2000e-16(d) of this title, and such compensatory damages as would be appropriate if awarded under section 1981 or sections 1981a(a) and 1981a(b)(2) of this title;

(2) may include, in the case of a determination that a violation of subsection (a)(2) of this section has occurred, such remedies as would be appropriate if awarded under section 633a(c) of title 29; and

(3) may not include punitive damages.

[Sec. 2000e-16c].

(a) The rights, protections, and remedies provided pursuant to section 2000e-16b of this title shall apply with respect to employment of any individual chosen or appointed, by a person elected to public office in any State or political subdivision of any State by the qualified voters thereof-

(1) to be a member of the elected official's personal staff;

(2) to serve the elected official on the policymaking level; or

(3) to serve the elected official as an immediate advisor with respect to the exercise of the constitutional or legal powers of the office.

15. Repealed by Pub. L. 104-331, §5(a), 110 Stat. 4072 (October 26, 1996).
16. *Id.*

(b)(1) In general. Any individual referred to in subsection (a) of this section may file a complaint alleging a violation, not later than 180 days after the occurrence of the alleged violation, with the Equal Employment Opportunity Commission, which, in accordance with the principles and procedures set forth in sections 554 through 557 of title 5, shall determine whether a violation has occurred and shall set forth its determination in a final order. If the Equal Employment Opportunity Commission determines that a violation has occurred, the final order shall also provide for appropriate relief.

(2) Referral to State and local authorities

(A) *Application.* Section 2000e-5(d) of this title shall apply with respect to any proceeding under this section.

(B) *Definition.* For purposes of the application described in subparagraph (A), the term "any charge filed by a member of the Commission alleging an unlawful employment practice" means a complaint filed under this section.

(c) Any party aggrieved by a final order under subsection (b) of this section may obtain a review of such order under chapter 158 of title 28. For the purpose of this review, the Equal Employment Opportunity Commission shall be an "agency" as that term is used in chapter 158 of title 28.

(d) To the extent necessary to decision and when presented, the reviewing court shall decide all relevant questions of law and interpret constitutional and statutory provisions. The court shall set aside a final order under subsection (b) of this section if it is determined that the order was-

(1) arbitrary, capricious, an abuse of discretion, or otherwise not consistent with law;

(2) not made consistent with required procedures; or

(3) unsupported by substantial evidence.

In making the foregoing determinations, the court shall review the whole record or those parts of it cited by a party, and due account shall be taken of the rule of prejudicial error.

(e) If the individual referred to in subsection (a) of this section is the prevailing party in a proceeding under this subsection, attorney's fees may be allowed by the court in accordance with the standards prescribed under section 2000e-5(k) of this title.[17]

SPECIAL PROVISIONS WITH RESPECT TO DENIAL, TERMINATION, AND SUSPENSION OF GOVERNMENT CONTRACTS

SEC. 718 [42 U.S.C. §2000e-17].

No Government contract, or portion thereof, with any employer, shall be denied, withheld, terminated, or suspended, by any agency or officer of the United States under any equal employment opportunity law or order, where such employer has an affirmative action plan which has previously been accepted by the Government for the same facility within the past twelve months without first according such employer full hearing and adjudication under the provisions of title 5, section 554, and the following pertinent sections: Provided, That if such employer has deviated substantially from such previously agreed to affirmative action plan, this section shall not apply: Provided further, That for the purposes of this section an affirmative action plan shall be deemed to have been accepted by the Government at the time the appropriate compliance agency has accepted such plan unless within forty-five days thereafter the Office of Federal Contract Compliance has disapproved such plan.

17. Added by Pub. L. 102-166, §§301-302, 321, 105 Stat. 1088, 1097 (November 21, 1991).

Selected Provisions of the Civil Rights Act of 1991

P.L. 102-166, (November 21, 1991) 105 Stat. 1071

42 U.S.C. § 1981 note

Sec. 1. Short Title.

This Act may be cited as the "Civil Rights Act of 1991".

Sec. 2. Findings.

The Congress finds that—

(1) additional remedies under Federal law are needed to deter unlawful harassment and intentional discrimination in the workplace;

(2) the decision of the Supreme Court in *Wards Cove Packing Co. v. Atonio*, 490 U.S. 642 (1989) has weakened the scope and effectiveness of Federal civil rights protections; and

(3) legislation is necessary to provide additional protections against unlawful discrimination in employment.

Sec. 3. Purposes.

The purposes of this Act are—

(1) to provide appropriate remedies for intentional discrimination and unlawful harassment in the workplace;

(2) to codify the concepts of "business necessity" and "job related" enunciated by the Supreme Court in *Griggs v. Duke Power Co.*, 401 U.S. 424 (1971), and in the other Supreme Court decisions prior to *Wards Cove Packing Co. v. Atonio*, 490 U.S. 642 (1989);

(3) to confirm statutory authority and provide statutory guidelines for the adjudication of disparate impact suits under title VII of the Civil Rights Act of 1964 (42 U.S.C. 2000e *et seq.*); and

(4) to respond to recent decisions of the Supreme Court by expanding the scope of relevant civil rights statutes in order to provide adequate protection to victims of discrimination.

Title I. Federal Civil Rights Remedies

* * *

Sec. 116. Lawful Court-Ordered Remedies, Affirmative Action, and Conciliation Agreements Not Affected.

Nothing in the amendments made by this title shall be construed to affect court-ordered remedies, affirmative action, or conciliation agreements, that are in accordance with the law.

Sec. 117. Coverage of House of Representative and the Agencies of the Legislative Branch. [2 U.S.C. § 60l].

(a) Coverage of the House of Representatives.—

(1) In general.—Notwithstanding any provision of title VII of the Civil Rights Act of 1964 (42 U.S.C. 2000e *et seq.*) or of other law, the purposes of such title shall, subject to paragraph (2), apply in their entirety to the House of Representatives.

(2) Employment in the house.—

(A) Application.—The rights and protections under title VII of the Civil Rights Act of 1964 (42 U.S.C. 2000e §.) shall, subject to subparagraph (B), apply with respect to any employee in an employment position in the House of Representatives and any employing authority of the House of Representatives.

(B) Administration.—

(i) In general.—In the administration of this paragraph, the remedies and procedures made applicable pursuant to the resolution described in clause (ii) shall apply exclusively.

(ii) Resolution.—The resolution referred to in clause (i) is the Fair Employment Practices Resolution (House Resolution *558* of the One Hundredth Congress, as agreed to October 4,1988), as incorporated into the Rules of the House of Representatives of the One Hundred Second Congress as Rule LI, or any other provision that continues in effect the provisions of such resolution.

(C) Exercise of rule making power.—The provisions of subparagraph (B) are enacted by the House of Representatives as an exercise of the rule making power of the House of Representatives, with full recognition of the right of the House to change its rules, in the same manner, and to the same extent as in the case of any other rule of the House.

(b) Instrumentalities of Congress.—

(1) In general.—The rights and protections under this title and title VII of the Civil Rights Act of 1964 (42 U.S.C. 2000e *et seq.*) shall, subject to paragraph (2), apply with respect to the conduct of each instrumentality of the Congress.

(2) Establishment of remedies and procedures by instrumentalities.—The chief official of each instrumentality of the Congress shall establish remedies and procedures to be utilized with respect to the rights and protections provided pursuant to paragraph (1). Such remedies and procedures shall apply exclusively, except for the employees who are defined as Senate employees, in section 301(c)(l).

(3) Report to Congress.—The chief official of each instrumentality of the Congress shall, after establishing remedies and procedures for purposes of paragraph (2), submit to the Congress a report describing the remedies and procedures.

(4) Definition of instrumentalities.—For purposes of this section, instrumentalities of the Congress include the following: the Architect of the Capitol, the Congressional Budget Office, the General Accounting Office, the Government Printing Office, the Office of Technology Assessment, and the United States Botanic Garden.

(5) Construction.—Nothing in this section shall alter the enforcement procedures for individuals protected under section 717 of title VII of the Civil Rights Act of 1964 (42 U.S.C. 2000e-16).

Sec. 118. Alternative Means of Dispute Resolution.

Where appropriate and to the extent authorized by law, the use of alternative means of dispute resolution, including settlement negotiations, conciliation, facilitation, mediation, fact finding, minitrials, and arbitration, is encouraged to resolve disputes arising under the Acts or provisions of Federal law amended by this title.

Title IV. General Provisions

42 U.S.C. § 1981 note

Sec. 401. Severability.

If any provision of this Act, or an amendment made by this Act, or the application of such provision to any person or circumstances is held to be invalid, the remainder of this Act and the amendments made by this Act, and the applications of such provision to other persons and circumstances, shall not be affected.

Sec. 402. Effective Date.

(a) In General.—Except as otherwise specifically provided, this Act and the amendments made by this Act shall take effect upon enactment.

(b) Certain Disparate Impact Cases.—Notwithstanding any other provisions of this Act, nothing in this Act shall apply to any disparate impact case for which a complaint was filed before March 1, 1975 and for which an initial decision was rendered after October 30, 1983.

Selected Provisions of the Lilly Ledbetter Fair Pay Act of 2009

Pub. L. No. 111-2, 123 Stat. 5 (2009)

Sec. 1. Short Title

This Act may be cited as the "Lilly Ledbetter Fair Pay Act of 2009".

Sec. 2. Finding

Congress finds the following:

(1) The Supreme Court in *Ledbetter v. Goodyear Tire & Rubber Co.*, 550 U.S. 618 (2007), significantly impairs statutory protections against discrimination in compensation that Congress established and that have been bedrock principles of American law for decades. The Ledbetter decision undermines those statutory protections by unduly restricting the time period in which victims of discrimination can challenge and recover for discriminatory compensation decisions or other practices, contrary to the intent of Congress

(2) The limitation imposed by the Court on the filing of discriminatory compensation claims ignores the reality of wage discrimination and is at odds with the robust application of the civil rights laws that Congress intended.

(3) With regard to any charge of discrimination under any law, nothing in this Act is intended to preclude or limit an aggrieved person's right to introduce evidence of an unlawful employment practice that has occurred outside the time for filing a charge of discrimination.

(4) Nothing in this Act is intended to change current law treatment of when pension distributions are considered paid.

* * *

Sec. 6. Effective Date

This Act, and the amendments made by this Act, take effect as if enacted on May 28, 2007, and apply to all claims of discrimination in compensation under title VII of the Civil Rights Act of 1964 (42 U.S.C. 2000e et seq.), the Age Discrimination in Employment Act of 1967 (29 U.S.C. 621 et seq.), title I and section 503 of the Americans with Disabilities Act of 1990, and sections 501 and 504 of the Rehabilitation Act of 1973, that are pending on or after that date.

Equal Employment Opportunity Commission Discrimination Guidelines

29 C.F.R. §§ 1604, 1605, 1606

Part 1604. Guidelines on Discrimination Because of Sex

1604.1 General principles.

(a) References to "employer" or "employers" in this Part 1604 state principles that are applicable not only to employers but also to labor organizations and to employment agencies insofar as their action or inaction may adversely affect employment opportunities.

(b) To the extent that the views expressed in prior Commission pronouncements are inconsistent with the views expressed herein, such prior views are hereby overruled.

(c) The Commission will continue to consider particular problems relating to sex discrimination on a case-by-case basis.

1604.2 Sex as a bona fide occupational qualification.

(a) The Commission believes that the bona fide occupational qualification exception as to sex should be interpreted narrowly. Labels—"Men's jobs" and "Women's jobs"—tend to deny employment opportunities unnecessarily to one sex or the other.

(1) The Commission will find that the following situations do not warrant the application of the bona fide occupational qualification exception:

(i) The refusal to hire a woman because of her sex based on assumptions of the comparative employment characteristics of women in general. For example, the assumption that the turnover rate among women is higher than among men.

(ii) The refusal to hire an individual based on stereotyped characterizations of the sexes. Such stereotypes include, for example, that men are less capable of assembling intricate equipment; that women are less capable of aggressive salesmanship. The principle of nondiscrimination requires that individuals be considered on the basis of individual capacities and not on the basis of any characteristics generally attributed to the group.

(iii) The refusal to hire an individual because of the preferences of coworkers, the employer, clients or customers except as covered specifically in subparagraph (2) of this paragraph.

(2) Where it is necessary for the purpose of authenticity or genuineness, the Commission will consider sex to be a bona fide occupational qualification, e.g., an actor or actress.

(b) Effect of sex-oriented State employment legislation.

(1) Many States have enacted laws or promulgated administrative regulations with respect to the employment of females. Among these laws are those which prohibit or limit the employment of females, e.g., the employment of females in certain occupations, in jobs requiring the lifting or carrying of weights exceeding certain prescribed limits, during certain hours of the night, for more than a specified number of hours per day or per week, and for certain periods of time before and after childbirth. The Commission has found that such laws and regulations do not take into account the capacities, preferences, and abilities of individual females and, therefore, discriminate on the basis of sex. The Commission has concluded that such laws and regulations conflict with

and are superseded by title VII of the Civil Rights Act of 1964. Accordingly, such laws will not be considered a defense to an otherwise established unlawful employment practice or as a basis for the application of the bona fide occupational qualification exception.

(2) The Commission has concluded that State laws and regulations which discriminate on the basis of sex with regard to the employment of minors are in conflict with and are superseded by title VII to the extent that such laws are more restrictive for one sex. Accordingly, restrictions on the employment of minors of one sex over and above those imposed on minors of the other sex will not be considered a defense to an otherwise established unlawful employment practice or as a basis for the application of the bona fide occupational qualification exception.

(3) A number of States require that minimum wage and premium pay for overtime be provided for female employees. An employer will be deemed to have engaged in an unlawful employment practice if:

(i) It refuses to hire or otherwise adversely affects the employment opportunities of female applicants or employees in order to avoid the payment of minimum wages or overtime pay required by State law; or

(ii) It does not provide the same benefits for male employees.

(4) As to other kinds of sex-oriented State employment laws, such as those requiring special rest and meal periods or physical facilities for women, provision of these benefits to one sex only will be a violation of title VII. An employer will be deemed to have engaged in an unlawful employment practice if:

(i) It refuses to hire or otherwise adversely affects the employment opportunities of female applicants or employees in order to avoid the provision of such benefits; or

(ii) It does not provide the same benefits for male employees. If the employer can prove that business necessity precludes providing these benefits to both men and women, then the State law is in conflict with and superseded by title VII as to this employer. In this situation, the employer shall not provide such benefits to members of either sex.

(5) Some States require that separate restrooms be provided for employees of each sex. An employer will be deemed to have engaged in an unlawful employment practice if it refuses to hire or otherwise adversely affects the employment opportunities of applicants or employees in order to avoid the provision of such restrooms for persons of that sex.

1604.3 Separate lines of progression and seniority systems.

(a) It is an unlawful employment practice to classify a job as "male" or "female" or to maintain separate lines of progression or separate seniority lists based on sex where this would adversely affect any employee unless sex is a bona fide occupational qualification for that job. Accordingly, employment practices are unlawful which arbitrarily classify jobs so that:

(1) A female is prohibited from applying for a job labeled "male," or for a job in a "male" line of progression; and vice versa.

(2) A male scheduled for layoff is prohibited from displacing a less senior female on a "female" seniority list; and vice versa.

(b) A seniority system or line of progression which distinguishes between "light" and "heavy" jobs constitutes an unlawful employment practice if it operates as a disguised form of classification by sex, or creates unreasonable obstacles to the advancement by members of either sex into jobs which members of that sex would reasonably be expected to perform.

1604.4 Discrimination against married women.

(a) The Commission has determined that an employer's rule which forbids or restricts the employment of married women and which is not applicable to married men is a discrimination based on sex prohibited by title VII of the Civil Rights Act. It does not seem to us relevant that the rule is not directed against all females, but only against married females, for so long as sex is a factor in the application of the rule, such application involves a discrimination based on sex.

(b) It may be that under certain circumstances, such a rule could be justified within the meaning of section 703(e)(1) of title VII. We express no opinion on this question at this time except to point out that sex as a bona fide occupational qualification must be justified in terms of the peculiar requirements of the particular job and not on the basis of a general principle such as the desirability of spreading work.

1604.5 Job opportunities advertising.

It is a violation of title VII for a help-wanted advertisement to indicate a preference, limitation, specification, or discrimination based on sex unless sex is a bona fide occupational qualification for the particular job involved. The placement of an advertisement in columns classified by publishers on the basis of sex, such as columns headed "Male" or "Female," will be considered an expression of a preference, limitation, specification, or discrimination based on sex.

1604.6 Employment agencies.

(a) Section 703(b) of the Civil Rights Act specifically states that it shall be unlawful for an employment agency to discriminate against any individual because of sex. The Commission has determined that private employment agencies which deal exclusively with one sex are engaged in an unlawful employment practice, except to the extent that such agencies limit their services to furnishing employees for particular jobs for which sex is a bona fide occupational qualification.

(b) An employment agency that receives a job order containing an unlawful sex specification will share responsibility with the employer placing the job order if the agency fills the order knowing that the sex specification is not based upon a bona fide occupational qualification. However, an employment agency will not be deemed to be in violation of the law, regardless of the determination as to the employer, if the agency does not have reason to believe that the employer's claim of bona fide occupations qualification is without substance and the agency makes and maintains a written record available to the Commission of each such job order. Such record shall include the name of the employer, the description of the job and the basis for the employer's claim of bona fide occupational qualification.

(c) It is the responsibility of employment agencies to keep informed of opinions and decisions of the Commission on sex discrimination.

1604.7 Pre-employment inquiries as to sex.

A pre-employment inquiry may ask "Male.... ...., Female........" or "Mr. Mrs. Miss," provided that the inquiry is made in good faith for a nondiscriminatory purpose. Any pre-employment inquiry in connection with prospective employment which expresses directly or indirectly any limitation, specification, or discrimination as to sex shall be unlawful unless based upon a bona fide occupational qualification.

1604.8 Relationship of Title VII to the Equal Pay Act.

(a) The employee coverage of the prohibitions against discrimination based on sex contained in title VII is coextensive with that of the other prohibitions contained in title VII and is not limited by section 703(h) to those employees covered by the Fair Labor Standards Act.

(b) By virtue of section 703(h), a defense based on the Equal Pay Act may be raised in a proceeding under title VII.

(c) Where such a defense is raised the Commission will give appropriate consideration to the interpretations of the Administrator, Wage and Hour Division, Department of Labor, but will not be bound thereby.

1604.9 Fringe benefits.

(a) "Fringe benefits," as used herein, includes medical, hospital, accident, life insurance and retirement benefits; profit-sharing and bonus plans; leave; and other terms, conditions, and privileges of employment.

(b) It shall be an unlawful employment practice for an employer to discriminate between men and women with regard to fringe benefits.

(c) Where an employer conditions benefits available to employees and their spouses and families on whether the employee is the "head of the household" or "principal wage earner" in the family unit, the benefits tend to be available only to male employees and their families. Due to the fact that such conditioning discriminatorily affects the rights of women employees, and that "head of household" or "principal wage earner" status bears no relationship to job performance, benefits which are so conditioned will be found a prima facie violation of the prohibitions against sex discrimination contained in the Act.

(d) It shall be an unlawful employment practice for an employer to make available benefits for the wives and families of male employees where the same benefits are not made available for the husbands and families of female employees; or to make available benefits for the wives of male employees which are not made available for female employees; or to make available benefits to the husbands of female employees which are not made available for male employees. An example of such an unlawful employment practice is a situation in which wives of male employees receive maternity benefits while female employees receive no such benefits.

(e) It shall not be a defense under title VII to a charge of sex discrimination in benefits that the cost of such benefits is greater with respect to one sex than the other.

(f) It shall be an unlawful employment practice for an employer to have a pension or retirement plan which establishes different optional or compulsory retirement ages based on sex, or which differentiates in benefits on the basis of sex. A statement of the General Counsel of September 13, 1968, providing for a phasing out of differentials with regard to optional retirement age for certain incumbent employees is hereby withdrawn.

1604.10 Employment policies relating to pregnancy and childbirth.

(a) A written or unwritten employment policy or practice which excludes from employment opportunities applicants or employees because of pregnancy, childbirth or related medical conditions is in prima facie violation of Title VII.

(b) Disabilities caused or contributed to by pregnancy, childbirth, or related medical conditions, for all job-related purposes, shall be treated the same as disabilities caused or contributed to by other medical conditions, under any health or disability insurance or sick leave plan available in connection with employment. Written or unwritten employment policies and practices involving matters such as the commencement and duration of leave, the availability of extensions, the accrual of seniority and other benefits and privileges, reinstatement, and payment under any health or disability insurance or sick leave plan, formal or informal, shall be applied to disability due to pregnancy, childbirth, or related medical conditions on the same terms and conditions as they are applied to other disabilities. Health insurance benefits for abortion, except where the life of the mother would be endangered if the fetus were carried to term or where medical complications have arisen from an abortion, are not required to be paid by an employer; nothing herein, however, precludes an employer from providing abortion benefits or otherwise affects bargaining agreements in regard to abortion.

(c) Where the termination of an employee who is temporarily disabled is caused by an employment policy under which insufficient or no leave is available, such a termination violates the Act if it has a disparate impact on employees of one sex and is not justified by business necessity.

(d) (1) Any fringe benefit program, or fund, or insurance program which is in effect on October 31, 1978, which does not treat women affected by pregnancy, childbirth, or related medical conditions the same as other persons not so affected but similar in their ability or inability to work, must be in compliance with the provisions of § 1604.10(b) by April 29, 1979. In order to come into compliance with the provisions of § 1604.10(b), there can be no reduction of benefits or compensation which were in effect on October 31, 1978, before October 31, 1979 or the expiration of a collective bargaining agreement in effect on October 31, 1978, whichever is later.

(2) Any fringe benefit program implemented after October 31, 1978, must comply with the provisions of § 1604.10(b) upon implementation.

1604.11 Sexual harassment.

(a) Harassment on the basis of sex is a violation of Sec. 703 of Title VII.[18] Unwelcome sexual advances, requests for sexual favors, and other verbal or physical conduct of a sexual nature constitute sexual harassment when (1) submission to such conduct is made either explicitly or implicitly a term or condition of an individual's employment, (2) submission to or rejection of such conduct by an individual is used as the basis for employment decisions affecting such individual, or (3) such conduct has the purpose or effect of unreasonably interfering with an individual's work performance or creating an intimidating, hostile, or offensive working environment.

(b) In determining whether alleged conduct constitutes sexual harassment, the Commission will look at the record as a whole and at the totality of the circumstances, such as the nature of the sexual advances and the context in which the alleged incidents occurred. The determination of the legality of a particular action will be made from the facts, on a case by case basis.

(c) [Removed and reserved by amendment at 64 Fed. Reg. 58333 effective October 29, 1999]

18. The principles involved here continue to apply to race, color, religion or national origin.

(d) With respect to conduct between fellow employees, an employer is responsible for acts of sexual harassment in the workplace where the employer (or its agents or supervisory employees) knows or should have known of the conduct, unless it can show that it took immediate and appropriate corrective action.

(e) An employer may also be responsible for the acts of nonemployees, with respect to sexual harassment of employees in the workplace, where the employer (or its agents or supervisory employees) knows or should have known of the conduct and fails to take immediate and appropriate corrective action. In reviewing these cases the Commission will consider the extent of the employer's control and any other legal responsibility which the employer may have with respect to the conduct of such non-employees.

(f) Prevention is the best tool for the elimination of sexual harassment. An employer should take all steps necessary to prevent sexual harassment from occurring, such as affirmatively raising the subject, expressing strong disapproval, developing appropriate sanctions, informing employees of their right to raise and how to raise the issue of harassment under Title VII, and developing methods to sensitize all concerned.

(g) Other related practices: Where employment opportunities or benefits are granted because of an individual's submission to the employer's sexual advances or requests for sexual favors, the employer may be held liable for unlawful sex discrimination against other persons who were qualified for but denied that employment opportunity or benefit.

Questions & Answers on the Pregnancy Discrimination Act

Pub. L. 95-555, 92 Stat. 2076 (1978)

Introduction

On October 31, 1978, President Carter signed into law the Pregnancy Discrimination Act (Pub. L. 95-955). The Act is an amendment to Title VII of the Civil Rights Act of 1964 which prohibits, among other things, discrimination in employment on the basis of sex. The Pregnancy Discrimination Act makes it clear that "because of sex" or "on the basis of sex" as used in Title VII, includes "because of or on the basis of pregnancy, childbirth or related medical conditions." Therefore, Title VII prohibits discrimination in employment against women affected by pregnancy or related conditions.

The basic principle of the Act is that women affected by pregnancy and related conditions must be treated the same as other applicants and employees on the basis of their ability or inability to work. A woman is therefore protected against such practices as being fired, or refused a job or promotion, merely because she is pregnant or has had an abortion. She usually cannot be forced to go on leave as long as she can still work. If other employees who take disability leave are entitled to get their jobs back when they are able to work again, so are women who have been unable to work because of pregnancy.

In the area of fringe benefits, such as disability benefits, sick leave and health insurance, the same principle applies. A woman unable to work for pregnancy-related reasons is entitled to disability benefits or sick leave on the same basis as employees unable to work for other medical reasons. Also, any health insurance provided must cover expenses for pregnancy-related conditions on the same basis as expenses for other medical conditions. However, health insurance for expenses arising from abortion is not required except where the life of the mother would be endangered if the fetus were carried to term, or where medical complications have arisen from an abortion.

Some questions and answers about the Pregnancy Discrimination Act follow. Although the questions and answers often use only the term "employer," the Act—and these questions and answers—apply also to unions and other entities covered by Title VII.

1. Q. What is the effective date of the Pregnancy Discrimination Act?

A. The Act became effective on October 31, 1978, except that with respect to fringe benefit programs in effect on that date, the Act will take effect 180 days thereafter, that is, April 29, 1979.

To the extent that Title VII already required employers to treat persons affected by pregnancy-related conditions the same as persons affected by other medical conditions, the Act does not change employee rights arising prior to October 31, 1978, or April 29, 1979. Most employment practices relating to pregnancy, childbirth and related conditions—whether concerning fringe benefits or other practices—were already controlled by Title VII prior to this Act. For example, Title VII has always prohibited an employer from firing, or refusing to hire or promote, a woman because of pregnancy or related conditions, and from failing to accord a woman on pregnancy-related leave the same seniority retention and accrual accorded those on other disability leaves.

2. Q. If an employer had a sick leave policy in effect on October 31, 1978, by what date must the employer bring its policy into compliance with the Act?

A. With respect to payment of benefits, an employer has until April 29, 1979, to bring into compliance any fringe benefit or insurance program, including a sick leave policy, which was in effect on October 31, 1978. However, any such policy or program created after October 31, 1978, must be in compliance when created.

With respect to all aspects of sick leave policy other than payment of benefits, such as the terms governing retention and accrual of seniority, credit for vacation, and resumption of former job on return from sick leave, equality of treatment was required by Title VII without the Amendment.

3. Q. Must an employer provide benefits for pregnancy-related conditions to an employee whose pregnancy begins prior to April 29, 1979, and continues beyond that date?

A. As of April 29, 1979, the effective date of the Act's requirements, an employer must provide the same benefits for pregnancy-related conditions as it provides for other conditions, regardless of when the pregnancy began. Thus, disability benefits must be paid for all absences on or after April 29, 1979, resulting from pregnancy-related temporary disabilities to the same extent as they are paid for absences resulting from other temporary disabilities. For example, if an employee gives birth before April 29, 1979, but is still unable to work on or after that date, she is entitled to the same disability benefits available to other employees. Similarily [sic], medical insurance benefits must be paid for pregnancy-related expenses incurred on or after April 29, 1979.

If an employer requires an employee to be employed for a predetermined period prior to being eligible for insurance coverage, the period prior to April 29, 1979, during which a pregnant employee has been employed must be credited toward the eligibility waiting period on the same basis as for any other employee.

As to any programs instituted for the first time after October 31, 1978, coverage for pregnancy-related conditions must be provided in the same manner as for other medical conditions.

4. Q. Would the answer to the preceding question be the same if the employee became pregnant prior to October 31,1978?

A. Yes.

5. Q. If, for pregnancy-related reasons, an employee is unable to perform the functions of her job, does the employer have to provide her an alternative job?

A. An employer is required to treat an employee temporarily unable to perform the functions of her job because of, her pregnancy-related condition in the same manner as it treats other temporarily disabled employees, whether by providing modified tasks, alternative assignments, disability leaves, leaves without pay, etc. For example, a woman's primary job function may be the operation of a machine, and, incidental to that function, she may carry materials to and from the machine. If other employees temporarily unable to lift are relieved of these functions, pregnant employees also unable to lift must be temporarily relieved of the function.

6. Q. What procedures may an employer use to determine whether to place on leave as unable to work a pregnant employee who claims she is able to work or deny leave to a pregnant employee who claims that she is disabled from work?

A. An employer may not single out pregnancy-related conditions for special procedures for determining an employee's ability to work. However, an employer may use any procedure 'used to determine the ability of all employees to work. For example, if an employer requires its employees to submit a doctor's statement concerning their inability to work before granting leave or paying sick benefits, the employer may require employees affected by pregnancy-related conditions to submit such statements. Similarly, if an employer allows its employees to obtain doctor's statements from their personal physicians for absences due to other disabilities or return dates from other disabilities it must accept doctor's statements from personal physicians for absences and return dates connected with pregnancy-related disabilities.

7. Q. Can an employer have a rule which prohibits an employee from returning to work for a predetermined length of time after childbirth?

A. No.

8. Q. If an employee has been absent from work as a result of a pregnancy-related condition and recovers, may her employer require her to remain on leave until after her baby is born?

A. No. An employee must be permitted to work at all times during pregnancy when she is able to perform her job.

9. Q. Must an employer hold open the job of an employee who is absent on leave because she is temporarily disabled by pregnancy-related conditions?

A. Unless the employee on leave has informed the employer that she does not intend to return to work, her job must be held open for her return on the same basis as jobs are held open for employees on sick or disability leave for other reasons.

10. Q. May an employer's policy concerning the accrual and crediting of seniority during absences for medical conditions be different for employees affected by pregnancy-related conditions than for other employees?

A. No. An employer's seniority policy must be the same for employees absent for pregnancy-related reasons as for those absent for other medical reasons.

11. Q. For purposes of calculating such matters as vacations and pay increases, may an employer credit time spent on leave for pregnancy-related reasons differently than time spent on leave for other reasons?

A. No. An employer's policy with respect to crediting time for the purpose of calculating such matters as vacations and pay increases cannot treat employees on leave for pregnancy-related reasons less favorably than employees on leave for other reasons. For example, if employees on leave for medical reasons are credited with the time spent on leave when computing entitlement to vacation or pay raises, an employee on leave for pregnancy-related disability is entitled to the same kind of time credit.

12. Q. Must an employer hire a woman who is medically unable, because of a pregnancy-related condition, to perform a necessary function of a job?

A. An employer cannot refuse to hire a woman because of her pregnancy- related condition so long as she is able to perform the major functions necessary to the job. Nor can an employer refuse to hire her because of its preferences against pregnant workers or the preferences of co-workers, clients, or customers.

13. Q. May an employer limit disability benefits for pregnancy-related conditions to married employees?

A. No.

14. Q. If an employer has an all female workforce or job classification, must benefits be provided for pregnancy-related conditions?

A. Yes. If benefits are provided for other conditions, they must also be provided for pregnancy-related conditions.

15. Q. For what length of time must an employer who provides income maintenance benefits for temporary disabilities provide such benefits for pregnancy-related disabilities?

A. Benefits should be provided for as long as the employee is unable to work for medical reasons unless some other limitation is set for all other temporary disabilities, in which case pregnancy-related disabilities should be treated the same as other temporary disabilities.

16. Q. Must an employer who provides benefits for long-term or permanent disabilities provide such benefits for pregnancy-related conditions?

A. Yes. Benefits for long term or permanent disabilities resulting from pregnancy-related conditions must be provided to the same extent that such benefits are provided for other conditions which result in long-term or permanent disability.

17. Q. If an employer provides benefits to employees on leave, such as installment purchase disability insurance, payment of premiums for health, life or other insurance, continued payments into pension, saving or profit sharing plans, must the same benefits be provided for those on leave for pregnancy-related conditions?

A. Yes, the employer must provide the same benefits for those on leave for pregnancy-related conditions as for those on leave for other reasons.

18. Q. Can an employee who is absent due to a pregnancy-related disability be required to exhaust vacation benefits before receiving sick leave pay or disability benefits?

A. No. If employees who are absent because of other disabling causes receive sick leave pay or disability benefits without any requirement that they first exhaust vacation benefits, the employer cannot impose this requirement on an employee absent for a pregnancy-related cause.

18(A). Q. Must an employer grant leave to a female employee for childcare purposes after she is medically able to return to work following leave necessitated by pregnancy, childbirth or related medical conditions?

A. While leave for childcare purposes is not covered by the Pregnancy Discrimination Act, ordinary Title VII principles would require that leave for childcare purposes be granted on the same basis as leave which is granted to employees for other non-medical reasons. For example, if an employer allows its employees to take leave without pay or accrued annual leave for travel or education which is not job related, the same type of leave must be granted to those who wish to remain on leave for infant care, even though they are medically able to return to work.

19. Q. If state law requires an employer to provide disability insurance for a specified period before and after childbirth, does compliance with the state law fulfill the employer's obligation under the Pregnancy Discrimination Act?

A. Not necessarily. It is an employer's obligation to treat employees temporarily disabled by pregnancy in the same manner as employees affected by other temporary disabilities. Therefore, any restrictions imposed by state law on benefits for pregnancy-related disabilities, but not for other disabilities, do not excuse the employer from treating the individuals in both groups of employees the same. If, for example, a state law requires an employer to pay a maximum of 26 weeks benefits for disabilities other than pregnancy-related ones but only six weeks for pregnancy-related disabilities, the employer must provide benefits for the additional weeks to an employee disabled by pregnancy-related conditions, up to the maximum provided other disabled employees.

20. Q. If a State or local government provides its own employees income maintenance benefits for disabilities, may it provide different benefits for disabilities arising from pregnancy-related conditions than for disabilities arising from other conditions?

A. No. State and local governments, as employers, are subject to the Pregnancy Discrimination Act in the same way as private employers and must bring their employment practices and programs into compliance with the Act, including disability and health insurance programs.

21. Q. Must an employer provide health insurance coverage for the medical expenses of pregnancy-related conditions of the spouses of male employees? Of the dependents of all employees?

A. Where an employer provides no coverage for dependents, the employer is not required to institute such coverage. However, if an employers s insurance program covers the medical expenses of spouses of female employees then it must equally cover the medical expenses of spouses of male employees, including those arising from pregnancy-related conditions.

But the insurance does not have to cover the pregnancy-related conditions of non-spouse dependents as long as it excludes the pregnancy-related conditions of such non-spouse dependents of male and female employees equally.

22. Q. Must an employer provide the same level of health insurance coverage for the pregnancy-related medical conditions of the spouses of male employees as it provides for its female employees?

A. No. It is not necessary to provide the same level of coverage for the pregnancy-related medical conditions of spouses of male employees as for female employees. However, where the employer provides coverage for the medical conditions of the spouses of its employees, then the level of coverage for pregnancy-related medical conditions of the spouses of male employees must be the same as the level of coverage for all other medical conditions of the spouses of female employees. For example, if the employer covers employees for 100 percent of reasonable and customary expenses sustained for a medical condition, but only covers dependent spouses for 50 percent of reasonable and customary expenses for their medical conditions, the pregnancy-related expenses of the male employee's spouse must be covered at the 50 percent level.

23. Q. May an employer offer optional dependent coverage which excludes pregnancy-related medical conditions or offers less coverage for pregnancy-related medical conditions where the total premium for the optional coverage is paid by the employee?

A. No. Pregnancy-related medical conditions must be treated the same as other medical conditions under any health or disability insurance or sick leave plan available in connection with employment, regardless of who pays the premiums.

24. Q. Where an employer provides its employees a choice among several health insurance plans, must coverage for pregnancy-related conditions be offered in all of the plans?

A. Yes. Each of the plans must cover pregnancy-related conditions. For example, an employee with a single coverage policy cannot be forced to purchase a more expensive family coverage policy in order to receive coverage for her own pregnancy-related condition.

25. Q. On what basis should an employee be reimbursed for medical expenses arising from pregnancy, childbirth or related conditions?

A. Pregnancy-related expenses should be reimbursed in the same manner as are expenses incurred for other medical conditions. Therefore, whether a plan reimburses the employees on a fixed basis, or a percentage of reasonable and customary charge basis, the same basis should be used for reimbursement of expenses incurred for pregnancy-related conditions. Furthermore, if medical costs for pregnancy-related conditions increase, reevaluation of the reimbursement level should be conducted in the same manner as are cost reevaluations of increases for other medical conditions.

Coverage provided by a health insurance program for other conditions must be provided for pregnancy-related conditions. For example, if a plan provides major medical coverage, pregnancy-related conditions must be so covered. Similarly, if a plan covers the cost of a private room for other conditions, the plan must cover the cost of a private room for pregnancy-related conditions. Finally, where a health insurance plan covers office visits to physicians, pre-natal and post-natal visits must be included in such coverage.

26. Q. May an employer limit payment of costs for pregnancy-related medical conditions to a specified dollar amount set forth in an insurance policy, collective bargaining agreement or other statement of benefits to which an employee is entitled?

A. The amounts payable for the costs incurred for pregnancy-related conditions can be limited only to the same extent as are costs for other conditions. Maximum recoverable dollar amounts may be specified for pregnancy-related conditions if such amounts are similarly specified for other conditions, and so long as the specified amounts in all instances cover the same proportion of actual costs. If, in addition to the scheduled amount for other procedures, additional costs are paid for, either directly or indirectly, by the employer, such additional payments must also be paid for pregnancy-related procedures.

27. Q. May an employer impose a different deductible for payment of costs for pregnancy-related medical conditions than for costs of other medical conditions?

A. No. Neither an additional deductible, an increase in the usual 'deductible, nor a larger deductible can be imposed for coverage for pregnancy-related medical costs, whether as a condition for inclusion of pregnancy-related costs in the policy or for payment of the costs when incurred. Thus, if pregnancy-related costs are the first incurred under the policy, the employee is required to pay only the same deductible as would otherwise be required had other medical costs been the first incurred. Once this deductible has been paid, no additional deductible can be required for other medical procedures. If the usual deductible has already been paid for other medical procedures, no additional deductible can be required when pregnancy-related costs are later incurred.

28. Q. If a health insurance plan excludes the payment of benefits for any conditions existing at the time the insured's coverage becomes effective (pre-existing condition clause), can benefits be denied for medical costs arising from a pregnancy existing at the time the coverage became effective?

A. Yes. However, such benefits cannot be denied unless the preexisting condition clause also excludes benefits for other pre-existing conditions in the same way.

29. Q. If an employer's insurance plan provides benefits after the insured's employment has ended (i.e. extended benefits) for costs connected with pregnancy and delivery where conception occurred while the insured was working for the employer, but not for the costs of any other medical condition which began prior to termination of employment, may an employer (a) continue to pay these extended benefits for pregnancy-related medical conditions but not for other medical conditions, or (b) terminate these benefits for pregnancy-related conditions?

A. Where a health insurance plan currently provides extended benefits for other medical conditions on a less favorable basis than for pregnancy-related medical conditions, extended benefits must be provided for other medical conditions on the same basis as for pregnancy-related medical conditions. Therefore, an employer can neither continue to provide less benefits for other medical conditions nor reduce benefits currently paid for pregnancy-related medical conditions.

30. Q. Where an employer's health insurance plan currently requires total disability as a prerequisite for payment of 'extended benefits for other medical conditions but not for pregnancy-related costs, may the employer now require total disability for payment of benefits for pregnancy-related medical conditions as well?

A. Since extended benefits cannot be reduced in order to come into compliance with the Act, a more stringent prerequisite for payment of extended benefits for pregnancy-related medical conditions, such as a requirement for total disability, cannot be imposed. Thus, in this instance, in order to comply with the Act, the employer must treat other medical conditions as pregnancy-related conditions are treated.

31. Q. Can the added costs of bringing benefit plans into compliance with the Act be apportioned between the employer and employee?

A. The added cost, if any, can be apportioned between the employer and employee in the same proportion that the cost of the fringe benefit plan was apportioned on October 31, 1978, if that apportionment was nondiscriminatory. If the costs were not apportioned on October 31, 1978, they may not be apportioned in order to come into compliance with the Act. However, in no circumstance may male or female employees be required to pay unequal apportionments on the basis of sex or pregnancy.

32. Q. In order to come into compliance with the Act, may an employer reduce benefits or compensation?

A. In order to come into compliance with the Act, benefits or compensation which an employer was paying on October 31, 1978 cannot be reduced before October 31, 1979 or before the expiration of a collective bargaining agreement in effect on October 31, 1978, whichever is later.

Where an employer has not been in compliance with the Act by the times specified in the Act, and attempts to reduce benefits, or compensation, the employer may be required to remedy its practices in accord with ordinary Title VII remedial principles.

33. Q. Can an employer self-insure benefits for pregnancy-related conditions if it does not self-insure benefits for other medical conditions?

A. Yes, so long as the benefits are the same. In measuring whether benefits are the same, factors other than the dollar coverage paid should be considered. Such factors include the range of choice of physicians and hospitals, and the processing and promptness of payment of claims.

34. Q. Can an employer discharge, refuse to hire or otherwise discriminate against a woman because she has had or is contemplating having an abortion?

A. No. An employer cannot discriminate in its employment practices against a woman who has had or is contemplating having an abortion.

35. Q. Is an employer required to provide fringe benefits for abortions if fringe benefits are provided for other medical conditions?

A. All fringe benefits other than health insurance, such as sick leave, which are provided for other medical conditions, must be provided for abortions. Health insurance, however, need be provided for abortions only where the life of the woman would be endangered if the fetus were carried to term or where medical complications arise from an abortion.

36. Q. If complications arise during the course of an abortion, as for instance excessive hemorrhaging, must an employer's health insurance plan cover the additional cost due to the complications of the abortion?

A. Yes. The plan is required to pay those additional costs attributable to the complications of the abortion. However, the employer is not required to pay for the abortion itself, except where the life of the mother would be endangered if the fetus were carried to term.

37. Q. May an employer elect to provide insurance coverage for abortions?

A. Yes. The Act specifically provides that an employer is not precluded from providing benefits for abortions whether directly or through a collective bargaining agreement, but if an employer decides to cover the costs of abortion, the employer must do so in the same manner and to the same degree as it covers other medical conditions.

Part 1605. Guidelines on Discrimination Because of Religion

1605.1 "Religious" nature of a practice or belief.

In most cases whether or not a practice or belief is religious is not at issue. However, in those cases in which the issue does exist, the Commission will define religious practices to include moral or ethical beliefs as to what is right and wrong which are sincerely held with the strength of traditional religious views. This standard was developed in *United States v. Seeger*, 380 U.S. 163 (1965) and *Welsh v. United States*, 398 U.S. 333 (1970). The Commission has consistently applied this standard in its decisions.[19] The fact that no religious group espouses such beliefs or the fact that the religious group to which the individual professes to belong may not accept such belief will not determine whether the

19. *See* CD 76-104 (1976), CCH (oblique) §6500; CD 7 1-2620 (1971), CCH (oblique) §6283; CD 7 1-779 (1970), CCH (oblique) §6180.

belief is a religious belief of the employee or prospective employee. The phrase "religious practice" as used in these Guidelines includes both religious observances and practices, as stated in Section 701(j), 42 U.S.C. 2000e(j).

1605.2 Reasonable accommodation without undue hardship as required by Section 701(j) of Title VII of the Civil Rights Act of 1964.

(a) *Purpose of this section.*

This section clarifies the obligation imposed by Title VII of the Civil Rights Act of 1964, as amended, (sections 701(j), 703 and 717) to accommodate the religious practices of employees and prospective employees. This section does not address other obligations under Title VII not to discriminate on grounds of religion, nor other provisions of Title VII. This section is not intended to limit any additional obligations to accommodate religious practices which may exist pursuant to constitutional, or other statutory provisions; neither is it intended to provide guidance for statutes which require accommodation on bases other than religion such as § 503 of the Rehabilitation Act of 1973. The legal principles which have been developed with respect to discrimination prohibited by Title VII on the bases of race, color, sex, and national origin also apply to religious discrimination in all circumstances other than where an accommodation is required.

(b) *Duty to accommodate.*

(1) Section 701(j) makes it an unlawful employment practice under § 703(a)(1) for an employer to fail to reasonably accommodate the religious practices of an employee or prospective employee, unless the employer demonstrates that accommodation would result in undue hardship on the conduct of its business.[20]

(2) Section 701(j) in conjunction with § 703(c), imposes an obligation on a labor organization to reasonably accommodate the religious practices of an employee or prospective employee, unless the labor organization demonstrates that accommodation would result in undue hardship.

(3) Section 1605.2 is primarily directed to obligations of employers or labor organizations, which are the entities covered by Title VII that will most often be required to make an accommodation. However, the principles of Section 1605.2 also apply when an accommodation can be required of other entities covered by Title VII, such as employment agencies (§ 703(b)) or joint labor-management committees controlling apprenticeship [sic] or other training or retraining (§ 703(d)). (*See, for example,* § 1605.3(a) "Scheduling of Tests or Other Selection Procedures.")

(c) *Reasonable Accommodation.*

(1) After an employee or prospective employee notifies the employer or labor organization of his or her need for a religious accommodation, the employer or labor organization has an obligation to reasonably accommodate the individual's religious practices. A refusal to accommodate is justified only when an employer or labor organization can demonstrate that an undue hardship would in fact result from each available alternative method of accommodation. A mere assumption that many more people, with the same religious practices as the person being accommodated, may also need accommodation is not evidence of undue hardship.

(2) When there is more than one method of accommodation available which would not cause undue hardship, the Commission will determine whether the accommodation offered is reasonable by examining:

---

20. *See Trans World Airlines, Inc. v. Hardison*, 432 U.S. 63, 74 (1977).

(i) The alternatives for accommodation considered by the employer or labor organization; and

(ii) The alternatives for accommodation, if any, actually offered to the individual requiring accommodation. Some alternatives for accommodating religious practices might disadvantage the individual with respect to his or her employment opportunities, such as compensation, terms, conditions, or privileges of employment. Therefore, when there is more than one means of accommodation which would not cause undue hardship, the employer or labor organization must offer the alternative which least disadvantages the individual with respect to his or her employment opportunities.

(d) *Alternatives for Accommodating Religious Practices.*

(1) Employees and prospective employees most frequently request an accommodation because their religious practices conflict with their work schedules. The following subsections are some means of accommodating the conflict between work schedules and religious practices which the Commission believes that employers and labor organizations should consider as part of the obligation to accommodate and which the Commission will consider in investigating a charge. These are not intended to be all-inclusive. There are often other alternatives which would reasonably accommodate an individual's religious practices when they conflict with a work schedule. There are also employment practices besides work scheduling which may conflict with religious practices and cause an individual to request an accommodation. See, for example, the Commission's finding number (3) from its Hearings on Religious Discrimination, in Appendix A to §§ 1605.2 and 1605.3. The principles expressed in these Guidelines apply as well to such requests for accommodation.

(i) Voluntary Substitutes and "Swaps."

Reasonable accommodation without undue hardship is generally possible where a voluntary substitute with substantially similar qualifications is available. One means of substitution is the voluntary swap. In a number of cases, the securing of a substitute has been left entirely up to the individual seeking the accommodation. The Commission believes that the obligation to accommodate requires that employers and labor organizations facilitate the securing of a voluntary substitute with substantially similar qualifications. Some means of doing this which employers and labor organizations should consider are: to publicize policies regarding accommodation and voluntary substitution; to promote an atmosphere in which such substitutions are favorably regarded; to provide a central file, bulletin board or other means for matching voluntary substitutes with positions for which substitutes are needed.

(ii) Flexible Scheduling.

One means of providing reasonable accommodation for the religious practices of employees or prospective employees which employers and labor organizations should consider is the creation of a flexible work schedule for individuals requesting accommodation.

The following list is an example of areas in which flexibility might be introduced: flexible arrival and departure time; floating or optional holidays; flexible work breaks; use of lunch time in exchange for early departure; staggered work hours; and permitting an employee to make up time lost due to the observance of religious practices.[21]

(iii) Lateral Transfer and Change of Job Assignments.

---

21. On September 29, 1978, Congress enacted such a provision for the accommodation of Federal employees' religious practices. *See* Pub. L. 95-390, 5 U.S.C. § 5550a "Compensatory Time Off for Religious Observances."

When an employee cannot be accommodated either as to his or her entire job or an assignment within the job, employers and labor organizations should consider whether or not it is possible to change the job assignment or give the employee a lateral transfer.

(2) Payment of Dues to a Labor Organization.

Some collective bargaining agreements include a provision that each employee must join the labor organization or pay the labor organization a sum equivalent to dues. When an employee's religious practices do not permit compliance with such a provision, the labor organization should accommodate the employee by not requiring the employee to join the organization and by permitting him or her to donate a sum equivalent to dues to a charitable organization.

(e) *Undue Hardship.*

(1) Costs.

An employer may assert undue hardship to justify a refusal to accommodate an employee's need to be absent from his or her scheduled duty hours if the employer can demonstrate that the accommodation would require "more than a de minimis cost".[22] The Commission will determine what constitutes "more than a de minimis cost" with due regard given to the identifiable cost in relation to the size and operating cost of the employer, and the number of individuals who will in fact need a particular accommodation. In general, the Commission interprets this phrase as it was used in the Hardison decision to mean that costs similar to the regular payment of premium wages of substitutes, which was at issue in Hardison, would constitute undue hardship. However, the Commission will presume that the infrequent payment of premium wages for a substitute or the payment of premium wages while a more permanent accommodation is being sought are costs which an employer can be required to bear as a means of providing a reasonable accommodation. Further, the Commission will presume that generally, the payment of administrative costs necessary for providing the accommodation will not constitute more than a de minimis cost. Administrative costs, for example, include those costs involved in rearranging schedules and recording substitutions for payroll purposes.

(2) Seniority Rights.

Undue hardship would also be shown where a variance from a bona fide seniority system is necessary in order to accommodate an employee's religious practices when doing so would deny another employee his or her job or shift preference guaranteed by that system. *Hardison, supra*, 432 U.S. at 80. Arrangements for voluntary substitutes and swaps (see paragraph (d)(1)(i) of this section) do not constitute an undue hardship to the extent the arrangements do not violate a bona fide seniority system. Nothing in the Statute or these Guidelines precludes an employer and a union from including arrangements for voluntary substitutes and swaps as part of a collective bargaining agreement.

1605.3 Selection practices.

(a) *Scheduling of Tests or Other Selection Procedures.* When a test or other selection procedure is scheduled at a time when an employee or prospective employee cannot attend because of his or her religious practices, the user of the test should be aware that the principles enunciated in these guidelines apply and that it has an obligation to accommodate such employee or prospective employee unless undue hardship would result.

22. *Hardison, supra*, 432 U.S. at 84.

(b) *Inquiries Which Determine An Applicant's Availability to Work During An Employer's Scheduled Working Hours.*

(1) The duty to accommodate pertains to prospective employees as well as current employees. Consequently, an employer may not permit an applicant's need for a religious accommodation to affect in any way its decision whether to hire the applicant unless it can demonstrate that it cannot reasonably accommodate the applicant's religious practices without undue hardship.

(2) As a result of the oral and written testimony submitted at the Commission's Hearings on Religious Discrimination, discussions with representatives of organizations interested in the issue of religious discrimination, and the comments received from the public on these Guidelines as proposed, the Commission has concluded that the use of pre-selection inquiries which determine an applicant's availability has an exclusionary effect on the employment opportunities of persons with certain religious practices. The use of such inquiries will, therefore, be considered to violate Title VII unless the employer can show that it:

(i) Did not have an exclusionary effect on its employees or prospective employees needing an accommodation for the same religious practices; or

(ii) Was otherwise justified by business necessity.

Employers who believe they have a legitimate interest in knowing the availability of their applicants prior to selection must consider procedures which would serve this interest and which would have a lesser exclusionary effect on persons whose religious practices need accommodation. An example of such a procedure is for the employer to state the normal work hours for the job and, after making it clear to the applicant that he or she is not required to indicate the need for any absences for religious practices during the scheduled work hours, ask the applicant whether he or she is otherwise available to work those hours. Then, after a position is offered, but before the applicant is hired, the employer can inquire into the need for a religious accommodation and determine, according to the principles of these Guidelines, whether an accommodation is possible. This type of inquiry would provide an employer with information concerning the availability of most of its applicants, while deferring until after a position is offered the identification of the usually small number of applicants who require an accommodation.

(3) The Commission will infer that the need for an accommodation discriminatorily influenced a decision to reject an applicant when: (i) prior to an offer of employment the employer makes an inquiry into an applicant's availability without having a business necessity justification; and (ii) after the employer has determined the applicant's need for an accommodation, the employer rejects a qualified applicant. The burden is then on the employer to demonstrate that factors other than the need for an accommodation were the reason for rejecting the qualified applicant, or that a reasonable accommodation without undue hardship was not possible.

Appendix A to §§ 1605.2 and 1605.3 — Background Information

In 1966, the Commission adopted guidelines on religious discrimination which stated that an employer had an obligation to accommodate the religious practices of its employees or prospective employees unless to do so would create a "serious inconvenience to the conduct of the business". 29 CFR 1605.1(a)(2), 31 FR 3870 (1966).

In 1967, the Commission revised these guidelines to state that an employer had an obligation to reasonably accommodate the religious practices of its employees or prospective employees, unless the employer could prove that to do so would create' an "undue hardship". 29 CFR 1605. 1(b)(c), 32 FR 10298.

In 1972, Congress amended Title VII to incorporate the obligation to accommodate expressed in the Commission's 1967 Guidelines by adding section 701(j).

In 1977, the United States Supreme Court issued its decision in the case of *Trans World Airlines, Inc. v. Hardison*, 432 U.S. 63 (1977). *Hardison* was brought under section 703 (a)(1) because it involved facts occurring before the enactment of Section 701(j). The Court applied the Commission's 1967 Guidelines, but indicated that the result would be the same under Section 701(j). It stated that Trans World Airlines had made reasonable efforts to accommodate the religious needs of its employee, Hardison. The Court held that to require Trans World Airlines to make further attempts at accommodations—by unilaterally violating a seniority provision of the collective bargaining agreement, paying premium wages on a regular basis to another employee to replace Hardison, or creating a serious shortage of necessary employees in another department in order to replace Hardison—would create an undue hardship on the conduct of Trans World Airlines' business, and would therefore, exceed the duty to accommodate Hardison.

In 1978, the Commission conducted public hearings on religious discrimination in New York City, Milwaukee, and Los Angeles in order to respond to the concerns raised by Hardison. Approximately 150 witnesses testified or submitted written statements.[23] The witnesses included employers, employees, representatives of religious and labor organizations and representatives of Federal, State and local governments.

The Commission found from the hearings that:

(1) There is widespread confusion concerning the extent of accommodation under the *Hardison* decision.

(2) The religious practices of some individuals and some groups of individuals are not being accommodated.

(3) Some of those practices which are not being accommodated are:

- Observance of a Sabbath or religious holidays;

- Need for prayer break during working hours;

- Practice of following certain dietary requirements;

- Practice of not working during a mourning period for a deceased relative;

- Prohibition against medical examinations;

- Prohibition against membership in labor and other organizations; and

- Practices concerning dress and other personal grooming habits.

(4) Many of the employers who testified had developed alternative employment practices which accommodate the religious practices of employees and prospective employees and which meet the employer's business needs.

(5) Little evidence was submitted by employers which showed actual attempts to accommodate religious practices with resultant unfavorable consequences to the employer's business. Employers appeared to have substantial anticipatory concerns but no, or very

23. The transcript of the Commission's Hearings on Religious Discrimination can be examined by the public at: The Equal Employment Opportunity Commission, 2401 E Street NW., Washington, D.C. 20506.

little, actual experience with the problems they theorized would emerge by providing reasonable accommodation for religious practices.

Based on these findings, the Commission is revising its Guidelines to clarify the obligation imposed by Section 701(j) to accommodate the religious practices of employees and prospective employees.

Part 1606. Guidelines on Discrimination Because of National Origin

1606.1 Definition of national origin discrimination.

The Commission defines national origin discrimination broadly as including, but not limited to, the denial of equal employment opportunity because of an individual's, or his or her ancestor's, place of origin; or because an individual has the physical, cultural or linguistic characteristics of a national origin group. The Commission will examine with particular concern charges alleging that individuals within the jurisdiction of the Commission have been denied equal employment opportunity for reasons which are grounded in national origin considerations, such as (a) marriage to or association with persons of a national origin group; (b) membership in, or association with an organization identified with or seeking to promote the interests of national origin groups; (c) attendance or participation in schools, churches, temples or mosques, generally used by persons of a national origin group; and (d) because an individual's name or spouse's name is associated with a national origin group. In examining these charges for unlawful national origin discrimination, the Commission will apply general Title VII principles, such as disparate treatment and adverse impact.

1606.2 Scope of Title VII protection.

Title VII of the Civil Rights Act of 1964, as amended, protects individuals against employment discrimination on the basis of race, color, religion, sex or national origin. The Title VII principles of disparate treatment and adverse impact equally apply to national origin discrimination. These Guidelines apply to all entities covered by Title VII (collectively referred to as "employer").

1606.3 The national security exception.

It is not an unlawful employment practice to deny employment opportunities to any individual who does not fulfill the national security requirements stated in section 703(g) of Title VII.[24]

1606.4 The bona fide occupational qualification exception.

The exception stated in Section 703(e) of Title VII, that national origin may be a bona fide occupational qualification, shall be strictly construed.

1606.5 Citizenship requirements.

(a) In those circumstances, where citizenship requirements have the purpose or effect of discriminating against an individual on the basis of national origin, they are prohibited by Title VII.[25]

---

24. *See also* 5 U.S.C. 7532, for the authority of the head of a federal agency or department to suspend or remove an employee on grounds of national security.

(b) Some State laws prohibit the employment of non-citizens. Where these laws are in conflict with Title VII, they are superseded under Section 708 of the Title.

1606.6 Selection procedures.

(a)(1) In investigating an employer's selection procedures (including those identified below) for adverse impact on the basis of national origin, the Commission will apply the Uniform Guidelines on Employee Selection Procedures (UGESP), 29 CFR part 1607. Employers and other users of selection procedures should refer to the UGESP for guidance on matters, such as adverse impact, validation and record keeping requirements for national origin groups.

(2) Because height or weight requirements tend to exclude individuals on the basis of national origin, [26] the user is expected to evaluate these selection procedures for adverse impact, regardless of whether the total selection process has an adverse impact based on national origin. Therefore, height or weight requirements are identified here, as they are in the UGESP,[27] as exceptions to the "bottom line" concept.

(b) The Commission has found that the use of the following selection procedures may be discriminatory on the basis of national origin. Therefore, it will carefully investigate charges involving these selection procedures for both disparate treatment and adverse impact on the basis of national origin. However, the Commission does not consider these to be exceptions to the "bottom line" concept:

(1) Fluency-in-English requirements, such as denying employment opportunities because of an individual's foreign accent,[28] or inability to communicate well in English.[29]

(2) Training or education requirements which deny employment opportunities to an individual because of his or her foreign training or education, or which require an individual to be foreign trained or educated.

1606.7 Speak-English-only rules.

(a) *When Applied at All Times.* A rule requiring employees to speak only English at all times in the workplace is a burdensome term and condition of employment. The primary language of an individual is often an essential national origin characteristic. Prohibiting employees at all times, in the workplace, from speaking their primary language or the language they speak most comfortably, disadvantages an individual's employment opportunities on the basis of national origin. It may also create an atmosphere of inferiority, isolation and intimidation based on national origin which could result in a discriminatory working environment.[30] Therefore, the Commission will presume that such a rule violates Title VII and will closely scrutinize it.

---

25. *See Espinoza v. Farah Mfg. Co.*, 414 U.S. 86, 92 (1973). *See also* E.O. 11935, 5 CFR Part 7.4; and 31 U.S.C. 699(b), for citizenship requirements in certain Federal employment.

26. *See* CD 71-1529 (1971), CCH EEOC Decisions §6231, 3 FEP Cases 952; CD 71 1418 (1971), CCH EEOC Decisions §6223, 3 FEP Cases 580; CD 74-25 (1973), CCH EEOC Decisions §6400, 10 FEP Cases 260; *Davis v. County of Los Angeles*, 566 F.2d 1334, 1341-42 (9th Cir. 1977), vacated and remanded as moot on other grounds, 440 U.S. 625 (1979). *See also Dothard v. Rawlinson*, 433 U.S. 321 (1977).

27. *See* Section 4C(2) of the Uniform Guidelines on Employee Selection Procedures, 29 CFR 1607.4C(2).

28. *See* CD AL68-1-155E (1969), CCH EEOC Decisions §6008, 1 FEP Cases 921.

29. *See* CD YAU9-048 (1969), CCH EEOC Decisions §6054, 2 FEP Cases 78.

30. *See* CD 7 1-446 (1970), CCH EEOC Decisions §6173, 2 FEP Cases, 1127; CD 72-0281(1971), CCH EEOC Decisions §6293.

(b) *When Applied Only at Certain Times.* An employer may have a rule requiring that employees speak only in English at certain times where the employer can show that the rule is justified by business necessity.

(c) *Notice of the Rule.* It is common for individuals whose primary language is not 'English to inadvertently change from speaking English to speaking their primary language. Therefore, if an employer believes it has a business necessity for a speak-English-only rule at certain times, the employer should inform its employees of the general circumstances when speaking only in English is required and of the consequences of violating the rule. If an employer fails to effectively notify its employees of the rule and makes an adverse employment decision against an individual based on a violation of the rule, the Commission will consider the employer's application of the rule as evidence of discrimination on the basis of national origin.

1606.8 Harassment.

(a) The Commission has consistently held that harassment on the basis of national origin is a violation of Title VII. An employer has an affirmative duty to maintain a working environment free of harassment on the basis of national origin.[31]

(b) Ethnic slurs and other verbal or physical conduct relating to an individual's national origin constitute harassment when this conduct: (1) Has the purpose or effect of creating an intimidating, hostile or offensive working environment; (2) has the purpose or effect of unreasonably interfering with an individual's work performance; or (3) otherwise adversely affects an individual's employment opportunities.

(c) [Removed and reserved by amendment at 64 Fed. Reg. 58333, effective October 29, 1999]

(d) With respect to conduct between fellow employees, an employer is responsible for acts of harassment in the workplace on the basis of national origin, where the employer, its agents or supervisory employees, knows or should have known of the conduct, unless the employer can show that it took immediate and appropriate corrective action.

(e) An employer may also be responsible for the acts of non-employees with respect to harassment of employees in the workplace on the basis of national origin, where the employer, its agents or supervisory employees, knows or should have known of the conduct and fails to take immediate and appropriate corrective action. In reviewing these cases, the Commission will consider the extent of the employer's control and any other legal responsibility which the employer may have with respect to the conduct of such non-employees.

Part 1608. Guidelines on Affirmative Action

1608.1 Statement of Purpose.

(a) *Need for Guidelines.* Since the passage of Title VII in 1964, many employers, labor organizations, and other persons subject to Title VII have changed their employment practices and systems to improve employment opportunities for minorities and women,

31. *See* CD CL68-12-431 EU (1969), CCH EEOC Decisions §6085, 2 FEP Cases 295; CD 72-0621 (1971), CCH EEOC Decisions §6311, 4 FEP Cases 312; CD 72-1561(1972), CCH EEOC Decisions §6354, 4 FEP Cases 852; CD 74-05 (1973), CCH EEOC Decisions §6387, 6 FEP Cases 834; CD 76-41 (1975), CCH EEOC Decisions §6632. *See also* Amendment to Guidelines on Discrimination Because of Sex, §16O4.11(a) n.1, 45 FR 7476 sy 74677 (November 10, 1980).

and this must continue. These changes have been undertaken either on the initiative of the employer, labor organization, or other person subject to Title VII, or as a result of conciliation efforts under Title VII, action under Executive Order No. 11246, as amended, or under other Federal, state, or local laws, or litigation. Many decisions taken pursuant to affirmative action plans or programs have been race, sex, or national origin conscious in order to achieve the Congressional purpose of providing equal employment opportunity. Occasionally these actions have been challenged as inconsistent with Title VII, because they took into account race, sex, or national origin. This is the so-called "reverse discrimination" claim. In such a situation, both the affirmative action undertaken to improve the conditions of minorities and women, and the objection to that action, are based upon the principles of Title VII. Any uncertainty as to the meaning and application of Title VII in such situations threatens the accomplishment of the clear Congressional intent to encourage voluntary affirmative action. The Commission believes that by the enactment of Title VII Congress did not intend to expose those who comply with the Act to charges that they are violating the very statute they are seeking to implement. Such a result would immobilize or reduce the efforts of many who would otherwise take action to improve the opportunities of minorities and women without litigation, thus frustrating the Congressional intent to encourage voluntary action and increasing the prospect of Title VII litigation. The Commission believes that it is now necessary to clarify and harmonize the principles of Title VII in order to achieve these Congressional objectives and protect those employers, labor organizations, and other persons who comply with the principles of Title VII.

(b) *Purposes of Title VII.* Congress enacted Title VII in order to improve the economic and social conditions of minorities and women by providing equality of opportunity in the work place. These conditions were part of a larger pattern of restriction, exclusion, discrimination, segregation, and inferior treatment of minorities and women in many areas of life.[32]

The Legislative Histories of Title VII, the Equal Pay Act, and the Equal Employment Opportunity Act of 1972 contain extensive analyses of the higher unemployment rate, the lesser occupational status, and the consequent lower income levels of minorities and women.[33]

The purpose of Executive Order No. 11246, as amended, is similar to the purpose of Title VII. In response to these economic and social conditions, Congress, by passage of Title VII, established a national policy against discrimination in employment on grounds of race, color, religion, sex, and national origin. In addition, Congress strongly encouraged

---

32. Congress has also addressed these conditions in other laws, including the Equal Pay Act of 1963, Pub.L. 88-38, 77 Stat. 56 (1963), as amended; the other Titles of the Civil Rights Act of 1964, Pub. L. 88-352, 78 Stat. 241 (1964), as amended; the Voting Rights Act of 1965, Pub. L. 89 110, 79 Stat. 437(1965), as amended; the Fair Housing Act of 1968, Pub. L. 90-284, Title VII, 82 Stat. 73, 81(1968), as amended; the Educational Opportunity Act (Title IX), Pub. L. 92-318, 86 Stat. 373 (1972), as amended; and the Equal Employment Opportunity Act of 1972, Pub. L. 92-26 1, 86 Stat. 103 (1972), as amended.

33. Equal Pay Act of 1963: 5. Rep. No. 176, 88th Cong., 1st Sess., 1-2 (1963). Civil Rights Act of 1964: H.R. Rep. No. 914, pt. 2, 88th Cong., 1st Sess. (1971). Equal Employment Opportunity Act of 1972: H.R. Rep. No. 92-238, 92d Cong., 1st Sess. (1971); 5. Rep. No. 92-415, 92d Cong., 1st Sess. (1971). *See also* Equal Employment Opportunity Commission, Equal Employment Opportunity Report—1975, Job Patterns for Women in Private Industry (1977); Equal Employment Opportunity Commission, Minorities and Women in State and Local Government—1975 (1977); United States Commission on Civil Rights, Social Indicators of Equality for Minorities and Women (1978).

employers, labor organizations, and other persons subject to Title VII (hereinafter referred to as "persons," see section 701(a) of the Act) to act on a voluntary basis to modify employment practices and systems which constituted barriers to equal employment opportunity, without awaiting litigation or formal government action. Conference, conciliation, and persuasion were the primary processes adopted by Congress in 1964, and reaffirmed in 1972, to achieve these objectives, with enforcement action through the courts or agencies as a supporting procedure where voluntary action did not take place and conciliation failed. *See* § 706 of Title VII.

(c) *Interpretation in furtherance of legislative purpose.* The principle of nondiscrimination in employment because of race, color, religion, sex, or national origin, and the principle that each person subject to Title VII should take voluntary action to correct the effects of past discrimination and to prevent present and future discrimination without awaiting litigation, are mutually consistent and interdependent methods of addressing social and economic conditions which precipitated the enactment of Title VII. Voluntary affirmative action to improve opportunities for minorities and women must be encouraged and protected in order to carry out the Congressional intent embodied in Title VII.[34]

Affirmative action under these principles means those actions appropriate to overcome the effects of past or present practices, policies, or other barriers to equal employment opportunity. Such voluntary affirmative action cannot be measured by the standard of whether it would have been required had there been litigation, for this standard would undermine the legislative purpose of first encouraging voluntary action without litigation. Rather, persons subject to Title VII must be allowed flexibility in modifying employment systems and practices to comport with the purposes of Title VII. Correspondingly, Title VII must be construed to permit such voluntary action, and those taking such action should be afforded the protection against Title VII liability which the Commission is authorized to provide under section 713(b)(l).

(d) *Guidelines interpret Title VII and authorize use of Section 713(b)(1).* These Guidelines describe the circumstances in which persons subject to Title VII may take or agree upon action to improve employment opportunities of minorities and women, and describe the kinds of actions they may take which are consistent with Title VII. These Guidelines constitute the Commission's interpretation of Title VII and will be applied in the processing of claims of discrimination which involve voluntary affirmative action plans and programs. In addition, these Guidelines state the circumstances under which the Commission will recognize that a person subject to Title VII is entitled to assert that actions were taken "in good faith, in conformity with, and in reliance upon a written interpretation or opinion of the Commission," including reliance upon the interpretation and opinion contained in these Guidelines, and thereby invoke the protection of section 713(b)(1) of Title VII.

(e) *Review of existing plans recommended.* Only affirmative action plans or programs adopted in good faith, in conformity with, and in reliance upon these Guidelines can receive the full protection of these Guidelines, including the section 713(b)(1) defense. *See* § 1608.10. Therefore, persons subject to Title VII who have existing affirmative action

---

34. Affirmative action often improves opportunities for all members of the workforce, as where affirmative action includes the posting of notices of job vacancies. Similarly, the integration of previously segregated jobs means that all workers will be provided opportunities to enter jobs previously restricted. *See, e.g., EEOC v. AT & T*, 419 F. Supp. 1022 (E.D.Pa. 1976), *aff'd*, 556 F. 2d 167 (3rd Cir. 1977), *cert. denied*, 98 S Ct. 3145 (1978).

plans, programs, or agreements are encouraged to review them in light of these Guidelines, to modify them to the extent necessary to comply with these Guidelines, and to readopt or reaffirm them.

1608.2 Written interpretation and opinion.

These Guidelines constitute "a written interpretation and opinion" of the Equal Employment Opportunity Commission as that term is used in section 713(b)(1) of Title VII of the Civil Rights Act of 1964, as amended, 42 U.S.C. 2000e-12(b)(1), and section 1601.33 of the Procedural Regulations of the Equal Employment Opportunity Commission (29 CFR 1601.30; 42 FR 55,394 (October 14, 1977)). Section 713(b)(1) provides:

> In any action or proceeding based on any alleged unlawful employment practice, no person shall be subject to any liability or punishment for or on account of (1) the commission by such person of an unlawful employment practice if he pleads and proves that the act or omission complained of was in good faith, in conformity with, and in reliance on any written interpretation or opinion of the Commission.... Such a defense, if established, shall be a bar to the action or proceeding, notwithstanding that ... after such act or omission, such interpretation or opinion is modified or rescinded or is determined by judicial authority to be invalid or of no legal effect....

The applicability of these Guidelines is subject to the limitations on use set forth in § 1608.11.

1608.3 Circumstances under which voluntary affirmative action is appropriate.

(a) *Adverse effect.* Title VII prohibits practices, procedures, or policies which have an adverse impact unless they are justified by business necessity. In addition, Title VII proscribes practices which "tend to deprive" persons of equal employment opportunities. Employers, labor organizations and other persons subject to Title VII may take affirmative action based on an analysis which reveals facts constituting actual or potential adverse impact, if such adverse impact is likely to result from existing or contemplated practices.

(b) *Effects of prior discriminatory practices.* Employers, labor organizations, or other persons subject to Title VII may also take affirmative action to correct the effects of prior discriminatory practices. The effects of prior discriminatory practices can be initially identified by a comparison between the employer's work force, or a part thereof, and an appropriate segment of the labor force.

(c) *Limited labor pool.* Because of historic restrictions by employers, labor organizations, and others, there are circumstances in which the available pool. particularly of qualified minorities and women, for employment or promotional opportunities is artificially limited. Employers, labor organizations, and other persons subject to Title VII may, and are encouraged to take affirmative action in such circumstances, including, but not limited to, the following:

(1) Training plans and programs, including on-the-job training, which emphasize providing minorities and women with the opportunity, skill, and experience necessary to perform the functions of skilled trades, crafts, or professions;

(2) Extensive and focused recruiting activity;

(3) Elimination of the adverse impact caused by invalidated selection criteria (*see* sections 3 and 6, Uniform Guidelines on Employee Selection Procedures (1978), 43 FR 30,290; 38,297; 39,299 (August 25, 1978));

(4) Modification through collective bargaining where a labor organization represents employees, or unilaterally where one does not, of promotion and layoff procedures.

1608.4 Establishing affirmative action plans.

An affirmative action plan or program under this section shall contain three elements: a reasonable self analysis; a reasonable basis for concluding action is appropriate; and reasonable action.

(a) *Reasonable self analysis.* The objective of a self analysis is to determine whether employment practices do, or tend to, exclude, disadvantage, restrict, or result in adverse impact or disparate treatment of previously excluded or restricted groups or leave uncorrected the effects of prior discrimination, and if so, to attempt to determine why. There is no mandatory method of conducting a self analysis. The employer may utilize techniques used in order to comply with Executive Order No. 11246, as amended, and its implementing regulations, including 41 CFR Part 60-2 (known as Revised Order 4), or related orders issued by the Office of Federal Contract Compliance Programs or its authorized agencies, or may use an analysis similar to that required under other Federal, state, or local laws or regulations prohibiting employment discrimination. In conducting a self analysis, the employer, labor organization, or other person subject to Title VII should be concerned with the effect on its employment practices of circumstances which may be the result of discrimination by other persons or institutions. *See Griggs v. Duke Power Co*, 401 U.S. 424 (1971).

(b) *Reasonable basis.* If the self analysis shows that one or more employment practices: (1) Have or tend to have an adverse effect on employment opportunities of members of previously excluded groups, or groups whose employment or promotional opportunities have been artificially limited, (2) leave uncorrected the effects of prior discrimination, or (3) result in disparate treatment, the person making the self analysis has a reasonable basis for concluding that action is appropriate. It is not necessary that the self analysis establish a violation of Title VII. This reasonable basis exists without any admission or formal finding that the person has violated Title VII, and without regard to whether there exists arguable defenses to a Title VII action.

(c) *Reasonable action.* The action taken pursuant to an affirmative action plan or program must be reasonable in relation to the problems disclosed by the self analysis. Such reasonable action may include goals and timetables or other appropriate employment tools which recognize the race, sex, or national origin of applicants or employees. It may include the adoption of practices which will eliminate the actual or potential adverse impact, disparate treatment, or effect of past discrimination by providing opportunities for members of groups which have been excluded, regardless of whether the persons benefited were themselves the victims of prior policies or procedures which produced the adverse impact or disparate treatment or which perpetuated past discrimination.

(1) *Illustrations of appropriate affirmative action.* Affirmative action plans or programs may include, but are not limited to, those described in the Equal Employment Opportunity Coordinating Council "Policy Statement on Affirmative Action Programs for State and Local Government Agencies." 41 FR 38,814 (September 13, 1976), reaffirmed and extended to all persons subject to Federal equal employment opportunity laws and orders, in the Uniform Guidelines on Employee Selection Procedures (1978) 43 FR 38,290; 38,300 (Aug. 25, 1978). That statement reads, in relevant part:

When an employer has reason to believe that its selection procedures have ... exclusionary effect..., it should initiate affirmative steps to remedy the situation. Such steps, which in design and execution may be race, color, sex or ethnic "conscious", include, but are not limited to, the following:

The establishment of a long term goal and short range, interim goals and timetables for the specific job classifications, all of which should take into account the availability of basically qualified persons in the relevant job market;

A recruitment program designed to attract qualified members of the group in question;

A systematic effort to organize work and re-design jobs in ways that provide opportunities for persons lacking "journeyman" level knowledge or skills to enter and, with appropriate training, to progress in a career field;

Revamping selection instruments or procedures which have not yet been validated in order to reduce or eliminate exclusionary effects on particular groups in particular job classifications;

The initiation of measures designed to assure that members of the affected group who are qualified to perform the job are included within the pool of persons from which the selecting official makes the selection;

A systematic effort to provide career advancement training, both classroom and on-the-job, to employees locked into dead end jobs; and

The establishment of a system for regularly monitoring the effectiveness of the particular affirmative action program, and procedures for making timely adjustments in this program where effectiveness is not demonstrated.

(2) *Standards of reasonable action.* In considering the reasonableness of a particular affirmative action plan or program, the Commission will generally apply the following standards:

(i) The plan should be tailored to solve the problems which were identified in the self analysis, see § 1608.4(a), *supra*, and to ensure that employment systems operate fairly in the future, while avoiding unnecessary restrictions on opportunities for the workforce as a whole. The race, sex, and national origin conscious provisions of the plan or program should be maintained only so long as is necessary to achieve these objectives.

I. Goals and timetables should be reasonably related to such considerations as the effects of past discrimination, the need for prompt elimination of adverse impact or disparate treatment, the availability of basically qualified or qualifiable applicants, and the number of employment opportunities expected to be available.

(d) *Written or unwritten plans or programs*—(1) *Written plans required for 713 (b)(1) Protection.* The protection of section 713(b) of Title VII will be accorded by the Commission to a person subject to Title VII only if the self analysis and the affirmative action plan are dated and in writing, and the plan otherwise meets the requirements of Section 713(b)(1). The Commission will not require that there be any written statement concluding that a Title VII violation exists.

(2) *Reasonable cause determinations.* Where an affirmative action plan or program is alleged to violate Title VII, or is asserted as a defense to a charge of discrimination, the Commission will investigate the charge in accordance with its usual procedures and pursuant to the standards set forth in these Guidelines, whether or not the analysis and plan are in writing. However, the absence of a written self analysis and a written affirmative action plan or program may make it more difficult to provide credible evidence that the analysis was conducted, and that action was taken pursuant to a plan or program based

on the analysis. Therefore, the Commission recommends that such analyses and plans be in writing.

1608.5 Affirmative action compliance programs under Executive Order No. 11246, as amended.

Under Title VII, affirmative action compliance programs adopted pursuant to Executive Order No. 11246, as amended, and its implementing regulations, including 41 CFR Part 60-2 (Revised Order 4), will be considered by the Commission in light of the similar purposes of Title VII and the Executive Order, and the Commission's responsibility under Executive Order No. 12067 to avoid potential conflict among Federal equal employment opportunity programs. Accordingly, the Commission will process Title VII complaints involving such affirmative action compliance programs under this section.

(a) *Procedures for review of Affirmative Action Compliance Programs.* If adherence to an affirmative action compliance program adopted pursuant to Executive Order No. 11246, as amended, and its implementing regulations, is the basis of a complaint filed under Title VII, or is alleged to be the justification for an action which is challenged under Title VII, the Commission will investigate to determine whether the affirmative action compliance program was adopted by a person subject to the Order and pursuant to the Order, and whether adherence to the program was the basis of the complaint or the justification.

(1) *Programs previously approved.* If the Commission makes the determination described in paragraph (a) of this section and also finds that the affirmative action program has been approved by an appropriate official of the Department of Labor or its authorized agencies, or is part of a conciliation or settlement agreement or an order of an administrative agency, whether entered by consent or after contested proceedings brought to enforce Executive Order No. 11246, as amended, the Commission will issue a determination of no reasonable cause.

(2) *Program not previously approved.* If the Commission makes the determination described in paragraph (a) of this section but the program has not been approved by an appropriate official of the Department of Labor or its authorized agencies, the Commission will: (i) Follow the procedure in § 1608.10(a) and review the program, or (ii) refer the plan to the Department of Labor for a determination of whether it is to be approved under Executive Order No. 11246, as amended, and its implementing regulations. If the Commission finds that the program does conform to these Guidelines, or the Department of Labor approves the affirmative action compliance program, the Commission will issue a determination of no reasonable cause under § 1608.10(a).

(b) *Reliance on these guidelines.* In addition, if the affirmative action compliance program has been adopted in good faith reliance on these Guidelines, the provisions of section 713(b)(1) of Title VII and of § 1608.10(b), below, may be asserted by the contractor.

1608.6 Affirmative action plans which are part of Commission conciliation or settlement agreements.

(a) *Procedures for review of plans.* If adherence to a conciliation or settlement agreement executed under Title VII and approved by a responsible official of the EEOC is the basis of a complaint filed under Title VII, or is alleged to be the justification for an action challenged under Title VII, the Commission will investigate to determine: (1) Whether the conciliation agreement or settlement agreement was approved by a responsible official of the EEOC, and (2) whether adherence to the agreement was the basis for the complaint or justification. If the Commission so finds, it will make a determination of no reasonable cause under § 1608.10(a) and will advise the respondent of its right under section 713(b)(1) of Title VII to rely on the conciliation agreement.

(b) *Reliance on these guidelines.* In addition, if the affirmative action plan or program has been adopted in good faith reliance on these Guidelines, the provisions of section 713(b)(1) of Title VII and of § 1608.10(b), below, may be asserted by the respondent.

1608.7 Affirmative action plans or programs under State or local law.

Affirmative action plans or programs executed by agreement with state or local government agencies, or by order of state or local government agencies, whether entered by consent or after contested proceedings, under statutes or ordinances described in Title VII, will be reviewed by the Commission in light of the similar purposes of Title VII and such statutes and ordinances. Accordingly, the Commission will process Title VII complaints involving such affirmative action plans or programs under this section.

(a) *Procedures for review of plans or programs.* If adherence to an affirmative action plan or program executed pursuant to a state statute or local ordinance described in Title VII is the basis of a complaint filed under Title VII or is alleged to be the justification for an action which is challenged under Title VII, the Commission will investigate to determine:

(1) Whether the affirmative action plan or program was executed by an employer, labor organization, or person subject to the statute or ordinance,

(2) whether the agreement was approved by an appropriate official of the state or local government, and

(3) whether adherence to the plan or program was the basis of the complaint or justification.

(1) *Previously Approved Plans or Programs.* If the Commission finds the facts described in paragraph (a) of this section, the Commission will, in accordance with the "substantial weight" provisions of section 706 of the Act, find no reasonable cause where appropriate.

(2) *Plans or Programs not previously approved.* If the plan or program has not been approved by an appropriate official of the state or local government, the Commission will follow the procedure of § 1608.10 of these Guidelines. If the Commission finds that the plan or program does conform to these Guidelines, the Commission will make a determination of no reasonable cause as set forth in § 1608.10(a).

(b) *Reliance on these guidelines.* In addition, if the affirmative action plan or program has been adopted in good faith reliance on these Guidelines, the provisions of section 713(b)(1) and § 1608.10(b), below, may be asserted by the respondent.

1608.8 Adherence to court order.

Parties are entitled to rely on orders of courts of competent jurisdiction. If adherence to an order of a United States District Court or other court of competent jurisdiction, whether entered by consent or after contested litigation, in a case brought to enforce a Federal, state, or local equal employment opportunity law or regulation, is the basis of a complaint filed under Title VII or is alleged to be the justification for an action which is challenged under Title VII, the Commission will investigate to determine: (a) Whether such an Order exists and (b) whether adherence to the affirmative action plan which is part of the Order was the basis of the complaint or justification. If the Commission so finds, it will issue a determination of no reasonable cause. The Commission interprets Title VII to mean that actions taken pursuant to the direction of a Court Order cannot give rise to liability under Title VII.

1608.9 Reliance on directions of other government agencies.

When a charge challenges an affirmative action plan or program, or when such a plan or program is raised as justification for an employment decision, and when the plan or program was developed pursuant to the requirements of a Federal or state law or regulation which in part seeks to ensure equal employment opportunity, the Commission will process the charge in accordance with § 1608.10(a). Other agencies with equal employment opportunity responsibilities may apply the principles of these Guidelines in the exercise of their authority.

1608.10 Standard of review.

(a) *Affirmative action plans or programs not specifically relying on these guidelines.* If, during the investigation of a charge of discrimination filed with the Commission, a respondent asserts that the action complained of was taken pursuant to and in accordance with a plan or program of the type described in these Guidelines, the Commission will determine whether the assertion is true, and if so, whether such a plan or program conforms to the requirements of these guidelines. If the Commission so finds, it will issue a determination of no reasonable cause and, where appropriate, will state that the determination constitutes a written interpretation or opinion of the Commission under section 713(b)(1). This interpretation may be relied upon by the respondent and asserted as a defense in the event that new charges involving similar facts and circumstances are thereafter filed against the respondent, which are based on actions taken pursuant to the affirmative action plan or program. If the Commission does not so find, it will proceed with the investigation in the usual manner.

(b) *Reliance on these guidelines.* If a respondent asserts that the action taken was pursuant to and in accordance with a plan or program which was adopted or implemented in good faith, in conformity with, and in reliance upon these Guidelines, and the self analysis and plan are in writing, the Commission will determine whether such assertion is true. If the Commission so finds, it will so state in the determination of no reasonable cause and will advise the respondent that:

(1) The Commission has found that the respondent is entitled to the protection of section 713(b)(1) of Title VII; and

(2) That the determination is itself an additional written interpretation or opinion of the Commission pursuant to section 713(b)(l).

1608.11 Limitations on the application of these guidelines.

(a) *No determination of adequacy of plan or program.* These Guidelines are applicable only with respect to the circumstances described in § 1608.1(d), above. They do not apply to, and the section 713(b)(1) defense is not available for the purpose of, determining the adequacy of an affirmative action plan or program to eliminate discrimination. Whether an employer who takes such affirmative action has done enough to remedy such discrimination will remain a question of fact in each case.

(b) *Guidelines inapplicable in absence of affirmative action.* Where an affirmative action plan or program is not the basis of the action complained of, these Guidelines are inapplicable.

(c) *Currency of plan or program.* Under section 713(b)(1), persons may rely on the plan or program only during the time when it is current. Currency is related to such factors as progress in correcting the conditions disclosed by the self analysis. The currency of the plan or program is a question of fact to be determined on a case by case basis. Programs developed under Executive Order No. 11246, as amended, will be deemed current in accordance with Department of Labor regulations at 41 CFR Chapter 60, or successor orders or regulations.

1608.12 Equal employment opportunity plans adopted pursuant to section 717 of Title VII.

If adherence to an Equal Employment Opportunity Plan, adopted pursuant to Section 717 of Title VII, and approved by an appropriate official of the U.S. Civil Service Commission, is the basis of a complaint filed under Title VII, or is alleged to be the justification for an action under Title VII, these Guidelines will apply in a manner similar to that set forth in § 1608.5. The Commission will issue regulations setting forth the procedure for processing such complaints.

Uniform Guidelines on Employee Selection Procedures

43 Fed. Reg. 38290 (1978)

Supplementary Information:

An Overview of the 1978 Uniform Guidelines on Employee Selection Procedures

I. BACKGROUND

One problem that confronted the Congress which adopted the Civil Rights Act of 1964 involved the effect of written preemployment tests on equal employment opportunity. The use of these test scores frequently denied employment to minorities in many cases without evidence that the tests were related to success on the job. Yet employers wished to continue to use such tests as practical tools to assist in the selection of qualified employees. Congress sought to strike a balance which would proscribe discrimination, but otherwise permit the use of tests in the selection of employees. Thus, in title VII, Congress authorized the use of "any professionally developed ability test provided that such test, its administration or action upon the results is not designed, intended or used to discriminate...."[35]

At first, some employers contended that, under this section, they could use any test which had been developed by a professional so long as they did not intend to exclude minorities, even if such exclusion was the consequence of the use of the test. In 1966, the Equal Employment Opportunity Commission (EEOC) adopted guidelines to advise employers and other users what the law and good industrial psychology practice required.[36]

The Department of Labor adopted the same approach in 1968 with respect to tests used by Federal contractors under Executive Order 11246 in a more detailed regulation. The Government's view was that the employer's intent was irrelevant. If tests or other practices had an adverse impact on protected groups, they were unlawful unless they could be justified. To justify a test which screened out a higher proportion of minorities, the employer would have to show that it fairly measured or predicted performance on the job. Otherwise, it would not be considered to be "professionally developed."

In succeeding years, the EEOC and the Department of Labor provided more extensive guidance which elaborated upon these principles and expanded the guidelines to emphasize all selection procedures. In 1971 in *Griggs v. Duke Power Co.*,[37] the Supreme Court announced the principle that employer practices which had an adverse impact on minorities and were not justified by business necessity constituted illegal discrimination under Title VII. Congress confirmed this interpretation in the 1972 amendments to Title VII. The elaboration of these principles by courts and agencies continued into the mid-1970's[38] but differences between the EEOC and the other agencies (Justice, Labor, and Civil Service Commission) produced two different sets of guidelines by the end of 1976.

With the advent of the Carter administration in 1977, efforts were intensified to produce a unified government position. The following document represents the result of that effort. This introduction is intended to assist those not familiar with these matters to un-

35. Section 703(h), 42 U.S.C. 2000e(2)(h).
36. *See* 35 U.S.L.W. 2137 (1966).
37. 401 U.S. 424 (1971).
38. *See, e.g.*, Albemarle Paper Co. v. Moody, 422 U.S. 405 (1975).

derstand the basic approach of the uniform guidelines. While the guidelines are complex and technical, they are based upon the principles which have been consistently upheld by the courts, the Congress, and the agencies.

The following discussion will cite the sections of the Guidelines which embody these principles.

II. ADVERSE IMPACT

The fundamental principle underlying the guidelines is that employer policies or practices which have an adverse impact on employment opportunities of any race, sex, or ethnic group are illegal under title VII and the Executive order unless justified by business necessity.[39] A selection procedure which has no adverse impact generally does not violate title VII or the Executive order.[40] This means that an employer may usually avoid the application of the guidelines by use of procedures which have no adverse impact.[41] If adverse impact exists, it must be justified on grounds of business necessity. Normally, this means by validation which demonstrates the relation between the selection procedure and performance on the job.

The guidelines adopt a "rule of thumb" as a practical means of determining adverse impact for use in enforcement proceedings. This rule is known as the "4/5 ths" or "80 percent" rule.[42] It is not a legal definition of discrimination, rather it is a practical device to keep the attention of enforcement agencies on serious discrepancies in hire or promotion rates or other employment decisions. To determine whether a selection procedure violates the "4/5 ths rule" an employer compares its hiring rates for different groups. [43] But this rule of thumb cannot be applied automatically. An employer who has conducted an extensive recruiting campaign may have a larger than normal pool of applicants, and the "4/5 ths rule" might unfairly expose it to enforcement proceedings.[44] On the other hand, an employer's reputation may have discouraged or "chilled" applicants of particular groups from applying because they believed application would be futile. The application of the "4/5 ths rule" in that situation would allow an employer to evade scrutiny because of its own discrimination[45]

III. IS ADVERSE IMPACT TO BE MEASURED BY THE OVERALL PROCESS?

In recent years some employers have eliminated the overall adverse impact of a selection procedure and employed sufficient numbers of minorities or women to meet this "4/5 ths rule of thumb". However, they might continue use of a component which does have an adverse impact. For example, an employer might insist on a minimum passing score on a written test which is not job related and which has an adverse impact on minorities.[46] However, the employer might compensate for this adverse impact by hiring a sufficient proportion of minorities who do meet its standards, so that its overall hiring is on a par with or higher than the applicant flow. Employers have argued that as long as their "bottom line" shows no overall adverse impact, there is no violation at all, regardless of the operation of a particular component of the process.

---

39. Griggs, note 3, *supra*; uniform guidelines on employees selection procedures (1978), section 3A, (hereinafter cited by section number only).
40. Furnco v. Waters, 98 S.Ct. 2943 (1978).
41. Section 6.
42. Section 4D.
43. Section 16R (definition of selection rate).
44. Section 4D (special recruiting programs).
45. *Ibid.* (user's actions have discouraged applicants).
46. *See, e.g.*, Griggs v. Duke Power Co., 401 U.S. 424 (1971).

Employee representatives have argued that rights under equal employment opportunity laws are individual, and the fact that an employer has hired some minorities does not justify discrimination against other minorities. Therefore, they argue that adverse impact is to be determined by examination of each component of the selection procedure, regardless of the "bottom line." This question has not been answered definitively by the courts. There are decisions pointing in both directions.

These guidelines do not address the underlying question of law. They discuss only the exercise of prosecutorial discretion by the Government agencies themselves.[47] The agencies have decided that, generally, their resources to combat discrimination should be used against those respondents whose practices have restricted or excluded the opportunities of minorities and women. If an employer is appropriately including all groups in the workforce, it is not sensible to spend Government time and effort on such a case, when there are so many employers whose practices do have adverse effects which should be challenged. For this reason, the guidelines provide that, in considering whether to take enforcement action, the Government will take into account the general posture of the employer concerning equal employment opportunity, including its affirmative action plan and results achieved under the plan.[48] There are some circumstances where the government may intervene even though the "bottom line" has been satisfied. They include the case where a component of a selection procedure restricts promotional opportunities of minorities or women who were discriminatorily assigned to jobs, and where a component, such as a height requirement, has been declared unlawful in other situations.[49]

What of the individual who is denied the job because of a particular component in a procedure which otherwise meets the "bottom line" standard? The individual retains the right to proceed through the appropriate agencies, and into Federal court.[50]

IV. WHERE ADVERSE IMPACT EXISTS: THE BASIC OPTIONS

Once an employer has established that there is adverse impact, what steps are required by the guidelines? As previously noted, the employer can modify or eliminate the procedure which produces the adverse impact, thus taking the selection procedure from the coverage of these guidelines. If the employer does not do that, then it must justify the use of the procedure on grounds of "business necessity."[51]

This normally means that it must show a clear relation between performance on the selection procedure and performance on the job. In the language of industrial psychology, the employer must validate the selection procedure. Thus the bulk of the guidelines consist of the Government's interpretation of standards for validation.

V. VALIDATION: CONSIDERATION OF ALTERNATIVES

The concept of validation as used in personnel psychology involves the establishment of the relationship between a test instrument or other selection procedure and performance on the job. Federal equal employment opportunity law has added a requirement to the

---

47. Section 4C.

48. Section 4E.

49. Section 4C.

50. The processing of individual cases is excluded from the operation of the bottom line concept by the definition of "enforcement action," section 161. Under section 4C, where adverse impact has existed, the employer must keep records of the effect of each component for 2 years after the adverse effect has dissipated.

51. A few practices may be used without validation even if they have adverse impact. *See, e.g.*, McDonnell Douglas v. Green, 411 U.S. 792 (1973) and section 6B.

process of validation. In conducting a validation study, the employer should consider available alternatives which will achieve its legitimate business purpose with lesser adverse impact.[52]

The employer cannot concentrate solely on establishing the validity of the instrument or procedure which it has been using in the past.

This same principle of using the alternative with lesser adverse impact is applicable to the manner in which an employer uses a valid selection procedure.[53]

The guidelines assume that there are at least three ways in which an employer can use scores on a selection procedure: (1) To screen out of consideration those who are not likely to be able to perform the job successfully; (2) to group applicants in accordance with the likelihood of their successful performance on the job, and (3) to rank applicants, selecting those with the highest scores for employment.[54]

The setting of a "cutoff score" to determine who will be screened out may have an adverse impact. If so, an employer is required to justify the initial cutoff score by reference to its need for a trustworthy and efficient work force.[55]

Similarly, use of results for grouping or for rank ordering is likely to have a greater adverse effect than use of scores solely to screen out unqualified candidates. If the employer chooses to use a rank order method, the evidence of validity must be sufficient to justify that method of use.[56]

VI. TESTING FOR HIGHER LEVEL JOBS

Normally, employers test for the job for which people are hired. However, there are situations where the first job is temporary or transient, and the workers who remain are promoted to work which involves more complex activities. The guidelines restrict testing for higher level jobs to users who promote a majority of the employees who remain with them to the higher level job within a reasonable period of time.[57]

VII. HOW IS VALIDATION TO BE CONDUCTED

Validation has become highly technical and complex, and yet is constantly changing as a set of concepts in industrial psychology. What follows here is a simple introduction to a highly complex field. There are three concepts which can be used to validate a selection procedure. These concepts reflect different approaches to investigating the job relatedness of selection procedures and may be interrelated in practice. They are (1) criterion-related validity,[58] **(2) content validity,**[59] and (3) construct validity.[60]

---

52. Albemarle Paper Co. v. Moody, 422 U.S. 405 (1975); Robinson v. Lorillard Corp., 444 F.2d 791 (4th Cir. 1971).

53. Sections 3B; 5G.

54. *Ibid.*

55. *See* sections 3B; SH. *See also* sections 14B(6) (criterion-related validity); 14C(9) (content validity); 14D(I) (construct validity).

56. Sections 5G, 14B(6); 14C(9); 14D(I).

57. Section 51.

58. Sections SB, (General Standards); 14B (Technical Standards); 15B (Documentation); 16F (Definition).

59. Sections SB (General Standards); 14C (Technical Standards); 15C (Documentation); 16D (Definition).

60. Sections SB (General Standards); 14D (Technical Standards); 15D (Documentation); 16E (Definition).

In criterion-related validity, a selection procedure is justified by a statistical relationship between scores on the test or other selection procedure and measures of job performance. In content validity, a selection procedure is justified by showing that it representatively samples significant parts of the job, such as a typing test for a typist. Construct validity involves identifying the psychological trait (the construct) which underlies successful performance on the job and then devising a selection procedure to measure the presence and degree of the construct. An example would be a test of "leadership ability."

The guidelines contain technical standards and documentation requirements for the application of each of the three approaches.[61] One of the problems which the guidelines attempt to meet is the "borderline" between "content validity" and "construct validity." The extreme cases are easy to understand. A secretary, for example, may have to type. Many jobs require the separation of important matters which must be handled immediately from those which can be handled routinely. For the typing function, a typing test is appropriate. It is justifiable on the basis of content validity because it is a sample of an important or critical part of the job. The second function can be viewed as involving a capability to exercise selective judgment in light of the surrounding circumstances, a mental process which is difficult to sample.

In addressing this situation, the guidelines attempt to make it practical to validate the typing test by a content strategy,[62] but do not allow the validation of a test measuring a construct such as "judgment" by a content validity strategy.

The bulk of the guidelines deals with questions such as those discussed in the above paragraphs. Not all such questions can be answered simply, nor can all problems be addressed in the single document. Once the guidelines are issued, they will have to be interpreted in light of changing factual, legal, and professional circumstances.

VIII. SIMPLIFICATION OF REPORTING AND RECORD KEEPING REQUIREMENTS

The reporting and record keeping provisions which appeared in the December 30 draft which was published for comment have been carefully reviewed in light of comments received and President Carter's direction to limit paperwork burdens on those regulated by Government to the minimum necessary for effective regulation. As a result of this review, two major changes have been made in the documentation requirements of the guidelines:

(1) A new section 15A(1) provides a simplified record keeping option for employers with fewer than 100 employees;

(2) Determinations of the adverse impact of selection procedures need not be made for groups which constitute less than 2 percent of the relevant labor force.

Also, the draft has been changed to make clear that users can assess adverse impact on an annual basis rather than on a continuing basis.

Analysis of comments. The uniform guidelines published today are based upon the proposition that the Federal Government should speak to the public and to those whom it regulates with one voice on this important subject; and that the Federal Government ought to impose upon itself obligations for equal employment opportunity which are at least as demanding as those it seeks to impose on others. These guidelines state a uniform Federal position on

61. Technical standards are in section 14; documentation requirements are in section 15.
62. Section 14C.

this subject, and are intended to protect the rights created by title VII of the Civil Rights Act of 1964, as amended, Executive Order 11246 as amended, and other provisions of Federal law. The uniform guidelines are also intended to represent "professionally acceptable methods" of the psychological profession for demonstrating whether a selection procedure validly predicts or measures performance for a particular job. *Albemarle Paper Co. v. Moody*, 442 U.S. 405, 425. They are also intended to be consistent with the decisions of the Supreme Court and authoritative decisions of other appellate courts.

Although the development of these guidelines preceded the issuance by President Jimmy Carter of Executive Order 12044 designed to improve the regulatory process, the spirit of his Executive order was followed in their development. Initial agreement among the Federal agencies was reached early in the fall of 1977, and the months from October 1977 until today have been spent in extensive consultation with civil rights groups whose clientele are protected by these guidelines; employers, labor unions, and State and local governments whose employment practices are affected by these guidelines; State and local government antidiscrimination agencies who share with the Federal Government enforcement responsibility for discriminatory practices; and appropriate members of the general public. For example, an earlier draft of these guidelines was circulated informally for comment on October 28, 1977, pursuant to 0MB Circular A-85. Many comments were received from representatives of State and local governments, psychologists, private employers, and civil rights groups. Those comments were taken into account in the draft of these guidelines which was published for comment December 30, 1977, 42 FR 66542.

More than 200 organizations and individuals submitted written comments on the December 30, 1977, draft. These comments were from representatives of private industry, public employers, labor organizations, civil rights groups, the American Psychological Association and components thereof, and many individual employers, psychologists, and personnel specialists. On March 3, 1978, notice was given of a public hearing and meeting to be held on April 10, 1978, 43 FR 9131. After preliminary review of the comments, the agencies identified four issues of particular interest, and invited testimony particularly on those issues, 43 FR 11812 (March 21, 1978). In the same notice the agencies published questions and answers on four issues of concern to the commenters. The questions and answers were designed to clarify the intent of the December 30, 1977, draft, so as to provide a sharper focus for the testimony at the hearing.

At a full day of testimony on April 10, 1978, representatives of private industry, State and local governments, labor organizations, and civil rights groups, as well as psychologists, personnel specialists, and others testified at the public hearing and meeting. The written comments, testimony, and views expressed in subsequent informal consultations have been carefully considered by the four agencies. We set forth below a summary of the comments, and the major issues raised in the comments and testimony, and attempt to explain how we have resolved those issues.

The statement submitted by the American Psychological Association (A.P.A.) stated that "these guidelines represent a major step forward and with careful interpretation can provide a sound basis for concerned professional work." Most of the A.P.A. comments were directed to clarification and interpretation of the present language of the proposal. However, the A.P.A. recommended substantive change in the construct validity section and in the definition of work behavior.

Similarly, the Division of Industrial and Organizational Psychology (division 14) of the A.P.A. described the technical standards of the guidelines as "superior" in terms of congruence with professional standards to "most previous orders and guidelines but numerous troublesome aspects remain." Division 14 had substantial concerns with a number of the provisions of the general principles of the draft.

Civil rights groups generally found the uniform guidelines far superior to the FEA guidelines, and many urged their adoption, with modifications concerning ranking and documentation. Others raised concerns about the "bottom line" concept and other provisions of the guidelines.

The Ad Hoc Group on Employee Selection Procedures representing many employers in private industry supported the concept of uniform guidelines, but had a number of problems with particular provisions, some of which are described below. The American Society for Personnel Administration (ASPA) and the International Personnel Management Association, which represents State and local governments, generally took the same position as the ad hoc group. Major industrial unions found that the draft guidelines were superior to the FEA guidelines, but they perceived them to be inferior to the EEOC guidelines. They challenged particularly the bottom line concept and the construct validity section.

The building trade unions urged an exclusion of apprenticeship programs from coverage of the guidelines. The American Council on Education found them inappropriate for employment decisions concerning faculty at institutions of higher education. Other particular concerns were articulated by organizations representing the handicapped, licensing and certifying agencies, and college placement offices.

General Principles

1. *Relationship between validation and elimination of adverse impact and affirmative action.* Federal equal employment opportunity law generally does not require evidence of validity for a selection procedure if there is no adverse impact; *e.g.*, *Griggs v. Duke Power Co*, 401 U.S. 424. Therefore, a user has the choice of complying either by providing evidence of validity (or otherwise justifying use in accord with Federal law), or by eliminating the adverse impact. These options have always been present under Federal law, 29 CFR 1607.3; 41 CFR 60-3.3(a); and the Federal Executive Agency Guidelines, 41 FR 51734 (November 23, 1976). The December 30 draft guidelines, however, clarified the nature of the two options open to users.

Psychologists expressed concern that the December 30 draft of section 6A encouraged the use of invalid procedures as long as there is no adverse impact. Employers added the concern that the section might encourage the use of illegal procedures not having an adverse impact against the groups who have historically suffered discrimination (minorities, women), even if they have an adverse impact on a different group (whites, males).

Section 6A was not so intended, and we have revised it to clarify the fact that illegal acts purporting to be affirmative action are not the goal of the agencies or of the guidelines; and that any employee selection procedure must be lawful and should be as job related as possible. The delineation of examples of alternative procedures was eliminated to avoid the implication that particular procedures are either prescribed or are necessarily appropriate. The basic thrust of section 6A, that elimination of adverse impact is an alternative to validation, is retained.

The inclusion of excerpts from the 1976 Equal Employment Opportunity Coordinating Council Policy Statement on Affirmative Action in section 13B of the December 30 draft was criticized as not belonging in a set of guidelines for the validation of selection procedures. Section 13 has been revised. The general statement of policy in support of voluntary affirmative action, and the reaffirmation of the policy statement have been retained, but this statement itself is now found in the appendix to the guidelines.

2. *The "bottom line" (section 4C).* The guidelines provide that when the overall selection process does not have an adverse impact the Government will usually not examine the individual components of that process for adverse impact or evidence of validity. The concept is based upon the view that the Federal Government should not generally concern itself with individual components of a selection process, if the overall effect of that process is nonexclusionary. Many commenters criticized the ambiguity caused by the word "generally" in the December 30 draft of section 4C which provided, "the Federal enforcement agencies generally will not take enforcement action based upon adverse impact of any component" of a process that does not have an overall adverse impact. Employer groups stated the position that the "bottom line" should be a rule prohibiting enforcement action by Federal agencies with respect to all or any part of a selection process where the bottom line does not show adverse impact. Civil rights and some labor union representatives expressed the opposing concerns that the concept may be too restrictive, that it may be interpreted as a matter of law, and that it might allow certain discriminatory conditions to go unremedied.

The guidelines have been revised to clarify the intent that the bottom line concept is based upon administrative and prosecutorial discretion. The Federal agencies cannot accept the recommendation that they never inquire into or take enforcement action with respect to any component procedure unless the whole process of which it is a part has an adverse impact. The Federal enforcement agencies believe that enforcement action may be warranted in unusual circumstances, such as those involving other discriminatory practices, or particular selection procedures which have no validity and have a clear adverse impact on a national basis. Other unusual circumstances may warrant a high level agency decision to proceed with enforcement actions although the "bottom line" has been satisfied. At the same time the agencies adhere to the bottom line concept of allocating resources primarily to those users whose overall selection processes have an adverse impact. See overview, above, part III.

3. *Investigation of alternatives selection procedures and alternative methods of use (section 3B).* The December 30 draft included an obligation on the user, when conducting a validity study, to investigate alternative procedures and uses, in order to determine whether there are other procedures which are substantially equally valid, but which have less adverse impact. The American Psychological Association stated:

> We would concur with the drafters of the guidelines that it is appropriate in the determination of a selection strategy to consider carefully a variety of possible procedures and to think carefully about the question of adverse impact with respect to each of these procedures. Nevertheless, we feel it appropriate to note that a rigid enforcement of these sections, particularly for smaller employers, would impose a substantial and expensive burden on these employers.

Since a reasonable consideration of alternatives is consistent with the underlying principle of minimizing adverse impact consistent with business needs, the provision is retained.

Private employer representatives challenged earlier drafts of these guidelines as being inconsistent with the decision of the Supreme Court in *Albemarle Paper Co. v. Moody*, 422 U.S. 405. No such inconsistency was intended. Accordingly, the first sentence of section 3B was revised to paraphrase the opinion in the Albemarle decision, so as to make it clear that section 3B is in accord with the principles of the Albemarle decision.

Section 3B was further revised to clarify the intent of the guidelines that the obligation to investigate alternative procedures is a part of conducting a validity study, so that alternative procedures should be evaluated in light of validity studies meeting professional standards, and that section 3B does not impose an obligation to search for alternatives if the user is not required to conduct a validity study.

Just as, under section 3B of the guidelines, a user should investigate alternative selection procedures as a part of choosing and validating a procedure, so should the user investigate alternative uses of the selection device chosen to find the use most appropriate to his needs. The validity study should address the question of what method of use (screening, grouping, or rank ordering) is appropriate for a procedure based on the kind and strength of the validity evidence shown, and the degree of adverse impact of the different uses.

4. *Establishment of cutoff scores and rank ordering.* Some commenters from civil rights groups believed that the December 30 draft guidelines did not provide sufficient guidance as to when it was permissible to use a selection procedure on a ranking basis rather than on a pass-fail basis. They also objected to section 5G in terms of setting cutoff scores. Other comments noted a lack of clarity as to how the determination of a cutoff score or the use of a procedure for ranking candidates relates to adverse impact.

As we have noted, users are not required to validate procedures which do not have an adverse impact. However, if one way of using a procedure (e.g., for ranking) results in greater adverse impact than another way (e.g., pass/fail), the procedure must be validated for that use. Similarly, cutoff scores which result in adverse impact should be justified. If the use of a validated procedure for ranking results in greater adverse impact than its use as a screening device, the evidence of validity and utility must be sufficient to warrant use of the procedures as a ranking device.

A new section 5G has been added to clarify these concepts. Section 5H (formerly section 5G) addresses the choice of a cutoff score when a procedure is to be used for ranking.

5. *Scope: Requests for exemptions for certain classes of users.* Some employer groups and labor organizations (e.g., academic institutions, large public employers, apprenticeship councils) argued that they should be exempted from all or some of the provisions of these guidelines because of their special needs. The intent of Congress as expressed in Federal equal employment opportunity law is to apply the same standards to all users, public and private.

These guidelines apply the same principles and standards to all employers. On the other hand, the nature of the procedures which will actually meet those principles and standards may be different for different employers, and the guidelines recognize that fact. Accordingly, the guidelines are applicable to all employers and other users who are covered by Federal equal employment opportunity law.

Organizations of handicapped persons objected to excluding from the scope of these guidelines the enforcement of laws prohibiting discrimination on the basis of handicap, in particular the Rehabilitation Act of 1973, sections 501, 503, and 504. While this issue has not been addressed in the guidelines, nothing precludes the adoption of the principles set forth in these guidelines for other appropriate situations.

Licensing and certification boards raised the question of the applicability of the guidelines to their licensing and certification functions. The guidelines make it clear that licensing and certification are covered "to the extent" that licensing and certification may be covered by Federal equal employment opportunity law.

Voluntary certification boards, where certification is not required by law, are not users as defined in section 16 with respect to their certifying functions and therefore are not subject to these guidelines. If an employer relies upon such certification in making employment decisions, the employer is the user and must be prepared to justify, under Federal law, that reliance as it would any other selection procedure.

6. *The "Four-Fifths Rule of Thumb" (section 4D).* Some representatives of employers and some professionals suggest that the basic test for adverse impact should be a test of statistical significance, rather than the four-fifths rule. Some civil rights groups, on the other hand, still regard the four-fifths rule as permitting some unlawful discrimination.

The Federal agencies believe that neither of these positions is correct. The great majority of employers do not hire, promote, or assign enough employees for most jobs to warrant primary reliance upon statistical significance. Many decisions in day-to-day life are made on the basis of information which does not have the justification of a test of statistical significance. Courts have found adverse impact without a showing of statistical significance. *Griggs v. Duke Power Co..supra*; *Vulcan Society of New York v. CSC of N.Y.*, 490 F.2d 387, 393 (2d Cir. 1973); *Kirkland v. New York St. Dept. of Corr. Serv.*, 520 F.2d 420, 425 (2d Cir. 1975).

Accordingly, the undersigned believe that while the four-fifths rule does not define discrimination and does not apply in all cases, it is appropriate as a rule of thumb in identifying adverse impact.

Technical Standards

7. *Criterion-related validity (section 14B).* This section of the guidelines found general support among the commenters from the psychological profession and, except for the provisions concerning test fairness (sometimes mistakenly equated with differential prediction or differential validity), generated relatively little comment.

The provisions of the guidelines concerning criterion-related validity studies call for studies of fairness of selection procedures where technically feasible.

Section 14B(8). Some psychologists and employer groups objected that the concept of test fairness or unfairness has been discredited by professionals and pointed out that the term is commonly misused. We recognize that there is serious debate on the question of test fairness; however, it is accepted professionally that fairness should be examined where feasible. The A.P.A. standards for educational and psychological tests, for example, direct users to explore the question of fairness on finding a difference in group performances (section E9, pp. 43-44). Similarly the concept of test fairness is one which is closely related to the basic thrust of Federal equal employment opportunity law; and that concept was endorsed by the Supreme Court in *Albemarle Paper Co. v. Moody*, 422 U.S. 405.

Accordingly, we have retained in the guidelines the obligation upon users to investigate test fairness where it is technically feasible to do so.

8. *Content validity.* The Division of the Industrial and Organizational Psychology of A.P.A. correctly perceived that the provisions of the draft guidelines concerning content validity, with their emphasis on observable work behaviors or work products, were "greatly concerned with minimizing the inferential leap between test and performance." That division expressed the view that the draft guidelines neglected situations where a knowledge, skill or ability is necessary to an outcome but where the work behavior cannot be replicated in a test. They recommended that the section be revised.

We believe that the emphasis on observable work behaviors or observable work products is appropriate; and that in order to show content validity, the gap between the test and performance on the job should be a small one. We recognize, however, that content validity may be appropriate to support a test which measures a knowledge, skill, or ability which is a necessary prerequisite to the performance of the job, even though the test might not be close enough to the work behavior to be considered a work sample, and the guidelines have been revised appropriately. On the other hand, tests of mental processes which are not directly observable and which may be difficult to determine on the basis of observable work behaviors or work products should not be supported by content validity.

Thus, the Principles for the Validation and Use of Personnel Selection Procedures (Division of Industrial and Organizational Psychology, American Psychological Association, 1975, p. 10), discuss the use of content validity to support tests of "specific items of knowledge, or specific job skills," but call attention to the inappropriateness of attempting to justify tests for traits or constructs on a content validity basis.

9. *Construct validity (section 14D).* Business 'groups and professionals expressed concern that the construct validity requirements in the December 30 draft were confusing and technically inaccurate. As section 14D indicates, construct validity is a relatively new procedure in the field of personnel selection and there is not yet substantial guidance in the professional literature as to its use in the area of employment practices. The provisions on construct validity have been revised to meet the concerns expressed by the A.P.A. The construct validity section as revised clarifies what is required by the Federal enforcement agencies at this stage in the development of construct validity. The guidelines leave open the possibility that different evidence of construct validity may be accepted in the future, as new methodologies develop and become incorporated in professional standards and other professional literature.

10. *Documentation (section 15).* Commenters stated that the documentation section did not conform to the technical requirements of the guidelines or was otherwise inadequate. Section 15 has been clarified and two significant changes have been made to minimize the record keeping burden. (See overview, part VIII.)

11. *Definitions (section 16).* The definition of work behavior in the December 30, 1977 draft was criticized by the A.P.A. and others as being too vague to provide adequate guidance to those using the guidelines who must identify work behavior as a part of any validation technique. Other comments criticized the absence or inadequacies of other definitions, especially "adverse impact." Substantial revisions of and additions to this section were therefore made.

Uniform Guidelines on Employee Selection Procedures (1978)

NOTE.—These guidelines are issued jointly by four agencies. Separate official adoptions follow the guidelines in this part IV as follows: Civil Service Commission, Department of Justice, Equal Employment Opportunity Commission, Department of Labor.

For official citation see section 18 of these guidelines.

SYNOPSIS

TABLE OF CONTENTS

(8) Operational Use
(9) Ranking Based on Content Validity Studies
D. Technical Standards for Construct Validity Studies
(1) Appropriateness of Construct Validity Studies
(2) Job Analysis for Construct Validity Studies
(3) Relationship to the Job
(4) Use of Construct Validity Study without New Criterion-Related Evidence
(a) Standards for Use
(b) Determination of Common work Behaviors

Documentation of Impact and Validity Evidence
15. Documentation of Impact and Validity Evidence
A. Required Information
(1) Simplified Record keeping for Users with Less Than 100 Employees
(2) Information on Impact
(a) Collection of Information on Impact
(b) When Adverse Impact Has Been Eliminated in the Total Selection Process
(c) When Data Insufficient to Determine Impact
(3) Documentation of Validity Evidence
(a) Type of Evidence
(b) Form of Report
(c) Completeness
B. Criterion-Related Validity Studies
(1) User(s), Location(s), and Date(s) of Study
(2) Problem and Setting
(3) Job Analysis or Review of Job Information
(4) Job Titles and Codes
(5) Criterion Measures
(6) Sample Description
(7) Description of Selection Procedure
(8) Techniques and Results
(9) Alternative Procedures Investigated
(10) Uses and Applications
(11) Source Data
(12) Contact Person
(13) Accuracy and Completeness
C. Content Validity Studies
(1) User(s), Location(s), and Date(s) of Study
(2) Problem and Setting
(3) Job Analysis—Content of the Job
(4) Selection Procedure and its Content
(5) Relationship Between Selection Procedure and the Job
(6) Alternative Procedures Investigated
(7) Uses and Applications
(8) Contact Person
(9) Accuracy and Completeness
D. Construct Validity Studies
(1) User(s), Location(s), and Date(s) of Study
(2) Problem and Setting
(3) Construct Definition

GENERAL PRINCIPLES

SEC. 1 *Statement of purpose.*—A. *Need for uniformity—Issuing agencies.* The Federal government s need for a uniform set of principles on the question of the use of tests and other selection procedures has long been recognized. The Equal Employment Opportunity Commission, the Civil Service Commission, the Department of Labor, and the Department of Justice jointly have adopted these uniform guidelines to meet that need, and to apply the same principles to the Federal Government as are applied to other employers.

B. *Purpose of guidelines.* These guidelines incorporate a single set of principles which are designed to assist employers, labor organizations, employment agencies, and licensing and certification boards to comply with requirements of Federal law prohibiting employment practices which discriminate on grounds of race, color, religion, sex, and national origin. They are designed to provide a framework for determining the proper use of tests and other selection procedures. These guidelines do not require a user to conduct validity studies of selection procedures where no adverse impact results. However, all users are encouraged to use selection procedures which are valid, especially users operating under merit principles.

C. *Relation to prior guidelines.* These guidelines are based upon and supersede previously issued guidelines on employee selection procedures. These guidelines have been built upon court decisions, the previously issued guidelines of the agencies, and the practical experience of the agencies, as well as the standards of the psychological profession. These guidelines are intended to be consistent with existing law.

SEC. 2. *Scope.*—A. *Application of guidelines.* These guidelines will be applied by the Equal Employment Opportunity Commission in the enforcement of title VII of the Civil Rights Act of' 1964, as amended by the Equal Employment Opportunity Act of 1972 (hereinafter "Title VII"); by the Department of Labor, and the contract compliance agencies until the transfer of authority contemplated by the President's Reorganization Plan No. 1 of 1978, in the administration and enforcement of Executive Order 11246, as amended by Executive Order 11375 (hereinafter "Executive Order 11246"); by the Civil Service Commission and other Federal agencies subject to section 717 of Title VII; by the Civil Service Commission in exercising its responsibilities toward State and local governments under section 208(b)(1) of the Intergovernmental-Personnel Act; by the Department of Justice in exercising its responsibilities under Federal law; by the Office of Revenue Sharing of the Department of the Treasury under the State and Local Fiscal Assistance Act of 1972, as amended; and by any other Federal agency which adopts them.

B. *Employment decisions.* These guidelines apply to tests and other selection procedures which are used as a basis for any employment decision. Employment decisions include but are not limited to hiring, promotion, demotion, membership (for example, in a labor organization), referral, retention, and licensing and certification, to the extent that licensing and certification may be covered by Federal equal employment opportunity law. Other selection decisions, such as selection for training or transfer, may also be considered employment decisions if they lead to any of the decisions listed above.

C. *Selection procedures.* These guidelines apply only to selection procedures which are used as a basis for making employment decisions. For example, the use of recruiting procedures designed to attract members of a particular race, sex, or ethnic group, which were previously denied employment opportunities or which are currently underutilized, may be necessary to bring an employer into compliance with Federal law, and is frequently an essential element of any effective affirmative action program; but recruitment practices are not considered by these guidelines to be selection procedures. Similarly, these guidelines do not pertain to the question of the lawfulness of a seniority system within the meaning of section 703(h), Executive Order 11246 or other provisions of Federal law or regulation, except to the extent that such systems utilize selection procedures to determine qualifications or abilities to perform the job. Nothing in these guidelines is intended or should be interpreted as discouraging the use of a selection procedure for the purpose of determining qualifications or for the purpose of selection on the basis of relative qualifications, if the selection procedure had been validated in accord with these guidelines for each such purpose for which it is to be used.

D. *Limitations.* These guidelines apply only to persons subject to Title VII, Executive Order 11246, or other equal employment opportunity requirements of Federal law. These guidelines do not apply to responsibilities under the Age Discrimination in Employment Act of 1967, as amended, not to discriminate on the basis of age, or under sections 501, 503, and 504 of the Rehabilitation Act of 1973, not to discriminate on the basis of handicap.

E. *Indian preference not affected.* These guidelines do not restrict any obligation imposed or right granted by Federal law to users to extend a preference in employment to Indians living on or near an Indian reservation in connection with employment opportunities on or near an Indian reservation.

SEC. 3. *Discrimination defined: Relationship between use of selection procedures and discrimination.*—A. *Procedure having adverse impact constitutes discrimination unless justified.* The use of any selection procedure which has an adverse impact on the hiring, promotion, or other employment or membership opportunities of members of any race, sex, or ethnic group will be considered to be discriminatory and inconsistent with these guidelines, unless the procedure has been validated in accordance with these guidelines, or the provisions of section 6 below are satisfied.

B. *Consideration of suitable alternative selection procedures.* Where two or more selection procedures are available which serve the user s legitimate interest in efficient and trustworthy workmanship, and which are substantially equally valid for a given purpose, the user should use the procedure which has been demonstrated to have the lesser adverse impact. Accordingly, whenever a validity study is called for by these guidelines, the user should include, as a part of the validity study, an investigation of suitable alternative selection procedures and suitable alternative methods of using the selection procedures which have as little adverse impact as possible, to determine the appropriateness of using or validating them in accord with these guidelines. If a user has made a reasonable effort to become aware of such alternative procedures and validity has been demonstrated in accord with these guidelines, the use of the test or other selection procedure may continue until such time as it should reasonably be reviewed for currency. Whenever the user is shown an alternative selection procedure with evidence of less adverse impact and substantial evidence of validity for the same job in similar circumstances, the user should investigate it to determine the appropriateness of using or validating it in accord with these guidelines. This subsection is not intended to preclude the combination of procedures into a significantly more valid procedure, if the use of such a combination has been shown to be in compliance with the guidelines.

SEC. 4. *Information on impact.*—A. *Records concerning impact.* Each user should maintain and have available for inspection records or other information which will disclose the impact which its tests and other selection procedures have upon employment opportunities of persons by identifiable race, sex, or ethnic group as set forth in subparagraph B below in order to determine compliance with these guidelines. Where there are large numbers of applicants and procedures are administered frequently, such information may be retained on a sample basis, provided that the sample is appropriate in terms of the applicant population and adequate in size.

B. *Applicable race, sex, and ethnic groups for record keeping.* The records called for by this section are to be maintained by sex, and the following races and ethnic groups: Blacks (Negroes), American Indians (including Alaskan Natives), Asians (including Pacific Islanders), Hispanic (including persons of Mexican, Puerto Rican, Cuban, Central or South American, or other Spanish origin or culture regardless of race), whites (Caucasians) other than Hispanic, and totals. The race, sex, and ethnic classifications called for by this section are consistent with the Equal Employment Opportunity Standard Form 100, Employer Information Report EEO-1 series of reports. The user should adopt safeguards to insure that the records required by this paragraph are used for appropriate purposes such as determining adverse impact, or (where required) for developing and monitoring affirmative action programs, and that such records are not used improperly. See sections 4E and 17(4) below.

C. *Evaluation of selection rates.* The "bottom line." If the information called for by sections 4A and B above shows that the total selection process for a job has an adverse impact, the individual components of the selection process should be evaluated for adverse impact. If this information shows that the total selection process does not have an adverse impact, the Federal enforcement agencies, in the exercise of their administrative and prosecutorial discretion, in usual circumstances, will not expect a user to evaluate the individual components for adverse impact, or to validate such individual components, and will not take enforcement action based upon adverse impact of any component of that process, including the separate parts of a multipart selection procedure or any separate procedure that is used as an alternative method of selection. However, in the following circumstances the Federal enforcement agencies will expect a user to evaluate the individual components for adverse impact and may, where appropriate, take enforcement action with respect to the individual components: (1) where the selection procedure is a significant factor in the continuation of patterns of assignments of incumbent employees caused by prior discriminatory employment practices, (2) where the weight of court decisions or administrative interpretations hold that a specific procedure (such as height or weight requirements or no-arrest records) is not job related in the same or similar circumstances. In unusual circumstances, other than those listed in (1) and (2) above, the Federal enforcement agencies may request a user to evaluate the individual components for adverse impact and may, where appropriate, take enforcement action with respect to the individual component.

D. *Adverse impact and the "four-fifths rule."* A selection rate for any race, sex, or ethnic group which is less than four-fifths *(4/5)* (or eighty percent) of the rate for the group with the highest rate will generally be regarded by the Federal enforcement agencies as evidence of adverse impact, while a greater than four-fifths rate will generally not be regarded by Federal enforcement agencies as evidence of adverse impact. Smaller differences in selection rate may nevertheless constitute adverse impact, where they are significant in both statistical and practical terms or where a user's actions have discouraged applicants disproportionately on grounds of race, sex, or ethnic group. Greater differences in selection rate may not constitute adverse impact where the differences are based on small numbers and are not statistically significant, or where special recruiting or other programs cause the pool of minority or female candidates to be atypical of the normal pool of applicants from that group. Where the user's evidence concerning the impact of a selection procedure indicates adverse impact but is based upon numbers which are too small to be reliable, evidence concerning the impact of the procedure over a longer period of time and/or evidence concerning the impact which the selection procedure had when used in the same manner in similar circumstances elsewhere may be considered in determining adverse impact. Where the user has not maintained data on adverse impact as required by the documentation section of applicable guidelines, the Federal enforcement agencies may draw an inference of adverse impact of the selection process from the failure of the user to maintain such data, if the user has an underutilization of a group in the job category, as compared to the group's representation in the relevant labor market or, in the case of jobs filled from within, the applicable work force.

E. *Consideration of user's equal employment opportunity posture.* In carrying out their obligations, the Federal enforcement agencies will consider the general posture of the user with respect to equal employment opportunity for the job or group of jobs in question. Where a user has adopted an affirmative action program, the Federal enforcement agencies will consider the provisions of that program, including the goals and timetables which the user has adopted and the progress which the user has made in carrying out that program and in meeting the goals and timetables. While such affirmative action programs may in design and execution be race, color, sex, or ethnic conscious, selection procedures under such programs should be based upon the ability or relative ability to do the work.

SEC. 5. *General standards for validity studies.—A. Acceptable types of validity studies.* For the purposes of satisfying these guidelines, users may rely upon criterion-related validity studies, content validity studies or construct validity studies, in accordance with the standards set forth in the technical standards of these guidelines, section 14 below. New strategies for showing the validity of selection procedures will be evaluated as they become accepted by the psychological profession.

B. *Criterion-related, content. and construct validity.* Evidence of the validity of a test or other selection procedure by a criterion-related validity study should consist of empirical data demonstrating that the selection procedure is predictive of or significantly correlated with important elements of job performance. See section 14B below. Evidence of the validity of a test or other selection procedure by a content validity study should consist of data showing that the content of the selection procedure is representative of important aspects of performance on the job for which the candidates are to be evaluated. See section 14C below. Evidence of the validity of a test or other selection procedure through a construct validity study should consist of data showing that the procedure measures the degree to which candidates have identifiable characteristics which have been determined to be important in successful performance in the job for which the candidates are to be evaluated. See section 14D below.

C. *Guidelines are consistent with professional standards.* The provisions of these guidelines relating to validation of selection procedures are intended to be consistent with generally accepted professional standards for evaluating standardized tests and other selection procedures, such as those described in the Standards for Educational and Psychological Tests prepared by a joint committee of the American Psychological Association, the American Educational Research Association, and the National Council on Measurement in Education (American Psychological Association, Washington, D.C., 1974) (hereinafter "A.P.A. Standards") and standard textbooks and journals in the field of personnel selection.

D. *Need for documentation of validity.* For any selection procedure which is part of a selection process which has an adverse impact and which selection procedure has an adverse impact, each user should maintain and have available such documentation as is described in section 15 below.

E. *Accuracy and standardization.* Validity studies should be carried out under conditions which assure insofar as possible the adequacy and accuracy of the research and the report. Selection procedures should be administered and scored under standardized conditions.

F. *Caution against selection on basis of knowledge, skills, or ability learned in brief orientation period.* In general, users should avoid making employment decisions on the basis of measures of knowledge, skills, or abilities which are normally learned in a brief orientation period, and which have an adverse impact.

G. *Method of use of selection procedures.* The evidence of both the validity and utility of a selection procedure should support the method the user chooses for operational use of the procedure, if that method of use has a greater adverse impact than another method of use. Evidence which may be sufficient to support the use of a selection procedure on a pass/fail (screening) basis may be insufficient to support the use of the same procedure on a ranking basis under these guidelines. Thus, if a user decides to use a selection procedure on a ranking basis, and that method of use has a greater adverse impact than use on an appropriate pass/fail basis (see section SH below), the user should have sufficient evidence of validity and utility to support the use on a ranking basis. See sections 3B, 14B (5) and (6), and 14C (8) and (9).

H. *Cutoff scores.* Where cutoff scores are used, they should normally be set so as to be reasonable and consistent with normal expectations of acceptable proficiency within the work force. Where applicants are ranked on the basis of properly validated selection procedures and those applicants scoring below a higher cutoff score than appropriate in light of such expectations have little or no chance of being selected for employment, the higher cutoff score may be appropriate, but the degree of adverse impact should be considered.

I. *Use of selection procedures for higher level jobs.* If job progression structures are so established that employees will probably, within a reasonable period of time and in a majority of cases, progress to a higher level, it may be considered that the applicants are being evaluated for a job or jobs at the higher level. However, where job progression is not so nearly automatic, or the time span is such that higher level jobs or employees potential may be expected to change in significant ways, it should be considered that applicants are being evaluated for a job at or near the entry level. A "reasonable period of time" will vary for different jobs and employment situations but will seldom be more than 5 years. Use of selection procedures to evaluate applicants for a higher level job would not be appropriate:

(1) If the majority of those remaining employed do not progress to the higher level job;

(2) If there is a reason to doubt that the higher level job will continue to require essentially similar skills during the progression period; or

(3) If the selection procedures measure knowledge, skills, or abilities required for advancement which would be expected to develop principally from the training or experience on the job.

J. *Interim use of selection procedures.* Users may continue the use of a selection procedure which is not at the moment fully supported by the required evidence of validity, provided: (1) The user has available substantial evidence of validity, and (2) the user has in progress, when technically feasible, a study which is designed to produce the additional evidence required by these guidelines within a reasonable time. If such a study is not technically feasible, see section 6B. If the study does not demonstrate validity, this provision of these guidelines for interim use shall not constitute a defense in any action, nor shall it relieve the user of any obligations arising under Federal law.

K. *Review of validity studies for currency.* Whenever validity has been shown in accord with these guidelines for the use of a particular selection procedure for a job or group of jobs, additional studies need not be performed until such time as the validity study is subject to review as provided in section 3B above. There are no absolutes in the area of determining the currency of a validity study. All circumstances concerning the study, including the validation strategy used, and changes in the relevant labor market and the job should be considered in the determination of when a validity study is outdated.

SEC. 6. *Use of selection procedures which have not been validated.*

A. *Use of alternate selection procedures to eliminate adverse impact.* A user may choose to utilize alternative selection procedures in order to eliminate adverse impact or as part of an affirmative action program. See section 13 below. Such alternative procedures should eliminate the adverse impact in the total selection process, should be lawful and should be as job related as possible.

B. *Where validity studies cannot or need not be performed.* There are circumstances in which a user cannot or need not utilize the validation techniques contemplated by these guidelines. In such circumstances, the user should utilize selection procedures which are as job related as possible and which will minimize or eliminate adverse impact, as set forth below.

(1) *Where informal or unscored procedures are used.* When an informal or unscored selection procedure which has an adverse impact is utilized, the user should eliminate the adverse impact, or modify the procedure to one which is a formal, scored or quantified measure or combination of measures and then validate the procedure in accord with these guidelines, or otherwise justify continued use of the procedure in accord with Federal law.

(2) *Where formal and scored procedures are used.* When a formal and scored selection procedure is used which has an adverse impact, the validation techniques contemplated by these guidelines usually should be followed if technically feasible. Where the user cannot or need not follow the validation techniques anticipated by these guidelines, the user should either modify the procedure to eliminate adverse impact or otherwise justify continued use of the procedure in accord with Federal law.

SEC. 7. *Use of other validity studies.*

A. *Validity studies not conducted by the user.* Users may, under certain circumstances, support the use of selection procedures by validity studies conducted by other users or conducted by test publishers or distributors and described in test manuals. While publishers of selection procedures have a professional obligation to provide evidence of validity which meets generally accepted professional standards (see section SC above), users are cautioned that they are responsible for compliance with these guidelines. Accordingly, users seeking to obtain selection procedures from publishers and distributors should be careful to determine that, in the event the user becomes subject to the validity requirements of these guidelines, the necessary information to support validity has been determined and will be made available to the user.

B. *Use of criterion-related validity evidence from other sources.* Criterion-related validity studies conducted by one test user, or described in test manuals and the professional literature, will be considered acceptable for use by another user when the following requirements are met:

(1) *Validity evidence.* Evidence from the available studies meeting the standards of section 14B below clearly demonstrates that the selection procedure is valid;

(2) *Job similarity.* The incumbents in the user s job and the incumbents in the job or group of jobs on which the validity study was conducted perform substantially the same major work behaviors, as shown by appropriate job analyses both on the job or group of jobs on which the validity study was performed and on the job for which the selection procedure is to be used; and

(3) *Fairness evidence.* The studies include a study of test fairness for each race, sex, and ethnic group which constitutes a significant factor in the borrowing user's relevant labor market for the job or jobs in question. If the studies under consideration satisfy (1) and (2) above but do not contain an investigation of test fairness, and it is not technically feasible for the borrowing user to conduct an internal study of test fairness, the borrowing user may utilize the study until studies conducted elsewhere meeting the requirements of these guidelines show test unfairness, or until such time as it becomes technically feasible to conduct an internal study of test fairness and the results of that study can be acted upon. Users obtaining selection procedures from publishers should consider, as one factor in the decision to purchase a particular selection procedure, the availability of evidence concerning test fairness.

C. *Validity evidence from multiunit study.* If validity evidence from a study covering more than one unit within an organization satisfies the requirements of section 14B below, evidence of validity specific to each unit will not be required unless there are variables which are likely to affect validity significantly.

D. *Other significant variables.* If there are variables in the other studies which are likely to affect the. validity significantly, the user may not rely upon such studies, but will be expected either to conduct an internal validity study or to comply with section 6 above.

SEC. 8. *Cooperative studies.*

A. *Encouragement of cooperative studies.* The agencies issuing these guidelines encourage employers, labor organizations, and employment agencies to cooperate in research, development, search for lawful alternatives, and validity studies in order to achieve procedures which are consistent with these guidelines.

B. *Standards for use of cooperative studies.* If validity evidence from a cooperative study satisfies the requirements of section 14 below, evidence of validity specific to each user will not be required unless there are variables in the user's situation which are likely to affect validity significantly.

SEC. 9. *No assumption of validity.*

A. *Unacceptable substitutes for evidence of validity.* Under no circumstances will the general reputation of a test or other selection procedures, its author or its publisher, or casual reports of its validity be accepted in lieu of evidence of validity. Specifically ruled out are: assumptions of validity based on a procedure's name or descriptive labels; all forms of promotional literature; data bearing on the frequency of a procedure's usage; testimonial statements and credentials of sellers, users, or consultants; and other nonempirical or anecdotal accounts of selection practices or selection outcomes.

B. *Encouragement of professional supervision.* Professional supervision of selection activities is encouraged but is not a substitute for documented evidence of validity. The enforcement agencies will take into account the fact that a thorough job analysis was conducted and that careful development and use of a selection procedure in accordance with professional standards enhance the probability that the selection procedure is valid for the job.

SEC. 10. *Employment agencies and employment services.*

A. *Where selection procedures are devised by agency.* An employment agency, including private employment agencies and State employment agencies, which agrees to a request by an employer or labor organization to devise and utilize a selection procedure should follow the standards in these guidelines for determining adverse impact. If adverse impact exists the agency should comply with these guidelines. An employment agency is not relieved of its obligation herein because the user did not request such validation or has requested the use of some lesser standard of validation than is provided in these guidelines. The use of an employment agency does not relieve an employer or labor organization or other user of its responsibilities under Federal law to provide equal employment opportunity or its obligations as a user under these guidelines.

B. *Where selection procedures are devised elsewhere.* Where an employment agency or service is requested to administer a selection procedure which has been devised elsewhere and to make referrals pursuant to the results, the employment agency or service should maintain and have available evidence of the impact of the selection and referral procedures which it administers. If adverse impact results the agency or service should comply with these guidelines. If the agency or service seeks to comply with these guidelines by reliance upon validity studies or other data in the possession of the employer, it should obtain and have available such information.

SEC. 11. *Disparate treatment.* The principles of disparate or unequal treatment must be distinguished from the concepts of validation. A selection procedure—even though validated against job performance in accordance with these guidelines—cannot be imposed upon members of a race, sex, or ethnic group where other employees, applicants, or members have not been subjected to that standard. Disparate treatment occurs where members of a race, sex, or ethnic group have been denied the same employment, promotion, membership, or other employment opportunities as have been available to other employees or applicants. Those employees or applicants who have been denied equal treatment, because of prior discriminatory practices or policies, must at least be afforded the same opportunities as had existed for other employees or applicants during the period of discrimination. Thus, the persons who were in the class of persons discriminated against during the period the user followed the discriminatory practices should be allowed the opportunity to qualify under less stringent selection procedures previously followed, unless the user demonstrates that the increased standards are required by business necessity. This section does not prohibit a user who has not previously followed merit standards from adopting merit standards which are in compliance with these guidelines; nor does it preclude a user who has previously used invalid or unvalidated selection procedures from developing and using procedures which are in accord with these guidelines.

SEC. 12. *Retesting of applicants.* Users should provide a reasonable opportunity for retesting and reconsideration. Where examinations are administered periodically with public notice, such reasonable opportunity exists, unless persons who have previously been tested are precluded from retesting. The user may however take reasonable steps to preserve the security of its procedures.

SEC. 13. *Affirmative action.*

A. *Affirmative action obligations.* The use of selection procedures which have been validated pursuant to these guidelines does not relieve users of any obligations they may have to undertake affirmative action to assure equal employment opportunity. Nothing in these guidelines is intended to preclude the use of lawful selection procedures which assist in remedying the effects of prior discriminatory practices, or the achievement of affirmative action objectives.

B. *Encouragement of voluntary affirmative action programs.* These guidelines are also intended to encourage the adoption and implementation of voluntary affirmative action programs by users who have no obligation under Federal law to adopt them; but are not intended to impose any new obligations in that regard. The agencies issuing and endorsing these guidelines endorse for all private employers and reaffirm for all governmental employers the Equal Employment Opportunity Coordinating Council s "Policy Statement on Affirmative Action Programs for State and Local Government Agencies" (41 FR 38814, September 13, 1976). That policy statement is attached hereto as appendix, section 17.

TECHNICAL STANDARDS

SEC. 14. *Technical standards for validity studies.* The following minimum standards, as applicable, should be met in conducting a validity study. Nothing in these guidelines is intended to preclude the development and use of other professionally acceptable techniques with respect to validation of selection procedures. Where it is not technically feasible for a user to conduct a validity study, the user has the obligation otherwise to comply with these guidelines. See sections 6 and 7 above.

A. *Validity studies should be based on review of information about the job.* Any validity study should be based upon a review of information about the job for which the selection procedure is to be used. The review should include a job analysis except as provided in section 14B(3) below with respect to criterion-related validity. Any method of job analysis may be used if it provides the information required for the specific validation strategy used.

B. *Technical standards for criterion-related validity studies.*

(1) *Technical feasibility.* Users choosing to validate a selection procedure by a criterion-related validity strategy should determine whether it is technically feasible (as defined

in section 16) to conduct such a study in the particular employment context. The determination of the number of persons necessary to permit the conduct of a meaningful criterion-related study should be made by the user on the basis of all relevant information concerning the selection procedure, the potential sample and the employment situation. Where appropriate, jobs with substantially the same major work behaviors may be grouped together for validity studies, in order to obtain an adequate sample. These guidelines do not require a user to hire or promote persons for the purpose of making it possible to conduct a criterion-related study.

(2) *Analysis of the job.* There should be a review of job information to determine measures of work behavior(s) or performance that are relevant to the job or group of jobs in question. These measures or criteria are relevant to the extent that they represent critical or important job duties, work behaviors or work outcomes as developed from the review of job information. The possibility of bias should be considered both in selection of the criterion measures and their application. In view of the possibility of bias in subjective evaluations, supervisory rating techniques and instructions to raters should be carefully developed. All criterion measures and the methods for gathering data need to be examined for freedom from factors which would unfairly alter scores of members of any group. The relevance of criteria and their freedom from bias are of particular concern when there are significant differences in measures of job performance for different groups.

(3) *Criterion measures.* Proper safeguards should be taken to insure that scores on selection procedures do not enter into any judgments of employee adequacy that are to be used as criterion measures. Whatever criteria are used should represent important or critical work behavior(s) or work outcomes. Certain criteria may be used without a full job analysis if the user can show the importance of the criteria to the particular employment context. These criteria include but are not limited to production rate, error rate, tardiness, absenteeism, and length of service. A standardized rating of overall work performance may be used where a study of the job shows that it is an appropriate criterion. Where performance in training is used as a criterion, success in training should be properly measured and the relevance of the training should be shown either through a comparison of the content of the training program with the critical or important work behavior(s) of the job(s), or through a demonstration of the relationship between measures of performance in training and measures of job performance. Measures of relative success in training include but are not limited to instructor evaluations, performance samples, or tests. Criterion measures consisting of paper and pencil tests will be closely reviewed for job relevance.

(4) *Representativeness of the sample.* Whether the study is predictive or concurrent, the sample subjects should insofar as feasible be representative of the candidates normally available in the relevant labor market for the job or group of jobs in question, and should insofar as feasible include the races, sexes, and ethnic groups normally available in the relevant job market. In determining the representativeness of the sample in a concurrent validity study, the user should take into account the extent to which the specific knowledges or skills which are the primary focus of the test are those which employees learn on the job.

Where samples are combined or compared, attention should be given to see that such samples are comparable in terms of the actual job they perform, the length of time on the job where time on the job is likely to affect performance, and other relevant factors likely to affect validity differences; or that these factors are included in the design of the study and their effects identified.

(5) *Statistical relationships.* The degree of relationship between selection procedure scores and criterion measures should be examined and computed, using professionally ac-

ceptable statistical procedures. Generally, a selection procedure is considered related to the criterion, for the purposes of these guidelines, when the relationship between performance on the procedure and performance on the criterion measure is statistically significant at the 0.05 level of significance, which means that it is sufficiently high as to have a probability of no more than one (1) in twenty (20) to have occurred by chance. Absence of a statistically significant relationship between a selection procedure and job performance should not necessarily discourage other investigations of the validity of that selection procedure.

(6) *Operational use of selection procedures.* Users should evaluate each selection procedure to assure that it is appropriate for operational use, including establishment of cutoff scores or rank ordering. Generally, if other factors remain the same, the greater the magnitude of the relationship (e.g., correlation coefficient) between performance on a selection procedure and one or more criteria of performance on the job, and the greater the importance and number of aspects of job performance covered by the criteria, the more likely it is that the procedure will be appropriate for use. Reliance upon a selection procedure which is significantly related to a criterion measure but which is based upon a study involving a large number of subjects and has a low correlation coefficient will be subject to close review if it has a large adverse impact. Sole reliance upon a single selection instrument which is related to only one of many job duties or aspects of job performance will also be subject to close review. The appropriateness of a selection procedure is best evaluated in each particular situation and there are no minimum correlation coefficients applicable to all employment situations. In determining whether a selection procedure is appropriate for operational use the following considerations should also be taken into account: The degree of adverse impact of the procedure, the availability of other selection procedures of greater or substantially equal validity.

(7) *Overstatement of validity findings.* Users should avoid reliance upon techniques which tend to overestimate validity findings as a result of capitalization on chance unless an appropriate safeguard is taken. Reliance upon a few selection procedures or criteria of successful job performance when many selection procedures or criteria of performance have been studied, or the use of optimal statistical weights for selection procedures computed in one sample, are techniques which tend to inflate validity estimates as a result of chance. Use of a large sample is one safeguard; cross-validation is another.

(8) *Fairness.* This section generally calls for studies of unfairness where technically feasible. The concept of fairness or unfairness of selection procedures is a developing concept. In addition, fairness studies generally require substantial numbers of employees in the job or group of jobs being studied. For these reasons, the Federal enforcement agencies recognize that the obligation to conduct studies of fairness imposed by the guidelines generally will be upon users or groups of users with' a large number of persons in a job class, or test developers; and that small users utilizing their own selection procedures will generally not be obligated to conduct such studies because it will be technically infeasible for them to do so.

(a) *Unfairness defined.* When members of one race, sex, or ethnic group characteristically obtain lower scores on a selection procedure than members of another group, and the differences in scores are not reflected in differences in a measure of job performance, use of the selection procedure may unfairly deny opportunities to members of the group that obtains the lower scores.

(b) *Investigation of fairness.* Where a selection procedure results in an adverse impact on a race, sex, or ethnic group identified in accordance with the classifications set forth in section 4 above and that group is a significant factor in the relevant labor market, the user generally should investigate the possible existence of unfairness for that group if it is technically feasible to do so. The greater the severity of the adverse impact on a group, the greater the need to investigate the possible existence of unfairness. Where the weight of evidence from other studies shows that the selection procedure predicts fairly for the group in question and for the same or similar jobs, such evidence may be relied on in connection with the selection procedure at issue.

(c) *General considerations in fairness investigations.* Users conducting a study of fairness should review the A.P.A. Standards regarding investigation of possible bias in testing. An investigation of fairness of a selection procedure depends on both evidence of validity and the manner in which the selection procedure is to be used in a particular employment context. Fairness of a selection procedure cannot necessarily be specified in advance without investigating these factors. Investigations of fairness of a selection procedure in samples where the range of scores on selection procedures or criterion measures is severely restricted for any subgroup sample (as compared to other subgroup samples) may produce misleading evidence of unfairness. That factor should accordingly be taken into account in conducting such studies and before reliance is placed on' the results.

(d) *When unfairness is shown.* If unfairness is demonstrated through a showing that members of a particular group perform better or poorer on the job than their scores on the selection procedure would indicate through comparison with how members of other groups perform, the user may either revise or replace the selection instrument in accordance with these guidelines, or may continue to use the selection instrument operationally with appropriate revisions in its use to assure compatibility between the probability of successful job performance and the probability of being selected.

(e) *Technical feasibility of fairness studies.* In addition to the general conditions needed for technical feasibility for the conduct of a criterion-related study (see section 16, below) an investigation of fairness requires the following:

(i) An adequate sample of persons in each group available for the study to achieve findings of statistical significance. Guidelines do not require a user to hire or promote persons on the basis of group classifications for the purpose of making it possible to conduct a study of fairness; but the user has the obligation otherwise to comply with these guidelines.

(ii) The samples for each group should be comparable in terms of the actual job they perform, length of time on the job where time on the job is likely to affect performance, and other relevant factors likely to affect validity differences; or such factors should be included in the design of the study and their effects identified.

(f) *Continued use of selection procedures when fairness studies not feasible.* If a study of fairness should otherwise be performed, but is not technically feasible, a selection procedure may be used which has otherwise met the validity standards of these guidelines, unless the technical infeasibility resulted from discriminatory employment practices which are demonstrated by facts other than past failure to conform with requirements for validation of selection procedures. However, when it becomes technically feasible for the user to perform a study of fairness and such a study is otherwise called for, the user should conduct the study of fairness.

C. *Technical standards for content validity studies.*

(1) *Appropriateness of content validity studies.* Users choosing to validate a selection procedure by a content validity strategy should determine whether it is appropriate to conduct such a study in the particular employment context. A selection procedure can be supported by a content validity strategy to the extent that it is a representative sample of

the content of the job. Selection procedures which purport to measure knowledges, skills, or abilities may in certain circumstances be justified by content validity, although they may not be representative samples, if the knowledge, skill, or ability measured by the selection procedure can be operationally defined as provided in section 14C(4) below, and if that knowledge, skill, or ability is a necessary prerequisite to successful job performance.

A selection procedure based upon inferences about mental processes cannot be supported solely or primarily on the basis of content validity. Thus, a content strategy is not appropriate for demonstrating the validity of selection procedures which purport to measure traits or constructs, such as intelligence, aptitude, personality, common sense, judgment, leadership, and spatial ability. Content validity is also not an appropriate strategy when the selection procedure involves knowledges, skills, or abilities which an employee will be expected to learn on the job.

(2) *Job analysis for content validity.* There should be a job analysis which includes an analysis of the important work behavior(s) required for successful performance and their relative importance and, if the behavior results in work product(s), an analysis of the work product(s). Any job analysis should focus on the work behavior(s) and the tasks associated with them. If work behavior(s) are not observable, the job analysis should identify and analyze those aspects of the behavior(s) that can be observed and the observed work products. The work behavior(s) selected for measurement should be critical work behavior(s) and/or important work behavior(s) constituting most of the job.

(3) *Development of selection procedures.* A selection procedure designed to measure the work behavior may be developed specifically from the job and job analysis in question, or may have been previously developed by the user, or by other users or by a test publisher.

(4) *Standards for demonstrating content validity.* To demonstrate the content validity of a selection procedure, a user should show that the behavior(s) demonstrated in the selection procedure are a representative sample of the behavior(s) of the job in question or that the selection procedure provides a representative sample of the work product of the job. In the case of a selection procedure measuring a knowledge, skill, or ability, the knowledge, skill, or ability being measured should be operationally defined. In the case of a selection procedure measuring a knowledge, the knowledge being measured should be operationally defined as that body of learned information which is used in and is a necessary prerequisite for observable aspects of work behavior of the job. In the case of skills or abilities, the skill or ability being measured should be operationally defined in terms of observable aspects of work behavior of the job. For any selection procedure measuring a knowledge, skill, or ability the user should show that (a) the selection procedure measures and is a representative sample of that knowledge, skill, or ability; and (b) that knowledge, skill, or ability is used in and is a necessary prerequisite to performance of critical or important work behavior(s). In addition, to be content valid, a selection procedure measuring a skill or ability should either closely approximate an observable work behavior, or its product should closely approximate an observable work product. If a test purports to sample a work behavior or to provide a sample of a work product, the manner and setting of the selection procedure and its level and complexity should closely approximate the work situation. The closer the content and the context of the selection procedure are to work samples or work behaviors, the stronger is the basis for showing content validity. As the content of the selection procedure less resembles a work behavior, or the setting and manner of the administration of the selection procedure less resemble the work situation, or the result less resembles a work product, the less likely the selection procedure is to be content valid, and the greater the need for other evidence of validity.

(5) *Reliability.* The reliability of selection procedures justified on the basis of content validity should be a matter of concern to the user. Whenever it is feasible, appropriate statistical estimates should be made of the reliability of the selection procedure.

(6) *Prior training or experience.* A requirement for or evaluation of specific prior training or experience based on content validity, including a specification of level or amount of training or experience, should be justified on the basis of the relationship between the content of the training or experience and the content of the job for which the training or experience is to be required or evaluated. The critical consideration is the resemblance between the specific behaviors, products, knowledges, skills, or abilities in the experience or training and the specific behaviors, products, knowledges, skills, or abilities required on the job, whether or not there is close resemblance between the experience or training as a whole and the job as a whole.

(7) *Content validity of training success.* Where a measure of success in a training program is used as a selection procedure and the content of a training program is justified on the basis of content validity, the use should be justified on the relationship between the content of the training program and the content of the job.

(8) *Operational use.* A selection procedure which is supported on the basis of content validity may be used for a job if it represents a critical work behavior (i.e., a behavior which is necessary for performance of the job) or work behaviors which constitute most of the important parts of the job.

(9) *Ranking based on content validity studies.* If a user can show, by a job analysis or otherwise, that a higher score on a content valid selection procedure is likely to result in better job performance, the results may be used to rank persons who score above minimum levels. Where a selection procedure supported solely or primarily by content validity is used to rank job candidates, the selection procedure should measure those aspects of performance which differentiate among levels of job performance.

D. *Technical standards for construct validity studies.*

(1) *Appropriateness of construct validity studies.* Construct validity is a more complex strategy than either criterion-related or content validity. Construct validation is a relatively new and developing procedure in the employment field, and there is at present a lack of substantial literature extending the concept to employment practices. The user should be aware that the effort to obtain sufficient empirical support for construct validity is both an extensive and arduous effort involving a series of research studies, which include criterion related validity studies and which may include content validity studies. Users choosing to justify use of a selection procedure by this strategy should therefore take particular care to assure that the validity study meets the standards set forth below.

(2) *Job analysis for construct validity studies.* There should be a job analysis. This job analysis should show the work behavior(s) required for successful performance of the job, or the groups of jobs being studied, the critical or important work behavior(s) in the job or group of jobs being studied, and an identification of the construct(s) believed to underlie successful performance of these critical or important work behaviors in the job or jobs in question. Each construct should be named and defined, so as to distinguish it from other constructs. If a group of jobs is being studied the jobs should have in common one or more critical or important work behaviors at a comparable level of complexity.

(3) *Relationship to the job.* A selection procedure should then be identified or developed which measures the construct identified in accord with subparagraph (2) above. The user should show by empirical evidence that the selection procedure is validly related to the

construct and that the construct is validly related to the performance of critical or important work behavior(s). The relationship between the construct as measured by the selection procedure and the related work behavior(s) should be supported by empirical evidence from one or more criterion-related studies involving the job or jobs in question which satisfy the provisions of section 14B above.

(4) *Use of construct validity study without new criterion-related evidence.*

(a) *Standards for use.* Until such time as professional literature provides more guidance on the use of construct validity in employment situations, the Federal agencies will accept a claim of construct validity without a criterion-related study which satisfies section 14B above only when the selection procedure has been used elsewhere in a situation in which a criterion-related study has been conducted and the use of a criterion-related validity study in this context meets the standards for transportability of criterion-related validity studies as set forth above in section 7. However, if a study pertains to a number of jobs having common critical or important work behaviors at a comparable level of complexity, and the evidence satisfies subparagraphs 14B (2) and (3) above for those jobs with criterion-related validity evidence for those jobs, the selection procedure may be used for all the jobs to which the study pertains. If construct validity is to be generalized to other jobs or groups of jobs not in the group studied, the Federal enforcement agencies will expect at a minimum additional empirical research evidence meeting the standards of subparagraphs section 14B (2) and (3) above for the additional jobs or groups of jobs.

(b) *Determination of common work behaviors.* In determining whether two or more jobs have one or more work behavior(s) in common, the user should compare the observed work behavior(s) in each of the jobs and should compare the observed work product(s) in each of the jobs. If neither the observed work behavior(s) in each of the jobs nor the observed work product(s) in each of the jobs are the same, the Federal enforcement agencies will presume that the work behavior(s) in each job are different. If the work behaviors are not observable, then evidence of similarity of work products and any other relevant research evidence will be considered in determining whether the work behavior(s) in the two jobs are the same.

DOCUMENTATION OF IMPACT AND VALIDITY EVIDENCE

SEC. 15. *Documentation of impact and validity evidence.*

A. *Required information.* Users of selection procedures other than those users complying with section 15A(1) below should maintain and have available for each job information on adverse impact of the selection process for that job and, where it is determined a selection process has an adverse impact, evidence of validity as set forth below.

(1) *Simplified record keeping for users with less than 100 employees.* In order to minimize record keeping burdens' on employers who employ one hundred (100) or fewer employees, and other users not required to file EEO-1, *et seq.*, reports, such users may satisfy the requirements of this section 1S if they maintain and have available records showing, for each year:

(a) The number of persons hired, promoted, and terminated for each job, by sex, and where appropriate by race and national origin;

(b) The number of applicants for hire and promotion by sex and where appropriate by race and national origin; and

(c) The selection procedures utilized (either standardized or not standardized).

These records should be maintained for each race or national origin group (see section 4 above) constituting more than two percent (2 %) of the labor force in the relevant labor area. However, it is not necessary to maintain records by race and/or national origin (see section 4 above) if one race or national origin group in the relevant labor area constitutes more than ninety-eight percent (98%) of the labor force in the area. If the user has reason to believe that a selection procedure has an adverse impact, the user should maintain any available evidence of validity for that procedure (see sections 7A and 8).

(2) *Information on impact.*

(a) *Collection of information on impact.* Users of selection procedures other than those complying with section lSA(1) above should maintain and have available for each job records or other information showing whether the total selection process for that job has an adverse impact on any of the groups for which records are called for by section 4B above. Adverse impact determinations should be made at least annually for each such group which constitutes at least 2 percent of the labor force of the applicable workforce. Where a total selection process for a job has an adverse impact, the user should maintain and have available records or other information showing which components have an adverse impact. Where the total selection process for a job does not have an adverse impact, information need not be maintained for individual components except in circumstances set forth in subsection 1SA(2)(b) below. If the determination of adverse impact is made using a procedure other than the "four-fifths rule," as defined in the first sentence of section 4D above, a justification, consistent with section 4D above, for the procedure used to determine adverse impact should be available.

(b) *When adverse impact has been eliminated in the total selection process.* Whenever the total selection process for a particular job has had an adverse impact, as defined in section 4 above, in any year, but no longer has an adverse impact, the user should maintain and have available the information on individual components of the section process required in the preceding paragraph for the period in which there was adverse impact. In addition, the user should continue to collect such information for at least two (2) years after the adverse impact has been eliminated.

(c) *When data insufficient to determine impact.* Where there has been an insufficient number of selections to determine whether there is an adverse impact of the total selection process for a particular job, the user should continue to collect, maintain and have available the information on individual components of the selection process required in section 1SA(2)(a) above until the information is sufficient to determine that the overall selection process does not have an adverse impact as defined in section 4 above, or until the job has changed substantially.

(3) *Documentation of validity evidence.*

(a) *Types of evidence.* Where a total selection process has an adverse impact (see section 4 above) the user should maintain and have available for each component of that process which has an adverse impact, one or more of the following types of documentation evidence:

(i) Documentation evidence showing criterion-related validity of the selection procedure (see section 15B, below).

(ii) Documentation evidence showing content validity of the selection procedure (see section 15C, below).

(iii) Documentation evidence showing construct validity of the selection procedure (see section 15D, below).

(iv) Documentation evidence from other studies showing validity of the selection procedure in the user s facility (see section 1SE, below).

(v) Documentation evidence showing why a validity study cannot or need not be performed and why continued use of the procedure is consistent with Federal law.

(b) *Form of report.* This evidence should be compiled in a reasonably complete and organized manner to permit direct evaluation of the validity of the selection procedure. Previously written employer or consultant reports of validity, or reports describing validity studies completed before the issuance of these guidelines, are acceptable if they are complete in regard to the documentation requirements contained in this section, or if they satisfied requirements of guidelines which were in effect when the validity study was completed. If they are not complete, the required additional documentation should be appended. If necessary information is not available the report of the validity study may still be used as documentation, but its adequacy will be evaluated in terms of compliance with the requirements of these guidelines.

(c) *Completeness.* In the event that evidence of validity is reviewed by an enforcement agency, the validation reports completed after the effective date of these guidelines are expected to contain the information set forth below. Evidence denoted by use of the word "(Essential)" is considered critical. If information denoted essential is not included, the report will be considered incomplete unless the user affirmatively demonstrates either its unavailability due to circumstances beyond the user s control or special circumstances of the user s study which make the information irrelevant. Evidence not so denoted is desirable but its absence will not be a basis for considering a report incomplete. The user should maintain and have available the information called for under the heading "Source Data" in sections ISB(1 1) and 15D(1 1). While it is a necessary part of the study, it need not be submitted with the report. All statistical results should be organized and presented in tabular or graphic form to the extent feasible.

B. *Criterion-related validity studies.* Reports of criterion-related validity for a selection procedure should include the following information:

(1) *User(s), location(s), and date(s) of study.* Dates and location(s) of the job analysis or review of job information, the date(s) and location(s) of the administration of the selection procedures and collection of criterion data, and the time between collection of data on selection procedures and criterion measures should be provided (essential). If the study was conducted at several locations, the address of each location, including city and State, should be shown.

(2) *Problem and setting.* An explicit definition of the purpose(s) of the study and the circumstances in which the study was conducted should be provided. A description of existing selection procedures and cutoff scores, if any, should be provided.

(3) *Job analysis or review of job information.* A description of the procedure used to analyze the job or group of jobs, or to review the job information should be provided (essential). Where a review of job information results in criteria which may be used without a full job analysis (see section 14B(3)), the basis for the selection of these criteria should be reported (essential). Where a job analysis is required a complete description of the work behavior(s) or work outcome(s), and measures of their criticality or importance should be provided (essential). The report should describe the basis on which the behavior(s) or outcome(s) were determined to be critical or important, such as the proportion of time spent on the respective behaviors, their level of difficulty, their frequency of performance, the consequences of error, or other appropriate factors (essential). Where two or more jobs are grouped for a validity study, the information called for in this subsection should be provided for each of the jobs, and the justification for the grouping (see section 14B(1)) should be provided (essential).

(4) *Job titles and codes.* It is desirable to provide the user s job title(s), for the job(s) in question and the corresponding job title(s) and code(s) from U.S. Employment Service s Dictionary of Occupational Titles.

(5) *Criterion measures.* The bases for the selection of the criterion measures should be provided, together with references to the evidence considered in making the selection of criterion measures (essential). A full description of all criteria on which data were collected and means by which they were observed, recorded, evaluated and quantified, should be provided (essential). If rating techniques are used as criterion measures, the appraisal form(s) and instructions to the rater(s) should be included as part of the validation evidence, or should be explicitly described and available (essential). All steps taken to insure that criterion measures are free from factors which would unfairly alter the scores of members of any group should be described (essential).

(6) *Sample description.* A description of how the research sample was identified and selected should be included (essential). The race, sex, and ethnic composition of the sample, including those groups set forth in section 4A above, should be described (essential). This description should include the size of each subgroup (essential). A description of how the research sample compares with the relevant labor market or work force, the method by which the relevant labor market or work force was defined, and a discussion of the likely effects on validity of differences between the sample and the relevant labor market or work force, are also desirable. Descriptions of educational levels, length of service, and age are also desirable.

(7) *Description of selection procedures.* Any measure, combination of measures, or procedure studied should be completely and explicitly described or attached (essential). If commercially available selection procedures are studied, they should be described by title, form, and publisher (essential). Reports of reliability estimates and how they were established are desirable.

(8) *Techniques and results.* Methods used in analyzing data should be described (essential). Measures of central tendency (e.g., means) and measures of dispersion (e.g., standard deviations and ranges) for all selection procedures and all criteria should be reported for each race, sex, and ethnic group which constitutes a significant factor in the relevant labor market (essential). The magnitude and direction of all relationships between selection procedures and criterion measures investigated should be reported for each relevant race, sex, and ethnic group and for the total group (essential). Where groups are too small to obtain reliable evidence of the magnitude of the relationship, it need not be reported separately. Statements regarding the statistical significance of results should be made (essential). Any statistical adjustments, such as for less than perfect reliability or for restriction of score range in the selection procedure or criterion, should be described and explained; and uncorrected correlation coefficients should also be shown (essential). Where the statistical technique categorizes continuous data, such as biserial correlation and the phi coefficient, the categories and the bases on which they were determined should be described and explained (essential). Studies of test fairness should be included where called for by the requirements of section 14B(8) (essential). These studies should include the rationale by which a selection procedure was determined to be fair to the group(s) in question. Where test fairness or unfairness has been demonstrated on the basis of other studies, a bibliography of the relevant studies should be included (essential). If the bibliography includes unpublished studies, copies of these studies, or adequate abstracts or summaries, should be attached (essential). Where revisions have been made in a selection procedure to assure compatibility between successful job performance and the probability of being selected, the studies underlying such revisions should be included

(essential). All statistical results should be organized and presented by relevant race, sex, and ethnic group (essential).

(9) *Alternative procedures investigated.* The selection procedures investigated and available evidence of their impact should be identified (essential). The scope, method, and findings of the investigation, and the conclusions reached in light of the findings, should be fully described (essential).

(10) *Uses and applications.* The methods considered for use of the selection procedure (e.g., as a screening device with a cutoff score, for grouping or ranking, or combined with other procedures in a battery) and available evidence of their impact should be described (essential). This description should include the rationale for choosing the method for operational use, and the evidence of the validity and utility of the procedure as it is to be used (essential). The purpose for which the procedure is to be used (e.g., hiring, transfer, promotion) should be described (essential). If weights are assigned to different parts of the selection procedure, these weights and the validity of the weighted composite should be reported (essential). If the selection procedure is used with a cutoff score, the user should describe the way in which normal expectations of proficiency within the work force were determined and the way in which the cutoff score was determined (essential).

(11) *Source data.* Each user should maintain records showing all pertinent information about individual sample members and raters where they are used, in studies involving the validation of selection procedures. These records should be made available upon request of a compliance agency. In the case of individual sample members these data should include scores on the selection procedure(s), scores on criterion measures, age, sex, race, or ethnic group status, and experience in the specific job on which the validation study was conducted, and may also include such things as education, training, and prior job experience, but should not include names and social security numbers. Records should be maintained which show the ratings given to each sample member by each rater.

(12) *Contact person.* The name, mailing address, and telephone number of the person who may be contacted for further information about the validity study should be provided (essential).

(13) *Accuracy and completeness.* The report should describe the steps taken to assure the accuracy and completeness of the collection, analysis, and report of data and results.

C. *Content validity studies.* Reports of content validity for a selection procedure should include the following information:

(1) *User(s), location(s) and date(s) of study.* Dates and location(s) of the job analysis should be shown (essential).

(2) *Problem and setting.* An explicit definition of the purpose(s) of the study and the circumstances in which the study was conducted should be provided. A description of existing selection procedures and cutoff scores, if any, should be provided.

(3) *Job analysis—Content of the job.* A description of the method used to analyze the job should be provided (essential). The work behavior(s), the associated tasks, and, if the behavior results in a work product, the work products should be completely described (essential). Measures of criticality and/or importance of the work behavior(s) and the method of determining these measures should be provided (essential). Where the job analysis also identified the knowledges, skills, and abilities used in work behavior(s), an operational definition for each knowledge in terms of a body of learned information and for each skill and ability in terms of observable behaviors and outcomes, and the relationship between each knowledge, skill, or ability and each work behavior, as well as the method

used to determine this relationship, should be provided (essential). The work situation should be described, including the setting in which work behavior(s) are performed, and where appropriate, the manner in which knowledges, skills, or abilities are used, and the complexity and difficulty of the knowledge, skill, or ability as used in the work behavior(s).

(4) *Selection procedure and its content.* Selection procedures, including those constructed by or for the user, specific training requirements, composites of selection procedures, and any other procedure supported by content validity, should be completely and explicitly described or attached (essential). If commercially available selection procedures are used, they should be described by title, form, and publisher (essential). The behaviors measured or sampled by the selection procedure should be explicitly described (essential). Where the selection procedure purports to measure a knowledge, skill, or ability, evidence that the selection procedure measures and is a representative sample of the knowledge, skill, or ability should be provided (essential).

(5) *Relationship between the selection procedure and the job.* The evidence demonstrating that the selection procedure is a representative work sample, a representative sample of the work behavior(s), or a representative sample of a knowledge, skill, or ability as used as a part of a work behavior and necessary for that behavior should be provided (essential). The user should identify the work behavior(s) which each item or part of the selection procedure is intended to sample or measure (essential). Where the selection procedure purports to sample a work behavior or to provide a sample of a work product, a comparison should be provided of the manner, setting, and the level of complexity of the selection procedure with those of the work situation (essential). If any steps were taken to reduce adverse impact on a race, sex, or ethnic group in the content of the procedure or in its administration, these steps should be described. Establishment of time limits, if any, and how these limits are related to the speed with which duties must be performed on the job, should be explained. Measures of central tendency (e.g., means) and measures of dispersion (e.g., standard deviations) and estimates of realibility [sic] should be reported for all selection procedures if available. Such reports should be made for relevant race, sex, and ethnic subgroups, at least on a statistically reliable sample basis.

(6) *Alternative procedures investigated.* The alternative selection procedures investigated and available evidence of their impact should be identified (essential). The scope, method, and findings of the investigation, and the conclusions reached in light of the findings, should be fully described (essential).

(7) *Uses and applications.* The methods considered for use of the selection procedure (e.g., as a screening device with a cutoff score, for grouping or ranking, or combined with other procedures in a battery) and available evidence of their impact should be described (essential). This description should include the rationale for choosing the method for operational use, and the evidence of the validity and utility of the procedure as it is to be used (essential). The purpose for which the procedure is to be used (e.g., hiring, transfer, promotion) should be described (essential). If the selection procedure is used with a cutoff score, the user should describe the way in which normal expectations of proficiency within the work force were determined and the way in which the cutoff score was determined (essential). In addition, if the selection procedure is to be used for ranking, the user should specify the evidence showing that a higher score on the selection procedure is likely to result in better job performance.

(8) *Contact person.* The name, mailing address, and telephone number of the person who may be contacted for further information about the validity study should be provided (essential).

(9) *Accuracy and completeness.* The report should describe the steps taken to assure the accuracy and completeness of the collection, analysis, and report of data and results.

D. *Construct validity studies.* Reports of construct validity for a selection procedure should include the following information:

(1) *User(s), location(s), and date(s) of study.* Date(s) and location(s) of the job analysis and the gathering of other evidence called for by these guidelines should be provided (essential).

(2) *Problem and setting.* An explicit definition of the purpose(s) of the study and circumstances in which the study was conducted should be provided. A description of existing selection procedures and cutoff scores, if any, should be provided.

(3) *Construct definition.* A clear definition of the construct(s) which are believed to underlie successful performance of the critical or important work behavior(s) should be provided (essential). This definition should include the levels of construct performance relevant to the job(s) for which the selection procedure is to be used (essential). There should be a summary of the position of the construct in the psychological literature, or in the absence of such a position, a description of the way in which the definition and measurement of the construct was developed and the psychological theory underlying it (essential). Any quantitative data which identify or define the job constructs, such as factor analyses, should be provided (essential).

(4) *Job analysis.* A description of the method used to analyze the job should be provided (essential). A complete description of the work behavior(s) and, to the extent appropriate, work outcomes and measures of their criticality and/or importance should be provided (essential). The report should also describe the basis on which the behavior(s) or outcomes were determined to be important, such as their level of difficulty, their frequency of performance, the consequences of error or other appropriate factors (essential). Where jobs are grouped or compared for the purposes of generalizing validity evidence, the work behavior(s) and work product(s) for each of the jobs should be described, and conclusions concerning the similarity of the jobs in terms of observable work behaviors or work products should be made (essential).

(5) *Job titles and codes.* It is desirable to provide the selection procedure user(s) job title(s) for the job(s) in question and the corresponding job title(s) and code(s) from the United States Employment Service s dictionary of occupational titles.

(6) *Selection procedure.* The selection procedure used as a measure of the construct [should] be completely and explicitly described or attached (essential). If commercially available selection procedures are used, they should be identified by title, form and publisher (essential). The research evidence of the relationship between the selection procedure and the construct, such as factor structure, should be included (essential). Measures of central tendency, variability and reliability of the selection procedure should be provided (essential). Whenever feasible, these measures should be provided separately for each relevant race, sex and ethnic group.

(7) *Relationship to job performance.* The criterion-related study(ies) and other empirical evidence of the relationship between the construct measured by the selection procedure and the related work behavior(s) for the job or jobs in question should be provided (essential). Documentation of the criterion-related study(ies) should satisfy the provisions of section 15B above or section 15E(1) below, except for studies conducted prior to the effective date of these guidelines (essential). Where a study pertains to a group of jobs, and, on the basis of the study, validity is asserted for a job in the group, the observed

work behaviors and the observed work products for each of the jobs should be described (essential). Any other evidence used in determining whether the work behavior(s) in each of the jobs is the same should be fully described (essential).

(8) *Alternative procedures investigated.* The alternative selection procedures investigated and available evidence of their impact should be identified (essential). The scope, method, and findings of the investigation, and the conclusions reached in light of the findings should be fully described (essential).

(9) *Uses and applications.* The methods considered for use of the selection procedure (e.g., as a screening device with a cutoff score, for grouping or ranking, or combined with other procedures in a battery) and available evidence of their impact should be described (essential). This description should include the rationale for choosing the method for operational use, and the evidence of the validity and utility of the procedure as it is to be used (essential). The purpose for which the procedure is to be used (e.g., hiring, transfer, promotion) should be described (essential). If weights are assigned to different parts of the selection procedure, these weights and the validity of the weighted composite should be reported (essential). If the selection procedure is used with a cutoff score, the user should describe the way in which normal expectations of proficiency within the work force were determined and the way in which the cutoff score was determined (essential).

(10) *Accuracy and completeness.* The report should describe the steps taken to assure the accuracy and completeness of the collection, analysis, and report of data and results.

(11) *Source data.* Each user should maintain records showing all pertinent information relating to its study of construct validity.

(12) *Contact person.* The name, mailing address, and telephone number of the individual who may be contacted for further information about the validity study should be provided (essential).

E. *Evidence of validity from other studies.* When validity of a selection procedure is supported by studies not done by the user, the evidence from the original study or studies should be compiled in a manner similar to that required in the appropriate section of this section 15 above. In addition, the following evidence should be supplied:

(1) *Evidence from criterion-related validity studies.*

a. *Job information.* A description of the important job behavior(s) of the user s job and the basis on which the behaviors were determined to be important should be provided (essential). A full description of the basis for determining that these important work behaviors are the same as those of the job in the original study (or studies) should be provided (essential).

b. *Relevance of criteria.* A full description of the basis on which the criteria used in the original studies are determined to be relevant for the user should be provided (essential).

c. *Other variables.* The similarity of important applicant pool or sample characteristics reported in the original studies to those of the user should be described (essential). A description of the comparison between the race, sex and ethnic composition of the user's relevant labor market and the sample in the original validity studies should be provided (essential).

d. *Use of the selection procedure.* A full description should be provided showing that the use to be made of the selection procedure is consistent with the findings of the original validity studies (essential).

e. *Bibliography.* A bibliography of reports of validity of the selection procedure for the job or jobs in question should be provided (essential). Where any of the studies included an investigation of test fairness, the results of this investigation should be provided (essential). Copies of reports published in journals that are not commonly available should be described in detail or attached (essential). Where a user is relying upon unpublished studies, a reasonable effort should be made to obtain these studies. If these unpublished studies are the sole source of validity evidence they should be described in detail or attached (essential). If these studies are not available, the name and address of the source, an adequate abstract or summary of the validity study and data, and a contact person in the source organization should be provided (essential).

(2) *Evidence from content validity studies.* See section 14C(3) and section 15C above.

(3) *Evidence from construct validity studies.* See sections 14D(2) and 15D above.

F. *Evidence of validity from cooperative studies.* Where a selection procedure has been validated through a cooperative study, evidence that the study satisfies the requirements of sections 7, 8 and 15E should be provided (essential).

G. *Selection for higher level job.* If a selection procedure is used to evaluate candidates for jobs at a higher level than those for which they will initially be employed, the validity evidence should satisfy the documentation provisions of this section 15 for the higher level job or jobs, and in addition, the user should provide: (1) a description of the job progression structure, formal or informal; (2) the data showing how many employees progress to the higher level job and the length of time needed to make this progression; and (3) an identification of any anticipated changes in the higher level job. In addition, if the test measures a knowledge, skill or ability, the user should provide evidence that the knowledge, skill or ability is required for the higher level job and the basis for the conclusion that the knowledge, skill or ability is not expected to develop from the training or experience on the job.

H. *Interim use of selection procedures.* If a selection procedure is being used on an interim basis because the procedure is not fully supported by the required evidence of validity, the user should maintain and have available (1) substantial evidence of validity for the procedure, and (2) a report showing the date on which the study to gather the additional evidence commenced, the estimated completion date of the study, and a description of the data to be collected (essential).

DEFINITIONS

SEC. 16. *Definitions.* The following definitions shall apply throughout these guidelines.

A. *Ability.* A present competence to perform an observable behavior or a behavior which results in an observable product.

B. *Adverse impact.* A substantially different rate of selection in hiring, promotion, or other employment decision which works to the disadvantage of members of a race, sex, or ethnic group. See section 4 of these guidelines.

C. *Compliance with these guidelines.* Use of a selection procedure is in compliance with these guidelines if such use has been validated in accord with these guidelines (as defined below), or if such use does not result in adverse impact on any race, sex, or ethnic group (see section 4, above), or, in unusual circumstances, if use of the procedure is otherwise justified in accord with Federal law. See section 6B, above.

D. *Content validity.* Demonstrated by data showing that the content of a selection procedure is representative of important aspects of performance on the job. See section SB and section 14C.

E. *Construct validity.* Demonstrated by data showing that the selection procedure measures the degree to which candidates have identifiable characteristics which have been determined to be important for successful job performance. See section SB and section 14D.

F. *Criterion-related validity.* Demonstrated by empirical data showing that the selection procedure is predictive of or significantly correlated with important elements of work behavior. See sections SB and 14B.

G. *Employer.* Any employer subject to the provisions of the Civil Rights Act of 1964, as amended, including State or local governments and any Federal agency subject to the provisions of section 717 of the Civil Rights Act of 1964, as amended, and any Federal contractor or subcontractor or federally assisted construction contractor or subcontractor covered by Executive Order 11246, as amended.

H. *Employment agency.* Any employment agency subject to the provisions of the Civil Rights Act of 1964, as amended.

I. *Enforcement action.* For the purposes of section 4 a proceeding by a Federal enforcement agency such as a lawsuit or an administrative proceeding leading to debarment from or withholding, suspension, or termination of Federal Government contracts or the suspension or withholding of Federal Government funds; but not a finding of reasonable cause or a conciliation process or the issuance of right to sue letters under Title VII or under Executive Order 11246 where such finding, conciliation, or issuance of notice of right to sue is based upon an individual complaint.

J. *Enforcement agency.* Any agency of the executive branch of the Federal Government which adopts these guidelines for purposes of the enforcement of the equal employment opportunity laws or which has responsibility for securing compliance with them.

K. *Job analysis.* A detailed statement of work behaviors and other information relevant to the job.

L. *Job description.* A general statement of job duties and responsibilities.

M. *Knowledge.* A body of information applied directly to the performance of a function.

N. *Labor organization.* Any labor organization subject to the provisions of the Civil Rights Act of 1964, as amended, and any committee subject thereto controlling apprenticeship or other training.

O. *Observable.* Able to be seen, heard, or otherwise perceived by a person other than the person performing the action.

P. *Race. sex. or ethnic group.* Any group of persons identifiable on the grounds of race, color, religion, sex, or national origin.

Q. *Selection procedure.* Any measure, combination of measures, or procedure used as a basis for any employment decision. Selection procedures include the full range of assessment techniques from traditional paper and pencil tests, performance tests, training programs, or probationary periods and physical, educational, and work experience requirements through informal or casual interviews and unscored application forms.

R. *Selection rate.* The proportion of applicants or candidates who are hired, promoted, or otherwise selected.

S. *Should.* The term "should" as used in these guidelines is intended to connote action which is necessary to achieve compliance with the guidelines, while recognizing that there are circumstances where alternative courses of action are open to users.

T. *Skill.* A present, observable competence to perform a learned psychomotor act.

U. *Technical feasibility*. The existence of conditions permitting the conduct of meaningful criterion-related validity studies. These conditions include: (1) An adequate sample of persons available for the study to achieve findings of statistical significance; (2) having or being able to obtain a sufficient range of scores on the selection procedure and job performance measures to produce validity results which can be expected to be representative of the results if the ranges normally expected were utilized; and (3) having or being able to devise unbiased, reliable and relevant measures of job performance or other criteria of employee adequacy. See section 14B(2). With respect to investigation of possible unfairness, the same considerations are applicable to each group for which the study is made. See section 14B(8).

V. *Unfairness of selection procedure*. A condition in which members of one race, sex, or ethnic group characteristically obtain lower scores on a selection procedure than members of another group, and the differences are not reflected in differences in measures of job performance. See section 14B(7).

W. *User*. Any employer, labor organization, employment agency, or licensing or certification board, to the extent it may be covered by Federal equal employment opportunity law, which uses a selection procedure as a basis for any employment decision. Whenever an employer, labor organization, or employment agency is required by law to restrict recruitment for any occupation to those applicants who have met licensing or certification requirements, the licensing or certifying authority to the extent it may be covered by Federal equal employment opportunity law will be considered the user with respect to those licensing or certification requirements. Whenever a State employment agency or service does no more than administer or monitor a procedure as permitted by Department of Labor regulations, and does so without making referrals or taking any other action on the basis of the results, the State employment agency will not be deemed to be a user.

X. *Validated in accord with these guidelines or properly validated*. A demonstration that one or more validity study or studies meeting the standards of these guidelines has been conducted, including investigation and, where appropriate, use of suitable alternative selection procedures as contemplated by section 3B, and has produced evidence of validity sufficient to warrant use of the procedure for the intended purpose under the standards of these guidelines.

Y. *Work behavior*. An activity performed to achieve the objectives of the job. Work behaviors involve observable (physical) components and unobservable (mental) components. A work behavior consists of the performance of one or more tasks. Knowledges, skills, and abilities are not behaviors, although they may be applied in work behaviors.

APPENDIX

SEC. 17. *Policy statement on affirmative action (see section 13B)*. The Equal Employment Opportunity Coordinating Council was established by Act of Congress in 1972, and charged with responsibility for developing and implementing agreements and policies designed, among other things, to eliminate conflict and inconsistency among the agencies of the Federal Government responsible for administering Federal law prohibiting discrimination on grounds of race, color, sex, religion, and national origin. This statement is issued as an initial response to the requests of a number of State and local officials for clarification of the Government s policies concerning the role of affirmative action in the overall equal employment opportunity program. While the Coordinating Council s adoption of this statement expresses only the views of the signatory agencies concerning this important subject, the principles set forth below should serve as policy guidance for other Federal agencies as well.

(1) Equal employment opportunity is the law of the land. In the public sector of our society this means that all persons, regardless of race, color, religion, sex, or national origin shall have equal access to positions in the public service limited only by their ability to do the job. There is ample evidence in all sectors of our society that such equal access frequently has been denied to members of certain groups because of their sex, racial, or ethnic characteristics. The remedy for such past and present discrimination is twofold.

On the one hand, vigorous enforcement of the laws against discrimination is essential. But equally, and perhaps even more important are affirmative, voluntary efforts on the part of public employers to assure that positions in the public service are genuinely and equally accessible to qualified persons, without regard to their sex, racial, or ethnic characteristics. Without such efforts equal employment opportunity is no more than a wish. The importance of voluntary affirmative action on the part of employers is underscored by title VII of the Civil Rights Act of 1964, Executive Order 11246, and related laws and regulations—all of which emphasize voluntary action to achieve equal employment opportunity.

As with most management objectives, a systematic plan based on sound organizational analysis and problem identification is crucial to the accomplishment of affirmative action objectives. For this reason, the Council urges all State and local governments to develop and implement results oriented affirmative action plans which deal with the problems so identified.

The following paragraphs are intended to assist State and local governments by illustrating the kinds of analyses and activities which may be appropriate for a public employer s voluntary affirmative action plan. This statement does not address remedies imposed after a finding of unlawful discrimination.

(2) Voluntary affirmative action to assure equal employment opportunity is appropriate at any stage of the employment process. The first step in the construction of any affirmative action plan should be an analysis of the employer's work force to determine whether percentages of sex, race, or ethnic groups in individual job classifications are substantially similar to the percentages of those groups available in the relevant job market who possess the basic job-related qualifications.

When substantial disparities are found through such analyses, each element of the overall selection process should be examined to determine which elements operate to exclude persons on the basis of sex, race, or ethnic group. Such elements include, but are not limited to, recruitment, testing, ranking, certification, interview, recommendations for selection, hiring, promotion, etc. The examination of each element of the selection process should at a minimum include a determination of its validity in predicting job performance.

(3) When an employer has reason to believe that its selection procedures have the exclusionary effect described in paragraph 2 above, it should initiate affirmative steps to remedy the situation. Such steps, which in design and execution may be race, color, sex, or ethnic "conscious," include, but are not limited to, the following:

(a) The establishment of a long-term goal, and short-range, interim goals and timetables for the specific job classifications, all of which should take into account the availability of basically qualified persons in the relevant job market;

(b) A recruitment program designed to attract qualified members of the group in question;

(c) A systematic effort to organize work and redesign jobs in ways that provide opportunities for persons lacking "journeyman" level knowledge or skills to enter and, with appropriate training, to progress in a career field;

(d) Revamping selection instruments or procedures which have not yet been validated in order to reduce or eliminate exclusionary effects on particular groups in particular job classifications;

(e) The initiation of measures designed to assure that members of the affected group who are qualified to perform the job are included within the pool of persons from which the selecting official makes the selection;

(f) A systematic effort to provide career advancement training, both classroom and on-the-job, to employees locked into dead end jobs; and

(g) The establishment of a system for regularly monitoring the effectiveness of the particular affirmative action program, and procedures for making timely adjustments in this program where effectiveness is not demonstrated.

(4) The goal of any affirmative action plan should be achievement of genuine equal employment opportunity for all qualified persons. Selection under such plans should be based upon the ability of the applicant(s) to do the work. Such plans should not require the selection of the unqualified, or the unneeded, nor should they require the selection of persons on the basis of race, color, sex, religion, or national origin. Moreover, while the Council believes that this statement should serve to assist State and local employers, as well as Federal agencies, it recognizes that affirmative action cannot be viewed as a standardized program which must be accomplished in the same way at all times in all places.

Accordingly, the Council has not attempted to set forth here either the minimum or maximum voluntary steps that employers may take to deal with their respective situations. Rather, the Council recognizes that under applicable authorities, State and local employers have flexibility formulate affirmative action plans that are best suited to their particular situations. In this manner, the Council believes that affirmative action programs will best serve the goal of equal employment opportunity ...

SEC. 18. *Citations.* The official title of these guidelines "Uniform Guidelines on Employee Selection Procedures (1978)."

Uniform Guidelines on Employee Selection Procedures (1978) are intended to establish a uniform Federal position in the area of prohibitive discrimination in employment practices on grounds of race, color, religion sex, or national origin. These guidelines have been adopted by the Equal Employment Opportunity Commission, the Department of Labor, 1 Department of Justice, and the Civil Service Commission.

The official citation is:

"Section ___, Uniform Guidelines on Employee Selection Procedure (1978); 43 FR-___ (August 25, 1978)."

The short form citation is:

"Section ___, U.G.E.S.P. (1978); 43 FR-___ (August 25, 1978)."

When the guidelines are cited in connection with the activities one of the issuing agencies, a specific citation to the regulations of the agency can be added at the end of the above citation. The specific additional citations are as follows:

Equal Employment Opportunity Commission
29 CFR Part 1607

Department of Labor
Office of Federal Contract Compliance Programs
41 CFR Part 60-3

Department of Justice
28 CFR 50.14

Civil Service Commission
5 CFR 300. 103(c)

The Equal Pay Act of 1963 [Selected Provisions from Fair Labor Standards Act of 1938]

77 Stat. 56, 29 U.S.C. § 206(d) (1976)

(d)(1) No employer having employees subject to any provisions of this section shall discriminate, within any establishment in which such employees are employed, between employees on the basis of sex by paying wages to employees in such establishment at a rate less than the rate at which he pays wages to employees of the opposite sex in such establishment for equal work on jobs the performance of which requires equal skill, effort, and responsibility, and which are performed under similar working conditions, except where such payment is made pursuant to (i) a seniority system; (ii) a merit system; (iii) a system which measures earnings by quantity or quality of production; or (iv) a differential based on any other factor other than sex: Provided, That an employer who is paying a wage rate differential in violation of this subsection shall not, in order to comply with the provisions of this subsection, reduce the wage rate of any employee.

(2) No labor organization, or its agents, representing employees of an employer having employees subject to any provisions of this section shall cause or attempt to cause such an employer to discriminate against an employee in violation of paragraph (1) of this subsection.

(3) For purposes of administration and enforcement, any amounts owing to any employee which have been withheld in violation of this subsection shall be deemed to be unpaid minimum wages or unpaid overtime compensation under this chapter.

(4) As used in this subsection, the term "labor organization" means any organization of any kind, or any agency or employee representation committee or plan, in which employees participate and which exists for the purpose, in whole or in part, of dealing with employers concerning grievances, labor disputes, wages, rates of pay, hours of employment, or conditions of work.

29 U.S.C. § 215(a)

After the expiration of one hundred and twenty days from June 25, 1938, it shall be unlawful for any person –

* * *

(2) to violate any of the provisions of section 206 or section 207 of this title ...

(3) to discharge or in any other manner discriminate against any employee because such employee has filed any complaint or instituted or caused to be instituted any proceeding under or related to this chapter, or has testified or is about to testify in any such proceeding, or has served or is about to serve on an industry committee;

29 U.S.C. § 16. Penalties

* * *

(b) Damages; right of action; attorney's fees and costs; termination of right of action

Any employer who violates the provisions of section 206 or section 207 of this title shall be liable to the employee or employees affected in the amount of their unpaid minimum wages, or their unpaid overtime compensation, as the case may be, and in an additional equal amount as liquidated damages. Any employer who violates the provisions of section 15(a)(3) of this title shall be liable for such legal or equitable relief as may be appropriate to effectuate the purposes of section 15(a)(3) of this title, including without limitation employment, reinstatement, promotion, and the payment of wages lost and an additional equal amount as liquidated damages. An action to recover the liability prescribed in either of the preceding sentences may be maintained against any employer (including a public agency) in any Federal or State court of competent jurisdiction by any one or more employees on behalf of himself or themselves and other employees similarly situated. No employee shall be a party plaintiff to any such action unless he gives his consent in writing to become such a party and such consent is filed in the court in which such action is brought. The court in such action shall in addition to any judgment awarded to the plaintiff or plaintiffs, allow a reasonable attorney's fee to be paid by the defendant, and the costs of the action. The right provided by this subsection to bring an action by or on behalf of any employee, and the right of any employee to become a party plaintiff to any such action, shall terminate upon the filing of a complaint by the Secretary of Labor in an action under section 217 of this title in which (1) restraint is sought of any further delay in the payment of unpaid minimum wages, or the amount of unpaid overtime compensation, as the case may be, owing to such employee under section 206 or section 207 of this title by an employer liable therefore under the provisions of this subsection or (2) legal or equitable relief is sought as a result of alleged violations of section 215(a)(3) of this title.

(c) Payment of wages and compensation; waiver of claims; actions by the Secretary; limitation of actions

The Secretary is authorized to supervise the payment of the unpaid minimum wages or the unpaid overtime compensation owing to any employee or employees under section 206 or section 207 of this title, and the agreement of any employee to accept such payment shall upon payment in full constitute a waiver by such employee of any right he may have under subsection (b) of this section to such unpaid minimum wages or unpaid overtime compensation and an additional equal amount as liquidated damages. The Secretary may bring an action in any court of competent jurisdiction to recover the amount of unpaid minimum wages or overtime compensation and an equal amount as liquidated damages. The right provided by subsection (b) of this section to bring an action by or on behalf of any employee to recover the liability specified in the first sentence of such subsection and of any employee to become a party plaintiff to any such action shall terminate upon the filing of a complaint by the Secretary in an action under this subsection in which a recovery is sought of unpaid minimum wages or unpaid overtime compensation under sections 206 and 207 of this title or liquidated or other damages provided by this subsection owing to such employee by an employer liable under the provisions of subsection (b) of this section, unless such action is dismissed without prejudice on motion of the Secretary. Any sums thus recovered by the Secretary of Labor on behalf of an employee pursuant to this subsection shall be held in a special deposit account and shall be paid, on order of the Secretary of Labor, directly to the employee or employees affected....

29 U.S.C. § 217. Injunction proceedings

The district courts ... shall have jurisdiction for cause shown, to restrain violations of section 215 or this title, including in the case of violations of section 215 of this title, including in the case of violations of section 215(a)(2) of this title the restraint of any withholding of payment of minimum wages or overtime compensation found by the court to be due to employees under this chapter ...

Age Discrimination in Employment Act, as Amended

81 Stat. 602 (1967), as amended 88 Stat. 74 (1974), 92 Stat.189 (1978), 96 Stat. 353 (1982), 98 Stat. 1792 (1984), 100 Stat. 170-1, 1973-5, 1979-80, 3342-5 (1986), 102 Stat. 78 (1988), 104 Stat. 978 (1990), 104 Stat. 1298 (1990), 105 Stat. 1071 (1991), 110 Stat. 3009-3023 (1996), and 112 Stat. 1834, 1835 (1998).

29 U.S.C. § 621 *et seq.*

621. Congressional statement of findings and purpose[2]

(a) The Congress hereby finds and declares that—

(1) in the face of rising productivity and affluence, older workers find themselves disadvantaged in their efforts to retain employment, and especially to regain employment when displaced from jobs;

(2) the setting of arbitrary age limits regardless of potential for job performance has become a common practice, and certain otherwise desirable practices may work to the disadvantage of older persons;

(3) the incidence of unemployment, especially long-term unemployment with resultant deterioration of skill, morale, and employer acceptability is, relative to the younger ages, high among older workers; their numbers are great and growing; and their employment problems grave;

(4) the existence in industries affecting commerce, of arbitrary discrimination in employment because of age, burdens commerce and the free flow of goods in commerce.

(b) It is therefore the purpose of this chapter to promote employment of older persons based on their ability rather than age; to prohibit arbitrary age discrimination in employment; to help employers and workers find ways of meeting problems arising from the impact of age on employment.

622. Education and research program; recommendation to Congress

(a) The Secretary of Labor shall undertake studies and provide information to labor unions, management, and the general public concerning the needs and abilities of older workers, and their potentials for continued employment and contribution to the economy. In order to achieve the purposes of this chapter, the Secretary of Labor shall carry on a continuing program of education and information, under which he may, among other measures—

(1) undertake research, and promote research, with a view to reducing barriers to the employment of older persons, and the promotion of measures for utilizing their skills;

(2) publish and otherwise make available to employers, professional societies, the various media of communication, and other interested persons the findings of studies and other materials for the promotion of employment;

---

2. Section 101 of the Older Workers Benefit Protection Act, Pub. L. 101-433, 104 Stat. 978 (1990), codified as a Note to § 621, states:

> The Congress finds that, as a result of the decision of the Supreme Court in Public Employees Retirement System of Ohio v. Betts, 109 S. Ct. 256 (1989), legislative action is necessary to restore the original congressional intent in passing and amending the Age Discrimination in Employment Act of 1967 (29 U.S.C. 621 et seq.), which was to prohibit discrimination against older workers in all employee benefits except when age-based reductions in employee benefit plans are justified by significant cost considerations.

(3) foster through the public employment service system and through cooperative effort the development of facilities of public and private agencies for expanding the opportunities and potentials of older persons;

(4) sponsor and assist State and community informational and educational programs.

(b) Not later than six months after the effective date of this chapter, the Secretary shall recommend to the Congress any measures he may deem desirable to change the lower or upper age limits set forth in section 631 of this title.

623. Prohibition of age discrimination[3]

(a) Employer practices

It shall be unlawful for an employer—

(1) to fail or refuse to hire or to discharge any individual or otherwise discriminate against any individual with respect to his compensation, terms, conditions, or privileges of employment, because of such individual's age;

(2) to limit, segregate, or classify his employees in any way which would deprive or tend to deprive any individual of employment opportunities or otherwise adversely affect his status as an employee, because of such individual's age; or

(3) to reduce the wage rate of any employee in order to comply with this chapter.

(b) Employment agency practices

It shall be unlawful for an employment agency to fail or refuse to refer for employment, or otherwise to discriminate against, any individual because of such individual's age, or to classify or refer for employment any individual on the basis of such individual's age.

(c) Labor organization practices

It shall be unlawful for a labor organization—

(1) to exclude or to expel from its membership, or otherwise to discriminate against, any individual because of his age;

(2) to limit, segregate, or classify its membership, or to classify or fail or refuse to refer for employment any individual, in any way which would deprive or tend to deprive any individual of employment opportunities, or would limit such employment opportunities or otherwise adversely affect his status as an employee or as an applicant for employment because of such individual's age;

(3) to cause or attempt to cause an employer to discriminate against an individual in violation of this section.

(d) Opposition to unlawful practices; participation in investigations, proceedings, or litigation

It shall be unlawful for an employer to discriminate against any of his employees or applicants for employment, for an employment agency to discriminate against any in-

3. Section 104 of the Older Workers Benefit Protection Act, Pub. L. 10 1-433, 104 Stat. 981 (1990), codified as a Note to §623, state:

"Sec. 104. Rules and Regulations.

Notwithstanding section 9 of the Age Discrimination in Employment Act of 1967 (29 U.S.C. 628), the Equal Employment Opportunity Commission may issue such rules and regulations as the Commission may consider necessary or appropriate for carrying out this title, and the amendments made by this title, only after consultation with the Secretary of the Treasury and the Secretary of Labor."

dividual, or for a labor organization to discriminate against any member thereof or applicant for membership, because such individual, member or applicant for membership has opposed any practice made unlawful by this section, or because such individual, member or applicant for membership has made a charge, testified, assisted, or participated in any manner in an investigation, proceeding, or litigation under this chapter.

(e) Printing or publication of notice or advertisement indicating preference, limitation, etc.

It shall be unlawful for an employer, labor organization, or employment agency to print or publish, or cause to be printed or published, any notice or advertisement relating to employment by such an employer or membership in or any classification or referral for employment by such a labor organization, or relating to any classification or referral for employment by such an employment agency, indicating any preference, limitation, specification, or discrimination, based on age.

(f) Lawful practices; age and occupational qualification; other reasonable factors; laws of foreign workplace; seniority system; employee benefit plans; discharge or discipline for good cause

It shall not be unlawful for any employer, employment agency, or labor organization—

(1) to take any action otherwise prohibited under subsections (a), (b), (c), or (e) of this section where age is a bona fide occupational qualification reasonably necessary to the normal operation of the particular business, or where the differentiation is based on reasonable factors other than age, or where such practices involve an employee in a workplace in a foreign country, and compliance with such subsections would cause such employer, or a corporation controlled by such employer, to violate the laws of the country in which such workplace is located;

(2) to take any action otherwise prohibited under subsection (a), (b), (c), or (e) of this section—

(A) to observe the terms of a bona fide seniority system that is not intended to evade the purposes of this Act, except that no such seniority system shall require or permit the involuntary retirement of any individual specified by section 12(a) because of the age of such individual; or

(B) to observe the terms of a bona fide employee benefit plan—

(i) where, for each benefit or benefit package, the actual amount of payment made or cost incurred on behalf of an older worker is no less than that made or incurred on behalf of a younger worker, as permissible under section 1625.10, title 29, Code of Federal Regulations (as in effect on June 22, 1989); or

(ii) that is a voluntary early retirement incentive plan consistent with the relevant purpose or purposes of this Act.

Notwithstanding clause (i) or (ii) of subparagraph (B), no such employee benefit plan or voluntary early retirement incentive plan shall excuse the failure to hire any individual, and no such employee benefit plan shall require or permit the involuntary retirement of any individual specified by section 12(a), because of the age of such individual. An employer, employment agency, or labor organization acting under subparagraph (A), or under clause (i) or (ii) of subparagraph (B), shall have the burden of proving that such actions are lawful in any civil enforcement proceeding brought under this Act; or

(3) to discharge or otherwise discipline an individual for good cause.

(g) Repealed. Replaced by Pub. L. No. 10 1-239, Sec. 6202(b). See 42 U.S.C. § 1395y.

(h) Practices of foreign corporations controlled by American employers; foreign persons not controlled by American employers; factors determining control

(1) If an employer controls a corporation whose place of incorporation is in a foreign country, any practice by such corporation prohibited under this section shall be presumed to be such practice by such employer.

(2) The prohibitions of this section shall not apply where the employer is a foreign person not controlled by an American employer.

(3) For the purpose of this subsection the determination of whether an employer controls a corporation shall be based upon the—

(A) interrelation of operations,

(B) common management,

(C) centralized control of labor relations, and

(D) common ownership or financial control, of the employer and the corporation.

(i) Employee pension benefit plans; cessation or reduction of benefit accrual or of allocation to employee account; distribution of benefits after attainment of normal retirement age; compliance; highly compensated employees

(1) Except as otherwise provided in this subsection, it shall be unlawful for an employer, an employment agency, a labor organization, or any combination thereof to establish or maintain an employee pension benefit plan which requires or permits-

(A) in the case of a defined benefit plan, the cessation of an employee's benefit accrual, or the reduction of the rate of an employee's benefit accrual, because of age, or

(B) in the case of a defined contribution plan, the cessation of allocations to an employee's account, or the reduction of the rate at which amounts are allocated to an employee's account, because of age.

(2) Nothing in this section shall be construed to prohibit an employer, employment agency, or labor organization from observing any provision of an employee pension benefit plan to the extent that such provision imposes (without regard to age) a limitation on the amount of benefits that the plan provides or a limitation on the number of years of service or years of participation which are taken into account for purposes of determining benefit accrual under the plan.

(3) In the case of any employee who, as of the end of any plan year under a defined benefit plan, has attained normal retirement age under such plan—

(A) if distribution of benefits under such plan with respect to such employee has commenced as of the end of such plan year, then any requirement of this subsection for continued accrual of benefits under such plan, with respect to such employee during such plan year shall be treated as satisfied to the extent of the actuarial equivalent of in-service distribution of benefits, and

(B) if distribution of benefits under such plan with respect to such employee has not commenced as of the end of such year in accordance with section 1056(a)(3) of this title and section 401(a)(14)(C) of title 26, and the payment of benefits under such plan with respect to such employee is not suspended during such plan year pursuant to section 1053(a)(3)(B) of this title or section 411 (a)(3)(B) of title 26, then any requirement of this subsection for continued accrual of benefits under such plan with respect to such employee during such plan year shall be treated as satisfied to the extent of any adjustment in the benefit payable under the plan during such plan year attributable to the delay in the distribution of benefits after the attainment of normal retirement age. The provisions of this paragraph shall apply in accordance with regulations of the Secretary of the Treasury. Such regulations shall provide for the application of the preceding provisions of this paragraph to all employee pension benefit plans subject to this subsection and may provide for the application of such provisions, in the case of any such employee, with respect to any period of time within a plan year.

(4) Compliance with the requirements of this subsection with respect to an employee pension benefit plan shall constitute compliance with the requirements of this section relating to benefit accrual under such plan.

(5) Paragraph (1) shall not apply with respect to any employee who is a highly compensated employee (within the meaning of section 414(q) of title 26) to the extent provided in regulations prescribed by the Secretary of the Treasury for purposes of precluding discrimination in favor of highly compensated employees within the meaning of subchapter D of chapter 1 of title 26.

(6) A plan shall not be treated as failing to meet the requirements of paragraph (1) solely because the subsidized portion of any early retirement benefit is disregarded in determining benefit accruals or it is a plan permitted by subsection (m) of this section.

(7) Any regulations prescribed by the Secretary of the Treasury pursuant to clause (v) of section 411(b)(1)(H) of title 26 and subparagraphs (C) and (D) of section 411(b)(2) of title 26 shall apply with respect to the requirements of this subsection in the same manner and to the same extent as such regulations apply with respect to the requirements of such sections 411(b)(1)(H) and 411(b)(2).

(8) A plan shall not be treated as failing to meet the requirements of this section solely because such plan provides a normal retirement age described in section 1002(24)(B) of this title and section 411(a)(8)(B) of title 26.

(9) For purposes of this subsection-

(A) The terms "employee pension benefit plan," "defined benefit plan," "defined contribution plan," and "normal retirement age" have the meanings provided such terms in section 1002 of this title.

(B) The term "compensation" has the meaning provided by section 414(s) of title 26.

(j) Employment as firefighter or law enforcement officer

It shall not be unlawful for an employer which is a State, a political subdivision of a State, an agency or instrumentality of a State or a political subdivision of a State, or an interstate agency to fail or refuse to hire or to discharge any individual because of such individual's age if such action is taken—

(1) with respect to the employment of an individual as a firefighter or as a law enforcement officer, the employer has complied with section 3(d)(2) of the Age Discrimination in Employment Amendments of 1996 if the individual was discharged after the date described in such section, and the individual has attained—

(A) the age of hiring or retirement, respectively, in effect under applicable State or local law on March 3, 1983; or

(B)(i) if the individual was not hired, the age of hiring in effect on the date of such failure or refusal to hire under applicable State or local law enacted after the date of enactment of the Age Discrimination in Employment Amendments of 1996; or

(ii) if applicable State or local law was enacted after the date of enactment of the Age Discrimination in Employment Amendments of 1996 and the individual was discharged, the higher of—

(I) the age of retirement in effect on the date of such discharge under such law; and

(II) age 55: and

(2) pursuant to a bona fide hiring or retirement plan that is not a subterfuge to evade the purposes of this chapter[4]

(k) A seniority system or employee benefit plan shall comply with this Act regardless of the date ofadoption of such system or plan.

(l) Lawful practices; minimum age as condition of eligibility for retirement benefits; deductions from severance pay; reduction of longterm disability benefits[5]

Notwithstanding clause (i) or (ii) of subsection (f)(2)(B)—

(1) It shall not be a violation of subsection (a), (b), (c), or (e) solely because—

(A) an employee pension benefit plan (as defined in section 3(2) of the Employee Retirement Income Security Act of 1974 (29 U.S.C. 1002(2))) provides for the attainment of a minimum age as a condition of eligibility for normal or early retirement benefits; or

(B) a defined benefit plan (as defined in section 3(35) of such Act) provides for—

(i) payments that constitute the subsidized portion of an early retirement benefit; or

(ii) social security supplements for plan participants that commence before the age and terminate at the age (specified by the plan) when participants are eligible to receive reduced or unreduced old-age insurance benefits under title II of the Social Security Act (42 U.S.C. 401 et seq.), and that do not exceed such old-age insurance benefits.

(2)(A) It shall not be a violation of subsection (a), (b), (c), or (e) solely because following a contingent event unrelated to age—

(i) the value of any retiree health benefits received by an individual eligible for an immediate pension;

(ii) the value of any additional pension benefits that are made available solely as a result of the contingent event unrelated to age and following which the individual is eligible for not less than an immediate and unreduced pension; or

(iii) the values described in both clauses (i) and (ii); are deducted from severance pay made available as a result of the contingent event unrelated to age.

---

4. Section 119, subsection 1 of Pub. L. No. 104-208 also provides as follows:

(c) CONSTRUCTION.—Nothing in the repeal, reenactment, and amendment made by subsections (a) and (b) shall be construed to make lawful the failure or refusal to hire, or the discharge of, an individual pursuant to a law that—

(1) was enacted after March 3, 1983 and before the date of enactment of the Age Discrimination in Employment Amendments of 1996; and

(2) lowered the age of hiring or retirement, respectively, for firefighters or law enforcement officers that was in effect under applicable State or local law on March 3, 1983.

5. As amended by the Older Workers Benefit Protection Act, Technical Amendment, Pub. L. 101-521, 104 Stat. 2287 (1990).

(B) For an individual who receive immediate pension benefits that are actuarially reduced under subparagraph (A)(i), the amount of the deduction available pursuant to subparagraph (A)(i) shall be reduced by the same percentage as the reduction in the pension benefits.

(C) For purposes of this paragraph, severance pay shall include that portion of supplemental unemployment compensation benefits (as described in section 501(c)(17) of the Internal Revenue Code of 1986) that—

(i) constitutes additional benefits of up to 52 weeks;

(ii) has the primary purpose and effect of continuing benefits until an individual becomes eligible for an immediate and unreduced pension; and

(iii) is discontinued once the individual becomes eligible for an immediate and unreduced pension.

(D) For purposes of this paragraph and solely in order to make the deduction authorized under this paragraph, the term "retiree health benefits" means benefits provided pursuant to a group health plan covering retirees, for which (determined as of the contingent event unrelated to age)—

(i) the package of benefits provided by the employer for the retirees who are below age 65 is at least comparable to benefits provided under title XVIII of the Social Security Act (42 U.S.C. 1395 et seq.);

(ii) the package of benefits provided by the employer for the retirees who are age 65 and above is at least comparable to that offered under a plan that provides a benefit package with one-fourth the value of benefits provided under title XVIII of such Act; or

(iii) the package of benefits provided by the employer is as described in clauses (i) and (ii).

(E)(i) If the obligation of the employer to provide retiree health benefits is of limited duration, the value for each individual shall be calculated at a rate of $3,000 per year for benefit years before age 65, and $750 per year for benefit years beginning at age 65 and above.

(ii) If the obligation of the employer to provide retiree health benefits is of unlimited duration, the value for each individual shall be calculated at a rate of $48,000 for individuals below age 65, and $24,000 for individuals age 65 and above.

(iii) The values described in clauses (i) and (ii) shall be calculated based on the age of the individual as of the date of the contingent event unrelated to age. The values are effective on the date of enactment of this subsection, and shall be adjusted on an annual basis, with respect to a contingent event that occurs subsequent to the first year after the date of enactment of this subsection, based on the medical component of the Consumer Price Index for all-urban consumers published by the Department of Labor.

(iv) If an individual is required to pay a premium for retiree health benefits, the value calculated pursuant to this subparagraph shall be reduced by whatever percentage of the overall premium the individual is required to pay.

(F) If an employer that has implemented a deduction pursuant to subparagraph (A) fails to fulfill the obligation described in subparagraph (E), any aggrieved individual may bring an action for specific performance of the obligation described in subparagraph (E). The relief shall be in addition to any other remedies provided under Federal or State law.

(3) It shall not be a violation of subsection (a), (b), (c), or (e) solely because an employer provides a bona fide employee benefit plan or plans under which long-term disability benefits received by an individual are reduced by any pension benefits (other than those attributable to employee contributions)—

(A) paid to the individual that the individual voluntarily elects to receive; or

(B) for which an individual who has attained the later of age 62 or normal retirement age is eligible.

(m) Voluntary retirement incentive plans

Notwithstanding subsection (f)(2)(b), it shall not be a violation of subsection (a), (b), (c), or (e) solely because a plan of an institution of higher education (as defined in section 1001 of Title 20) offers employees who are serving under a contract of unlimited tenure (or similar arrangement providing for unlimited tenure) supplemental benefits upon voluntary retirement that are reduced or eliminated on the basis of age, if-

(1) such institution does not implement with respect to such employees any age-based reduction or cessation of benefits that are not such supplemental benefits, except as permitted by other provisions of this chapter.

(2) such supplemental benefits are in addition to any retirement or severance benefits which have been offered generally to employees serving under a contract of unlimited tenure (or similar arrangement providing for unlimited tenure), independent of any early retirement or exit-incentive plan, within the preceding 365 days; and

(3) any employee who attains the minimum age and satisfies all non-age-based conditions for receiving a benefit under the plan has an opportunity lasting not less than 180 days to elect to retire and to receive the maximum benefit that could then be elected by a younger but otherwise similarly situated employee, and the plan does not require retirement to occur sooner than 180 days after such election.

624. Study by Secretary of Labor; reports to President and Congress; scope of study; implementation of study; transmittal date of reports

(a)(1) The Secretary of Labor is directed to undertake an appropriate study of institutional and other arrangements giving rise to involuntary retirement, and report his findings and any appropriate legislative recommendations to the President and to the Congress.

Such study shall include—

(A) an examination of the effect of the amendment made by section 3(a) of the Age Discrimination in Employment Act Amendments of 1978 in raising the upper age limitation established by section 63 1(a) of this title to 70 years of age;

(B) a determination of the feasibility of eliminating such limitation;

(C) a determination of the feasibility of raising such limitation above 70 years of age; and

(D) an examination of the effect of the exemption contained in section 631(c) of this title, relating to certain executive employees, and the exemption contained in section 63 1(d) of this title, relating to tenured teaching personnel.

(2) The Secretary may undertake the study required by paragraph (1) of this subsection directly or by contract or other arrangement.

(b) The report required by subsection (a) of this section shall be transmitted to the President and to the Congress as an interim report not later than January 1, 1981, and in final form not later than January 1, 1982.

625. Administration

The Commission shall have the power—

(a) to make delegations, to appoint such agents and employees, and to pay for technical assistance on a fee for service basis, as he deems necessary to assist him in the performance of his functions under this chapter;

(b) to cooperate with regional, State, local, and other agencies, and to cooperate with and furnish technical assistance to employers, labor organizations, and employment agencies to aid in effectuating the purposes of this chapter.

626. Recordkeeping, investigation, and enforcement

(a) The Commission shall have the power to make investigations and require the keeping of records necessary or appropriate for the administration of this chapter in accordance with the powers and procedures provided in sections 209 and 211 of this title.

(b) The provisions of this chapter shall be enforced in accordance with the powers, remedies, and procedures provided in sections 211(b), 216 (except for subsection (a) thereof), and 217 of this title, and subsection (c) of this section. Any act prohibited under section 623 of this title shall be deemed to be a prohibited act under section 215 of this title. Amounts owing to a person as a result of a violation of this chapter shall be deemed to be unpaid minimum wages or unpaid overtime compensation for purposes of sections 216 and 217 of this title: *Provided*, That liquidated damages shall be payable only in cases of willful violations of this chapter. In any action brought to enforce this chapter the court shall have jurisdiction to grant such legal or equitable relief as may be appropriate to effectuate the purposes of this chapter, including without limitation judgments compelling employment, reinstatement or promotion, or enforcing the liability for amounts deemed to be unpaid minimum wages or unpaid overtime compensation under this section. Before instituting any action under this section, the Commission shall attempt to eliminate the discriminatory practice or practices alleged, and to effect voluntary compliance with the requirements of this chapter through informal methods of conciliation, conference, and persuasion.

(c)(1) Any person aggrieved may bring a civil action in any court of competent jurisdiction for such legal or equitable relief as will effectuate the purposes of this chapter: Provided, That the right of any person to bring such action shall terminate upon the commencement of an action by the Commission to enforce the right of such employee under this chapter.

(2) In an action brought under paragraph (1), a person shall be entitled to a trial by jury of any issue of fact in any such action for recovery of amounts owing as a result of a violation of this chapter, regardless of whether equitable relief is sought by any party in such action.

(d) No civil action may be commenced by an individual under this section until 60 days after a charge alleging unlawful discrimination has been filed with the Commission. Such a charge shall be filed—

(1) within 180 days after the alleged unlawful practice occurred; or

(2) in a case to which section 633(b) of this title applies, within 300 days after the alleged unlawful practice occurred, or within 30 days after receipt by the individual of notice of termination of proceeding under State law, whichever is earlier.

Upon receiving such a charge, the Commission shall promptly notify all persons named in such charge as prospective defendants in the action and shall promptly seek to eliminate any alleged unlawful practice by informal methods of conciliation, conference, and persuasion.

(e) Section 259 of this title shall apply to actions under this chapter. If a charge filed with the Commission under this Act is dismissed or the proceedings of the Commission are otherwise terminated by the Commission, the Commission shall notify the person aggrieved. A civil action may be brought under this section by a person defined in section 630(a) against the respondent named in the charge within 90 days after the date of the receipt of such notice.

(f)(1)[6] An individual may not waive any right or claim under this Act unless the waiver is knowing and voluntary. Except as provided in paragraph (2), a waiver may not be considered knowing and voluntary unless at a minimum—

(A) the waiver is part of an agreement between the individual and the employer that is written in a manner calculated to be understood by such individual, or by the average individual eligible to participate;

(B) the waiver specifically refers to rights or claims arising under this Act;

(C) the individual does not waive rights or claims that may arise after the date the waiver is executed;

(D) the individual waives rights or claims only in exchange for consideration in addition to anything of value to which the individual already is entitled;

(E) the individual is advised in writing to consult with an attorney prior to executing the agreement;

(F)(i) the individual is given a period of at least 21 days within which to consider the agreement; or

(ii) if a waiver is requested in connection with an exit incentive or other employment termination program offered to a group or class of employees, the individual is given a period of at least 45 days within which to consider the agreement;

(G) the agreement provides that for a period of at least 7 days following the execution of such agreement, the individual may revoke the agreement, and the agreement shall not become effective or enforceable until the revocation period has expired;

(H) if a waiver is requested in connection with an exit incentive or other employment termination program offered to a group or class of employees, the employer (at the commencement of the period specified in subparagraph (F)) informs the individual in writing in a manner calculated to be understood by the average individual eligible to participate, as to—

(i) any class, unit, or group of individuals covered by such program, any eligibility factors for such program, and any time limits applicable to such program; and

(ii) the job titles and ages of all individuals eligible or selected for the program, and the ages of all individuals in the same job classification or organizational unit who are not eligible or selected for the program.

---

6. Added by Section 201 of the Older Workers Benefit Protection Act, Pub. L. 101-433, 104 Stat. 984 (1990).

(2) A waiver in settlement of a charge filed with the Equal Employment Opportunity Commission, or an action filed in court by the individual or the individual's representative, alleging age discrimination of a kind prohibited under section 4 or 15 may not be considered knowing and voluntary unless at a minimum—

(A) subparagraphs (A) through (E) of paragraph (1) have been met; and

(B) the individual is given a reasonable period of time within which to consider the settlement agreement.

(3) In any dispute that may arise over whether any of the requirements, conditions, and circumstances set forth in subparagraph (A), (B), (C), (D), (E), (F), (G), or (H) of paragraph (1), or subparagraph (A) or (B) of paragraph (2), have been met, the party asserting the validity of a waiver shall have the burden of proving in a court of competent jurisdiction that a waiver was knowing and voluntary pursuant to paragraph (1) or (2).

(4) No waiver agreement may affect the Commission's rights and responsibilities to enforce this Act. No waiver may be used to justify interfering with the protected right of an employee to file a charge or participate in an investigation or proceeding conducted by the Commission.

627. Notices to be posted

Every employer, employment agency, and labor organization shall post and keep posted in conspicuous places upon its premises a notice to be prepared or approved by the Commission setting forth information as the Commission deems appropriate to effectuate the purposes of this chapter.

628. Rules and regulations; exemptions

In accordance with the provisions of subchapter II of chapter 5 of Title 5, the Equal Employment Opportunity Commission may issue such rules and regulations as it may consider necessary or appropriate for carrying out this chapter, and may establish such reasonable exemptions to and from any or all provisions of this chapter as it may find necessary and proper in the public interest.

629. Criminal penalties

Whoever shall forcibly resist, oppose, impede, intimidate or interfere with a duly authorized representative of the Equal Employment Opportunity Commission while it is engaged in the performance of duties under this chapter shall be punished by a fine of not more than $500 or by imprisonment for not more than one year, or by both: Provided, however, That no person shall be imprisoned under this section except when there has been a prior conviction hereunder.

630. Definitions

For the purposes of this chapter—

(a) The term "person" means one or more individuals, partnerships, associations, labor organizations, corporations, business trusts, legal representatives, or any organized groups of persons.

(b) The term "employer" means a person engaged in an industry affecting commerce who has twenty or more employees for each working day in each of twenty or more calendar weeks in the current or preceding calendar year: Provided, That prior to June 30, 1968, employers having fewer than fifty employees shall not be considered employers.

The term also means (1) any agent of such a person, and (2) a State or political subdivision of a State and any agency or instrumentality of a State or a political subdivision of a State, and any interstate agency, but such term does not include the United States, or a corporation wholly owned by the Government of the United States.

(c) The term "employment agency" means any person regularly undertaking with or without compensation to procure employees for an employer and includes an agent of such a person; but shall not include an agency of the United States.

(d) The term "labor organization" means a labor organization engaged in an industry affecting commerce, and any agent of such an organization, and includes any organization of any kind, any agency, or employee representation committee, group, association, or plan so engaged in which employees participate and which exists for the purpose, in whole or in part, of dealing with employers concerning grievances, labor disputes, wages, rates of pay, hours, or other terms or conditions of employment, and any conference, general committee, joint or system board, or joint council so engaged which is subordinate to a national or international labor organization.

(e) A labor organization shall be deemed to be engaged in an industry affecting commerce if (1) it maintains or operates a hiring hall or hiring office which procures employees for an employer or procures for employees opportunities to work for an employer, or (2) the number of its members (or, where it is a labor organization composed of other labor organizations or their representatives, if the aggregate number of the members of such other labor organization) is fifty or more prior to July 1, 1968, or twenty-five or more on or after July 1, 1968, and such labor organization—(1) is the certified representative of employees under the provisions of the National Labor Relations Act, as amended, or the Railway Labor Act, as amended; or (2) although not certified, is a national or international labor organization or a local labor organization recognized or acting as the representative of employees of an employer or employers engaged in an industry affecting commerce; or (3) has chartered a local labor organization or subsidiary body which is representing or actively seeking to represent employees of employers within the meaning of paragraph (1) or (2); or (4) has been chartered by a labor organization representing or actively seeking to represent employees within the meaning of paragraph (1) or (2) as the local or subordinate body through which such employees may enjoy membership or become affiliated with such labor organization; or (5) is a conference, general committee, joint or system board, or joint council subordinate to a national or international labor organization, which includes a labor organization engaged in an industry affecting commerce within the meaning of any of the preceding paragraphs of this subsection.

(f) The term "employee" means an individual employed by any employer except that the term "employee" shall not include any person elected to public office in any State or political subdivision of any State by the qualified voters thereof, or any person chosen by such officer to be on such officer's personal staff, or an appointee on the policymaking level or an immediate adviser with respect to the exercise of the constitutional or legal powers of the office. The exemption set forth in the preceding sentence shall not include employees subject to the civil service laws of a State government, governmental agency, or political subdivision. The term "employee" includes any individual who is a citizen of the United States employed by an employer in a workplace in a foreign country.

(g): The term "commerce" means trade, traffic, commerce, transportation, transmission, or communication among the several States; or between a State and any place outside thereof; or within the District of Columbia, or a possession of the United States; or between points in the same State but through a point outside thereof.

(h) The term "industry affecting commerce" means any activity, business, or industry in commerce or in which a labor dispute would hinder or obstruct commerce or the free flow of commerce and includes any activity or industry "affecting commerce" within the meaning of the Labor-Management Reporting and Disclosure Act of 1959.

(i) The term "State" includes a State of the United States, the District of Columbia, Puerto Rico, the Virgin Islands, American Samoa, Guam, Wake Island, the Canal Zone, and Outer Continental Shelf lands defined in the Outer Continental Shelf Lands Act.

(j) The term "firefighter" means an employee, the duties of whose position are primarily to perform work directly connected with the control and extinguishment of fires or the maintenance and use of firefighting apparatus and equipment, including an employee engaged in this activity who is transferred to a supervisory or administrative position.

(k) The term "law enforcement officer" means an employee, the duties of whose position are primarily the investigation, apprehension, or detention of individuals suspected or convicted of offenses against the criminal laws of a State, including an employee engaged in this activity who is transferred to a supervisory or administrative position. For the purpose of this subsection, "detention" includes the duties of employees assigned to guard individuals incarcerated in any penal institution.

(l) The term "compensation, terms, conditions, or privileges of employment" encompasses all employee benefits, including such benefits provided pursuant to a bona fide employee benefit plan.

631. Age limits

(a) The prohibitions in this chapter shall be limited to individuals who are at least 40 years of age.

(b) In the case of any personnel action affecting employees or applicants for employment which is subject to the provisions of section 633a of this title, the prohibitions established in section 633a of this title shall be limited to individuals who are at least 40 years of age.

(c)(1) Nothing in this chapter shall be construed to prohibit compulsory retirement of any employee who has attained 65 years of age who, for the 2-year period immediately before retirement, is employed in a bona fide executive or a high policymaking position, if such employee is entitled to an immediate nonforfeitable annual retirement benefit from a pension, profit-sharing, savings, or deferred compensation plan, or any combination of such plans, of the employer of such employee, which equals, in the aggregate, at least $44,000.

(2) In applying the retirement benefit test of paragraph (1) of this subsection, if any such retirement benefit is in a form other than a straight life annuity (with no ancillary benefits), or if employees contribute to any such plan or make rollover contributions, such benefit shall be adjusted in accordance with regulations prescribed by the Secretary, after consultation with the Secretary of the Treasury, so that the benefit is the equivalent of a straight life annuity (with no ancillary benefits) under a plan to which employees do not contribute and under which no rollover contributions are made.

632. [Omitted]

633. Federal-State relationship

(a) Nothing in this chapter shall affect the jurisdiction of any agency of any State performing like functions with regard to discriminatory employment practices on account of age except that upon commencement of action under this chapter such action shall supersede any State action.

(b) In the case of an alleged unlawful practice occurring in a State which has a law prohibiting discrimination in employment because of age and establishing or authorizing a State authority to grant or seek relief from such discriminatory practice, no suit may be brought under section 626 of this title before the expiration of sixty days after proceedings have been commenced under the State law, unless such proceedings have been earlier terminated: *Provided*, That such sixty-day period shall be extended to one hundred and twenty days during the first year after the effective date of such State law. If any requirement for the commencement of such proceedings is imposed by a State authority other than a requirement of the filing of a written and signed statement of the facts upon which the proceeding is based, the proceeding shall be deemed to have been commenced for the purposes of this subsection at the time such statement is sent by registered mail to the appropriate State authority.

633a. Nondiscrimination on account of age in Federal Government employment

(a) All personnel actions affecting employees or applicants for employment who are at least 40 years of age (except personnel actions with regard to aliens employed outside the limits of the United States) in military departments as defined in section 102 of Title 5, in executive agencies as defined in section 105 of Title 5 (including employees and applicants for employment who are paid from nonappropriated funds), in the United States Postal Service and the Postal Rate Commission, in those units in the government of the District of Columbia having positions in the competitive service, and in those units of the legislative and judicial branches of the Federal Government having positions in the competitive service, and in the Library of Congress shall be made free from any discrimination based on age.

(b) Except as otherwise provided in this subsection, the Equal Employment Opportunity Commission is authorized to enforce the provisions of subsection (a) of this section through appropriate remedies, including reinstatement or hiring of employees with or without backpay, as will effectuate the policies of this section. The Civil Service Commission shall issue such rules, regulations, orders, and instructions as it deems necessary and appropriate to carry out its responsibilities under this section. The Equal Employment Opportunity Commission shall—

(1) be responsible for the review and evaluation of the operation of all agency programs designed to carry out the policy of this section periodically obtaining and publishing (on at least a semiannual basis) progress reports from each department, agency, or unit referred to in subsection (a) of this section;

(2) consult with and solicit the recommendations of interested individuals, groups, and organizations relating to nondiscrimination in employment on account of age; and

(3) provide for the acceptance and processing of complaints of discrimination in Federal employment on account of age. The head of each such department, agency, or unit shall comply with such rules, regulations, orders, and instructions of the Equal Employment Opportunity Commission which shall include a provision that an employee or applicant for employment shall be notified of any final action taken on any complaint of discrimination filed by him thereunder. Reasonable exemptions to the provisions of this section may be established by the Commission but only when the Commission has established a maximum age requirement on the basis of a determination that age is a bona fide occupational qualification necessary to the performance of the duties of the position. With respect to employment in the Library of Congress, authorities granted in this subsection to the Equal Employment Opportunity Commission shall be exercised by the Librarian of Congress.

(c) Any person aggrieved may bring a civil action in any Federal district court of competent jurisdiction for such legal or equitable relief as will effectuate the purposes of this chapter.

(d) When the individual has not filed a complaint concerning age discrimination with the Commission, no civil action may be commenced by any individual under this section until the individual has given the Commission not less than thirty days' notice of an intent to file such action. Such notice shall be filed within one hundred and eighty days after the alleged unlawful practice occurred. Upon receiving a notice of intent to sue, the Commission shall promptly notify all persons named therein as prospective defendants in the action and take any appropriate action to assure the elimination of any unlawful practice.

(e) Nothing contained in this section shall relieve any Government agency or official of the responsibility to assure nondiscrimination on account of age in employment as required under any provision of Federal law.

(f) Any personnel action of any department, agency, or other entity referred to in subsection (a) of this section shall not be subject to, or affected by, any provision of this chapter, other than the provisions of section 631(b) of this title and the provisions of this section.

(g)(1) The Equal Employment Opportunity Commission shall undertake a study relating to the effects of the amendments made to this section by the Age Discrimination in Employment Act Amendments of 1978, and the effects of section 631(b) of this title. (2) The Equal Employment Opportunity Commission shall transmit a report to the President and to the Congress containing the findings of the Commission resulting from the study of the Commission under paragraph (1) of this subsection. Such report shall be transmitted no later than January 1, 1980.

634. Authorization of appropriations

There are hereby authorized to be, appropriated such sums as may be necessary to carry out this chapter.

Interpretations—Age Discrimination in Employment Act

29 C.F.R. Part 1625

1625.1 Definitions.

The Equal Employment Opportunity Commission is hereinafter referred to as the "Commission." The terms "person," "employer," "employment agency," "labor organization," and "employee" shall have the meanings set forth in Section 11 of the Age Discrimination in Employment Act of 1967, as amended, 29 U.S.C. 621 et seq., hereinafter referred to as the "Act". References to "employers" in this part state principles that are applicable not only to employers but also to labor organizations and to employment agencies.

1625.2 Discrimination between individuals protected by the Act.

(a) It is unlawful in situations where this Act applies, for an employer to discriminate in hiring or in any other way by giving preference because of age between individuals 40 and over. Thus, if two people apply for the same position, and one is 42 and the other 52, the employer may not lawfully turn down either one on the basis of age, but must make such decision on the basis of some other factor.

(b) The extension of additional benefits, such as increased severance pay, to older employees within the protected group may be lawful if an employer has a reasonable basis to conclude that those benefits will counteract problems related to age discrimination. The extension of those additional benefits may not be used as a means to accomplish practices otherwise prohibited by the Act.

1625.3 Employment agency.

(a) As long as an employment agency regularly procures employees for at least one covered employer, it qualifies under section 11(c) of the Act as an employment agency with respect to all of its activities whether or not such activities are for employers covered by the act.

(b)The prohibitions of section 4(b) of the Act apply not only to the referral activities of a covered employment agency but also to the agency's own employment practices, regardless of the number of employees the agency may have.

1625.4 Help wanted notices or advertisements.

(a) When help wanted notices or advertisements contains terms and phrases such as "age 25 to 35," "young," "college student," "recent college graduate," "boy," "girl," or others of a similar nature, such a term or phrase deters the employment of older persons and is a violation of the Act, unless one of the exceptions applies. Such phrases as "age 40 to 50," "age over 65," "retired person," or "supplement your pension discriminate against others within the protected group and, therefore, are prohibited unless one of the exceptions applies.

(b) The use of the phrase "state age" in help wanted notices or advertisements is not, in itself, a violation of the Act. But because the request that an applicant state his age may tend to deter older applicants or otherwise indicate discrimination based on age, employment notices or advertisements which include that phrase "state age," or any similar term, will be closely scrutinized to assure that the request is for a lawful purpose.

1625.5 Employment applications.

A request on the part of an employer for information such as "Date of Birth" or "State Age" on an employment application form is not, in itself, a violation of the Act. But because the request that an applicant state his age may tend to deter older applicants or otherwise indicate discrimination based on age, employment application forms which request such information will be closely scrutinized to assure that the request is for a permissible purpose and not for purposes proscribed by the Act. That the purpose is not one proscribed by the statute should be made known to the applicant, either by a reference on the application form to the statutory prohibition in language to the following effect: "The Age Discrimination in Employment Act of 1967 prohibits discrimination on the basis of age with respect to individuals who are at least 40 years of age," or by other means. The term "employment applications," refers to all written inquiries about employment or applications for employment or promotion including, but not limited to, resumes or other summaries of the applicant's background. It relates not only to written preemployment inquiries, but to inquiries by employees concerning terms, conditions, or privileges of employment as specified in section 4 of the Act.

1625.6 Bona fide occupational qualifications.

(a) Whether occupational qualifications will be deemed to be "bona fide" to a specific job and "reasonably necessary to the normal operation of the particular business," will be determined on the basis of all the pertinent facts surrounding each particular situation. It is anticipated that this concept of a bona fide occupational qualification will have limited scope and application. Further, as this is an exception to the Act it must be narrowly construed.

(b) An employer asserting a BFOQ defense has the burden of proving that (1) the age limit is reasonably necessary to the essence of the business, and either (2) that all or substantially all individuals excluded from the job involved are in fact disqualified, or (3) that some of the individuals so excluded possess a disqualifying trait that cannot be ascertained except by reference to age. If the employer's objective in asserting a BFOQ is the goal of public safety, the employer must prove that the challenged practice does indeed effectuate that goal and that there is no acceptable alternative which would better advance it or equally advance it with less discriminatory impact.

(c) Many State and local governments have enacted laws or administrative regulations which limit employment opportunities based on age. Unless these laws meet the standards for the establishment of a valid bona fide occupational qualification under section 4(f)(1) of the Act, they will be considered in conflict with and effectively superseded by the ADEA.

1625.7 Differentiations based on reasonable factors other than age.

(a) Section 4(f)(1) of the Act provides that

> ... it shall not be unlawful for an employer, employment agency, or labor organization ... to take any action otherwise prohibited under paragraphs (a), (b),(c), or (e) of this section ... where the differentiation is based on reasonable factors other than age....

(b) No precise and unequivocal determination can be made as to the scope of the phrase "differentiation based on reasonable factors other than age." Whether such differentiations exist must be decided on the basis of all the particular facts and circumstances surrounding each individual situation.

(c) When an employment practice uses age as a limiting criterion, the defense that the practice is justified by a reasonable factor other than age is unavailable.

(d) When an employment practice, including a test, is claimed as a basis for different treatment of employees or applicants for employment on the grounds that it is a "factor other than" age, and such a practice has an adverse impact on individuals within the protected age group, it can only be justified as a business necessity. Tests which are asserted as "reasonable factors other than age" will be scrutinized in accordance with the standards set forth at Part 1607 of this Title.

(e) When the exception of "a reasonable factor other than age" is raised against an individual claim of discriminatory treatment, the employer bears the burden of showing that the "reasonable factor other than age" exists factually.

(f) A differentiation based on the average cost of employing older employees as a group is unlawful except with respect to employee benefit plans which qualify for the section 4(f)(2) exception to the Act.

1625.8 Bona fide seniority systems.

Section 4(f)(2) of the Act provides that

... It shall not be unlawful for an employer, employment agency, or labor organization ... to observe the terms of a bona fide seniority system ... which is not a subterfuge to evade the purposes of this Act except that no such seniority system ... shall require or permit the involuntary retirement of any individual specified by section 12(a) of this Act because of the age of such individual ...

(In the case of employees covered by a collective bargaining agreement which was in effect on September 1,1977, which was entered into by a labor organization (as defined by section 6(d)(4) of the Fair Labor Standards Act), the provisions of this section with respect to involuntary retirement of individuals between the ages of 6S and 70 were effective upon the termination of the collective bargaining agreement or January 1, 1980, whichever occurred first.) (See also § 1625.9(d), (e), and (f).)

(a) Though a seniority system may be qualified by such factors as merit, capacity, or ability, any bona fide seniority system must be based on length of service as the primary criterion for the equitable allocation of available employment opportunities and prerogatives among younger and older workers.

(b) Adoption of a purported seniority system which gives those with longer service lesser rights, and results in discharge or less favored treatment to those within the protection of the Act, may, depending upon the circumstances, be a "subterfuge to evade the purposes" of the Act.

(c) Unless the essential terms and conditions of an alleged seniority system have been communicated to the affected employees and can be shown to be applied uniformly to all of those affected, regardless of age, it will not be considered a bona fide seniority system within the meaning of the Act.

(d) It should be noted that seniority systems which segregate, classify, or otherwise discriminate against individuals on the basis of race, color, religion, sex, or national origin, are prohibited under Title VII of the Civil Rights Act of 1964, where that Act otherwise applies. The "bona fides" of such a system will be closely scrutinized to ensure that such a system is, in fact, bona fide under the ADEA.

1625.9 Prohibition of involuntary retirement.

(a)(1) As originally enacted in 1967, section 4(f)(2) of the Act provided: "It shall not be unlawful ... to observe the terms of a bona fide seniority system or any bona fide employee benefit plan such as a retirement, pension, or insurance plan, which is not a subterfuge to evade the purposes of this Act, except that no such employee benefit plan shall excuse the failure to hire any individual...." The Department of Labor interpreted the provision as "Authoriz[ing] involuntary retirement irrespective of age: Provided. That such retirement is pursuant to the terms of a retirement or pension plan meeting the requirements of section 4(f)(2)." See 29 CFR 860.110(a), 34 FR 9709 (June 21, 1969). The Department took position that in order to meet the requirements of section 4(f)(2), the involuntary retirement provision had to be (i) contained in a bona fide pension or retirement plan, (ii) required by the terms of the plan and not optional, and (iii) essential to the plan's economic survival or to some other legitimate business purpose—i.e., the provision was not in the plan as the result of arbitrary discrimination on the basis of age.

(2) As revised by the 1978 amendments, section 4(f)(2) was amended by adding the following clause at the end: "and no such seniority system or employee benefit plan shall require or permit the involuntary retirement of any individual specified by section 12(a) of this Act because of the age of such individual...." The Conference Committee Report expressly states that this amendment is intended "to make absolutely clear one of the original purposes of this provision, namely, that the exception does not authorize an employer to require or permit involuntary retirement of an employee within the protected age group on account of age" (H.R. Rept. No. 95-950, p. 8).

(b)(1) The amendment applies to all new and existing seniority systems and employee benefit plans. Accordingly, any system or plan provision requiring or permitting involuntary retirement is unlawful, regardless of whether the provision antedates the 1967 Act or the 1978 amendments.

(2) Where lawsuits pending on the date of enactment (April 6, 1978) or filed thereafter challenge involuntary retirements which occurred either before or after that date, the amendment applies.

(c)(1) The amendment protects all individuals covered by section 12(a) of the Act. Section 12(a) was amended in October of 1986 by the Age Discrimination in Employment Amendments of 1986, Pub. L. 99-S92, 100 Stat. 3342 (1986), which removed the age 70 limit. Section 12(a) provides that the Act's prohibitions shall be limited to individuals who are at least forty years of age. Accordingly, unless a specific exemption applies, an employer can no longer force retirement or otherwise discriminate on the basis of age against an individual because (s)he is 70 or older.

(2) The amendment to section 12(a) of the Act became effective on January 1, 1987, except with respect to any employee subject to a collective bargaining agreement containing a provision that would be superseded by such amendment that was in effect on June 30, 1986, and which terminates after January 1, 1987. In that case, the amendment is effective on the termination of the agreement or January 1, 1990, whichever comes first.

(d) Neither section 4(f)(2) nor any other provision of the Act makes it unlawful for a plan to permit individuals to elect early retirement at a specified age at their own option. Nor is it unlawful for a plan to require early retirement for reasons other than age.

1625.10 Costs and benefits under employee benefit plans.

(a)(1) *General.* Section 4(f)(2) of the Act provides that it is not unlawful for an employer, employment agency, or labor organization "to observe the terms of ... any bona fide employee benefit plan such as a retirement, pension, or insurance plan, which is not a subterfuge to evade the purposes of this Act, except that no such employee benefit plan shall excuse the failure to hire any individual, and no such ... employee benefit plan shall require or permit the involuntary retirement of any individual specified by section 12(a) of this Act because of the age of such individuals." The legislative history of this provision indicates that its purpose is to permit age-based reductions in employee benefit plans where such reductions are justified by significant cost considerations. Accordingly, section 4(f)(2) does not apply, for example, to paid vacations and uninsured paid sick leave, since reductions in these benefits would not be justified by significant cost considerations. Where employee benefit plans do meet the criteria in section 4(f)(2), benefit levels for older workers may be reduced to the extent necessary to achieve approximate equivalency in cost for older and younger workers. A benefit plan will be considered in compliance with the statute where the actual amount of payment made, or cost incurred, in behalf of an older worker is equal to that made or incurred in behalf of a younger worker, even though the older worker may thereby receive a lesser amount of benefits or insurance coverage. Since section 4(f)(2) is an exception from the general nondiscrimination provisions of the Act, the burden is on the one seeking to invoke the exception to show that every element has been clearly and unmistakably met. The exception must be narrowly construed. The following sections explain three key elements of the exception: (i) What a "bona fide employee benefit plan" is; (ii) what it means to "observe the terms" of such a plan; and (iii) what kind of plan, or plan provision, would be considered "a subterfuge to evade the purposes of [the] Act." There is also a discussion of the application of the general rules governing all plans with respect to specific kinds of employee benefit plans.

(2) *Relation of section 4(f)(2) to sections 4(a), 4(b) and 4(c).* Sections 4(a), 4(b) and 4(c) prohibit specified acts of discrimination on the basis of age. Section 4(a) in

particular makes it unlawful for an employer to "discriminate against any individual with respect to his compensation, terms, conditions, or privileges of employment, because of such individual's age...." Section 4(f)(2) is an exception to this general prohibition. Where an employer under an employee benefit plan provides the same level of benefits to older workers as to younger workers, there is no violation of section 4(a), and accordingly the practice does not have to be justified under section 4(f)(2).

(b) "*Bona fide employee benefit plan.*" Section 4(f)(2) applies only to bona fide employee benefit plans. A plan is considered "bona fide" if its terms (including cessation of contributions or accruals in the case of retirement income plans) have been accurately described in writing to all employees and if it actually provides the benefits in accordance with the terms of the plan. Notifying employees promptly of provisions and changes in an employee benefit plan is essential if they are to know how the plan affects them. For these purposes, it would be sufficient under the ADEA for employers to follow the disclosure requirements of ERISA and the regulations thereunder. The plan must actually provide the benefits its provisions describe, since otherwise the notification of the provisions to employees is misleading and inaccurate. An "employee benefit plan" is a plan, such as a retirement, pension, or insurance plan, which provides employees with what are frequently referred to as "fringe benefits." The term does not refer to wages or salary in cash; neither section 4(f)(2) nor any other section of the Act excuses the payment of lower wages or salary to older employees on account of age. Whether or not any particular employee benefit plan may lawfully provide lower benefits to older employees on account of age depends on whether all of the elements of the exception have been met. An "employee-pay-all" employee benefit plan is one of the "terms, conditions, or privileges of employment" with respect to which discrimination on the basis of age is forbidden under section 4(a)(1). In such a plan, benefits for older workers may be reduced only to the extent and according to the same principles as apply to other plans under section 4(f)(2).

(c) "*To observe the terms*" *of a plan.* In order for a bona fide employee benefit plan which provides lower benefits to older employees on account of age to be within the section 4(f)(2) exception, the lower benefits must be provided in "obser[ance of] the terms of" the plan. As this statutory text makes clear, the section 4(f)(2) exception is limited to otherwise discriminatory actions which are actually prescribed by the terms of a bona fide employee benefit plan. Where the employer, employment agency, or labor organization is not required by the express provisions of the plan to provide lesser benefits to older workers, section 4(f)(2) does not apply. Important purposes are served by this requirement. Where a discriminatory policy is an express term of a benefit plan, employees presumably have some opportunity to know of the policy and to plan (or protest) accordingly. Moreover, the requirement that the discrimination actually be prescribed by a plan assures that the particular plan provision will be equally applied to all employees of the same age. Where a discriminatory provision is an optional term of the plan, it permits individual, discretionary acts of discrimination, which do not fall within the section 4(f)(2) exception.

(d) "*Subterfuge.*"

In order for a bona fide employee benefit plan which prescribes lower benefits for older employees on account of age to be within the section 4(f)(2) exception, it must not be "a subterfuge to evade the purposes of [the] Act." In general, a plan or plan provision which prescribes lower benefits for older employees on account of age is not a "subterfuge" within the meaning of section 4(f)(2), provided that the lower level of benefits is justified by age-related cost considerations. (The only exception to this general rule is with respect to certain retirement plans. See paragraph (f)(4) of this section.) There are certain other requirements that must be met in order for a plan not to be a subterfuge. These requirements are set forth below.

(1) *Cost data—General.* Cost data used in justification of a benefit plan which provides lower benefits to older employees on account of age must be valid and reasonable. This standard is met where an employer has cost data which show the actual cost to it of providing the particular benefit (or benefits) in question over a representative period of years. An employer may rely in cost data for its own employees over such a period, or on cost data for a larger group of similarly situated employees. Sometimes, as a result of experience rating or other causes, an employer incurs costs that differ significantly from costs for a group of similarly situated employees. Such an employer may not rely on cost data for the similarly situated employees where such reliance would result in significantly lower benefits for its own older employees. Where reliable cost information is not available, reasonable projections made from existing cost data meeting the standards set forth above will be considered acceptable.

(2) *Cost data—Individual benefit basis and "benefit package" basis.* Cost comparisons and adjustments under section 4(f)(2) must be made on a benefit-by-benefit basis or on a "benefit package" basis, as described below.

(i) *Benefit-by-benefit basis.* Adjustments made on a benefit-by-benefit basis must be made in the amount or level of a specific form of benefit for a specific event or contingency. For example, higher group term life insurance costs for older workers would justify a corresponding reduction in the amount of group term life insurance coverage for older workers, on the basis of age. However, a benefit-by-benefit approach would not justify the substitution of one form of benefit for another, even though both forms of benefit are designed for the same contingency, such as death. See paragraph (f)(1) of this section.

(ii) *"Benefit package" basis.* As an alternative to the benefit-by-benefit basis, cost comparisons and adjustments under section 4(f)(2) may be made on a limited "benefit package" basis. Under this approach, subject to the limitations described below, cost comparisons and adjustments can be made with respect to section 4(f)(2) plans in the aggregate. This alternative basis provides greater flexibility than a benefit-by-benefit basis in order to carry out the declared statutory purpose "to help employers and workers find ways of meeting problems arising from the impact of age on employment." A "benefit package" approach is an alternative approach consistent with this purpose and with the general purpose of section 4(f)(2) only if it is not used to reduce the cost to the employer or the favorability to the employees of overall employee benefits for older employees. A "benefit package" approach used for either of these purposes would be a subterfuge to evade the purposes of the Act. In order to assure that such a "benefit package" approach is not abused and is consistent with the legislative intent, it is subject to the limitations described in paragraph (f), which also includes a general example.

(3) *Cost data—Five year maximum basis.* Cost comparisons and adjustments under section 4(f)(2) may be made on the basis of age brackets of up to 5 years. Thus a particular benefit may be reduced for employees of any age within the protected age group by an amount no greater than that which could be justified by the additional cost to provide them with the same level of the benefit as younger employees within a specified five-year age group immediately preceding theirs. For example, where an employer chooses to provide unreduced group term life insurance benefits until age 60, benefits for employees who are between 60 and 65 years of age may be reduced

only to the extent necessary to achieve approximate equivalency in costs with employees who are 55 to 60 years old. Similarly, any reductions in benefit levels for 65 to 70 year old employees cannot exceed an amount which is proportional to the additional costs for their coverage over 60 to 65 year old employees.

(4) *Employee contributions in support of employee benefit plans—*

(i) As a condition of employment. An older employee within the protected age group may not be required as a condition of employment to make greater contributions than a younger employee in support of an employee benefit plan. Such a requirement would be in effect a mandatory reduction in take-home pay, which is never authorized by section 4(f)(2), and would impose an impediment to employment in violation of the specific restrictions in section 4(f)(2).

(ii) *As a condition of participation in a voluntary employee benefit plan.* An older employee within the protected age group may be required as a condition of participation in a voluntary employee benefit plan to make a greater contribution than a younger employee only if the older employee is not thereby required to bear a greater proportion of the total premium cost (employer-paid and employee-paid) than the younger employee. Otherwise the requirement would discriminate against the older employee by making compensation in the form of an employer contribution available on less favorable terms than for the younger employee and denying that compensation altogether to an older employee unwilling or unable to meet the less favorable terms. Such discrimination is not authorized by section 4(f)(2). This principle applies to three different contribution arrangements as follows:

(ii)(A) *Employee-pay-all plans.* Older employees, like younger employees, may be required to contribute as a condition of participation up to the full premium cost for their age.

(B) *Non-contributory ("employer-pay-all") plans.* Where younger employees are not required to contribute any portion of the total premium cost, older employees may not be required to contribute any portion.

(C) *Contributory plans.* In these plans employers and participating employees share the premium cost. The required contributions of participants may increase with age so long as the proportion of the total premium required to be paid by the participants does not increase with age.

(iii) *As an option in order to receive an unreduced benefit.* An older employee may be given the option, as an individual, to make the additional contribution necessary to receive the same level of benefits as a younger employee (provided that the contemplated reduction in benefits is otherwise justified by section 4(f)(2).

(5) *Forfeiture clauses.* Clauses in employee benefit plans which state that litigation or participation in any manner in a formal proceeding by an employee will result in the forfeiture of his rights are unlawful insofar as they may be applied to those who seek redress under the Act. This is by reason of section 4(d) which provides that it is unlawful for an employer, employment agency, or labor organization to discriminate against any individual because such individual "has made a charge, testified, assisted, or participated in any manner in an investigation, proceeding, or litigation under this Act."

(6) *Refusal to hire clauses.* Any provision of an employee benefit plan which requires or permits the refusal to hire an individual specified in section 12(a) of the Act on the basis of age is a subterfuge to evade the purposes of the Act and cannot be excused under section 4(f)(2).

(7) *Involuntary retirement clauses.* Any provision of an employee benefit plan which requires or permits the involuntary retirement of any individual specified in section 12(a) of the Act on the basis of age is a subterfuge to evade the purpose of the Act and cannot be excused under section 4(f)(2).

(e) *Benefits provided by the Government.* An employer does not violate the Act by permitting certain benefits to be provided by the Government, even though the availability of such benefits may be based on age. For example, it is not necessary for an employer to provide health benefits which are otherwise provided to certain employees by Medicare. However, the availability of benefits from the Government will not justify a reduction in employer-provided benefits if the result is that, taking the employer-provided and Government-provided benefits together, an older employee is entitled to a lesser benefit of any type (including coverage for family and/or dependents) than a similarly situated younger employee. For example, the availability of certain benefits to an older employee under Medicare will not justify denying an older employee a benefit which is provided to younger employees and is not provided to the older employee by Medicare.

(f) *Application of section 4(f)(2) to various employees benefit plans*—

(1) *Benefit-by-benefit approach.* This portion of the interpretation discusses how a benefit-by-benefit approach would apply to four of the most common types of employee benefit plans.

(i) *Life insurance.* It is not uncommon for life insurance coverage to remain constant until a specified age, frequently 65, and then be reduced. This practice will not violate the Act (even if reductions start before age 65), provided that the reduction for an employee of a particular age is no greater than is justified by the increased cost of coverage for that employee's specific age bracket encompassing no more than five years. It should be noted that a total denial of life insurance, on the basis of age, would not be justified under a benefit-by-benefit analysis. However, it is not unlawful for life insurance coverage to cease upon separation from service.

(ii) *Long-term disability.* Under a benefit-by-benefit approach, where employees who are disabled at younger ages are entitled to long-term disability benefits, there is no cost-based justification for denying such benefits altogether, on the basis of age, to employees who are disabled at older ages. It is not unlawful to cut off long-term disability benefits and coverage on the basis of some non-age factor, such as recovery from disability. Reductions on the basis of age in the level or duration of benefits available for disability are justifiable only on the basis of age-related cost considerations as set forth elsewhere in this section. An employer which provides long-term disability coverage to all employees may avoid any increases in the cost to it that such coverage for older employees would entail by reducing the level of benefits available to older employees. An employer may also avoid such cost increases by reducing the duration of benefits available to employees who become disabled at older ages, without reducing the level of benefits. In this connection, the Department would not assert a violation where the level of benefits is not reduced and the duration of benefits is reduced in the following manner:

(A) With respect to disabilities which occur at age 60 or less, benefits cease at age 65.

(B) With respect to disabilities which occur after age 60, benefits cease 5 years after disablement. Cost data may be produced to support other patterns of reduction as well.

(iii) *Retirement plans.* (A) *Participation.* No employee hired prior to normal retirement age may be excluded from a defined contribution plan. With respect to defined benefit plans not subject to the Employee Retirement Income Security Act (ERISA), Pub. L. 93-406, 29 U.S.C. 1001, 1003(a) and (b), an employee hired at an age more than 5 years prior to normal retirement age may not be excluded from such a plan unless the exclusion is justifiable on the basis of cost considerations as set forth elsewhere in this section. With respect to defined benefit plans subject to ERISA, such an exclusion would be unlawful in any case. An employee hired less than 5 years prior to normal retirement age may be excluded from a defined benefit plan, regardless of whether or not the plan is covered by ERISA. Similarly, any employee hired after normal retirement age may be excluded from a defined benefit plan.

(2) *"Benefit Package" approach.* A "benefit package" approach to compliance under section 4(f)(2) offers greater flexibility than a benefit-by-benefit approach by permitting deviations from a benefit-by-benefit approach so long as the overall result is no lesser cost to the employer and no less favorable benefits for employees. As previously noted, in order to assure that such an approach is used for the benefit of older workers and not to their detriment, and is otherwise consistent with the legislative intent, it is subject to limitations as set forth below:

(i) A benefit package approach shall apply only to employee benefit plans which fall within section 4(f)(2).

(ii) A benefit package approach shall not apply to a retirement or pension plan. The 1978 legislative history sets forth specific and comprehensive rules governing such plans, which have been adopted above. These rules are not tied to actuarially significant cost considerations but are intended to deal with the special funding arrangements of retirement or pension plans. Variations from these special rules are therefore not justified by variations from the cost-based benefit-by-benefit approach in other benefit plans, nor may variations from the special rules governing pension and retirement plans justify variations from the benefit-by-benefit approach in other benefit plans.

(iii) A benefit package approach shall not be used to justify reductions in health benefits greater than would be justified under a benefit-by-benefit approach. Such benefits appear to be of particular importance to older workers in meeting "problems arising from the impact of age" and were of particular concern to Congress. Therefore, the "benefit package" approach may not be used to reduce health insurance benefits by more than is warranted by the increase in the cost to the employer of those benefits alone. Any greater reduction would be a subterfuge to evade the purpose of the Act.

(iv) A benefit reduction greater than would be justified under a benefit-by-benefit approach must be offset by another benefit available to the same employees. No employees may be deprived because of age of one benefit without an offsetting benefit being made available to them.

(v) Employers who wish to justify benefit reductions under a benefit package approach must be prepared to produce data to show that those reductions are fully justified. Thus employers must be able to show that deviations from a benefit-by-benefit approach do not result in lesser cost to them or less favorable benefits to their employees. A general example consistent with these limitations may be given. Assume two employee benefit plans, providing Benefit "A" and Benefit "B." Both plans fall within section 4(f)(2), and neither is a retirement or pension plan subject to special rules. Both benefits are available to all employees. Age-based cost increases would justify a 10% decrease in both benefits on a benefit-by-benefit basis. The affected employees would, however, find it more favorable—that is, more consistent with meeting their needs—for no reduction to be made in Benefit "A" and a greater reduction to be made in Benefit "B." This "trade-off" would not result in a reduction in health benefits. The "trade-off" may therefore be made. The details of the "trade-off" depend on data on the relative cost to the employer of the two benefits. If the data show that Benefit "A" and Benefit "B" cost the same, Benefit "B" may be reduced up to 20% if Benefit "A" is unreduced. If the data show that Benefit "A" costs only half as much as Benefit "B", however, Benefit "B" may be reduced up to only 15% if Benefit "A" is unreduced, since a greater reduction in Benefit "B" would result in an impermissible reduction in total benefit costs.

(g) *Relation of ADEA to State laws.* The ADEA does not preempt State age discrimination in employment laws. However, the failure of the ADEA to preempt such laws does not affect the issue of whether section 514 of the Employee Retirement Income Security Act (ERISA) preempts State laws which related to employee benefit plans.

* * *

1625.12 Exemption for bona fide executive or high policymaking employees.

(a) Section 12(c)(1) of the Act, added by the 1978 amendments and as amended in 1984 and 1986, provides: "Nothing in this Act shall be construed to prohibit compulsory retirement of any employee who has attained 65 years of age, and who, for the 2-year period immediately before retirement, is employed in a bona fide executive or higher policymaking position, if such employee is entitled to an immediate nonforfeitable annual retirement benefit from a pension, profit-sharing, savings, or deferred compensation plan, or any combination of such plans, of the employer of such employee which equals, in the aggregate, at least $44,000."

(b) Since this provision is an exemption from the nondiscrimination requirements of the Act, the burden is on the one seeking to invoke the exemption to show that every element has been clearly and unmistakably met. Moreover, as with other exemptions from the Act, this exemption must be narrowly construed.

(c) An employee within the exemption can lawfully be forced to retire on account of age at age 65 or above. In addition, the employer is free to retain such employees, either in the same position or status or in a different position or status. For example, an employee who falls within the exemption may be offered a position of lesser status or a part-time position. An employee who accepts such a new status or position, however, may not be treated any less favorably, on account of age, than any similarly situated younger employee.

(d)(1) In order for an employee to qualify as a "bona fide executive," the employer must initially show that the employee satisfies the definition of a bona fide executive set forth in § 541.1 of this chapter. Each of the requirements in paragraphs (a) through (e) of § 541.1 must be satisfied, regardless of the level of the employee's salary or compensation.

(2) Even if an employee qualifies as an executive under the definition in § 541.1 of this chapter, the exemption from the ADEA may not be claimed unless the employee also meets the further criteria specified in the Conference Committee Report in the form of examples (see H.R. Rept. No. 95-950, p. 9). The examples are intended to make clear that the exemption does not apply to middle-management employees, no matter how great their retirement income, but only to a very few top level employees who exercise substantial executive authority over a significant number of employees and a large volume of business. As stated in the Conference Report (H.R. Rept. No. 95-950, p. 9):

> Typically the head of a significant and substantial local or regional operation of a corporation [or other business organization], such as a major production facility or retail establishment, but not the head of a minor branch, warehouse or retail store, would be covered by the term "bona fide executive. Individuals at higher levels in the corporate organizational structure who possess comparable or greater levels of responsibility and authority as measured by established and recognized criteria would also be covered.
>
> The heads of major departments or divisions of corporations [or other business organizations] are usually located at corporate or regional headquarters. With respect to employees whose duties are associated with corporate headquarters operations, such as finance, marketing, legal, production and manufacturing (or in a corporation organized on a product line basis, the management of product lines), the definition would cover employees who head those divisions.
>
> In a large organization the immediate subordinates of the heads of these divisions sometimes also exercise executive authority, within the meaning of this exemption. The conferees intend the definition to cover such employees if they possess responsibility which is comparable to or greater than that possessed by the head of a significant and substantial local operation who meets the definition.

(e) The phrase "high policymaking position," according to the Conference Report (H.R. Rept. No. 95-950, p. 10), is limited to " ... certain top level employees who are not 'bona fide executives...." Specifically, these are:

> ... individuals who have little or no line authority but whose position and responsibility are such that they play a significant role in the development of corporate policy and effectively recommend the implementation thereof.
>
> For example, the chief economist or the chief research scientist of a corporation typically has little line authority. His duties would be primarily intellectual as opposed to executive or managerial. His responsibility would be to evaluate significant economic or scientific trends and issues, to develop and recommend policy direction to the top executive officers of the corporation, and he would have a significant impact on the ultimate decision on such policies by virtue of his expertise and direct access to the decision makers. Such an employee would meet the definition of a "high policymaking employee."

On the other hand, as this description makes clear, the support personnel of a "high policymaking" employee would not be subject to the exemption even if they supervise the development, and draft the recommendation, of various policies submitted by their supervisors.

(f) In order for the exemption to apply to a particular employee, the employee must have been in a "bona fide executive or high policymaking position," as those terms are defined in this section, for the two-year period immediately before retirement. Thus, an employee who holds two or more different positions during the two-year period is subject to the exemption only if each such job is an executive or high policymaking position.

(g) The Conference Committee Report expressly states that the exemption is not applicable to Federal employees covered by section 15 of the Act (H.R. Rept. No. 95-950, p. 10).

(h) The "annual retirement benefit," to which covered employees must be entitled, is the sum of amounts payable during each one-year period from the date on which such benefits first become receivable by the retiree. Once established, the annual period upon which calculations are based may not be changed from year to year.

(i) The annual retirement benefit must be immediately available to the employee to be retired pursuant to the exemption. For purposes of determining compliance, "immediate" means that the payment of plan benefits (in a lump sum or the first of a series of periodic payments) must occur not later than 60 days after the effective date of the retirement in question. The fact that an employee will receive benefits only after expiration of the 60-day period will not preclude his retirement pursuant to the exemption, if the employee could have elected to receive benefits within that period.

(j)(1) The annual retirement benefit must equal, in the aggregate, at least $44,000. The manner of determining whether this requirement has been satisfied is set forth in § 1627.17(c).

(2) In determining whether the aggregate annual retirement benefit equals at least $44,000, the only benefits which may be counted are those authorized by and provided under the terms of a pension, profit-sharing, savings, or deferred compensation plan. (Regulations issued pursuant to section 12(c)(2) of the Act, regarding the manner of calculating the amount of qualified retirement benefits for purposes of the exemption, are set forth in § 1627.17 of this chapter.)

(k)(1) The annual retirement benefit must be "nonforfeitable." Accordingly, the exemption may not be applied to any employee subject to plan provisions which could cause the cessation of payments to a retiree or result in the reduction of benefits to less than $44,000 in any one year. For example, where a plan contains a provision under which benefits would be suspended if a retiree engages in litigation against the former employer, or obtains employment with a competitor of the former employer, the retirement benefit will be deemed to be forfeitable. However, retirement benefits will not be deemed forfeitable solely because the benefits are discontinued or suspended for reasons permitted under section 41 1(a)(3) of the Internal Revenue Code.

(2) An annual retirement benefit will not be deemed forfeitable merely because the minimum statutory benefit level is not guaranteed against the possibility of plan bankruptcy or is subject to benefit restrictions in the event of early termination of the plan in accordance with Treasury Regulation 1.401-4(c). However, as of the effective date of the retirement in question, there must be at least a reasonable expectation that the plan will meet its obligations.

1625.21 Apprenticeship programs.

All apprenticeship programs, including those apprenticeship programs created or maintained by joint labor—management organizations, are subject to the prohibitions of sec. 4 of the Age Discrimination in Employment Act of 1967, as amended, 29 U.S.C. § 623. Age limitations in apprenticeship programs are valid only if excepted under sec. 4(f)(1) of the Act, 29 U.S.C. § 623(f)(1), or exempted by the Commission under sec. 9 of the Act, 29 U.S.C. § 628, in accordance with the procedures set forth in 29 C.F.R. § 1627.15.

1625.22 Waivers of rights and claims under the ADEA.

(a) *Introduction.*

(1) Congress amended the ADEA in 1990 to clarify the prohibitions against discrimination on the basis of age. In Title II of OWBPA, Congress addressed waivers of rights and claims under the ADEA, amending section 7 of the ADEA by adding a new subsection (f).

(2) Section 7(f)(1) of the ADEA expressly provides that waivers may be valid and enforceable under the ADEA only if the waiver is "knowing and voluntary". Sections

7(f)(1) and 7(f)(2) of the ADEA set out the minimum requirements for determining whether a waiver is knowing and voluntary.

(3) Other facts and circumstances may bear on the question of whether the waiver is knowing and voluntary, as, for example, if there is a material mistake, omission, or misstatement in the information furnished by the employer to an employee in connection with the waiver.

(4) The rules in this section apply to all waivers of ADEA rights and claims, regardless of whether the employee is employed in the private or public sector, including employment by the United States Government.

(b) *Wording of Waiver Agreements.*

(1) Section 7(f)(1)(A) of the ADEA provides, as part of the minimum requirements for a knowing and voluntary waiver, that: The waiver is part of an agreement between the individual and the employer that is written in a manner calculated to be understood by such individual, or by the average individual eligible to participate.

(2) The entire waiver agreement must be in writing.

(3) Waiver agreements must be drafted in plain language geared to the level of understanding of the individual party to the agreement or individuals eligible to participate. Employers should take into account such factors as the level of comprehension and education of typical participants. Consideration of these factors usually will require the limitation or elimination of technical jargon and of long, complex sentences.

(4) The waiver agreement must not have the effect of misleading, misinforming, or failing to inform participants and affected individuals. Any advantages or disadvantages described shall be presented without either exaggerating the benefits or minimizing the limitations.

(5) Section 7(f)(1)(H) of the ADEA, relating to exit incentive or other employment termination programs offered to a group or class of employees, also contains a requirement that information be conveyed "in writing in a manner calculated to be understood by the average participant." The same standards applicable to the similar language in section 7(f)(1)(A) of the ADEA apply here as well.

(6) Section 7(f)(1)(B) of the ADEA provides, as part of the minimum requirements for a knowing and voluntary waiver, that "the waiver specifically refers to rights or claims under this Act." Pursuant to this subsection, the waiver agreement must refer to the Age Discrimination in Employment Act (ADEA) by name in connection with the waiver.

(7) Section 7(f)(1)(E) of the ADEA requires that an individual must be "advised in writing to consult with an attorney prior to executing the agreement."

(c) *Waiver of future rights.*

(1) Section 7(f)(1)(C) of the ADEA provides that:

> A waiver may not be considered knowing and voluntary unless at a minimum ... the individual does not waive rights or claims that may arise after the date the waiver is executed.

(2) The waiver of rights or claims that arise following the execution of a waiver is prohibited. However, section 7(f)(1)(C) of the ADEA does not bar, in a waiver that otherwise is consistent with statutory requirements, the enforcement of agreements to perform future employment related actions such as the employee's agreement to retire or otherwise terminate employment at a future date.

(d) *Consideration.*

(1) Section 7(f)(1)(D) of the ADEA states that:

> A waiver may not be considered knowing and voluntary unless at a minimum ... the individual waives rights or claims only in exchange for consideration in addition to anything of value to which the individual already is entitled.

(2) "Consideration in addition" means anything of value in addition to that to which the individual is already entitled in the absence of a waiver.

(3) If a benefit or other thing of value was eliminated in contravention of law or contract, express or implied, the subsequent offer of such benefit or thing of value in connection with a waiver will not constitute "consideration" for purposes of section 7(f)(1) of the ADEA. Whether such elimination as to one employee or group of employees is in contravention of law or contract as to other employees, or to that individual employee at some later time, may vary depending on the facts and circumstances of each case.

(4) An employer is not required to give a person age 40 or older a greater amount of consideration than is given to a person under the age of 40, solely because of that person's membership in the protected class under the ADEA.

(e) *Time periods.*

(1) Section 7(f)(1)(F) of the ADEA states that:

> A waiver may not be considered knowing and voluntary unless at a minimum ...
>
> (i) The individual is given a period of at least 21 days within which to consider the agreement; or
>
> (ii) If a waiver is requested in connection with an exit incentive or other employment termination program offered to a group or class of employees, the individual is given a period of at least 45 days within which to consider the agreement.

(2) Section 7(f)(1)(G) of the ADEA states:

> A waiver may not be considered knowing and voluntary unless at a minimum ... the agreement provides that for a period of at least 7 days following the execution of such agreement, the individual may revoke the agreement, and the agreement shall not become effective or enforceable until the revocation period has expired.

(3) The term "exit incentive or other employment termination program" includes both voluntary and involuntary programs.

(4) The 21 or 45 day period runs from the date of the employer's final offer. Material changes to the final offer restart the running of the 21 or 45 day period; changes made to the final offer that are not material do not restart the running of the 21 or 45 day period. The parties may agree that changes, whether material or immaterial, do not restart the running of the 21 or 45 day period.

(5) The 7 day revocation period cannot be shortened by the parties, by agreement or otherwise.

(6) An employee may sign a release prior to the end of the 21 or 45 day time period, thereby commencing the mandatory 7 day revocation period. This is permissible as long as the employee's decision to accept such shortening of time is knowing and voluntary and is not induced by the employer through fraud, misrepresentation, a threat to withdraw or alter the offer prior to the expiration of the 21 or 45 day time period, or by providing different terms to employees who sign the release prior to the

expiration of such time period. However, if an employee signs a release before the expiration of the 21 or 45 day time period, the employer may expedite the processing of the consideration provided in exchange for the waiver.

(f) *Informational requirements.*

(1) Introduction. (i) Section 7(f)(1)(H) of the ADEA provides that:

> A waiver may not be considered knowing and voluntary unless at a minimum... if a waiver is requested in connection with an exit incentive or other employment termination program offered to a group or class of employees, the employer (at the commencement of the period specified in subparagraph (F)) [which provides time periods for employees to consider the waiver] informs the individual in writing in a manner calculated to be understood by the average individual eligible to participate, as to—
>
> (i) Any class, unit, or group of individuals covered by such program, any eligibility factors for such program, and any time limits applicable to such program; and
>
> (ii) The job titles and ages of all individuals eligible or selected for the program, and the ages of all individuals in the same job classification or organizational unit who are not eligible or selected for the program.

(ii) Section 7(f)(1)(H) of the ADEA addresses two principal issues: to whom information must be provided, and what information must be disclosed to such individuals.

(iii)(A) Section 7(f)(1)(H) of the ADEA references two types of "programs" under which employers seeking waivers must make written disclosures: "exit incentive programs" and "other employment termination programs." Usually an "exit incentive program" is a voluntary program offered to a group or class of employees where such employees are offered consideration in addition to anything of value to which the individuals are already entitled (hereinafter in this section, "additional consideration") in exchange for their decision to resign voluntarily and sign a waiver. Usually "other employment termination program" refers to a group or class of employees who were involuntarily terminated and who are offered additional consideration in return for their decision to sign a waiver.

(B) The question of the existence of a "program" will be decided based upon the facts and circumstances of each case. A "program" exists when an employer offers additional consideration for the signing of a waiver pursuant to an exit incentive or other employment termination (e.g., a reduction in force) to two or more employees. Typically, an involuntary termination program is a standardized formula or package of benefits that is available to two or more employees, while an exit incentive program typically is a standardized formula or package of benefits designed to induce employees to sever their employment voluntarily. In both cases, the terms of the programs generally are not subject to negotiation between the parties.

(C) Regardless of the type of program, the scope of the terms "class," "unit," "group," "job classification," and "organizational unit" is determined by examining the "decisional unit" at issue. (See paragraph (f)(3) of this section, "The Decisional Unit.")

(D) A "program" for purposes of the ADEA need not constitute an "employee benefit plan" for purposes of the Employee Retirement Income Security Act of 1974 (ERISA). An employer may or may not have an ERISA severance plan in connection with its OWBPA program.

(iv) The purpose of the informational requirements is to provide an employee with enough information regarding the program to allow the employee to make an informed choice whether or not to sign a waiver agreement.

(2) To whom must the information be given. The required information must be given to each person in the decisional unit who is asked to sign a waiver agreement.

(3) The decisional unit. (i)(A) The terms "class," "unit," or "group" in section 7(f)(1)(H)(i) of the ADEA and "job classification or organizational unit" in section 7(f)(1)(H)(ii) of the ADEA refer to examples of categories or groupings of employees affected by a program within an employer's particular organizational structure. The terms are not meant to be an exclusive list of characterizations of an employer's organization.

(B) When identifying the scope of the "class, unit, or group," and "job classification or organizational unit," an employer should consider its organizational structure and decision-making process. A "decisional unit" is that portion of the employer's organizational structure from which the employer chose the persons who would be offered consideration for the signing of a waiver and those who would not be offered consideration for the signing of a waiver. The term "decisional unit" has been developed to reflect the process by which an employer chose certain employees for a program and ruled out others from that program.

(ii)(A) The variety of terms used in section 7(f)(1)(H) of the ADEA demonstrates that employers often use differing terminology to describe their organizational structures. When identifying the population of the decisional unit, the employer acts on a case-by-case basis, and thus the determination of the appropriate class, unit, or group, and job classification or organizational unit for purposes of section 7(f)(1)(H) of the ADEA also must be made on a case-by-case basis.

(B) The examples in paragraph (f)(3)(iii), of this section demonstrate that in appropriate cases some subgroup of a facility's work force may be the decisional unit. In other situations, it may be appropriate for the decisional unit to comprise several facilities. However, as the decisional unit is typically no broader than the facility, in general the disclosure need be no broader than the facility. "Facility" as it is used throughout this section generally refers to place or location. However, in some circumstances terms such as "school," "plant," or "complex" may be more appropriate.

(C) Often, when utilizing a program an employer is attempting to reduce its workforce at a particular facility in an effort to eliminate what it deems to be excessive overhead, expenses, or costs from its organization at that facility. If the employer's goal is the reduction of its workforce at a particular facility and that employer undertakes a decision making process by which certain employees of the facility are selected for a program, and others are not selected for a program, then that facility generally will be the decisional unit for purposes of section 7(f)(1)(H) of the ADEA.

(D) However, if an employer seeks to terminate employees by exclusively considering a particular portion or subgroup of its operations at a specific facility, then that subgroup or portion of the workforce at that facility will be considered the decisional unit.

(E) Likewise, if the employer analyzes its operations at several facilities, specifically considers and compares ages, seniority rosters, or similar factors at differing facilities, and determines to focus its workforce reduction at a particular facility, then by the nature of that employer's decision making process the decisional unit would include all considered facilities and not just the facility selected for the reductions.

(iii) The following examples are not all inclusive and are meant only to assist employers and employees in determining the appropriate decisional unit. Involuntary reductions in force typically are structured along one or more of the following lines:

(A) *Facility wide*: Ten percent of the employees in the Springfield facility will be terminated within the next ten days;

(B) *Division wide*: Fifteen of the employees in the Computer Division will be terminated in December;

(C) *Department wide*: One half of the workers in the Keyboard Department of the Computer Division will be terminated in December;

(D) *Reporting*: Ten percent of the employees who report to the Vice President for Sales, wherever the employees are located, will be terminated immediately;

(E) *Job Category*: Ten percent of all accountants, wherever the employees are located, will be terminated next week.

(iv) In the examples in paragraph (f)(3)(iii) of this section, the decisional units are, respectively:

(A) The Springfield facility;

(B) The Computer Division;

(C) The Keyboard Department;

(D) All employees reporting to the Vice President for Sales; and

(E) All accountants.

(v) While the particular circumstances of each termination program will determine the decisional unit, the following examples also may assist in determining when the decisional unit is other than the entire facility:

(A) A number of small facilities with interrelated functions and employees in a specific geographic area may comprise a single decisional unit;

(B) If a company utilizes personnel for a common function at more than one facility, the decisional unit for that function (i.e., accounting) may be broader than the one facility;

(C) A large facility with several distinct functions may comprise a number of decisional units; for example, if a single facility has distinct internal functions with no employee overlap (i.e., manufacturing, accounting, human resources), and the program is confined to a distinct function, a smaller decisional unit may be appropriate.

(vi)(A) For purposes of this section, higher level review of termination decisions generally will not change the size of the decisional unit unless the reviewing process alters its scope. For example, review by the Human Resources Department to monitor compliance with discrimination laws does not affect the decisional unit. Similarly, when a regional manager in charge of more than one facility reviews the termination decisions regarding one of those facilities, the review does not alter the decisional unit, which remains the one facility under consideration.

(B) However, if the regional manager in the course of review determines that persons in other facilities should also be considered for termination, the decisional unit becomes the population of all facilities considered. Further, if, for example, the regional manager and his three immediate subordinates jointly review the termination decisions, taking into account more than one facility, the decisional unit becomes the populations of all facilities considered.

(vii) This regulatory section is limited to the requirements of section 7(f)(1)(H) and is not intended to affect the scope of discovery or of substantive proceedings in the processing of charges of violation of the ADEA or in litigation involving such charges.

(4) Presentation of information.

(i) The information provided must be in writing and must be written in a manner calculated to be understood by the average individual eligible to participate.

(ii) Information regarding ages should be broken down according to the age of each person eligible or selected for the program and each person not eligible or selected for the program. The use of age bands broader than one year (such as "age 2030") does not satisfy this requirement.

(iii) In a termination of persons in several established grade levels and/or other established subcategories within a job category or job title, the information shall be broken down by grade level or other subcategory.

(iv) If an employer in its disclosure combines information concerning both voluntary and involuntary terminations, the employer shall present the information in a manner that distinguishes between voluntary and involuntary terminations.

(v) If the terminees are selected from a subset of a decisional unit, the employer must still disclose information for the entire population of the decisional unit. For example, if the employer decides that a 10% RIF in the Accounting Department will come from the accountants whose performance is in the bottom one-third of the Division, the employer still must disclose information for all employees in the Accounting Department, even those who are the highest rated.

(vi) An involuntary termination program in a decisional unit may take place in successive increments over a period of time. Special rules apply to this situation. Specifically, information supplied with regard to the involuntary termination program should be cumulative, so that later terminees are provided ages and job titles or job categories, as appropriate, for all persons in the decisional unit at the beginning of the program and all persons terminated to date. There is no duty to supplement the information given to earlier terminees so long as the disclosure, at the time it is given, conforms to the requirements of this section.

(vii) The following example demonstrates one way in which the required information could be presented to the employees. (This example is not presented as a prototype notification agreement that automatically will comply with the ADEA. Each information disclosure must be structured based upon the individual case, taking into account the corporate structure, the population of the decisional unit, and the requirements of section 7(f)(1)(H) of the ADEA): Example: Y Corporation lost a major construction contract and determined that it must terminate 10% of the employees in the Construction Division. Y decided to offer all terminees $20,000 in severance pay in exchange for a waiver of all rights. The waiver provides the section 7(f)(1)(H) of the ADEA information as follows:

(A) The decisional unit is the Construction Division.

(B) All persons in the Construction Division are eligible for the program. All persons who are being terminated in our November RIF are selected for the program.

(C) All persons who are being offered consideration under a waiver agreement must sign the agreement and return it to the Personnel Office within 45 days after receiving the waiver. Once the signed waiver is returned to the Personnel Office, the employee has 7 days to revoke the waiver agreement.

(D) The following is a listing of the ages and job titles of persons in the Construction Division who were and were not selected for termination and the offer of consideration for signing a waiver:

	Job Title	Age	No. Selected	No. Not Selected
(1)	Mechanical Engineers, I	25	21	48
		26	11	73
		63	4	18
		64	3	11
(2)	Mechanical Engineers, II	28	3	10
		29	11	17
	Etc., for all ages			
(3)	Structural Engineers, I	21	5	8
	Etc., for all ages			
(4)	Structural Engineers, II	23	2	4
	Etc., for all ages			
(5)	Purchasing Agents	26	10	11
	Etc., for all ages			

(g) *Waivers settling charges and lawsuits.* (1) Section 7(f)(2) of the ADEA provides that:

A waiver in settlement of a charge filed with the Equal Employment Opportunity Commission, or an action filed in court by the individual or the individual's representative, alleging age discrimination of a kind prohibited under section 4 or 15 may not be considered knowing and voluntary unless at a minimum-

(A) Subparagraphs (A) through (E) of paragraph (1) have been met; and

(B) The individual is given a reasonable period of time within which to consider the settlement agreement.

(2) The language in section 7(f)(2) of the ADEA, "discrimination of a kind prohibited under section 4 or 15" refers to allegations of age discrimination of the type prohibited by the ADEA.

(3) The standards set out in paragraph (f) of this section for complying with the provisions of section 7(f)(1) (A)(E) of the ADEA also will apply for purposes of complying with the provisions of section 7(f)(2)(A) of the ADEA.

(4) The term "reasonable time within which to consider the settlement agreement" means reasonable under all the circumstances, including whether the individual is represented by counsel or has the assistance of counsel.

(5) However, while the time periods under section 7(f)(1) of the ADEA do not apply to subsection 7(f)(2) of the ADEA, a waiver agreement under this subsection that provides an employee the time periods specified in section 7(f)(1) of the ADEA will be considered "reasonable" for purposes of section 7(f)(2)(B) of the ADEA.

(6) A waiver agreement in compliance with this section that is in settlement of an EEOC charge does not require the participation or supervision of EEOC.

(h) *Burden of proof.* In any dispute that may arise over whether any of the requirements, conditions, and circumstances set forth in section 7(f) of the ADEA, subparagraph (A), (B), (C), (D), (E), (F), (G), or (H) of paragraph (1), or subparagraph (A) or (B) of paragraph (2), have been met, the party asserting the validity of a waiver shall have the burden of proving in a court of competent jurisdiction that a waiver was knowing and voluntary pursuant to paragraph (1) or (2) of section 7(f) of the ADEA.

(i) *EEOC's enforcement powers.* (1) Section 7(f)(4) of the ADEA states:

> No waiver agreement may affect the Commission's rights and responsibilities to enforce [the ADEA]. No waiver may be used to justify interfering with the protected right of an employee to file a charge or participate in an investigation or proceeding conducted by the Commission.

(2) No waiver agreement may include any provision prohibiting any individual from:

(i) Filing a charge or complaint, including a challenge to the validity of the waiver agreement, with EEOC, or

(ii) Participating in any investigation or proceeding conducted by EEOC.

(3) No waiver agreement may include any provision imposing any condition precedent, any penalty, or any other limitation adversely affecting any individual's right to:

(i) File a charge or complaint, including a challenge to the validity of the waiver agreement, with EEOC, or

(ii) Participate in any investigation or proceeding conducted by EEOC.

(j) *Effective date of this section.* (1) This section is effective July 6, 1998.

(2) This section applies to waivers offered by employers on or after the effective date specified in paragraph (j)(1) of this section.

(3) No inference is to be drawn from this section regarding the validity of waivers offered prior to the effective date.

(k) *Statutory authority.* The regulations in this section are legislative regulations issued pursuant to section 9 of the ADEA and Title II of OWBPA.

1625.23 Waivers of rights and claims: Tender back of consideration.

(a) An individual alleging that a waiver agreement, covenant not to sue, or other equivalent arrangement was not knowing and voluntary under the ADEA is not required to tender back the consideration given for that agreement before filing either a lawsuit or a charge of discrimination with EEOC or any state or local fair employment practices agency acting as an EEOC referral agency for purposes of filing the charge with EEOC. Retention of consideration does not foreclose a challenge to any waiver agreement, covenant not to sue, or other equivalent arrangement; nor does the retention constitute the ratification of any waiver agreement, covenant not to sue, or other equivalent arrangement.

(b) No ADEA waiver agreement, covenant not to sue, or other equivalent arrangement may impose any condition precedent, any penalty, or any other limitation adversely affecting any individual's right to challenge the agreement. This prohibition includes, but is not limited to, provisions requiring employees to tender back consideration received, and provisions allowing employers to recover attorneys' fees and/or damages because of the filing of an ADEA suit. This rule is not intended to preclude employers from recovering attorneys' fees or costs specifically authorized under federal law.

(c) *Restitution, recoupment, or setoff.*

(1) Where an employee successfully challenges a waiver agreement, covenant not to sue, or other equivalent arrangement, and prevails on the merits of an ADEA claim, courts have the discretion to determine whether an employer is entitled to restitution, recoupment or setoff (hereinafter, "reduction") against the employee's monetary award. A reduction never can exceed the amount recovered by the employee, or the consideration the employee received for signing the waiver agreement, covenant not to sue, or other equivalent arrangement, whichever is less.

(2) In a case involving more than one plaintiff, any reduction must be applied on a plaintiff-by-plaintiff basis. No individual's award can be reduced based on the consideration received by any other person.

(d) No employer may abrogate its duties to any signatory under a waiver agreement, covenant not to sue, or other equivalent arrangement, even if one or more of the signatories or the EEOC successfully challenges the validity of that agreement under the ADEA.

1627.15 Administrative exemptions; procedures.

(a) Section 9 of the Act provides that, "In accordance with the provisions of subchapter II of chapter 5, of title 5, United States Code, the Secretary of Labor ... may establish such reasonable exemptions to and from any or all provisions of this Act as he may find necessary and proper in the public interest."

(b) The authority conferred on the Commission by section 9 of the Act to establish reasonable exemptions will be exercised with caution and due regard for the remedial purpose of the statute to promote employment of older persons based on their ability rather than age and to prohibit arbitrary age discrimination in employment. Administrative action consistent with this statutory purpose may be taken under this section, with or without a request therefor, when found necessary and proper in the public interest in accordance with the statutory standards. No formal procedures have been prescribed for requesting such action. However, a reasonable exemption from the Act's provisions will be granted only if it is decided, after notice published in the Federal Register giving all interested persons an opportunity to present data, views, or arguments, that a strong and affirmative showing has been made that such exemption is in fact necessary and proper in the public interest. Request for such exemption shall be submitted in writing to the Commission.

1627.16 Specific exemptions.

(a) Pursuant to the authority contained in section 9 of the Act and in accordance with the procedure provided therein and in § 1627.15(b) of this part, it has been found necessary and proper in the public interest to exempt from all prohibitions of the Act all activities and programs under Federal contracts or grants, or carried out by the public employment services of the several States, designed exclusively to provide employment for, or to encourage the employment of, persons with special employment problems, including employment activities and programs under the Manpower Development and Training Act of 1962, as amended, and the Economic Opportunity Act of 1964, as amended, for persons among the long-term unemployed, handicapped, members of minority groups, older workers, or youth. Questions concerning the application of this exemption shall be referred to the Commission for decision.

(b) Any employer, employment agency, or labor organization the activities of which are exempt from the prohibitions of the Act under paragraph (a) of this section shall maintain and preserve records containing the same information and data that is required of employers, employment agencies, and labor organizations under §§ 1627.3, 1627.4, and 1627.5, respectively.

1627.17 Calculating the amount of qualified retirement benefits for purposes of the exemption for bona fide executives or high policymaking employees.

(a) Section 12(c)(1) of the Act, added by the 1978 amendments and amended in 1984 and 1986, provides: "Nothing in this Act shall be construed to prohibit compulsory retirement of any employee who has attained 65 years of age, and who, for the 2-year period immediately before retirement, is employed in a bona fide executive or high policymaking position, if such employee is entitled to an immediate nonforfeitable annual retirement benefit from a pension, profit-sharing, savings, or deferred compensation plan, or any combination of such plans, of the employer of such employee, which equals, in the aggregate, at least $44,000." The Commission's interpretative statements regarding this exemption are set forth in section 1625 of this chapter.

(b) Section 12(c)(2) of the Act provides:

> In applying the retirement benefit test of paragraph (a) of this subsection, if any such retirement benefit is in a form other than a straight life annuity (with no ancillary benefits), or if employees contribute to any such plan or make rollover contributions, such benefit shall be adjusted in accordance with regulations prescribed by the Commission, after consultation with the Secretary of the Treasury, so that the benefit is the equivalent of a straight life annuity (with no ancillary benefits) under a plan to which employees do not contribute and under which no rollover contributions are made.

(c)(1) The requirement that an employee be entitled to the equivalent of a $44,000 straight life annuity (with no ancillary benefits) is satisfied in any case where the employee has the option of receiving, during each year of his or her lifetime following retirement, an annual payment of at least $44,000, or periodic payments on a more frequent basis which, in the aggregate, equal at least $44,000 per year: Provided, however, that the portion of the retirement income figure attributable to Social Security, employee contributions, rollover contributions and contributions of prior employers is excluded in the manner described in paragraph (e) of this section. (A retirement benefit which excludes these amounts is sometimes referred to herein as a "qualified" retirement benefit.)

(2) The requirement is also met where the employee has the option of receiving, upon retirement, a lump sum payment with which it is possible to purchase a single life annuity (with no ancillary benefits) yielding at least $44,000 per year as adjusted.

(3) The requirement is also satisfied where the employee is entitled to receive, upon retirement, benefits whose aggregate value, as of the date of the employee's retirement, with respect to those payments which are scheduled to be made within the period of life expectancy of the employee, is $44,000 per year as adjusted.

(4) Where an employee has one or more of the options described in paragraphs (c)(1) through (3) of this section, but instead selects another option (or options), the test is also met. On the other hand, where an employee has no choice but to have certain benefits provided after his or her death, the value of these benefits may not be included in this determination.

(5) The determination of the value of those benefits which may be counted towards the $44,000 requirement must be made on the basis of reasonable actuarial assumptions with respect to mortality and interest. For purposes of excluding from this determination any benefits which are available only after death, it is not necessary to determine the

life expectancy of each person on an individual basis. A reasonable actuarial assumption with respect to mortality will suffice.

(6) The benefits computed under paragraphs (c)(1), (2) and (3) of this section shall be aggregated for purposes of determining whether the $44,000 requirement has been met.

(d) The only retirement benefits which may be counted towards the $44,000 annual benefit are those from a pension, profit-sharing, savings, or deferred compensation plan, or any combination of such plans. Such plans include, but are not limited to, stock bonus, thrift and simplified employee pensions. The value of benefits from any other employee benefit plans, such as health or life insurance, may not be counted.

(e) In calculating the value of a pension, profit-sharing, savings, or deferred compensation plan (or any combination of such plans), amounts attributable to Social Security, employee contributions, contributions of prior employers, and rollover contributions must be excluded. Specific rules are set forth below.

(1) *Social Security.* Amounts attributable to Social Security must be excluded. Since these amounts are readily determinable, no specific rules are deemed necessary.

(2) *Employee contributions.* Amounts attributable to employee contributions must be excluded. The regulations governing this requirement are based on section 411(c) of the Internal Revenue Code and Treasury Regulations thereunder (§ 1.41 l(c)-(1)), relating to the allocation of accrued benefits between employer and employee contributions. Different calculations are needed to determine the amount of employee contributions, depending upon whether the retirement income plan is a defined contribution plan or a defined benefit plan. Defined contribution plans (also referred to as individual account plans) generally provide that each participant has an individual account and the participant's benefits are based solely on the account balance. No set benefit is promised in defined contribution plans, and the final amount is a result not only of the actual contributions, but also of other factors, such as investment gains and losses. Any retirement income plan which is not an individual account plan is a defined benefit plan. Defined benefit plans generally provide a definitely determinable benefit, by specifying either a flat monthly payment or a schedule of payments based on a formula (frequently involving salary and years of service), and they are funded according to actuarial principles over the employee's period of participation.

(i) *Defined contribution plans*

(A) *Separate accounts maintained.* If a separate account is maintained with respect to an employee's contributions and all income, expenses, gains and losses attributable thereto, the balance in such an account represents the amount attributable to employee contributions.

(B) *Separate accounts not maintained.* If a separate account is not maintained with respect to an employee's contributions and the income, expenses, gains and losses attributable thereto, the proportion of the total benefit attributable to employee contributions is determined by multiplying that benefit by a fraction:

(1) The numerator of which is the total amount of the employee's contributions under the plan (less withdrawals), and

(2) The denominator of which is the sum of the numerator and the total contributions made under the plan by the employer on behalf of the employee (less withdrawals).

Example: A defined contribution plan does not maintain separate accounts for employee contributions. An employee's annual retirement benefit under the plan is $40,000. The employee has contributed $96,000 and the employer has contributed $ 144,000 to the employee's individual account; no withdrawals have been made. The amount of the $40,000 annual benefit attributable to employee contributions is $40,000 =$16,000. Hence the employer's share of the $40,000 annual retirement benefit is $40,000 minus $16,000 or $24,000—too low to fall within the exemption.

(ii) *Defined benefit plans*—

(A) *Separate accounts maintained.* If a separate account is maintained with respect to an employee's contributions and all income, expenses, gains and losses attributable thereto, the balance in such an account represents the amount attributable to employee contributions.

(B) *Separate accounts not maintained.* If a separate account is not maintained with respect to an employee's contributions and the income, expenses, gains and losses attributable thereto, all of the contributions made by an employee must be converted actuarially to a single life annuity (without ancillary benefits) commencing at the age of forced retirement. An employee's accumulated contributions are the sum of all contributions (mandatory and, if not separately accounted for, voluntary) made by the employee, together with interest on the sum of all such contributions compounded annually at the rate of 5 percent per annum from the time each such contribution was made until the date of retirement. *Provided, however,* That prior to the date any plan became subject to section 411(c) of the Internal Revenue Code, interest will be credited at the rate (if any) specified in the plan. The amount of the employee's accumulated contribution described in the previous sentence must be multiplied by an "appropriate conversion factor" in order to convert it to a single life annuity (without ancillary benefits) commencing at the age of actual retirement. The appropriate conversion factor depends upon the age of retirement. In accordance with Rev. Rul. 76-47, 1976-2 C.B. 109, the following conversion factors shall be used with respect to the specified retirement ages:

Retirement Age	Conversion factor percent
65 through 66	10
67 through 68	11
69	12

Example: An employee is scheduled to receive a pension from a defined benefit plan of $50,000 per year. Over the years he has contributed $150,000 to the plan, and at age 65 this amount, when contributions have been compounded at appropriate annual interest rates, is equal to $240,000. In accordance with Rev. Rul. 76-47, 10 percent is an' appropriate conversion factor. When the $240,000 is multiplied by this conversion factor, the product is $24,000, which represents that part of the $50,000 annual pension payment which is attributable to employee contributions. The difference—$26,000—represents the employer's contribution, which is too low to meet the test in the exemption.

(3) *Contributions of prior employers.* Amounts attributable to contributions of prior employers must be excluded.

(i) *Current employer distinguished from prior employers.* Under the section 12(c) exemption, for purposes of excluding contributions of prior employers, a prior employer is every previous employer of the employee except those previous employers which are members of a "controlled group of corporations" with, or "under common control" with, the employer which forces the employee to retire, as those terms are used in sections 414 (b) and 414(c) of the Internal Revenue Code, as modified by section 414(h)(26 U.S.C. 414(b), (c) and (h)).

(ii) *Benefits attributable to current employer and to prior employers.* Where the current employer maintains or contributes to a plan which is separate from plans maintained or contributed to by prior employers, the amount of the employee's benefit attributable to those prior employers can be readily determined. However, where the current employer maintains or contributes to the same plan as prior employers, the following rule shall apply. The benefit attributable to the current employer shall be the total benefit received by the employee, reduced by the benefit that the employee would have received from the plan if he or she had never worked for the current employer. For purposes of this calculation, it shall be assumed that all benefits have always been vested, even if benefits accrued as a result of service with a prior employer had not in fact been vested.

(4) *Rollover contributions.* Amounts attributable to rollover contributions must be excluded. For purposes of § 1627.17(e), a rollover contribution (as defined in sections *402(a)(5),* 403(a)(4), 408(d)(3) and 409(b)(3)(C) of the Internal Revenue Code) shall be treated as an employee contribution. These amounts have already been excluded as a result of the computations set forth in § 1627.17(e)(2). Accordingly, no separate calculation is necessary to comply with this requirement.

Executive Order 11246—Equal Employment Opportunity [as Amended]

SOURCE: Executive Order 11246, 30 F.R. 12319, Sept. 28, 1965; 30 F.R. 12935, Oct. 12, 1965, as amended by the following: E.O. 11375, 32 F.R. 14303, Oct. 17, 1967; E.O. 11478, 34 F.R. 12985, Aug. 12, 1969; E.O. 12086, 43 F.R. 46501, Oct. 5, 1978; E.O. 13279, 67 F.R. 77141, Dec. 12, 2002.\; E.O. 13672, July 21, 2014

Under and by virtue of the authority vested in me as President of the United States by the Constitution and statutes of the United States, it is ordered as follows:

PART I—NONDISCRIMINATION IN GOVERNMENT EMPLOYMENT

EDITORIAL NOTE: Part I as amended by E.O. 11375, 32 F.R. 14303, Oct. 17, 1967, was superseded by E.O. 11478, 34 F.R. 12985, Aug. 12, 1969.

PART II—NONDISCRIMINATION IN EMPLOYMENT BY GOVERNMENT CONTRACTORS AND SUBCONTRACTORS

SUBPART A—DUTIES OF TILE SECRETARY OF LABOR

SEC. 201. The Secretary of Labor shall be responsible for the administration of Parts II and III of this Order and shall adopt such rules and regulations and issue such orders as are deemed necessary and appropriate to achieve the purposes of Parts II and III of this Order.

SUBPART B—CONTRACTORS' AGREEMENTS

SEC. 202. Except in contracts exempted in accordance with Section 204 of this Order, all Government contracting agencies shall include in every Government contract hereafter entered into the following provisions: "During the performance of this contract, the contractor agrees as follows:

"(1) The contractor will not discriminate against any employee or applicant for employment because of race, color, religion, sex, sexual orientation, gender identity or national origin. The contractor will take affirmative action to ensure that applicants are employed, and that employees are treated during employment, without regard to their race, color, religion, sex, sexual orientation, gender identity or national origin. Such action shall include, but not be limited to the following: employment, upgrading, demotion, or transfer; recruitment or recruitment advertising; layoff or termination; rates of pay or other forms of compensation; and selection for training, including apprenticeship. The contractor agrees to post in conspicuous places, available to employees and applicants for employment, notices to be provided by the contracting officer setting forth the provisions of this nondiscrimination clause.

"(2) The contractor will, in all solicitations or advertisements for employees placed by or on behalf of the contractor, state that all qualified applicants will receive consideration for employment without regard to race, color, religion, sex, sexual orientation, gender identity or national origin." [Paragraphs (1) and (2) of the contract revised by E.O. 11375, 32 F.R. 14304, Oct. 17, 1967. Effective one year after October 13, 1967]

"(3) The contractor will send to each labor union or representative of workers with which he has a collective bargaining agreement or other contract or understanding, a notice, to be provided by the agency contracting officer, advising the labor union or workers' representative of the contractor's commitments under

Section 202 of Executive Order No. 11246 of September 24, 1965, and shall post copies of the notice in conspicuous places available to employees and applicants for employment.

"(4) The contractor will comply with all provisions of Executive Order No. 11246 of Sept. 24, 1965, and of the rules, regulations, and relevant orders of the Secretary of Labor.

"(5) The contractor will furnish all information and reports required by Executive Order No. 11246 of September 24, 1965, and by the rules, regulations, and orders of the Secretary of Labor, or pursuant thereto, and will permit access to his books, records, and accounts by the contracting agency and the Secretary of Labor for purposes of investigation to ascertain compliance with such rules, regulations, and orders.

"(6) In the event of the contractor's noncompliance with the nondiscrimination clauses of this contract or with any of such rules, regulations, or orders, this contract may be cancelled, terminated or suspended in whole or in part and the contractor may be declared ineligible for further Government contracts in accordance with procedures authorized in Executive Order No. 11246 of Sept. 24, 1965, and such other sanctions may be imposed and remedies invoked as provided in Executive Order No. 11246 of September 24, 1965, or by rule, regulation, or order of the Secretary of Labor, or as otherwise provided by law.

"(7) The contractor will include the provisions of Paragraphs (1) through (7) in every subcontract or purchase order unless exempted by rules, regulations, or orders of the Secretary of Labor issued pursuant to Section 204 of Executive Order No. 11246 of Sept. 24, 1965, so that such provisions will be binding upon each subcontractor or vendor. The contractor will take such action with respect to any subcontract or purchase order as may be directed by the Secretary of Labor as a means of enforcing such provisions including sanctions for noncompliance: Provided, however, That in the event the contractor becomes involved in, or is threatened with, litigation with a subcontractor or vendor as a result of such direction the contractor may request the United States to enter into such litigation to protect the interests of the United States."

SEC. 203. (a) Each contractor having a contract containing the provisions prescribed in Section 202 shall file, and shall cause each of his subcontractors to file, Compliance Reports with the contracting agency or the Secretary of Labor as may be directed. Compliance Reports shall be filed within such times and shall contain such information as to the practices, policies, programs, and employment policies programs, and employment statistics of the contractor and each subcontractor, and shall be in such form, as the Secretary of Labor may prescribe.

(b) Bidders or prospective contractors or subcontractors may be required to state whether they have participated in any previous contracts subject to the provisions of this Order, or any preceding similar Executive order, and in that event to submit, on behalf of themselves and their proposed subcontractors, Compliance Reports prior to or as an initial part of their bid or negotiation of a contract.

(c) Whenever the contractor or subcontractor has a collective bargaining agreement or other contract or understanding with a labor union or an agency referring workers or providing or supervising apprenticeship or training for such workers, the Compliance Report shall include such information as to such labor union's or agency's practices and policies affecting compliance as the Secretary of Labor may prescribe: Provided. That to the extent such information is within the exclusive possession of a labor union or an agency referring workers or providing or supervising apprenticeship or training and such labor union or agency shall refuse to furnish such information to the contractor, the contractor shall so certify to the Secretary of Labor as part of its Compliance Report and shall set forth what efforts he has made to obtain such information.

(d) The Secretary of Labor may direct that any bidder or prospective contractor or subcontractor shall submit, as part of his Compliance Report, a statement in writing, signed by an authorized officer or agent on behalf of any labor union or any agency referring workers or providing or supervising apprenticeship or other training, with which the bidder or prospective contractor deals, with supporting information, to the effect that the signer's practices and policies do not discriminate on the grounds of race, color, religion, sex, sexual orientation, gender identity or national origin, and that the signer either will affirmatively cooperate in the implementation of the policy and provisions of this order or that it consents and agrees that recruitment, employment, and the terms and conditions of employment under the proposed contract shall be in accordance with the purposes and provisions of the order. In the event that the union, or the agency shall refuse to execute such a statement, the Compliance Report shall so certify and set forth what efforts have been made to secure such a statement and such additional factual material as the Secretary of Labor may require. [Paragraph (d) revised by E.O. 11375, 32 F.R. 14304, Oct. 17, 1967. Effective one year after October 13, 1967]

SEC. 204. (a) The Secretary of Labor may, when the Secretary deems that special circumstances in the national interest so require, exempt a contracting agency from the requirement of including any or all of the provisions of Section 202 of this Order in any specific contract, subcontract, or purchase order.

(b) The Secretary of Labor may, by rule or regulation, exempt certain classes of contracts, subcontracts, or purchase orders

(1) whenever work is to be or has been performed outside the United States and no recruitment of workers within the limits of the United States is involved;

(2) for standard commercial supplies or raw materials;

(3) involving less than specified amounts of money or specified numbers of workers; or

(4) to the extent that they involve subcontracts below a specified tier.

(c) Section 202 of this Order shall not apply to a Government contractor or subcontractor that is a religious corporation, association, educational institution, or society, with respect to the employment of individuals of a particular religion to perform work connected with the carrying on by such corporation, association, educational institution, or society of its activities. Such contractors and subcontractors are not exempted or excused from complying with the other requirements contained in this Order.

(d) The Secretary of Labor may also provide, by rule, regulation, or order, for the exemption of facilities of a contractor that are in all respects separate and distinct from activities of the contractor related to the performance of the contract: provided, that such an exemption will not interfere with or impede the effectuation of the purposes of this Order: and provided further, that in the absence of such an exemption all facilities shall be covered by the provisions of this Order.

SUBPART C—POWERS AND DUTIES OF THE SECRETARY OF LABOR AND THE CONTRACTING AGENCIES

SEC. 205. The Secretary of Labor shall be responsible for securing compliance by all Government contractors and subcontractors with this Order and any implementing rules or regulations. All contracting agencies shall comply with the terms of this Order and any implementing rules, regulations, or orders of the Secretary of Labor. Contracting agencies shall cooperate with the Secretary of Labor and shall furnish such information and assistance as the Secretary may require.

SEC. 206. (a) The Secretary of Labor may investigate the employment practices of any Government contractor or subcontractor to determine whether or not the contractual provisions specified in Section 202 of this Order have been violated. Such investigation shall be conducted in accordance with the procedures established by the Secretary of Labor.

(b) The Secretary of Labor may receive and investigate complaints by employees or prospective employees of a Government contractor or subcontractor which allege discrimination contrary to the contractual provisions specified in Section 202 of this Order.

SEC. 207. The Secretary of Labor shall use his best efforts, directly and through interested Federal, State, and local agencies, contractors, and all other available instrumentalities to cause any labor union engaged in work under Government contracts or any agency referring workers or providing or supervising apprenticeship or training for or in the course of such work to cooperate in the implementation of the purposes of this Order. The Secretary of Labor shall, in appropriate cases, notify the Equal Employment Opportunity Commission, the Department of Justice, or other appropriate Federal agencies whenever it has reason to believe that the practices of any such labor organization or agency violate Title VI or Title VII of the Civil Rights Act of 1964 or other provision of Federal law.

SEC. 208. (a) The Secretary of Labor, or any agency, officer, or employee in the executive branch of the Government designated by rule, regulation, or order of the Secretary, may hold such hearings, public or private, as the Secretary may deem advisable for compliance, enforcement, or educational purposes.

(b) The Secretary of Labor may hold, or cause to be held, hearings in accordance with Subsection (a) of this Section prior to imposing, ordering, or recommending the imposition of penalties and sanctions under this Order. No order for debarment of any contractor from further Government contracts under Section 209 (a)(6) shall be made without affording the contractor an opportunity for a hearing.

SUBPART D—SANCTIONS AND PENALTIES

SEC. 209. (a) In accordance with such rules, regulations, or orders as the Secretary of Labor may issue or adopt, the Secretary may:

(1) Publish, or cause to be published, the names of contractors or unions which it has concluded have complied or have failed to comply with the provisions of this Order or of the rules, regulations, and orders of the Secretary of Labor.

(2) Recommend to the Department of Justice that, in cases in which there is substantial or material violation or the threat of substantial or material violation of the contractual provisions set forth in Section 202 of this Order, appropriate proceedings be brought to enforce those provisions, including the enjoining, within the limitations of applicable law, of organizations, individuals, or groups who prevent directly or indirectly, or seek to prevent directly or indirectly, compliance with the provisions of this Order.

(3) Recommend to the Equal Employment Opportunity Commission or the Department of Justice that appropriate proceedings be instituted under Title VII of the Civil Rights Act of 1964.

(4) Recommend to the Department of Justice that criminal proceedings be brought for the furnishing of false information to any contracting agency or to the Secretary of Labor as the case may be.

(5) After consulting with the contracting agency, direct the contracting agency to cancel, terminate, suspend, or cause to be cancelled, terminated, or suspended, any contract, or any portion or portions thereof, for failure of the contractor or subcontractor to comply with equal employment opportunity provisions of the contract. Contracts may be cancelled, terminated, or suspended absolutely or continuance of contracts may be conditioned upon a program for future compliance approved by the Secretary of Labor.

(6) Provide that any contracting agency shall refrain from entering into further contracts, or extensions or other modifications of existing contracts, with any noncomplying contractor, until such contractor has satisfied the Secretary of Labor that such contractor has established and will carry out personnel and employment policies in compliance with the provisions of this Order.

(b) Pursuant to rules and regulations prescribed by the Secretary of Labor, the Secretary shall make reasonable efforts, within a reasonable time limitation, to secure compliance with the contract provisions of this Order by methods of conference, conciliation, mediation, and persuasion before proceedings shall be instituted under subsection (a)(2) of this Section, or before a contract shall be cancelled or terminated in whole or in part under subsection (a)(5) of this Section.

SEC. 210. Whenever the Secretary of Labor makes a determination under Section 209, the Secretary shall promptly notify the appropriate agency. The agency shall take the action directed by the Secretary and shall report the results of the action it has taken to the Secretary of Labor within such time as the Secretary shall specify. If the contracting agency fails to take the action directed within thirty days, the Secretary may take the action directly.

SEC. 211. If the Secretary of Labor shall so direct, contracting agencies shall not enter into contracts with any bidder or prospective contractor unless the bidder or prospective contractor has satisfactorily complied with the provisions of this Order or submits a program for compliance acceptable to the Secretary of Labor.

SEC. 212. When a contract has been cancelled or terminated under Section 209(a) (5) or a contractor has been debarred from further Government contracts under Section 209(a)(6) of this Order, because of noncompliance with the contract provisions specified in Section 202 of this Order, the Secretary of Labor shall promptly notify the Comptroller General of the United States.

SUBPART E—CERTIFICATES OF MERIT

SEC. 213. The Secretary of Labor may provide for issuance of a United States Government Certificate of Merit to employers or labor unions, or other agencies Which are or may hereafter be engaged in work under Government contracts, if the Secretary is satisfied that the personnel and employment practices of the employer, or that the personnel, training, apprenticeship, membership, grievance and representation, upgrading, and other practices and policies of the labor union or other agency conform to the purposes and provisions of this Order.

SEC. 214. Any Certificate of Merit may at any time be suspended or revoked by the Secretary of Labor if the holder thereof, in the judgment of the Secretary, has failed to comply with the provisions of this Order.

SEC. 215. The Secretary of Labor may provide for the exemption of any employer, labor union, or other agency from any reporting requirements imposed under or pursuant to this Order if such employer, labor union, or other agency has been awarded a Certificate of Merit which has not been suspended or revoked.

PART III—NONDISCRIMINATION PROVISIONS IN FEDERALLY ASSISTED CONSTRUCTION CONTRACTS

SEC. 301. Each executive department and agency which administers a program involving Federal financial assistance shall require as a condition for the approval of any grant, contract, loan, insurance, or guarantee thereunder, which may involve a construction contract, that the applicant for Federal assistance undertake and agree to incorporate, or cause to be incorporated, into all construction contracts paid for in whole or in part with funds obtained from the Federal Government or borrowed on the credit of the Federal Government pursuant to such grant, contract, loan, insurance, or guarantee, or undertaken pursuant to any Federal program involving such grant, contract, loan, insurance, or guarantee, the provisions prescribed for Government contracts by Section 202 of this Order or such modification thereof, preserving in substance the contractor's obligations thereunder, as may be approved by the Secretary of Labor, together with such additional provisions as the Secretary deems appropriate to establish and protect the interest of the United States in the enforcement of those obligations. Each such applicant shall also undertake and agree (1) to assist and cooperate actively with the Secretary of Labor in obtaining the compliance of contractors and subcontractors with those contract provisions and with the rules, regulations and relevant orders of the Secretary, (2) to obtain and to furnish to the Secretary of Labor such information as the Secretary may require for the supervision of such compliance, (3) to carry out sanctions and penalties for violation of such obligations imposed upon contractors and subcontractors by the Secretary of Labor pursuant to Part II, Subpart D, of this Order and (4) to refrain from entering into any contract subject to this Order, or extension or other modification of such a contract with a contractor debarred from Government contracts under Part II, Subpart D, of this Order.

SEC. 302. (a) "Construction contract" as used in this Order means any contract for the construction, rehabilitation, alteration, conversion, extension, or repair of buildings, highways, or other improvements to real property.

(b) The provisions of Part II of this Order shall apply to such construction contracts, and for purposes of such application the administering, department or agency shall be considered the contracting agency referred to therein.

(c) The term "applicant" as used in this Order means an applicant for Federal assistance or, as determined by agency regulation, other program participant, with respect to whom an application for any grant, contract, loan, insurance, or guarantee is not finally acted upon prior to the effective date of this Part, and it includes such an applicant after he becomes a recipient of such Federal assistance.

SEC. 303. (a) The Secretary of Labor shall be responsible for obtaining the compliance of such applicants with their undertakings under this Order. Each administering department and agency is directed to cooperate with the Secretary of Labor and to furnish the Secretary such information and assistance as the Secretary may require in the performance of the Secretary's functions under this Order.

(b) In the event an applicant fails and refuses to comply with the applicant's undertakings pursuant to this Order, the Secretary of Labor may, after consulting with the administering department or agency, take any or all of the following actions:

(1) direct any administering department or agency to cancel, terminate, or suspend in whole or in part the agreement, contract or other arrangement with such applicant with respect to which the failure or refusal occurred;

(2) direct any administering department or agency to refrain from extending any further assistance to the applicant under the program with respect to which the

failure or refusal occurred until satisfactory assurance of future compliance has been received by the Secretary of Labor from such applicant; and

(3) refer the case to the Department of Justice or the Equal Employment Opportunity Commission for appropriate law enforcement or other proceedings.

(c) In no case shall action be taken with respect to an applicant pursuant to clause (1) or (2) of subsection (b) without notice and opportunity for hearing.

SEC. 304. Any executive department or agency which imposes by rule, regulation, or order requirements of nondiscrimination in employment, other than requirements imposed pursuant to this Order, may delegate to the Secretary of Labor by agreement such responsibilities with respect to compliance standards, reports, and procedures as would tend to bring the administration of such requirements into conformity with the administration of requirements imposed under this Order: Provided, That actions to effect compliance by recipients of Federal financial assistance with requirements imposed pursuant to Title VI of the Civil Rights Act of 1964 shall be taken in conformity with the procedures and limitations prescribed in Section 602 thereof and the regulations of the administering department or agency issued thereunder.

PART IV—MISCELLANEOUS

SEC. 401. The Secretary of Labor may delegate to any officer, agency, or employee in the Executive branch of the Government, any function or duty of the Secretary under Parts II and III of this Order.

SEC. 402. The Secretary of Labor shall provide administrative support for the execution of the program known as the "Plans for Progress."

SEC. 403. (a) Executive Orders Nos. 10590 (January 19, 1955), 10722 (August 5, 1957), 10925 (March 6,1961), 11114 (June 22, 1963), and 11162 (July 28, 1964), are hereby superseded and the President's Committee on Equal Employment Opportunity established by Executive Order No. 10925 is hereby abolished. All records and property in the custody of the Committee shall be transferred to the Civil Service Commission and the Secretary of Labor, as appropriate.

(b) Nothing in this Order shall be deemed to relieve any person of any obligation assumed or imposed under or pursuant to any Executive Order superseded by this Order. All rules, regulations, orders, instructions, designations, and other directives issued by the President's Committee on Equal Employment Opportunity and those issued by the heads of various departments or agencies under or pursuant to any of the Executive orders superseded by this Order, shall, to the extent that they are not inconsistent with this Order, remain in full force and effect unless and until revoked or superseded by appropriate authority. References in such directives to provisions of the superseded orders shall be deemed to be references to the comparable provisions of this Order.

SEC. 404. The General Services Administration shall take appropriate action to revise the standard Government contract forms to accord with the provisions of this Order and of the rules and regulations of the Secretary of Labor.

SEC. 405. This Order shall become effective thirty days after the date of this Order. [Dated: September 24, 1965.]

Office of Federal Contract Compliance Programs

41 C.F.R. § 60-1.1 *et seq.*

Part 60-1. Obligations of Contractors and Subcontractors

SUBPART A. PRELIMINARY MATTERS; EQUAL OPPORTUNITY CLAUSE; COMPLIANCE REPORTS

60-1.1 Purpose and application.

The purpose of the regulations in this part is to achieve the aims of parts II, III, and IV of Executive Order 11246 for the promotion and insuring of equal opportunity for all persons, without regard to race, color, religion, sex, or national origin, employed or seeking employment with Government contractors or with contractors performing under federally assisted construction contracts. The regulations in this part apply to all contracting agencies of the Government and to contractors and subcontractors who perform under Government contracts, to the extent set forth in this part. The regulations in this part also apply to all agencies of the Government administering programs involving Federal financial assistance which may include a construction contract, and to all contractors and subcontractors performing under construction contracts which are related to any such programs. The procedures set forth in the regulations in this part govern all disputes relative to a contractor's compliance with his obligations under the equal opportunity clause regardless of whether or not his contract contains a "Disputes" clause. Failure of a contractor or applicant to comply with any provision of the regulations in this part shall be grounds for the imposition of any or all of the sanctions authorized by the order. The regulations in this part do not apply to any action taken to effect compliance with respect to employment practices subject to title VI of the Civil Rights Act of 1964. The rights and remedies of the Government hereunder are not exclusive and do not affect rights and remedies provided elsewhere by law, regulation, or contract; neither do the regulations limit the exercise by the Secretary or Government agencies of powers not herein specifically set forth, but granted to them by the order.

60-1.2 Administrative responsibility.

The Deputy Assistant Secretary has been delegated authority and assigned responsibility for carrying out the responsibilities assigned to the Secretary under the Executive order. All correspondence regarding the order should be directed to the Deputy Assistant Secretary, Office of Federal Contract Compliance Programs, Employment Standards Administration, U.S. Department of Labor, 200 Constitution Avenue NW., Washington, DC 20210.

60-1.3 Definitions.

Administering agency means any department, agency and establishment in the executive branch of the Government, including any wholly owned Government corporation, which administers a program involving federally assisted construction contracts.

Administrative law judge means an administrative law judge appointed as provided in 5 U.S.C. 3105 and Subpart B of Part 930 of Title 5 of the Code of Federal Regulations (see 37 FR 16787) and qualified to preside at hearings under 5 U.S.C. 557.

Agency means any contracting or any administering agency of the Government.

Applicant means an applicant for Federal assistance involving a construction contract, or other participant in a program involving a construction contract as determined by regulation of an administering agency. The term also includes such persons after they become recipients of such Federal assistance.

Compliance evaluation means any one or combination of actions OFCCP may take to examine a Federal contractor or subcontractor's compliance with one or more of the requirements of Executive Order 11246.

Construction work means the construction, rehabilitation, alteration, conversion, extension, demolition or repair of buildings, highways, or other changes or improvements to real property, including facilities providing utility services. The term also includes the supervision, inspection, and other onsite functions incidental to the actual construction.

Contract means any Government contract or subcontract or any federally assisted construction contract or subcontract.

Contracting agency means any department, agency, establishment, or instrumentality in the executive branch of the Government, including any wholly owned Government corporation, which enters into contracts.

Contractor means, unless otherwise indicated, a prime contractor or subcontractor.

Deputy Assistant Secretary means the Deputy Assistant Secretary for Federal Contract Compliance, United States Department of Labor, or his or her designee.

Equal opportunity clause means the contract provisions set forth in Sec. 601.4 (a) or (b), as appropriate.

Federally assisted construction contract means any agreement or modification thereof between any applicant and a person for construction work which is paid for in whole or in part with funds obtained from the Government or borrowed on the credit of the Government pursuant to any Federal program involving a grant, contract, loan, insurance, or guarantee, or undertaken pursuant to any Federal program involving such grant, contract, loan, insurance, or guarantee, or any application or modification thereof approved by the Government for a grant, contract, loan, insurance, or guarantee under which the applicant itself participates in the construction work.

Government means the government of the United States of America.

Government contract means any agreement or modification thereof between any contracting agency and any person for the purchase, sale or use of personal property or nonpersonal services. The term "personal property," as used in this section, includes supplies, and contracts for the use of real property (such as lease arrangements), unless the contract for the use of real property itself constitutes real property (such as easements). The term "nonpersonal services" as used in this section includes, but is not limited to, the following services: Utilities, construction, transportation, research, insurance, and fund depository. The term *Government contract* does not include:

(1) Agreements in which the parties stand in the relationship of employer and employee; and

(2) Federally assisted construction contracts.

Internet applicant.

(1) Internet applicant means any individual as to whom the following four criteria are satisfied:

(i) The individual submits an expression of interest in employment through the Internet or related electronic data technologies;

(ii) The contractor considers the individual for employment in a particular position;

(iii) The individual's expression of interest indicates the individual possesses the basic qualifications for the position; and

(iv) The individual at no point in the contractor's selection process prior to receiving an offer of employment from the contractor, removes himself or herself from further consideration or otherwise indicated that he or she is no longer interested in the position.

(2) For purposes of paragraph (1)(i) of this definition, "submits an expression of interest in employment through the Internet or related electronic data technologies" includes all expressions of interest, regardless of the means or manner in which the expression of interest is made, if the contractor considers expressions of interest made

through the Internet or related electronic data technologies in the recruiting or selection processes for that particular position.

(i) Example A: Contractor posts on its web site an opening for a Mechanical Engineer position and encourages potential applicants to complete an online profile if they are interested in being considered for that position. The web site also advises potential applicants that they can send a hard copy resume to the HR Manager with a cover letter identifying the position for which they would like to be considered. Because Contractor A considers both Internet and traditional expressions of interest for the Mechanical Engineer position, both the individuals who completed a personal profile and those who sent a paper resume and cover letter to contractor A meet this part of the definition of *Internet applicant* for this position.

(ii) Example B: Contractor B posts on its web site an opening for the Accountant II position and encourages potential applicants to complete an online profile if they are interested in being considered for that position. Contractor B also receives a large number of unsolicited paper resumes in the mail each year. Contractor B scans these paper resumes into an internal resume database that also includes all the online profiles that individuals completed for various jobs (including possibly for the Accountant II position) throughout the year. To find potential applicants for the Accountant II position, Contractor B searches the internal database for individuals who have the basic qualifications for the Accountant II position. Because Contractor B considers both Internet and traditional expressions of interest for the Accountant II position, both the individuals who completed a personal profile and those who sent a paper resume and cover letter to the employer meet this part of the definition of Internet Applicant for this position.

(iii) Example C: Contractor C advertises for Mechanics in a local newspaper and instructs interested candidates to mail their resumes to the employer's address. Walk-in applications also are permitted. Contractor C considers only paper resumes and application forms for the Mechanic position; therefore, no individual meets this part of the definition of an Internet Applicant for this position.

(3) For purposes of paragraph (1)(ii) of this definition, "considers the individual for employment in a particular position" means that the contractor assesses the substantive information provided in the expression of interest with respect to any qualifications involved with a particular position. A contractor may establish a protocol under which it refrains from considering expressions of interest that are not submitted in accordance with standard procedures the contractor establishes. Likewise, a contractor may establish a protocol under which it refrains from considering expressions of interest, such as unsolicited resumes, that are not submitted with respect to a particular position. If there are a large number of expressions of interest, the contractor does not "consider the individual for employment in a particular position" by using data management techniques that do not depend on assessment of qualification, such as random sampling or absolute numerical limits, to reduce the number of expression of interest to be considered, provided that the sample is appropriate in terms of the pool of these submitting expressions of interest.

(4) For purposes of paragraph (1)(iii) of this definition, "basic qualifications" means qualification-

(i)(A) That the contractor advertises (e.g., posts on its web site a description of the job and the qualifications involved) to potential applicants that they must possess in order to be considered for the position; or

(B) For which the contractor establishes criteria in advance by making and maintaining a record of such qualifications for the position prior to considering any expression of interest for that particular position if the contractor does not advertise for the position but instead uses an alternative device to find individuals for consideration (e.g., through an external resume database), and

(ii) That meet all of the following three conditions:

(A) The qualifications must be noncomparative features of a job seeker. For example, a qualification of three years' experience in a particular position is a noncomparative qualification; a qualification that an individual have one of the top five number of years' experience among a pool of job seekers is a comparative qualification.

(B) The qualifications must be objective; they do not depend on the contractor's subjective judgment. For example, "a Bachelor's degree in Accounting" is objective, while "a technical degree from a good school" is not. A basic qualification is objective if a third party, with the contractor's technical knowledge, would be able to evaluate whether the job seeker possesses the qualification without more information about the contractor's judgment.

(C) The qualifications must be relevant to performance of the particular position and enable the contractor to accomplish business-related goals.

(5) For purposes of paragraph (1)(iv) of this definition, a contractor may conclude that an individual has removed himself or herself from further consideration, or has otherwise indicated that he or she is no longer interested in the position for which the contractor has considered the individual, based on the individual's express statement that he or she is no longer interested in the position, or on the individual's passive demonstration of disinterest shown through repeated non-responsiveness to inquiries from the contractor about interest in the position. A contractor also may determine that an individual has removed himself or herself from further consideration or otherwise indicated that he or she is no longer interested in the position for which the contractor has considered the individual based on information the individual provided in the expression of interest, such as salary requirements or preferences as to type of work or location of work, provided that the contractor has a uniformly and consistently applied policy or procedure of not considering similarly situated job seekers. If a large number of management techniques, such as random sampling or absolute numerical limits, to limit the number of individuals who must be contacted to determine their interest in the position, provided that the sample is appropriate in terms of the pool of these meeting the basic qualifications.

Minority group as used herein shall include, where appropriate, female employees and prospective female employees.

Modification means any alteration in the terms and conditions of a contract, including supplemental agreements, amendments, and extensions.

Order, Executive order, or Executive Order 11246 means parts II, III, and IV of the Executive Order 11246 dated September 24, 1965 (30 FR 12319), any Executive order amending such order, and any other Executive order superseding such order.

Person means any natural person, corporation, partnership, unincorporated association, State or local government, and any agency, instrumentality, or subdivision of such a government.

Prime contractor means any person holding a contract and, for the purposes of Subpart B of this part, any person who has held a contract subject to the order.

Recruiting and training agency means any person who refers workers to any contractor or subcontractor or who provides for employment by any contractor or subcontractor.

Rules, regulations, and relevant orders of the Secretary of Labor used in paragraph (4) of the equal opportunity clause means rules, regulations, and relevant orders of the Secretary of Labor or his designee issued pursuant to the order.

Secretary means the Secretary of Labor, U.S. Department of Labor, or his or her designee.

Site of construction means the general physical location of any building, highway, or other change or improvement to real property which is undergoing construction, rehabilitation, alteration, conversion, extension, demolition, or repair and any temporary location or facility at which a contractor, subcontractor, or other participating party meets a demand or performs a function relating to the contract or subcontract.

Subcontract means any agreement or arrangement between a contractor and any person (in which the parties do not stand in the relationship of an employer and an employee):

(1) For the purchase, sale or use of personal property or nonpersonal services which, in whole or in part, is necessary to the performance of any one or more contracts; or

(2) Under which any portion of the contractor's obligation under any one or more contracts is performed, undertaken or assumed.

Subcontractor means any person holding a subcontract and, for the purposes of Subpart B of this part, any person who has held a subcontract subject to the order. The term "first-tier subcontractor" refers to a subcontractor holding a subcontract with a prime contractor.

United States as used herein shall include the several States, the District of Columbia, the Commonwealth of Puerto Rico, the Panama Canal Zone, and the possessions of the *United States* as used herein shall include the several States, the District of Columbia, the Virgin Islands, the Commonwealth of Puerto Rico, Guam, American Samoa, the Commonwealth of the Northern Mariana Islands, and Wake Island.

60-1.4 Equal opportunity clause.

(a) *Government contracts.* Except as otherwise provided, each contracting agency shall include the following equal opportunity clause contained in section 202 of the order in each of its Government contracts (and modifications thereof if not included in the original contract):

During the performance of this contract, the contractor agrees as follows:

(1) The contractor will not discriminate against any employee or applicant for employment because of race, color, religion, sex, or national origin. The contractor will take affirmative action to ensure that applicants are employed, and that employees are treated during employment, without regard to their race, color, religion, sex, or national origin. Such action shall include, but not be limited to the following: Employment, upgrading, demotion, or transfer, recruitment or recruitment advertising; layoff or termination; rates of pay or other forms of compensation; and selection for training, including apprenticeship. The contractor agrees to post in conspicuous places, available to employees and applicants for employment, notices to be provided by the contracting officer setting forth the provisions of this nondiscrimination clause.

(2) The contractor will, in all solicitations or advertisements for employees placed by or on behalf of the contractor, state that all qualified applicants will receive consideration for employment without regard to race, color, religion, sex, or national origin.

(3) The contractor will send to each labor union or representative of workers with which he has a collective bargaining agreement or other contract or understanding, a

notice to be provided by the agency contracting officer, advising the labor union or workers' representative of the contractor's commitments under section 202 of Executive Order 11246 of September 24, 1965, and shall post copies of the notice in conspicuous places available to employees and applicants for employment.

(4) The contractor will comply with all provisions of Executive Order 11246 of September 24, 1965, and of the rules, regulations, and relevant orders of the Secretary of Labor.

(5) The contractor will furnish all information and reports required by Executive Order 11246 of September 24, 1965, and by the rules, regulations, and orders of the Secretary of Labor, or pursuant thereto, and will permit access to his books, records, and accounts by the contracting agency and the Secretary of Labor for purposes of investigation to ascertain compliance with such rules, regulations, and orders.

(6) In the event of the contractor's noncompliance with the nondiscrimination clauses of this contract or with any of such rules, regulations, or orders, this contract may be canceled, terminated or suspended in whole or in part and the contractor may be declared ineligible for further Government contracts in accordance with procedures authorized in Executive Order 11246 of September 24, 1965, and such other sanctions may be imposed and remedies invoked as provided in Executive Order 11246 of September 24, 1965, or by rule, regulation, or order of the Secretary of Labor, or as otherwise provided by law.

(7) the contractor will include the provisions of paragraphs (1) through (7) in every subcontract or purchase order unless exempted by rules, regulations, or orders of the Secretary of Labor issued pursuant to section 204 of Executive Order 11246 of September 24, 1965, so that such provisions will be binding upon each subcontractor or vendor. The contractor will take such action with respect to any subcontract or purchase order as may be directed by the Secretary of Labor as a means of enforcing such provisions including sanctions for noncompliance: Provided, however, that in the event the contractor becomes involved in, or is threatened with, litigation with a subcontractor or vendor as a result of such direction, the contractor may request the United States to enter into such litigation to protect the interests of the United States.

(b) *Federally assisted construction contracts.* (1) Except as otherwise provided, each administering agency shall require the inclusion of the following language as a condition of any grant, contract, loan, insurance, or guarantee involving federally assisted construction which is not exempt from the requirements of the equal opportunity clause:

The applicant hereby agrees that it will incorporate or cause to be incorporated into any contract for construction work, or modification thereof, as defined in the regulations of the Secretary of Labor at 41 CFR Chapter 60, which is paid for in whole or in part with funds obtained from the Federal Government or borrowed on the credit of the Federal Government pursuant to a grant, contract, loan insurance, or guarantee, or undertaken pursuant to any Federal program involving such grant, contract, loan, insurance, or guarantee, the following equal opportunity clause:

During the performance of this contract, the contractor agrees as follows:

(1) The contractor will not discriminate against any employee or applicant for employment because of race, color, religion, sex, or national origin. The contractor will take affirmative action to ensure that applicants are employed, and that employees are treated during employment without regard to their race, color, religion, sex, or national origin. such action shall include, but not be limited to the following: Employment, upgrading, demotion, or transfer; recruitment or recruitment advertising;

layoff or termination; rates of pay or other forms of compensation; and selection for training, including apprenticeship. The contractor agrees to post in conspicuous places, available to employees and applicants for employment, notices to be provided setting forth the provisions of this nondiscrimination clause.

(2) The contractor will, in all solicitations or advertisements for employees placed by or on behalf of the contractor, state that all qualified applicants will receive considerations for employment without regard to race, color, religion, sex, or national origin.

(3) The contractor will send to each labor union or representative of workers with which he has a collective bargaining agreement or other contract or understanding, a notice to be provided advising the said labor union or workers' representatives of the contractor's commitments under this section, and shall post copies of the notice in conspicuous places available to employees and applicants for employment.

(4) The contractor will comply with all provisions of Executive Order 11246 of September 24, 1965, and of the rules, regulations, and relevant orders of the Secretary of Labor.

(5) The contractor will furnish all information and reports required by Executive Order 11246 of September 24, 1965, and by rules, regulations, and orders of the Secretary of Labor, or pursuant thereto, and will permit access to his books, records, and accounts by the administering agency and the Secretary of Labor for purposes of investigation to ascertain compliance with such rules, regulations, and orders.

(6) In the event of the contractor's noncompliance with the nondiscrimination clauses of this contract or with any of the said rules, regulations, or orders, this contract may be canceled, terminated, or suspended in whole or in part and the contractor may be declared ineligible for further Government contracts or federally assisted construction contracts in accordance with procedures authorized in Executive Order 11246 of September 24, 1965, and such other sanctions may be imposed and remedies invoked as provided in Executive Order 11246 of September 24, 1965, or by rule, regulation, or order of the Secretary of Labor, or as otherwise provided by law.

(7) The contractor will include the portion of the sentence immediately preceding paragraph (1) and the provisions of paragraphs (1) through (7) in every subcontract or purchase order unless exempted by rules, regulations, or orders of the Secretary of Labor issued pursuant to section 204 of Executive Order 11246 of September 24, 1965, so that such provisions will be binding upon each subcontractor or vendor. The contractor will take such action with respect to any subcontract or purchase order as the administering agency may direct as a means of enforcing such provisions, including sanctions for noncompliance: Provided, however, That in the event a contractor becomes involved in, or is threatened with, litigation with a subcontractor or vendor as a result of such direction by the administering agency the contractor may request the United States to enter into such litigation to protect the interests of the United States.

The applicant further agrees that it will be bound by the above equal opportunity clause with respect to its own employment practices when it participates in federally assisted construction work: Provided, That if the applicant so participating is a State or local government, the above equal opportunity clause is not applicable to any agency, instrumentality or subdivision of such government which does not participate in work on or under the contract.

The applicant agrees that it will assist and cooperate actively with the administering agency and the Secretary of Labor in obtaining the compliance of contractors and subcontractors with the equal opportunity clause and the rules, regulations, and relevant orders of the Secretary of Labor, that it will furnish the administering agency and the Secretary of Labor such information as they may require for the supervision of such compliance, and that it will otherwise assist the administering agency in the discharge of the agency's primary responsibility for securing compliance.

The applicant further agrees that it will refrain from entering into any contract or contract modification subject to Executive Order 11246 of September 24, 1965, with a contractor debarred from, or who has not demonstrated eligibility for, Government contracts and federally assisted construction contracts pursuant to the Executive order and will carry out such sanctions and penalties for violation of the equal opportunity clause as may be imposed upon contractors and subcontractors by the administering agency or the Secretary of Labor pursuant to Part II, Subpart D of the Executive order. In addition, the applicant agrees that if it fails or refuses to comply with these undertakings, the administering agency may take any or all of the following actions: Cancel, terminate, or suspend in whole or in part this grant (contract, loan, insurance, guarantee); refrain from extending any further assistance to the applicant under the program with respect to which the failure or refund occurred until satisfactory assurance of future compliance has been received from such applicant; and refer the case to the Department of Justice for appropriate legal proceedings.

(c) *Subcontracts.* Each nonexempt prime contractor or subcontractor shall include the equal opportunity clause in each of its nonexempt subcontracts.

(d) *Incorporation by reference.* The equal opportunity clause may be incorporated by reference in all Government contracts and subcontracts, including Government bills of lading, transportation requests, contracts for deposit of Government funds, and contracts for issuing and paying U.S. savings bonds and notes, and such other contracts and subcontracts as the Deputy Assistant Secretary may designate.

(e) *Incorporation by operation of the order.* By operation of the order, the equal opportunity clause shall be considered to be a part of every contract and subcontract required by the order and the regulations in this part to include such a clause whether or not it is physically incorporated in such contracts and whether or not the contract between the agency and the contractor is written.

(f) *Adaptation of language.* Such necessary changes in language may be made in the equal opportunity clause as shall be appropriate to identify properly the parties and their undertakings.

60-1.5 Exemptions.

(a) *General-(1) Transactions of $10,000 or under.* Contracts and subcontracts not exceeding $10,000, other than Government bills of lading, and other than contracts and subcontracts with depositories of Federal funds in any amount and with financial institutions which are issuing and paying agents for U.S. savings bonds and savings notes, are exempt from the requirements of the equal opportunity clause. In determining the applicability of this exemption to any federally assisted construction contract, or subcontract thereunder, the amount of such contract or subcontract rather than the amount of the Federal financial assistance shall govern. No agency, contractor, or subcontractor shall procure supplies or services in a manner so as to avoid applicability of the equal opportunity clause: Provided, that where a contractor has contracts or subcontracts with the Government in any 12month period which have an aggregate total value (or can reasonably be expected to have an aggregate total value) exceeding $10,000, the $10,000 or under exemption does not apply, and the contracts are subject to the order and the regulations issued pursuant thereto regardless of whether any single contract exceeds $10,000.

(2) *Contracts and subcontracts for indefinite quantities.* With respect to contracts and subcontracts for indefinite quantities (including, but not limited to, open end contracts, requirement type contracts, Federal Supply Schedule contracts, "call type" contracts, and purchase notice agreements), the equal opportunity clause shall be included unless the purchaser has reason to believe that the amount to be ordered in any year under such contract will not exceed $10,000. The applicability of the equal opportunity clause shall be determined by the purchaser at the time of award for the first year, and annually thereafter for succeeding years, if any. Notwithstanding the above, the equal opportunity clause shall be applied to such contract whenever the amount of a single order exceeds $10,000. Once the equal opportunity clause is determined to be applicable, the contract shall continue to be subject to such clause for its duration, regardless of the amounts ordered, or reasonably expected to be ordered in any year.

(3) *Work outside the United States.* Contracts and subcontracts are exempt from the requirements of the equal opportunity clause with regard to work performed outside the United States by employees who were not recruited within the United States.

(4) *Contracts with State or local governments.* The requirements of the equal opportunity clause in any contract or subcontract with a State or local government (or any agency, instrumentality or subdivision thereof) shall not be applicable to any agency, instrumentality or subdivision of such government which does not participate in work on or under the contract or subcontract. In addition, any agency, instrumentality or subdivision of such government, except for educational institutions and medical facilities, are exempt from the requirements of filing the annual compliance report provided for by Sec. 601.7(a)(1) and maintaining a written affirmative action compliance program prescribed by Sec. 601.40 and Part 602 of this chapter.

(5) *Contracts with religious entities.* Section 202 of Executive Order 11246, as amended, shall not apply to a Government contractor or subcontractor that is a religious corporation, association, educational institution, or society, with respect to the employment of individuals of a particular region to perform work connected with the carrying on by such corporation, association, educational institution, or society of its activities. Such contractors and subcontractors are not exempted or excused from complying with the other requirements contained in this Order.

(6) *Contracts with certain educational institutions.* It shall not be a violation of the equal opportunity clause for a school, college, university, or other educational institution or institution of learning to hire and employ employees of a particular religion if such school, college, university, or other educational institution or institution of learning is, in whole or in substantial part, owned, supported, controlled, or managed by a particular religion or by a particular religious corporation, association, or society, or if the curriculum of such school, college, university, or other educational institution or institution of learning is directed toward the propagation of a particular religion. The primary thrust of this provision is directed at religiously oriented colleges and universities and should be so interpreted.

(7) *Work on or near Indian reservations.* It shall not be a violation of the equal opportunity clause for a construction or nonconstruction contractor to extend a publicly announced preference in employment to Indians living on or near an Indian reservation in connection with employment opportunities on or near an Indian reservation. The use of the word "near" would include all that area where a person seeking employment could reasonably be expected to commute to and from in the course of a work day. Contractors or subcontractors extending such a preference shall not, however,

discriminate among Indians on the basis of religion, sex, or tribal affiliation, and the use of such a preference shall not excuse a contractor from complying with the other requirements contained in this chapter.

(b) *Specific contracts and facilities*-(1) *Specific contracts.* The Deputy Assistant Secretary may exempt an agency or any person from requiring the inclusion of any or all of the equal opportunity clause in any specific contract or subcontract when he deems that special circumstances in the national interest so require. The Deputy Assistant Secretary may also exempt groups or categories of contracts or subcontracts of the same type where he finds it impracticable to act upon each request individually or where group exemptions will contribute to convenience in the administration of the order.

(2) *Facilities not connected with contracts.* The Deputy Assistant Secretary may exempt from the requirements of the equal opportunity clause any of a prime contractor's or subcontractor's facilities which he finds to be in all respects separate and distinct from activities of the prime contractor or subcontractor related to the performance of the contract or subcontract, provided that he also finds that such an exemption will not interfere with or impede the effectuation of the order.

(c) *National security.* Any requirement set forth in these regulations in this part shall not apply to any contract or subcontract whenever the head of an agency determines that such contract or subcontract is essential to the national security and that its award without complying with such requirement is necessary to the national security. Upon making such a determination, the head of the agency will notify the Deputy Assistant Secretary in writing within 30 days.

(d) *Withdrawal of exemption.* When any contract or subcontract is of a class exempted under this section, the Deputy Assistant Secretary may withdraw the exemption for a specific contract or subcontract or group of contracts or subcontracts when in his judgment such action is necessary or appropriate to achieve the purposes of the order. Such withdrawal shall not apply to contracts or subcontracts awarded prior to the withdrawal, except that in procurements entered into by formal advertising, or the various forms of restricted formal advertising, such withdrawal shall not apply unless the withdrawal is made more than 10 calendar days before the date set for the opening of the bids.

60-1.6 [Reserved].

60-1.7 Reports and other required information.

(a) *Requirements for prime contractors and subcontractors.*

(1) Each prime contractor and subcontractor shall file annually, on or before the September 30, complete and accurate reports on Standard Form 100 (EEO1) promulgated jointly by the Office of Federal Contract Compliance Programs, the Equal Employment Opportunity Commission and Plans for Progress or such form as may hereafter be promulgated in its place if such prime contractor or subcontractor (i) is not exempt from the provisions of these regulations in accordance with Sec. 601.5; (ii) has 50 or more employees; (iii) is a prime contractor or first tier subcontractor; and (iv) has a contract, subcontract or purchase order amounting to $50,000 or more or serves as a depository of Government funds in any amount, or is a financial institution which is an issuing and paying agent for U.S. savings bonds and savings notes: Provided, That any subcontractor below the first tier which performs construction work at the site of construction shall be required to file such a report if it meets requirements of paragraphs (a)(1) (i), (ii), and (iv) of this section.

(2) Each person required by Sec. 601.7(a)(1) to submit reports shall file such a report with the contracting or administering agency within 30 days after the award to him of a contract or subcontract, unless such person has submitted such a report within 12 months preceding the date of the award. Subsequent reports shall be submitted annually in accordance with Sec. 601.7(a)(1), or at such other intervals as the Deputy Assistant Secretary may require. The Deputy Assistant Secretary may extend the time for filing any report.

(3) The Deputy Assistant Secretary or the applicant, on their own motions, may require a contractor to keep employment or other records and to furnish, in the form requested, within reasonable limits, such information as the Deputy Assistant Secretary or the applicant deems necessary for the administration of the order.

(4) Failure to file timely, complete and accurate reports as required constitutes noncompliance with the prime contractor's or subcontractor's obligations under the equal opportunity clause and is ground for the imposition by the Deputy Assistant Secretary, an applicant, prime contractor or subcontractor, of any sanctions as authorized by the order and the regulations in this part.

(b) *Requirements for bidders or prospective contractors*-(1) *Certification of compliance with Part 60-2: Affirmative Action Programs.* Each agency shall require each bidder or prospective prime contractor and proposed subcontractor, where appropriate, to state in the bid or in writing at the outset of negotiations for the contract: (i) Whether it has developed and has on file at each establishment affirmative action programs pursuant to Part 602 of this chapter; (ii) whether it has participated in any previous contract or subcontract subject to the equal opportunity clause; (iii) whether it has filed with the Joint Reporting Committee, the Deputy Assistant Secretary or the Equal Employment Opportunity Commission all reports due under the applicable filing requirements.

(2) *Additional information.* A bidder or prospective prime contractor or proposed subcontractor shall be required to submit such information as the Deputy Assistant Secretary requests prior to the award of the contract or subcontract. When a determination has been made to award the contract or subcontract to a specific contractor, such contractor shall be required, prior to award, or after the award, or both, to furnish such other information as the applicant or the Deputy Assistant Secretary requests.

(c) *Use of reports.* Reports filed pursuant to this section shall be used only in connection with the administration of the order, the Civil Rights Act of 1964, or in furtherance of the purposes of the order and said Act.

60-1.8 Segregated facilities.

To comply with its obligations under the Order, a contractor must ensure that facilities provided for employees are provided in such a manner that segregation on the basis of race, color, religion, sex or national origin cannot result. The contractor may neither require such segregated use by written or oral policies nor tolerate such use by employee custom. The contractor's obligation extends further to ensuring that its employees are not assigned to perform their services at any location, under the contractor's control, where the facilities are segregated. This obligation extends to all contracts containing the equal opportunity clause regardless of the amount of the contract. The term "facilities," as used in this section, means waiting rooms, work areas, restaurants and other eating areas, time clocks, restrooms, wash rooms, locker rooms, and other storage or dressing areas, parking lots, drinking fountains, recreation or entertainment areas, transportation, and housing provided for employees; Provided, That separate or single-user restrooms and necessary dressing or sleeping areas shall be provided to assure privacy between the sexes.

60-1.9 Compliance by labor unions and by recruiting and training agencies.

(a) Whenever compliance with the equal opportunity clause may necessitate a revision of a collective bargaining agreement the labor union or unions which are parties to such an agreement shall be given an adequate opportunity to present their views to the Deputy Assistant Secretary.

(b) The Deputy Assistant Secretary shall use his best efforts, directly and through agencies, contractors, subcontractors, applicants, State and local officials, public and private agencies, and all other available instrumentalities, to cause any labor union, recruiting and training agency or other representative of workers who are or may be engaged in work under contracts and subcontracts to cooperate with, and to comply in the implementation of, the purposes of the order.

(c) In order to effectuate the purposes of paragraph (a) of this section, the Deputy Assistant Secretary may hold hearings, public or private, with respect to the practices and policies of any such labor union or recruiting and training agency.

(d) The Deputy Assistant Secretary may notify any Federal, State, or local agency of his conclusions and recommendations with respect to any such labor organization or recruiting and training agency which in his judgment has failed to cooperate with himself, agencies, prime contractors, subcontractors, or applicants in carrying out the purposes of the order. The Deputy Assistant Secretary also may notify the Equal Employment Opportunity Commission, the Department of Justice, or other appropriate Federal agencies whenever he has reason to believe that the practices of any such labor organization or agency violates title VII of the Civil Rights Act of 1964 or other provisions of Federal law.

60-1.10 Foreign government practices.

Contractors shall not discriminate on the basis of race, color, religion, sex, or national origin when hiring or making employee assignments for work to be performed in the United States or abroad. Contractors are exempted from this obligation only when hiring persons outside the United States for work to be performed outside the United States (see 41 CFR 601.5(a)(3)). Therefore, a contractor hiring workers in the United States for either Federal or nonfederally connected work shall be in violation of Executive Order 11246, as amended, by refusing to employ or assign any person because of race, color, religion, sex, or national origin regardless of the policies of the country where the work is to be performed or for whom the work will be performed. Should any contractor be unable to acquire a visa of entry for any employee or potential employee to a country in which or with which it is doing business, and which refusal it believes is due to the race, color, religion, sex, or national origin of the employee or potential employee, the contractor must immediately notify the Department of State and the Deputy Assistant Secretary of such refusal.

60-1.11 Payment or reimbursement of membership fees and other expenses to private clubs.

Effective date deferred until further notice. 46 Fed. Reg. 18951 (March 27, 1981).

(a)(1) A contractor which maintains a policy or practice of paying membership fees or other expenses for employee participation in private clubs or organizations shall ensure that the policy or practice is administered without regard to the race, color, religion, sex, or national origin of employees.

(2) Payment or reimbursement by contractors of membership fees and other expenses for participation by their employees in a private club or organization which bars, restricts

or limits its membership on the basis of race, color, sex, religion, or national origin constitutes a violation of Executive Order 11246 except where the contractor can provide evidence that such restrictions or limitations do not abridge the promotional opportunities, status, compensation or other terms and conditions of employment of those of its employees barred from membership because of their race, color, religion, sex, or national origin. OFCCP shall provide the contractor with the opportunity to present evidence in defense of its actions.

(b) The contractor has the responsibility of determining whether the club or organization restricts membership on the basis of race, color, religion, sex, or national origin. The contractor may make separate determinations for different chapters of an organization, and where it does so, may limit any necessary corrective action to the particular chapters which observe discriminatory membership policies and practices.

60-1.12 Record retention.

(a) *General requirements.* Any personnel or employment record made or kept by the contractor shall be preserved by the contractor for a period of not less than two years from the date of the making of the record or the personnel action involved, whichever occurs later. However, if the contractor has fewer than 150 employees or does not have a Government contract of at least $150,000, the minimum record retention period shall be one year from the date of the making of the record or the personnel action involved, whichever occurs later. Such records include, but are not necessarily limited to, records pertaining to hiring, assignment, promotion, demotion, transfer, lay off or termination, rates of pay or other terms of compensation, and selection for training or apprenticeship, and other records having to do with requests for reasonable accommodation, the results of any physical examination, job advertisements and postings, applications resumes and any and all expressions of interest through the Internet or related electronic data technologies as to which the contractor considered the individual for a particular position, such as online resumes or internal resume databases, records identifying job seekers contacted regarding their interest in a particular position (for purposes of recordkeeping with respect to internal resume databases, the contractor must maintain a record of each resume added to the database, a record of the date each resume was added to the data base, the position for which each search of the database was made, and corresponding to each search, the substantive search criteria used and the date of the search; for purposes of recordkeeping with respect to external resume databases, the contractor must maintain a record of the position for which each search of the database was made, and corresponding to each search, the substantive search criteria used, the date of the search, and the resumes of job seekers who met the basic qualifications for the particular position who are considered by the contractor), regardless of whether the individual qualifies as an Internet applicant under Sec. 60-1.3, tests and test results, and interview notes. In the case of involuntary termination of an employee, the personnel records of the individual terminated shall be kept for a period of not less than two years from the date of the termination, except that contractors that have fewer than 150 employees or that do not have a Government contract of at least $150,000 shall keep such records for a period of not less than one year from the date of the termination. Where the contractor has received notice that a complaint of discrimination has been filed, that a compliance evaluation has been initiated, or that an enforcement action has been commenced, the contractor shall preserve all personnel records relevant to the complaint, compliance evaluation or enforcement action until final disposition of the complaint, compliance evaluation or enforcement action. The term "personnel records relevant to the complaint," for example, would include personnel or employment records relating to the complainant and to all other employees holding positions similar to that held or sought by the complainant and application forms or test papers submitted by unsuccessful applicants and by all other candidates for the same position as that for which the complainant unsuccessfully applied. Where a compliance evaluation has been initiated, all personnel and employment records described above are relevant until OFCCP makes a final disposition of the evaluation.

(b) *Affirmative action programs.* A contractor establishment required under Sec. 60-1.40 to develop and maintain a written affirmative action program (AAP) must maintain its current AAP and documentation of good faith effort, and must preserve its AAP and documentation of good faith effort for the immediately preceding AAP year, unless it was not then covered by the AAP requirement.

(c) *Contractor identification of record.*

(1) For any record the contractor maintains pursuant to this section, the contractor must be able to identify:

(i) The gender, race, and ethnicity of each employee; and

(ii) Where possible, the gender, race, and ethnicity of each applicant of Internet Applicant as defined in Sec. 60-1.3, whichever is applicable to the particular position.

(2) The contractor must supply this information to the Office of Federal Contract Compliance Programs upon request.

(d) *Adverse impact evaluations.* When evaluating whether a contractor has maintained information on impact and conducted an adverse impact analysis under Part 60-3 with respect to Internet hiring procedures, OFCCP will require only those records relating to the analyses of the impact of employee selection procedures on Internet Applicants, as defined in Sec. 60-1.3, and those records relating to the analyses of the impact of employment tests that are used as employee selection procedures, without regard to whether the tests were administered to Internet Applicants, as defined in Sec. 60-1.3

(e) *Failure to preserve records.* Failure to preserve complete and accurate records as required by paragraphs (a) through (c) of this section constitutes noncompliance with the contractor's obligations under the Executive Order and this part. Where the contractor has destroyed or failed to preserve records as required by this section, there may be a presumption that the information destroyed or not preserved would have been unfavorable to the contractor. *Provided,* That this presumption shall not apply where the contractor shows that the destruction or failure to preserve records results from the circumstances that are outside of the contractor's control.

Subpart B. General Enforcement; Compliance Review and Complaint Procedure

60-1.20 Compliance evaluations.

(a) OFCCP may conduct compliance evaluations to determine if the contractor maintains nondiscriminatory hiring and employment practices and is taking affirmative action to ensure that applicants are employed and that employees are placed, trained, upgraded, promoted, and otherwise treated during employment without regard to race, color, religion, sex, or national origin. A compliance evaluation may consist of any one or any combination of the following investigative procedures:

(1) *Compliance review.* A comprehensive analysis and evaluation of the hiring and employment practices of the contractor, the written affirmative action program, and the results of the affirmative action efforts undertaken by the contractor. A compliance review may proceed in three stages:

(i) A desk audit of the written AAP and supporting documentation to determine whether all elements required by the regulations in this part are included, whether the AAP meets agency standards of reasonableness, and whether the AAP and supporting documentation satisfy agency standards of acceptability. The desk audit is conducted at OFCCP offices, except in the case of preaward reviews. In a preaward review, the desk audit normally is conducted at the contractor's establishment.

(ii) An on-site review, conducted at the contractor's establishment to investigate unresolved problem areas identified in the AAP and supporting documentation during the desk audit, to verify that the contractor has implemented the AAP and has complied with those regulatory obligations not required to be included in the AAP, and to examine potential instances or issues of discrimination. An onsite review normally will involve an examination of the contractor's personnel and employment policies, inspection and copying of documents related to employment actions, and interviews with employees, supervisors, managers, hiring officials; and

(iii) Where necessary, an off-site analysis of information supplied by the contractor or otherwise gathered during or pursuant to the on-site review.

(2) *Off-site review of records.* An analysis and evaluation of the AAP (or any part thereof) and supporting documentation, and other documents related to the contractor's personnel policies and employment actions that may be relevant to a determination of whether the contractor has complied with the requirements of the Executive Order and regulations;

(3) *Compliance check.* A determination of whether the contractor has maintained records consistent with Sec. 60-1.12; at the contractor's option, the documents may be provided either on-site or off-site; or a visit to the establishment to ascertain whether data and other information previously submitted by the contractor are complete and accurate; whether the contractor has maintained records consistent with Sec. 60-1.12; and/or whether the contractor has developed an AAP consistent with Sec. 60-1.40; or

(4) *Focused review.* An on-site review restricted to one or more components of the contractor's organization or one or more aspects of the contractor's employment practices.

(b) Where deficiencies are found to exist, reasonable efforts shall be made to secure compliance through conciliation and persuasion. Before the contractor can be found to be in compliance with the order, it must make a specific commitment, in writing, to correct any such deficiencies. The commitment must include the precise action to be taken and dates for completion. The time period allotted shall be no longer than the minimum period necessary to effect such changes. Upon approval of the commitment, the contractor may be considered in compliance, on condition that the commitments are faithfully kept. The contractor shall be notified that making such commitments does not preclude future determinations of noncompliance based on a finding that the commitments are not sufficient to achieve compliance.

(c) [Reserved]

(d) *Preaward compliance evaluations.* Each agency shall include in the invitation for bids for each formally advertised nonconstruction contract or state at the outset of negotiations for each negotiated contract, that if the award, when let, should total $10 million or more, the prospective contractor and its known first-tier subcontractors with subcontracts of $10 million or more shall be subject to a compliance evaluation before the award of the contract unless OFCCP has conducted an evaluation and found them to be in compliance with the Order within the preceding 24 months. The awarding agency will notify OFCCP and request appropriate action and findings in accordance with this subsection. Within 15 days of the notice OFCCP will inform the awarding agency of its intention to conduct a preaward compliance evaluation. If OFCCP does not inform the awarding agency within that period of its intention to conduct a preaward compliance evaluation, clearance shall be presumed and the awarding agency is authorized to proceed with the award. If OFCCP informs the awarding agency of its intention to conduct a preaward compliance evaluation, OFCCP shall be allowed an additional 20 days after the date that it so informs the awarding agency to provide its conclusions. If OFCCP does not provide the awarding agency with its conclusions within that period, clearance shall be presumed and the awarding agency is authorized to proceed with the award.

(e) *Submission of Documents; Standard Affirmative Action Formats.* Each prime contractor or subcontractor with 50 or more employees and a contract of $50,000 or more is required to develop a written affirmative action program for each of its establishments (Sec. 60-1.40). If a contractor fails to submit an affirmative action program and supporting documents, including the workforce analysis, within 30 days of a request, the enforcement procedures specified in Sec. 60-1.26(b) shall be applicable. Contractors may reach agreement with OFCCP on nationwide AAP formats or on frequency of updating statistics.

(f) *Confidentiality and relevancy of information.* If the contractor is concerned with the confidentiality of such information as lists of employee names, reasons for termination, or pay data, then alphabetic or numeric coding or the use of an index of pay and pay ranges, consistent with the ranges assigned to each job group, are acceptable for purposes of the compliance evaluation. The contractor must provide full access to all relevant data on-site as required by Sec. 60-1.43. Where necessary, the compliance officer may take information made available during the on-site evaluation off-site for further analysis. An off-site analysis should be conducted where issues have arisen concerning deficiencies or an apparent violation which, in the judgment of the compliance officer, should be more thoroughly analyzed off-site before a determination of compliance is made. The contractor must provide all data determined by the compliance officer to be necessary for off-site analysis. Such data may only be coded if the contractor makes the key to the code available to the compliance officer. If the contractor believes that particular information which is to be taken off-site is not relevant to compliance with the Executive Order, the contractor may request a ruling by the OFCCP District/Area Director. The OFCCP District/Area Director shall issue a ruling within 10 days. The contractor may appeal that ruling to the OFCCP Regional Director within 10 days. The Regional Director shall issue a final ruling within 10 days. Pending a final ruling, the information in question must be made available to the compliance officer off-site, but shall be considered a part of the investigatory file and subject to the provisions of paragraph (g) of this section. The agency shall take all necessary precautions to safeguard the confidentiality of such information until a final determination is made. Such information may not be copied by OFCCP and access to the information shall be limited to the compliance officer and personnel involved in the determination of relevancy. Data determined to be not relevant to the investigation will be returned to the contractor immediately.

(g) *Public access to information.* OFCCP will treat information obtained in the compliance evaluation as confidential to the maximum extent the information is exempt from public disclosure under the Freedom of Information Act, 5 U.S.C. 552. It is the practice of OFCCP not to release data where the contractor is still in business, and the contractor indicates, and through the Department of Labor review process it is determined, that the data are confidential and sensitive and that the release of data would subject the contractor to commercial harm.

60-1.21 Filing complaints.

Complaints shall be filed within 180 days of the alleged violation unless the time for filing is extended by the Deputy Assistant Secretary for good cause shown.

60-1.22 Where to file.

Complaints may be filed with the OFCCP, 200 Construction Avenue, N.W., Washington, D.C. 20210, or with any OFCCP regional or area office.

60-1.23 Contents of complaint.

(a) The complaint shall include the name, address, and telephone number of the complainant, the name and address of the contractor or subcontractor committing the alleged discrimination, a description of the acts considered to be discriminatory, and any other pertinent information which will assist in the investigation and resolution of the complaint. The complaint shall be signed by the complainant or his/her authorized representative. Complaints alleging class type violations which do not identify the alleged discriminatee or discriminatees will be accepted, provided the other requirements of this paragraph are met.

(b) If a complaint contains incomplete information, OFCCP shall seek the needed information from the complainant. In the event such information is not furnished to the Deputy Assistant Secretary within 60 days of the date of such request, the case may be closed.

60-1.24 Processing of matters.

(a) *Complaints.* OFCCP may refer appropriate complaints to the Equal Employment Opportunity Commission (EEOC) for processing under Title VII of the Civil Rights Act of 1964, as amended, rather than processing under E.O. 11246 and the regulations in this chapter. Upon referring complaints to the EEOC, OFCCP shall promptly notify complainant(s) and the contractor of such referral.

(b) *Complaint investigations.* In conducting complaint investigations, OFCCP shall, as a minimum, conduct a thorough evaluation of the allegations of the complaint and shall be responsible for developing a complete case record. The case record should contain the name, address, and telephone number of each person interviewed, the interview statements, copies, transcripts, or summaries (where appropriate) of pertinent documents, a reference to at least one covered contract, and a narrative report of the investigation with references to exhibits and other evidence which relate to the alleged violations.

(c)(1) [Reserved]

(2) If any complaint investigation or compliance review indicates a violation of the equal opportunity clause, the matter should be resolved by informal means whenever possible. Such informal means may include the holding of a compliance conference.

(3) Where any complaint investigation or compliance review indicates a violation of the equal opportunity clause and the matter has not been resolved by informal means, the Deputy Assistant Secretary shall proceed in accordance with Sec. 60-1.26.

(4) When a prime contractor or subcontractor, without a hearing, shall have complied with the recommendations or orders of the Deputy Assistant Secretary and believes such recommendations or orders to be erroneous, he shall, upon filing a request therefor within ten days of such compliance, be afforded an opportunity for a hearing and review of the alleged erroneous action.

(5) For reasonable cause shown, the Deputy Assistant Secretary may reconsider or cause to be reconsidered any matter on his/her own motion or pursuant to a request.

(d) *Reports to the Deputy Assistant Secretary.*

(1) With the exception of complaints which have been referred to EEOC, within 60 days from receipt of a complaint or within such additional time as may be allowed by the Deputy Assistant Secretary for good cause shown, the complaint shall be processed and the case record developed containing the following information:

(i) Name and address of the complainant;

(ii) Brief summary of findings, including a statement regarding the contractor's compliance or noncompliance with the requirements of the equal opportunity clause;

(iii) A statement of the disposition of the case, including any corrective action taken and any sanctions or penalties imposed or, whenever appropriate, the recommended corrective action and sanctions or penalties.

(2) A written report of every preaward compliance review required by this regulation or otherwise required by the Deputy Assistant Secretary, shall be developed and maintained.

(3) A written report of every other compliance review or any other matter processed involving an apparent violation of the equal opportunity clause shall be made. Such report shall contain a brief summary of the findings, including a statement of conclusions regarding the contractor's compliance or noncompliance with the requirements of the order, and a statement of the disposition of the case, including any corrective action taken or recommended and any sanctions or penalties imposed or recommended.

60-1.25 Assumption of jurisdiction by or referrals to the Deputy Assistant Secretary.

The Deputy Assistant Secretary may inquire into the status of any matter pending before an agency. Where he considers it necessary or appropriate to the achievement of the purposes of the order, he may assume jurisdiction over the matter and proceed as provided herein. Whenever the Deputy Assistant Secretary assumes jurisdiction over any matter, or an agency refers any matter he may conduct, or have conducted, such investigations, hold such hearings, make such findings, issue such recommendations and directives, order such sanctions and penalties, and take such other action as may be necessary or appropriate to achieve the purposes of the order. The Deputy Assistant Secretary shall promptly notify the agency of any corrective action to be taken or any sanctions to be taken or any sanction to be imposed by the agency. The agency shall take such action, and report the results thereof to the Deputy Assistant Secretary within the time specified.

60-1.26 Enforcement proceedings.

(a) *General.*

(1) Violations of the Order, the equal opportunity clause, the regulations in this chapter, or applicable construction industry equal employment opportunity requirements, may result in the institution of administrative or judicial enforcement proceedings. Violations may be found based upon, inter alia, any of the following:

(i) The results of a complaint investigation;

(ii) The results of a compliance evaluation;

(iii) Analysis of an affirmative action program;

(iv) The results of an onsite review of the contractor's compliance with the Order and its implementing regulations;

(v) A contractor's refusal to submit an affirmative action program;

(vi) A contractor's refusal to allow an onsite compliance evaluation to be conducted;

(vii) A contractor's refusal to provide data for offsite review or analysis as required by the regulations in this chapter;

(viii) A contractor's refusal to establish, maintain and supply records or other information as required by the regulations in this chapter or applicable construction industry requirements;

(ix) A contractor's alteration or falsification of records and information required to be maintained by the regulations in this chapter; or

(x) Any substantial or material violation or the threat of a substantial or material violation of the contractual provisions of the Order, or of the rules or regulations in this chapter.

(2) OFCCP may seek back pay and other make whole relief for victims of discrimination identified during a complaint investigation or compliance evaluation. Such individuals need not have filed a complaint as a prerequisite to OFCCP seeking such relief on their behalf. Interest on back pay shall be calculated from the date of the loss and compounded quarterly at the percentage rate established by the Internal Revenue Service for the underpayment of taxes.

(b) *Administrative enforcement.* (1) OFCCP may refer matters to the Solicitor of Labor with a recommendation for the institution of administrative enforcement proceedings, which may be brought to enjoin violations, to seek appropriate relief, and to impose appropriate sanctions. The referral may be made when violations have not been corrected in accordance with the conciliation procedures in this chapter, or when OFCCP determines that referral for consideration of formal enforcement (rather than settlement) is appropriate. However, if a contractor refuses to submit an affirmative action program, or refuses to supply records or other requested information, or refuses to allow OFCCP access to its premises for an onsite review, and if conciliation efforts under this chapter are unsuccessful, OFCCP may immediately refer the matter to the Solicitor, notwithstanding other requirements of this chapter.

(2) Administrative enforcement proceedings shall be conducted under the control and supervision of the Solicitor of Labor and under the Rules of Practice for Administrative Proceedings to Enforce Equal Opportunity under Executive Order 11246 contained in part 6030 of this chapter and the Rules of Evidence set out in the Rules of Practice and Procedure for Administrative Hearings Before the Office of Administrative Law Judges contained in 29 CFR part 18, subpart B: Provided, That a Final Administrative Order shall be issued within on year from the date of the issuance of the recommended findings, conclusions and decision of the Administrative Law Judge, or the submission of any exceptions and responses to exceptions to such decision (if any), whichever is later.

(c) Referrals to the Department of Justice. (1) The Deputy Assistant Secretary may refer matters to the Department of Justice with a recommendation for the institution of judicial enforcement proceedings. There are no procedural prerequisites to a referral to the Department of Justice. Such referrals may be accomplished without proceeding through the conciliation procedures in this chapter, and a referral may be made at any stage in the procedures under this chapter.

(2) Whenever a matter has been referred to the Department of Justice for consideration of judicial enforcement, the Attorney General may bring a civil action in the appropriate

district court of the United States requesting a temporary restraining order, preliminary or permanent injunction (including relief against noncontractors, including labor unions, who seek to thwart the implementation of the Order and regulations), and an order for such additional sanctions or relief, including back pay, deemed necessary or appropriate to ensure the full enjoyment of the rights secured by the Order, or any of the above in this paragraph (c)(2).

(3) The Attorney General is authorized to conduct such investigation of the facts as he/she deem necessary or appropriate to carry out his/her responsibilities under the regulations in this chapter.

(4) Prior to the institution of any judicial proceedings, the Attorney General, on behalf of the Deputy Assistant Secretary, is authorized to make reasonable efforts to secure compliance with the contract provisions of the Order. The Attorney General may do so by providing the contractor and any other respondent with reasonable notice of his/her findings, his/her intent to file suit, and the actions he/she believes necessary to obtain compliance with the contract provisions of the Order without contested litigation, and by offering the contractor and any other respondent a reasonable opportunity for conference and conciliation, in an effort to obtain such compliance without contested litigation.

(5) As used in the regulations in this Part, the Attorney General shall mean the Attorney General, the Assistant Attorney General for Civil Rights, or any other person authorized by regulations or practice to act for the Attorney General with respect to the enforcement of equal employment opportunity laws, orders and regulations generally, or in a particular matter or case.

(6) The Deputy Assistant Secretary or his/her designee, and representatives of the Attorney General may consult from time to time to determine what investigations should be conducted to determine whether contractors or groups of contractors or other persons may be engaged in patterns or practices in violation of the Executive Order or these regulations, or of resistance to or interference with the full enjoyment of any of the rights secured by them, warranting judicial proceedings.

(d) *Initiation of lawsuits by the Attorney General without referral from the Deputy Assistant Secretary.* In addition to initiating lawsuits upon referral under this section, the Attorney General may, subject to approval by the Deputy Assistant Secretary, initiate independent investigations of contractors which he/she has reason to believe may be in violation of the Order or the rules and regulations issued pursuant thereto. If, upon completion of such an investigation, the Attorney General determines that the contractor has in fact violated the Order or the rules and regulations issued thereunder, he/she shall make reasonable efforts to secure compliance with the contract provisions of the Order. He/she may do so by providing the contractor and any other respondent with reasonable notice of the Department of Justice's findings, its intent to file suit, and the actions that the Attorney General believes are necessary to obtain compliance with the contract provisions of the Order without contested litigation, and by offering the contractor and any other respondent a reasonable opportunity for conference and conciliation in an effort to obtain such compliance without contested litigation. If these efforts are unsuccessful, the Attorney General may, upon approval by the Deputy Assistant Secretary, bring a civil action in the appropriate district court of the United States requesting a temporary restraining order, preliminary or permanent injunction, and an order for such additional sanctions or equitable relief, including back pay, deemed necessary or appropriate to ensure the full enjoyment of the rights secured by the Order or any of the above in this paragraph (d).

(e) To the extent applicable, this section and part 60-30 of this chapter shall govern proceedings resulting from any Deputy Assistant Secretary's determinations under Sec. 60-2.2(b) of this chapter.

60-1.27 Sanctions.

(a) *General.* The sanctions described in subsections (1), (5), and (6) of section 209(a) of the Order may be exercised only by or with the approval of the Deputy Assistant Secretary. Referral of any matter arising under the Order to the Department of Justice or to the Equal Employment Opportunity Commission shall be made by the Deputy Assistant Secretary.

(b) *Debarment.* A contractor may be debarred from receiving future contracts or modifications or extensions of existing contracts, subject to reinstatement pursuant to Sec. 60-1.31, for any violation of Executive Order 11246 or the implementing rules, regulations and orders of the Secretary of Labor. Debarment may be imposed for an indefinite term or for a fixed minimum period of at least six months.

60-1.28 Show cause notices.

When the Deputy Assistant Secretary has reasonable cause to believe that a contractor has violated the equal opportunity clause he may issue a notice requiring the contractor to show cause, within 30 days, why monitoring, enforcement proceedings or other appropriate action to ensure compliance should not be instituted.

60-1.29 Preaward notices.

(a) *Preaward compliance reviews.* Upon the request of the Deputy Assistant Secretary, agencies shall not enter into contracts or approve the entry into contracts or subcontracts with any bidder, prospective prime contractor, or proposed subcontractor named by the Deputy Assistant Secretary until a preaward compliance review has been conducted and the Deputy Assistant Secretary or his designee has approved a determination that the bidder, prospective prime contractor or proposed subcontractor will be able to comply with the provisions of the equal opportunity clause.

(b) *Other special preaward procedures.* Upon the request of the Deputy Assistant Secretary, agencies shall not enter into contracts or approve the entry into subcontracts with any bidder; prospective prime contractor or proposed subcontractor specified by the Deputy Assistant Secretary until the agency has complied with the directions contained in the request.

60-1.30 Notification of agencies.

The Deputy Assistant Secretary shall ensure that the heads of all agencies are notified of any debarment taken against any contractor.

60-1.31 Reinstatement of ineligible contractors.

A contractor debarred from further contracts for an indefinite period under the Order may request reinstatement in a letter filed with the Deputy Assistant Secretary at any time after the effective date of the debarment. A contractor debarred for a fixed period may request reinstatement in a letter filed with the Deputy Assistant Secretary 30 days prior to the expiration of the fixed debarment period, or at any time thereafter. The filing of a reinstatement request 30 days before a fixed debarment period ends will not result in early reinstatement. In connection with the reinstatement proceedings, all debarred contractors shall be required to show that they have established and will carry out employment policies and practices in compliance with the Order and implementing regulations. Before reaching a decision, the Deputy Assistant Secretary may conduct a compliance evaluation of the contractor and may require the contractor to supply additional information regarding the request for reinstatement. The Deputy Assistant Secretary shall issue a written decision on the request.

60-1.32 Intimidation and interference.

(a) The contractor, subcontractor or applicant shall not harass, intimidate, threaten, coerce, or discriminate against any individual because the individual has engaged in or may engage in any of the following activities:

(1) Filing a complaint;

(2) Assisting or participating in any manner in an investigation, compliance evaluation, hearing, or any other activity related to the administration of the Order or any other Federal, state or local law requiring equal opportunity;

(3) Opposing any act or practice made unlawful by the Order or any other Federal, state or local law requiring equal opportunity; or

(4) Exercising any other right protected by the Order.

(b) The contractor, subcontractor or applicant shall ensure that all persons under its control do not engage in such harassment, intimidation, threats, coercion or discrimination. The sanctions and penalties contained in this part may be exercised by OFCCP against any contractor, subcontractor or applicant who violates this obligation.

60-1.33 Conciliation agreements.

If a compliance review, complaint investigation or other review by OFCCP or its representative indicates a material violation of the equal opportunity clause, and (1) if the contractor, subcontractor or bidder is willing to correct the violations and/or deficiencies, and (2) if OFCCP or its representative determines that settlement (rather than referral for consideration of formal enforcement) is appropriate, a written agreement shall be required. The agreement shall provide for such remedial action as may be necessary to correct the violations and/or deficiencies noted, including, where appropriate (but not necessarily limited to), remedies such as back pay and retroactive seniority.

60-1.34 Violation of a conciliation agreement.

When a conciliation agreement has been violated, the following procedures are applicable:

(a) A written notice shall be sent to the contractor setting forth the violations alleged and summarizing the supporting evidence. The contractor shall have 15 days from receipt of the notice to respond, except in those cases in which such a delay would result in irreparable injury to the employment rights of affected employees or applicants.

(b) During the 15-day period the contractor may demonstrate in writing that it has not violated its commitments.

(c) If the contractor is unable to demonstrate that it has not violated its commitments, or if the complaint alleges irreparable injury, enforcement proceedings may be initiated immediately without issuing a show cause notice or proceeding through any other requirement contained in this chapter.

(d) In any proceeding involving an alleged violation of a conciliation agreement, OFCCP may seek enforcement of the agreement itself and shall not be required to present proof of the underlying violations resolved by the agreement.

Subpart C. Ancillary Matters

60-1.40 Affirmative action programs.

(a)(1) Each nonconstruction (supply and service) contractor must develop and maintain a written affirmative action program for each of its establishments, if it has 50 or more employees and:

(i) Has a contract of $50,000 or more; or

(ii) Has Government bills of lading which, in any 12-month period, total or can reasonably be expected to total $50,000 or more; or

(iii) Serves as a depository of Government funds in any amount; or

(iv) Is a financial institution which is an issuing and paying agent for U.S. savings bonds and savings notes in any amount.

(2) Each contractor and subcontractor must require each nonconstruction subcontractor to develop and maintain a written affirmative action program for each of its establishments if it has 50 or more employees and:

(i) Has a subcontract of $50,000 or more; or

(ii) Has Government bills of lading which, in any 12-month period, total or can reasonably be expected to total $50,000 or more; or

(iii) Serves as a depository of Government funds in any amount; or

(iv) Is a financial institution which is an issuing and paying agent for U.S. savings bonds and savings notes in any amount.

(b) Nonconstruction contractors should refer to Part 60-2 for specific affirmative action requirements. Construction contractors should refer to Part 60-4 for specific affirmative action requirements.

60-1.41 Solicitations or advertisements for employees.

In solicitations or advertisements for employees placed by or on behalf of a prime contractor or subcontractor, the requirements of paragraph (2) of the equal opportunity clause shall be satisfied whenever the prime contractor or subcontractor complies with any of the following:

(a) States expressly in the solicitations or advertising that all qualified applicants will receive consideration for employment without regard to race, color, religion, sex, or national origin;

(b) Uses display or other advertising, and the advertising includes an appropriate insignia prescribed by the Deputy Assistant Secretary. The use of the insignia is considered subject to the provisions of 18 U.S.C. 701;

(c) Uses a single advertisement, and the advertisement is grouped with other advertisements under a caption which clearly states that all employers in the group assure all qualified applicants equal consideration for employment without regard to race, color, religion, sex, or national origin;

(d) Uses a single advertisement in which appears in clearly distinguishable type the phrase "an equal opportunity employer."

60-1.42 Notices to be posted.

(a) Unless alternative notices are prescribed by the Deputy Assistant Secretary, the notices which contractors are required to post by paragraphs (1) and (3) of the equal opportunity clause in Sec. 601.4 will contain the following language and be provided by the contracting or administering agencies:

EQUAL EMPLOYMENT OPPORTUNITY IS THE LAW—DISCRIMINATION IS PROHIBITED BY THE CIVIL RIGHTS ACT OF 1964 AND BY EXECUTIVE ORDER NO. 11246

Title VII of the Civil Rights Act of 1964-*Administered by*:

THE EQUAL EMPLOYMENT OPPORTUNITY COMMISSION

Prohibits discrimination because of Race, Color, Religion, Sex, or National Origin by Employers with 15 or more employees, by Labor Organizations, by Employment Agencies, and by Apprenticeship or Training Programs

Any person Who believes he or she has been discriminated against should contact

The Equal Employment Opportunity Commission
1801 L Street NW., Washington, DC 20507

Executive Order No. 11246-*Administered by*:

THE OFFICE OF FEDERAL CONTRACT COMPLIANCE PROGRAMS

Prohibits discrimination because of Race, Color, Religion, Sex, or National Origin, and requires affirmative action to ensure equality of opportunity in all aspects of employment. By all Federal Government Contractors and Subcontractors, and by Contractors Performing Work Under a Federally Assisted Construction Contract, regardless of the number of employees in either case. Any person Who believes he or she has been discriminated against Should Contact The Office of Federal Contract Compliance Programs U.S. Department of Labor, Washington, DC 20210

(b) The requirements of paragraph (3) of the equal opportunity clause will be satisfied whenever the prime contractor or subcontractor posts copies of the notification prescribed by or pursuant to paragraph (a) of this section in conspicuous places available to employees, applicants for employment, and representatives of each labor union or other organization representing his employees with which he has a collective bargaining agreement or other contract or understanding.

60-1.43 Access to records and site of employment.

Each contractor shall permit access during normal business hours to its premises for the purpose of conducting onsite compliance evaluations and complaint investigations. Each contractor shall permit the inspecting and copying of such books and accounts and records, including computerized records, and other material as may be relevant to the matter under investigation and pertinent to compliance with the Order, and the rules and regulations promulgated pursuant thereto by the agency, or the Deputy Assistant Secretary. Information obtained in this manner shall be used only in connection with the administration of the Order, the Civil Rights Act of 1964 (as amended), and any other law that is or may be enforced in whole or in part by OFCCP.

60-1.44 Rulings and interpretations.

Rulings under or interpretations of the order or the regulations contained in this part shall be made by the Secretary or his designee.

60-1.45 Existing contracts and subcontracts.

All contracts and subcontracts in effect prior to October 24, 1965, which are not subsequently modified shall be administered in accordance with the nondiscrimination provisions of any prior applicable Executive orders. Any contract or subcontract modified on or after October 24, 1965, shall be subject to Executive Order 11246. Complaints received by and violations coming to the attention of agencies regarding contracts and subcontracts which were subject to Executive Orders 10925 and 11114 shall be processed as if they were complaints regarding violations of this order.

60-1.46 Delegation of authority by the Deputy Assistant Secretary.

The Deputy Assistant Secretary is authorized to redelegate the authority given to him by the regulations in this part. The authority redelegated by the Deputy Assistant Secretary pursuant to the regulations in this part shall be exercised under his general direction and control.

* * *

Part 60-2. Affirmative Action Programs

SUBPART A. GENERAL

60-2.1 Scope and application.

(a) *General.* The requirements of this part apply to nonconstruction (supply and service) contractors. The regulations prescribe the contents of affirmative action programs, standards and procedures for evaluating the compliance of affirmative action programs implemented pursuant to this part, and related matters.

(b) *Who must develop affirmative action programs.*

(1) Each nonconstruction contractor must develop and maintain a written affirmative action program for each of its establishments if it has 50 or more employees and:

(i) Has a contract of $50,000 or more; or

(ii) Has Government bills of lading which, in any 12-month period, total or can reasonably be expected to total $50,000 or more; or

(iii) Serves as a depository of Government funds in any amount; or

(iv) Is a financial institution which is an issuing and paying agent for U.S. savings bonds and savings notes in any amount.

(2) Each contractor and subcontractor must require each nonconstruction subcontractor to develop and maintain a written affirmative action program for each of its establishments if it has 50 or more employees and:

(i) Has a subcontract of $50,000 or more; or

(ii) Has Government bills of lading which, in any 12-month period, total or can reasonably be expected to total $50,000 or more; or

(iii) Serves as a depository of Government funds in any amount; or

(iv) Is a financial institution which is an issuing and paying agent for U.S. savings bonds and savings notes in any amount.

(c) *When affirmative action programs must be developed.* The affirmative action programs required under paragraph (b) of this section must be developed within 120 days from the commencement of a contract and must be updated annually.

(d) *Who is included in affirmative action programs.* Contractors subject to the affirmative action program requirements must develop and maintain a written affirmative action program for each of their establishments. Each employee in the contractor's workforce must be included in an affirmative action program. Each employee must be included in the affirmative action program of the establishment at which he or she works, except that:

(1) Employees who work at establishments other than that of the manager to whom they report must be included in the affirmative action program of their manager.

(2) Employees who work at an establishment where the contractor employs fewer than 50 employees may be included under any of the following three options: In an affirmative action program which covers just that establishment; in the affirmative action program which covers the location of the personnel function which supports the establishment; or in the affirmative action program which covers the location of the official to whom they report.

(3) Employees for whom selection decisions are made at a higher level establishment within the organization must be included in the affirmative action program of the establishment where the selection decision is made.

(4) If a contractor wishes to establish an affirmative action program other than by establishment, the contractor may reach agreement with OFCCP on the development and use of affirmative action programs based on functional or business units. The Deputy Assistant Secretary, or his or her designee, must approve such agreements. Agreements allowing the use of functional or business unit affirmative action programs cannot be construed to limit or restrict how the OFCCP structures its compliance evaluations.

(e) *How to identify employees included in affirmative action programs other than where they are located.* If pursuant to paragraphs (d)(1) through (3) of this section employees are included in an affirmative action program for an establishment other than the one in which the employees are located, the organizational profile and job group analysis of the affirmative action program in which the employees are included must be annotated to identify the actual location of such employees. If the establishment at which the employees actually are located maintains an affirmative action program, the organizational profile and job group analysis of that program must be annotated to identify the program in which the employees are included.

60-2.2 Agency action.

(a) Any contractor required by § 60-2.1 to develop and maintain a written affirmative action program at each of its establishments that has not complied with that section is not in full compliance with Executive Order 11246, as amended. When a contractor is required to submit its affirmative action program to OFCCP (e.g., for a compliance evaluation), the affirmative action program will be deemed to have been accepted by the Government at the time OFCCP notifies the contractor of completion of the compliance evaluation or other action, unless within 45 days thereafter the Deputy Assistant Secretary has disapproved such program.

(b) If, in determining such contractor's responsibility for an award of a contract, it comes to the contracting officer's attention, through sources within his/her agency or through the OFCCP or other Government agencies, that the contractor does not have an affirmative action program at each of its establishments, or has substantially deviated from such an approved affirmative action program, or has failed to develop or implement an affirmative action program which complies with the regulations in this chapter, the contracting officer must declare the contractor/bidder nonresponsible and so notify the contractor and the Deputy Assistant Secretary, unless the contracting officer otherwise affirmatively determines that the contractor is able to comply with the equal employment obligations. Any contractor/bidder which has been declared nonresponsible in accordance with the provisions of this section may request the Deputy Assistant Secretary to determine that the responsibility of the contractor/bidder raises substantial issues of law or fact to the extent that a hearing is required. Such request shall set forth the basis upon which the contractor/bidder seeks such a determination. If the Deputy Assistant Secretary,, in his/her sole discretion, determines that substantial issues of law or fact exist, an administrative or judicial proceeding may be commenced in accordance with the regulations contained in §60-1.26; or the Deputy Assistant Secretary may require the investigation or compliance review be developed further or additional conciliation be conducted: *Provided*, That during any pre-award conferences, every effort will be made through the processes of conciliation, mediation, and persuasion to develop an acceptable affirmative action program meeting the standards and guidelines set forth in this part so that, in the performance of the contract, the contractor is able to meet its equal employment obligations in accordance with the equal opportunity clause and applicable rules, regulations, and orders: *Provided further*, That a contractor/bidder may not be declared nonresponsible more than twice due to past noncompliance with the equal opportunity clause at a particular establishment or facility without receiving prior notice and an opportunity for a hearing.

(c)(1) Immediately upon finding that a contractor has no affirmative action program, or has deviated substantially from an approved affirmative action program, or has failed to develop or implement an affirmative action program which complies with the requirements of the regulations in this chapter, that fact shall be recorded in the investigation file. Except as provided in §60-1.26(b)(1), whenever administrative enforcement is contemplated, the notice to the contractor shall be issued giving the contractor 30 days to show cause why enforcement proceedings under section 209(a) of Executive Order 11246, as amended, should not be instituted. The notice to show cause should contain:

(i) An itemization of the sections of the Executive Order and of the regulations with which the contractor has been found in apparent violation, and a summary of the conditions, practices, facts, or circumstances which give rise to each apparent violation;

(ii) The corrective actions necessary to achieve compliance or, as may be appropriate, the concepts and principles of an acceptable remedy and/or the corrective action results anticipated;

(iii) A request for a written response to the findings, including commitments to corrective action or the presentation of opposing facts and evidence; and

(iv) A suggested date for the conciliation conference.

(2) If the contractor fails to show good cause for its failure or fails to remedy that failure by developing and implementing an acceptable affirmative action program within 30 days, the case file shall be processed for enforcement proceedings pursuant to § 60-1.26 of this chapter. If an administrative complaint is filed, the contractor shall have 20 days to request a hearing. If a request for hearing has not been received within 20 days from the filing of the administrative complaint, the matter shall proceed in accordance with Part 60-30 of this chapter.

(3) During the "show cause" period of 30 days, every effort will be made through conciliation, mediation, and persuasion to resolve the deficiencies which led to the determination of nonresponsibility. If satisfactory adjustments designed to bring the contractor into compliance are not concluded, the case shall be processed for enforcement proceedings pursuant to § 60-1.26 of this chapter.

(d) During the "show cause" period and formal proceedings, each contracting agency must continue to determine the contractor's responsibility in considering whether or not to award a new or additional contract.

SUBPART B. PURPOSE AND CONTENTS OF AFFIRMATIVE ACTION PROGRAMS

60-2.10 General purpose and contents of affirmative action programs.

(a) *Purpose.*

(1) An affirmative action program is a management tool designed to ensure equal employment opportunity. A central premise underlying affirmative action is that, absent discrimination, over time a contractor's workforce, generally, will reflect the gender, racial and ethnic profile of the labor pools from which the contractor recruits and selects. Affirmative action programs contain a diagnostic component which includes a number of quantitative analyses designed to evaluate the composition of the workforce of the contractor and compare it to the composition of the relevant labor pools. Affirmative action programs also include action-oriented programs. If women and minorities are not being employed at a rate to be expected given their availability in the relevant labor pool, the contractor's affirmative action program includes specific practical steps designed to address this underutilization. Effective affirmative action programs also include internal auditing and reporting systems as a means of measuring the contractor's progress toward achieving the workforce that would be expected in the absence of discrimination.

(2) An affirmative action program also ensures equal employment opportunity by institutionalizing the contractor's commitment to equality in every aspect of the employment process. Therefore, as part of its affirmative action program, a contractor monitors and examines its employment decisions and compensation systems to evaluate the impact of those systems on women and minorities.

(3) An affirmative action program is, thus, more than a paperwork exercise. An affirmative action program includes those policies, practices, and procedures that the contractor implements to ensure that all qualified applicants and employees are receiving an equal opportunity for recruitment, selection, advancement, and every other term and privilege associated with employment. Affirmative action, ideally, is a part of the way the contractor regularly conducts its business. OFCCP has found that when an

affirmative action program is approached from this perspective, as a powerful management tool, there is a positive correlation between the presence of affirmative action and the absence of discrimination.

(b) *Contents of affirmative action programs.*

(1) An affirmative action program must include the following quantitative analyses:

(i) Organizational profile-§ 60-2.11;

(ii) Job group analysis-§ 60-2.12;

(iii) Placement of incumbents in job groups-§ 60-2.13;

(iv) Determining availability-§ 60-2.14;

(v) Comparing incumbency to availability-§ 60-2.15; and

(vi) Placement goals-§ 60-2.16.

(2) In addition, an affirmative action program must include the following components specified in § 60-2.17 of this part:

(i) Designation of responsibility for implementation;

(ii) Identification of problem areas;

(iii) Action-oriented programs; and

(iv) Periodic internal audits.

(c) *Documentation.* Contractors must maintain and make available to OFCCP documentation of their compliance with §§ 60-2.11 through 60-2.17.

60-2.11 Organizational profile.

(a) *Purpose.* An organizational profile is a depiction of the staffing pattern within an establishment. It is one method contractors use to determine whether barriers to equal employment opportunity exist in their organizations. The profile provides an overview of the workforce at the establishment that may assist in identifying organizational units where women or minorities are underrepresented or concentrated. The contractor must use either the organizational display or the workforce analysis as its organizational profile:

(b) *Organizational display.*

(1) An organizational display is a detailed graphical or tabular chart, text, spreadsheet or similar presentation of the contractor's organizational structure. The organizational display must identify each organizational unit in the establishment, and show the relationship of each organizational unit to the other organizational units in the establishment.

(2) An organizational unit is any component that is part of the contractor's corporate structure. In a more traditional organization, an organizational unit might be a department, division, section, branch, group or similar component. In a less traditional organization, an organizational unit might be a project team, job family, or similar component. The term includes an umbrella unit (such as a department) that contains a number of subordinate units, and it separately includes each of the subordinate units (such as sections or branches).

(3) For each organizational unit, the organizational display must indicate the following:

(i) The name of the unit;

(ii) The job title, gender, race, and ethnicity of the unit supervisor (if the unit has a supervisor);

(iii) The total number of male and female incumbents; and

(iv) The total number of male and female incumbents in each of the following groups: Blacks, Hispanics, Asians/Pacific Islanders, and American Indians/Alaskan Natives.

(c) *Workforce analysis.*

(1) A workforce analysis is a listing of each job title as appears in applicable collective bargaining agreements or payroll records ranked from the lowest paid to the highest paid within each department or other similar organizational unit including departmental or unit supervision.

(2) If there are separate work units or lines of progression within a department, a separate list must be provided for each such work unit, or line, including unit supervisors. For lines of progression there must be indicated the order of jobs in the line through which an employee could move to the top of the line.

(3) Where there are no formal progression lines or usual promotional sequences, job titles should be listed by department, job families, or disciplines, in order of wage rates or salary ranges.

(4) For each job title, the total number of incumbents, the total number of male and female incumbents, and the total number of male and female incumbents in each of the following groups must be given: Blacks, Hispanics, Asians/Pacific Islanders, and American Indians/Alaskan Natives. The wage rate or salary range for each job title must be given. All job titles, including all managerial job titles, must be listed.

60-2.12 Job group analysis.

(a) *Purpose.* A job group analysis is a method of combining job titles within the contractor's establishment. This is the first step in the contractor's comparison of the representation of minorities and women in its workforce with the estimated availability of minorities and women qualified to be employed.

(b) In the job group analysis, jobs at the establishment with similar content, wage rates, and opportunities, must be combined to form job groups. Similarity of content refers to the duties and responsibilities of the job titles which make up the job group. Similarity of opportunities refers to training, transfers, promotions, pay, mobility, and other career enhancement opportunities offered by the jobs within the job group.

(c) The job group analysis must include a list of the job titles that comprise each job group. If, pursuant to §§60-2.1(d) and (e) the job group analysis contains jobs that are located at another establishment, the job group analysis must be annotated to identify the actual location of those jobs. If the establishment at which the jobs actually are located maintains an affirmative action program, the job group analysis of that program must be annotated to identify the program in which the jobs are included.

(d) Except as provided in §60-2.1(d), all jobs located at an establishment must be reported in the job group analysis of that establishment.

(e) *Smaller employers.* If a contractor has a total workforce of fewer than 150 employees, the contractor may prepare a job group analysis that utilizes EEO-1 categories as job groups. EEO-1 categories refers to the nine occupational groups used in the Standard Form 100, the Employer Information EEO-1 Survey: Officials and managers, professionals, technicians, sales, office and clerical, craft workers (skilled), operatives (semiskilled), laborers (unskilled), and service workers.

60-2.13 Placement of incumbents in job groups.

The contractor must separately state the percentage of minorities and the percentage of women it employs in each job group established pursuant to § 60-2.12.

60-2.14 Determining availability.

(a) *Purpose.* Availability is an estimate of the number of qualified minorities or women available for employment in a given job group, expressed as a percentage of all qualified persons available for employment in the job group. The purpose of the availability determination is to establish a benchmark against which the demographic composition of the contractor's incumbent workforce can be compared in order to determine whether barriers to equal employment opportunity may exist within particular job groups.

(b) The contractor must separately determine the availability of minorities and women for each job group.

(c) In determining availability, the contractor must consider at least the following factors:

(1) The percentage of minorities or women with requisite skills in the reasonable recruitment area. The reasonable recruitment area is defined as the geographical area from which the contractor usually seeks or reasonably could seek workers to fill the positions in question.

(2) The percentage of minorities or women among those transferable and trainable within the contractor's organization. Trainable refers to those employees within the contractor's organization who could, with appropriate training which the contractor is reasonably able to provide, become promotable or transferable during the AAP year.

(d) The contractor must use the most current and discrete statistical information available to derive availability figures. Examples of such information include census data, data from local job service offices, and data from colleges or other training institutions.

(e) The contractor may not draw its reasonable recruitment area in such a way as to have the effect of excluding minorities or women. For each job group, the reasonable recruitment area must be identified, with a brief explanation of the rationale for selection of that recruitment area.

(f) The contractor may not define the pool of transferable and trainable employees in such a way as to have the effect of excluding minorities or women. For each job group, the pool of promotable, transferable, and trainable employees must be identified with a brief explanation of the rationale for the selection of that pool.

(g) Where a job group is composed of job titles with different availability rates, a composite availability figure for the job group must be calculated. The contractor must separately determine the availability for each job title within the job group and must determine the proportion of job group incumbents employed in each job title. The contractor must weight the availability for each job title by the proportion of job group incumbents employed in that job group. The sum of the weighted availability estimates for all job titles in the job group must be the composite availability for the job group.

60-2.15 Comparing incumbency to availability.

(a) The contractor must compare the percentage of minorities and women in each job group determined pursuant to § 60-2.13 with the availability for those job groups determined pursuant to § 60-2.14.

(b) When the percentage of minorities or women employed in a particular job group is less than would reasonably be expected given their availability percentage in that particular job group, the contractor must establish a placement goal in accordance with § 60-2.16.

60-2.16 Placement goals.

(a) *Purpose.* Placement goals serve as objectives or targets reasonably attainable by means of applying every good faith effort to make all aspects of the entire affirmative action program work. Placement goals also are used to measure progress toward achieving equal employment opportunity.

(b) A contractor's determination under § 60-2.15 that a placement goal is required constitutes neither a finding nor an admission of discrimination.

(c) Where, pursuant to § 60-2.15, a contractor is required to establish a placement goal for a particular job group, the contractor must establish a percentage annual placement goal at least equal to the availability figure derived for women or minorities, as appropriate, for that job group.

(d) The placement goal-setting process described above contemplates that contractors will, where required, establish a single goal for all minorities. In the event of a substantial disparity in the utilization of a particular minority group or in the utilization of men or women of a particular minority group, a contractor may be required to establish separate goals for those groups.

(e) In establishing placement goals, the following principles also apply:

(1) Placement goals may not be rigid and inflexible quotas, which must be met, nor are they to be considered as either a ceiling or a floor for the employment of particular groups. Quotas are expressly forbidden.

(2) In all employment decisions, the contractor must make selections in a nondiscriminatory manner. Placement goals do not provide the contractor with a justification to extend a preference to any individual, select an individual, or adversely affect an individual's employment status, on the basis of that person's race, color, religion, sex, or national origin.

(3) Placement goals do not create set-asides for specific groups, nor are they intended to achieve proportional representation or equal results.

(4) Placement goals may not be used to supersede merit selection principles. Affirmative action programs prescribed by the regulations in this part do not require a contractor to hire a person who lacks qualifications to perform the job successfully, or hire a less qualified person in preference to a more qualified one.

(f) A contractor extending a publicly announced preference for American Indians as is authorized in 41 CFR 60-1.5(a)(6) may reflect in its placement goals the permissive employment preference for American Indians living on or near an Indian reservation.

60-2.17 Additional required elements of affirmative action programs.

In addition to the elements required by § 60-2.10 through § 60-2.16, an acceptable affirmative action program must include the following:

(a) *Designation of responsibility.* The contractor must provide for the implementation of equal employment opportunity and the affirmative action program by assigning responsibility and accountability to an official of the organization. Depending upon the size of the contractor, this may be the official's sole responsibility. He or she must have the authority, resources, support of and access to top management to ensure the effective implementation of the affirmative action program.

(b) *Identification of problem areas.* The contractor must perform in-depth analyses of its total employment process to determine whether and where impediments to equal employment opportunity exist. At a minimum the contractor must evaluate:

(1) the workforce by organizational unit and job group to determine whether there are problems of minority or female utilization (i.e., employment in the unit or group), or of minority or female distribution (i.e., placement in the different jobs within the unit or group);

(2) personnel activity (applicant flow, hires, terminations, promotions, and other personnel actions) to determine whether there are selection disparities;

(3) compensation system(s) to determine whether there are gender-, race-, or ethnicity-based disparities;

(4) selection, recruitment, referral, and other personnel procedures to determine whether they result in disparities in the employment or advancement of minorities or women; and

(5) any other areas that might impact the success of the affirmative action program.

(c) *Action-oriented programs.* The contractor must develop and execute action-oriented programs designed to correct any problem areas identified pursuant to § 60-2.17(b) and to attain established goals and objectives. In order for these action-oriented programs to be effective, the contractor must ensure that they consist of more than following the same procedures which have previously produced inadequate results. Furthermore, a contractor must demonstrate that it has made good faith efforts to remove identified barriers, expand employment opportunities, and produce measurable results.

(d) *Internal audit and reporting system.* The contractor must develop and implement an auditing system that periodically measures the effectiveness of its total affirmative action program. The actions listed below are key to a successful affirmative action program:

(1) Monitor records of all personnel activity, including referrals, placements, transfers, promotions, terminations, and compensation, at all levels to ensure the nondiscriminatory policy is carried out;

(2) Require internal reporting on a scheduled basis as to the degree to which equal employment opportunity and organizational objectives are attained;

(3) Review report results with all levels of management; and

(4) Advise top management of program effectiveness and submit recommendations to improve unsatisfactory performance.

60-2.18 Equal Opportunity Survey.

(a) *Survey requirement.* Each year, OFCCP will designate a substantial portion of all nonconstruction contractor establishments to prepare and file an Equal Opportunity Survey. OFCCP will notify those establishments required to prepare and file the Equal Opportunity Survey. The Survey will provide OFCCP compliance data early in the compliance evaluation process, thus allowing the agency to more effectively identify contractor establishments for further evaluation. The Survey will also provide contractors with a useful tool for self-evaluation.

(b) *Survey format.* The Equal Opportunity Survey must be prepared in accordance with the format specified by the Deputy Assistant Secretary. The Equal Opportunity Survey will include information that will allow for an accurate assessment of contractor personnel activities, pay practices, and affirmative action performance. At a minimum, this will include such data elements as applicants, hires, promotions, terminations, compensation, and tenure by race and gender. As use of the EO Survey develops and evolves, the Department may at some time determine that one or more of the data elements currently included in the EO Survey should be altered or deleted. In the event consideration is given to changing a data element requirement, the following circumstances must exist:

(1) The Secretary must clearly demonstrate through statistical analyses of EO Survey submissions that the data element in question is no longer of value; and

(2) The Secretary must follow Notice and Comment procedures.

(c) *How, when, and where to file.* Contractors are encouraged to submit the Equal Opportunity Survey via the Internet. The Equal Opportunity Survey may also be submitted via facsimile to the telephone number indicated in the Survey instructions. Paper versions of the Equal Opportunity Survey must be mailed to the address indicated in the Survey instructions. The filing deadline will be specified by the Deputy Assistant Secretary.

(d) *Confidentiality.* OFCCP will treat information contained in the Equal Opportunity Survey as confidential to the maximum extent the information is exempt from public disclosure under the Freedom of Information Act, 5 U.S.C. 552. It is the practice of OFCCP not to release data where the contractor is still in business, and the contractor indicates, and through the Department of Labor review process it is determined, that the data are confidential and sensitive and that the release of data would subject the contractor to commercial harm.

SUBPART C. MISCELLANEOUS

60-2.30 Corporate management compliance evaluations.

(a) *Purpose.* Corporate Management Compliance Evaluations are designed to ascertain whether individuals are encountering artificial barriers to advancement into mid-level and senior corporate management, i.e., glass ceiling. During Corporate Management Compliance Evaluations, special attention is given to those components of the employment process that affect advancement into mid-and senior-level positions.

(b) If, during the course of a Corporate Management Compliance Evaluation, it comes to the attention of OFCCP that problems exist at establishments outside the corporate headquarters, OFCCP may expand the compliance evaluation beyond the headquarters establishment. At its discretion, OFCCP may direct its attention to and request relevant data for any and all areas within the corporation to ensure compliance with Executive Order 11246.

60-2.31 Program summary.

The affirmative action program must be summarized and updated annually. The program summary must be prepared in a format which will be prescribed by the Deputy Assistant Secretary and published in the **Federal Register** as a notice before becoming effective. Contractors and subcontractors must submit the program summary to OFCCP each year on the anniversary date of the affirmative action program.

60-2.32 Affirmative action records.

The contractor must make available to the Office of Federal Contract Compliance Programs, upon request, records maintained pursuant to § 60-1.12 of this chapter and written or otherwise documented portions of AAPs maintained pursuant to § 60-2.10 for such purposes as may be appropriate to the fulfillment of the agency's responsibilities under Executive Order 11246.

60-2.33 Preemption.

To the extent that any state or local laws, regulations or ordinances, including those that grant special benefits to persons on account of sex, are in conflict with Executive Order 11246, as amended, or with the requirements of this part, they will be regarded as preempted under the Executive Order.

60-2.34 Supersedure.

All orders, instructions, regulations, and memorandums of the Secretary of Labor, other officials of the Department of Labor and contracting agencies are hereby superseded to the extent that they are inconsistent with this Part 60-2.

60-2.35 Compliance status.

No contractor's compliance status will be judged alone by whether it reaches its goals. The composition of the contractor's workforce (i.e., the employment of minorities or women at a percentage rate below, or above, the goal level) does not, by itself, serve as a basis to impose any of the sanctions authorized by Executive Order 11246 and the regulations in this chapter. Each contractor's compliance with its affirmative action obligations will be determined by reviewing the nature and extent of the contractor's good faith affirmative action activities as required under § 60-2.17, and the appropriateness of those activities to identified equal employment opportunity problems. Each contractor's compliance with its nondiscrimination obligations will be determined by analysis of statistical data and other non-statistical information which would indicate whether employees and applicants are being treated without regard to their race, color, religion, sex, or national origin.

Part 60-4. Construction Contractors— Affirmative Action Requirements

60-4.1 Scope and application.

This part applies to all contractors and subcontractors which hold any Federal or federally assisted construction contract in excess of $10,000. The regulations in this part are applicable to all of a construction contractor's or subcontractor's construction employees who are engaged in on site construction including those construction employees who work on a non-Federal or nonfederally assisted construction site. This part also establishes procedures which all Federal contracting officers and all applicants, as applicable, shall follow in soliciting for and awarding Federal or federally assisted construction contracts. Procedures also are established which administering agencies shall follow in making any grant, contract, loan, insurance, or guarantee involving federally assisted construction which is not exempt from the requirements of Executive Order 11246, as amended.

In addition, this part applies to construction work performed by construction contractors and subcontractors for Federal nonconstruction contractors and subcontractors if the construction work is necessary in whole or in part to the performance of a nonconstruction contract or subcontract.

60-4.2 Solicitations.

(a) All Federal contracting officers and all applicants shall include the notice set forth in paragraph (d) of this section and the Standard Federal Equal Employment Opportunity Construction Contract Specifications set forth in § 60-4.3 of this part in all solicitations for offers and bids on all Federal and federally assisted construction contracts or subcontracts to be performed in geographical areas designated by the Director pursuant to § 60-4.6 of this part. Administering agencies shall require the inclusion of the notice set forth in paragraph (d) of this section and the specifications set forth in § 60-4.3 of this part as a condition of any grant, contract, subcontract, loan, insurance or guarantee involving federally assisted construction covered by this part 60-4.

(b) All nonconstruction contractors covered by Executive Order 11246 and the implementing regulations shall include the notice in paragraph (d) of this section in all construction agreements which are necessary in whole or in part to the performance of the covered nonconstruction contract.

(c) Contracting officers, applicants and nonconstruction contractors shall give written notice to the Director within 10 working days of award of a contract subject to these provisions. The notification shall include the name, address and telephone number of the contractor; employer identification number; dollar amount of the contract, estimated starting and completion dates of the contract; the contract number; and geographical area in which the contract is to be performed.

(d) The following notice shall be included in, and shall be a part of, all solicitations for offers and bids on all Federal and federally assisted construction contracts or subcontracts in excess of $10,000 to be performed in geographical areas designed by the Director pursuant to § 60-4.6 of this part (see 41 CFR 60-4.2(a)):

NOTICE OF REQUIREMENT FOR AFFIRMATIVE ACTION TO ENSURE EQUAL EMPLOYMENT OPPORTUNITY (EXECUTIVE ORDER 11246)

1. The Offeror's or Bidder's attention is called to the "Equal Opportunity Clause" and the "Standard Federal Equal Employment Opportunity Construction Contract Specifications" set forth herein.

2. The goals and timetables for minority and female participation, expressed in percentage terms for the Contractor's aggregate workforce in each trade on all construction work in the covered area, are as follows:

Timetables	Goals for minority participation for each trade	Goals for female participation in each trade
	Insert goals for each year	Insert goals for each year.

These goals are applicable to all the Contractor's construction work (whether or not it is Federal or federally assisted) performed in the covered area.

The Contractor's compliance with the Executive Order and the regulations in 41 CFR Part 60-4 shall be based on its implementation of the Equal Opportunity Clause, specific affirmative action obligations required by the specifications set forth in 41 CFR 60-4.3(a), and its efforts to meet the goals established for the geographical area where the contract resulting from this solicitation is to be performed. The hours of minority and female employment and training must be substantially uniform throughout the length of the contract, and in each trade, and the contractor shall make a good faith effort to employ minorities and women evenly on each of its projects. The transfer of minority or female employees or trainees from Contractor to Contractor or from project to project for the sole purpose of meeting the Contractor's goals shall be a violation of the contract, the Executive Order and the regulations in 41 CFR Part 60-4. Compliance with the goals will be measured against the total work hours performed.

3. The Contractor shall provide written notification to the Director of the Office of Federal Contract Compliance Programs within 10 working days of award of any construction subcontract in excess of $10,000 at any tier for construction work under the contract resulting from this solicitation. The notification shall list the name, address and telephone number of the subcontractor; employer identification number; estimated dollar amount of the subcontract; estimated starting and completion dates of the subcontract; and the geographical area in which the contract is to be performed.

4. As used in this Notice, and in the contract resulting from this solicitation, the "covered area" is (insert description of the geographical areas where the contract is to be performed giving the state, county and city, if any).

60-4.3 Equal opportunity clauses.

(a) The equal opportunity clause published at 41 CFR 60-1.4(a) of this chapter is required to be included in, and is part of, all nonexempt Federal contracts and subcontracts, including construction contracts and subcontracts. The equal opportunity clause published at 41 CFR 60-1.4(b) is required to be included in, and is a part of, all nonexempt federally assisted construction contracts and subcontracts. In addition to the clauses described above, all Federal contracting officers, all applicants and all nonconstruction contractors, as applicable, shall include the specifications set forth in this section in all Federal and federally assisted construction contracts in excess of $10,000 to be performed in geographical areas designated by the Director pursuant to § 60-4.6 of this part and in construction subcontracts in excess of $10,000 necessary in whole or in part to the performance of nonconstruction Federal contracts and subcontracts covered under the Executive Order.

STANDARD FEDERAL EQUAL EMPLOYMENT OPPORTUNITY CONSTRUCTION CONTRACT SPECIFICATIONS (EXECUTIVE ORDER 11246)

1. As used in these specifications:

a. "Covered area" means the geographical area described in the solicitation from which this contract resulted;

b. "Director" means Director, Office of Federal Contract Compliance Programs, United States Department of Labor, or any person to whom the Director delegates authority;

c. "Employer identification number" means the Federal Social Security number used on the Employer's Quarterly Federal Tax Return, U.S. Treasury Department Form 941.

d. "Minority" includes:

(i) Black (all persons having origins in any of the Black African racial groups not of Hispanic origin);

(ii) Hispanic (all persons of Mexican, Puerto Rican, Cuban, Central or South American or other Spanish Culture or origin, regardless of race);

(iii) Asian and Pacific Islander (all persons having origins in any of the original peoples of the Far East, Southeast Asia, the Indian Subcontinent, or the Pacific Islands); and

(iv) American Indian or Alaskan Native (all persons having origins in any of the original peoples of North America and maintaining identifiable tribal affiliations through membership and participation or community identification).

2. Whenever the Contractor, or any Subcontractor at any tier, subcontracts a portion of the work involving any construction trade, it shall physically include in each subcontract in excess of $10,000 the provisions of these specifications and the Notice which contains the applicable goals for minority and female participation and which is set forth in the solicitations from which this contract resulted.

3. If the Contractor is participating (pursuant to 41 CFR 60-4.5) in a Hometown Plan approved by the U.S. Department of Labor in the covered area either individually or through an association, its affirmative action obligations on all work in the Plan area (including goals and timetables) shall be in accordance with that Plan for those trades which have unions participating in the Plan. Contractors must be able to demonstrate their participation in and compliance with the provisions of any such Hometown Plan. Each Contractor or Subcontractor participating in an approved Plan is individually required to comply with its obligations under the EEO clause, and to make a good faith effort to achieve each goal under the Plan in each trade in which it has employees. The overall good faith performance by other Contractors or Subcontractors toward a goal in an approved Plan does not excuse any covered Contractor's or Subcontractor's failure to take good faith efforts to achieve the Plan goals and timetables.

4. The Contractor shall implement the specific affirmative action standards provided in paragraphs 7a through p of these specifications. The goals set forth in the solicitation from which this contract resulted are expressed as percentages of the total hours of employment and training of minority and female utilization the Contractor should reasonably be able to achieve in each construction trade in which it has employees in the covered area. The Contractor is expected to make substantially uniform progress toward its goals in each craft during the period specified.

5. Neither the provisions of any collective bargaining agreement, nor the failure by a union with whom the Contractor has a collective bargaining agreement, to refer either minorities or women shall excuse the Contractor's obligations under these specifications, Executive Order 11246, or the regulations promulgated pursuant thereto.

6. In order for the nonworking training hours of apprentices and trainees to be counted in meeting the goals, such apprentices and trainees must be employed by the Contractor during the training period, and the Contractor must have made a commitment to employ the apprentices and trainees at the completion of their training, subject to the availability of employment opportunities. Trainees must be trained pursuant to training programs approved by the U.S. Department of Labor.

7. The Contractor shall take specific affirmative actions to ensure equal employment opportunity. The evaluation of the Contractor's compliance with these specifications shall be based upon its effort to achieve maximum results from its actions. The Contractor shall document these efforts fully, and shall implement affirmative action steps at least as extensive as the following:

a. Ensure and maintain a working environment free of harassment, intimidation, and coercion at all sites, and in all facilities at which the Contractor's employees are assigned to work. The Contractor, where possible, will assign two or more women to each construction project. The Contractor shall specifically ensure that all foremen, superintendents, and other on-site supervisory personnel are aware of and carry out the Contractor's obligation to maintain such a working environment, with specific attention to minority or female individuals working at such sites or in such facilities.

b. Establish and maintain a current list of minority and female recruitment sources, provide written notification to minority and female recruitment sources and to community organizations when the Contractor or its unions have employment opportunities available, and maintain a record of the organizations' responses.

c. Maintain a current file of the names, addresses and telephone numbers of each minority and female off-the-street applicant and minority or female referral from a union, a recruitment source or community organization and of what action was taken with respect to each such individual. If such individual was sent to the union hiring hall for referral and was not referred back to the Contractor by the union or, if referred, not employed by the Contractor, this shall be documented in the file with the reason therefore, along with whatever additional actions the Contractor may have taken.

d. Provide immediate written notification to the Director when the union or unions with which the Contractor has a collective bargaining agreement has not referred to the Contractor a minority person or woman sent by the Contractor, or when the Contractor has other information that the union referral process has impeded the Contractor's efforts to meet its obligations.

e. Develop on-the-job training opportunities and/or participate in training programs for the area which expressly include minorities and women, including upgrading programs and apprenticeship and trainee programs relevant to the Contractor's employment needs, especially those programs funded or approved by the Department of Labor. The Contractor shall provide notice of these programs to the sources complied under 7b above.

f. Disseminate the Contractor's EEO policy by providing notice of the policy to unions and training programs and requesting their cooperation in assisting the Contractor in meeting its EEO obligations; by including it in any policy manual and collective bargaining agreement; by publicizing it in the company newspaper, annual report, etc.; by specific review of the policy with all management personnel and with all minority and female employees at least once a year; and by posting the company EEO policy on bulletin boards accessible to all employees at each location where construction work is performed.

g. Review, at least annually, the company's EEO policy and affirmative action obligations under these specifications with all employees having any responsibility for hiring, assignment, layoff, termination or other employment decisions including specific review of these items with on-site supervisory personnel such as Superintendents, General Foremen, etc., prior to the initiation of construction work at any job site. A written record shall be made and maintained identifying the time and place of these meetings, persons attending, subject matter discussed, and disposition of the subject matter.

h. Disseminate the Contractor's EEO policy externally by including it in any advertising in the news media, specifically including minority and female news media, and providing written notification to and discussing the Contractor's EEO policy with other Contractors and Subcontractors with whom the Contractor does or anticipates doing business.

i. Direct its recruitment efforts, both oral and written, to minority, female and community organizations, to schools with minority and female students and to minority and female recruitment and training organizations serving the Contractor's recruitment area and employment needs. Not later than one month prior to the date for the acceptance of applications for apprenticeship or other training by any recruitment source, the Contractor shall send written notification to organizations such as the above, describing the openings, screening procedures, and tests to be used in the selection process.

j. Encourage present minority and female employees to recruit other minority persons and women and, where reasonable, provide after school, summer and vacation employment to minority and female youth both on the site and in other areas of a Contractor's work force.

k. Validate all tests and other selection requirements where there is an obligation to do so under 41 CFR Part 60-3.

l. Conduct, at least annually, an inventory and evaluation at least of all minority and female personnel for promotional opportunities and encourage these employees to seek or to prepare for, through appropriate training, etc., such opportunities.

m. Ensure that seniority practices, job classifications, work assignments and other personnel practices, do not have a discriminatory effect by continually monitoring all personnel and employment related activities to ensure that the EBO policy and the Contractor's obligations under these specifications are being carried out.

n. Ensure that all facilities and company activities are nonsegregated except that separate or single-user toilet and necessary changing facilities shall be provided to assure privacy between the sexes.

o. Document and maintain a record of all solicitations of offers for subcontracts from minority and female construction contractors and suppliers, including circulation of solicitations to minority and female contractor associations and other business associations.

p. Conduct a review, at least annually, of all supervisors adherence to and performance under the Contractor's EEO policies and affirmative action obligations.

8. Contractors are encouraged to participate in voluntary associations which assist in fulfilling one or more of their affirmative action obligations (7a through p). The efforts of a contractor association, joint contractor-union, contractor-community, or other similar group of which the Contractor is a member and participant, may be asserted as fulfilling any one or more of its obligations under 7a through p of these Specifications provided that the contractor actively participates in the group, makes every effort to assure that the group has a positive impact on the employment of minorities and women in the industry, ensures that the concrete benefits of the program are reflected in the Contractor's minority and female work force participation, makes a good faith effort to meet its individual goals and timetables, and can provide access to documentation which demonstrates the effectiveness of actions taken on behalf of the Contractor. The obligation to comply, however, is the Contractor's and failure of such a group to fulfill an obligation shall not be a defense for the Contractor's noncompliance.

9. A single goal for minorities and a separate single goal for women have been established. The Contractor, however, is required to provide equal employment opportunity and to take affirmative action for all minority groups, both male and female, and all women, both minority and non-minority. Consequently, the Contractor may be in violation of the Executive Order if a particular group is employed in a substantially disparate manner

(for example, even though the Contractor has achieved its goals for women generally, the Contractor may be in violation of the Executive Order if a specific minority group of women is underutilized).

10. The Contractor shall not use the goals and timetables or affirmative action standards to discriminate against any person because of race, color, religion, sex, or national origin.

11. The Contractor shall not enter into any Subcontract with any person or firm debarred from Government contracts pursuant to Executive Order 11246.

12. The Contractor shall carry out such sanctions and penalties for violation of these specifications and of the Equal Opportunity Clause, including suspension, termination and cancellation of existing subcontracts as may be imposed or ordered pursuant to Executive Order 11246, as amended, and its implementing regulations, by the Office of Federal Contract Compliance Programs. Any Contractor who fails to carry out such sanctions and penalties shall be in violation of these specifications and Executive Order 11246, as amended.

13. The Contractor, in fulfilling its obligations under these specifications, shall implement specific affirmative action steps, at least as extensive as those standards prescribed in paragraph 7 of these specifications, so as to achieve maximum results from its efforts to ensure equal employment opportunity. If the Contractor fails to comply with the requirements of the Executive Order, the implementing regulations, or these specifications, the Director shall proceed in accordance with 41 CFR 60-4.8.

14. The Contractor shall designate a responsible official to monitor all employment related activity to ensure that the company EEO policy is being carried out, to submit reports relating to the provisions hereof as may be required by the Government and to keep records. Records shall at least include for each employee the name, address, telephone numbers, construction trade, union affiliation if any, employee identification number when assigned, social security number, race, sex, status (e.g., mechanic, apprentice trainee, helper, or laborer), dates of changes in status, hours worked per week in the indicated trade, rate of pay, and locations at which the work was performed. Records shall be maintained in an easily understandable and retrievable form; however, to the degree that existing records satisfy this requirement, contractors shall not be required to maintain separate records.

15. Nothing herein provided shall be construed as a limitation upon the application of other laws which establish different standards of compliance or upon the application of requirements for the hiring of local or other area residents (e.g., those under the Public Works Employment Act of 1977 and the Community Development Block Grant Program).

(b) The notice set forth in 41 CFR 60-4.2 and the specifications set forth in 41 CFR 60-4.3 replace the New Form for Federal Equal Employment Opportunity Bid Conditions for Federal and Federally Assisted Construction published at 41 FR 32482 and commonly known as the Model Federal EEO Bid Conditions, and the New Form shall not be used after the regulations in 41 CFR Part 60-4 become effective.

60-4.4 Affirmative action requirements.

(a) To implement the affirmative action requirements of Executive Order 11246 in the construction industry, the Office of Federal Contract Compliance Programs previously has approved affirmative action programs commonly referred to as "Hometown Plans," has promulgated affirmative action plans referred to as "Imposed Plans" and has approved "Special Bid Conditions" for high impact projects constructed in areas not covered by a

Hometown or an Imposed Plan. All solicitations for construction contracts made after the effective date of the regulations in this part shall include the notice specified in § 60-4.2 of this part and the specifications in § 60-4.3 of this part in lieu of the Hometown and Imposed Plans including the Philadelphia Plan and Special Bid Conditions. Until the Director has issued an order pursuant to § 60-4.6 of this part establishing goals and timetables for minorities in the appropriate geographical areas or for a project covered by Special Bid Conditions, the goals and timetables for minorities to be inserted in the Notice required by 41 CFR 60-4.2 shall be the goals and timetables contained in the Hometown Plan, Imposed Plan or Special Bid Conditions presently covering the respective geographical area or project involved.

(b) Signatories to a Hometown Plan (including heavy highway affirmative action plans) shall have 45 days from the effective date of the regulations in this part to submit under such a Plan (for the director's approval) goals and timetables for women and to include female representation on the Hometown Plan Administrative Committee. Such goals for female representation shall be at least as high as the goals established for female representation in the notice issued pursuant to 41 CFR 60-4.6. Failure of the signatories, within the 45-day period, to include female representation and to submit goals for women or a new plan, as appropriate, shall result in an automatic termination of the Office of Federal Contract Compliance Program's approval of the Hometown Plan. At any time the Office of Federal Contract Compliance Programs terminates or withdraws its approval of a Hometown Plan, or when the plan expires and another plan is not approved, the contractors signatory to the plan shall be covered automatically by the specifications set forth in §_60-4.3 of this part and by the goals and timetables established for that geographical area pursuant to § 60-4.6 of this part.

60-4.5 Hometown plans.

(a) A contractor participating, either individually or through an association, in an approved Hometown Plan (including heavy highway affirmative action plans) shall comply with its affirmative action obligations under Executive Order 11246 by complying with its obligations under the plan: Provided, That each contractor or subcontractor participating in an approved plan is individually required to comply with the equal opportunity clause set forth in 41 CFR 60-1.4; to make a good faith effort to achieve the goals for each trade participating in the plan in which it has employees; and that the overall good performance by other contractors or subcontractors toward a goal in an approved plan does not excuse any covered contractor's or subcontractor's failure to take good faith efforts to achieve the plan's goals and timetables. If a contractor is not participating in an approved Hometown Plan it shall comply with the specifications set forth in § 60-4.3 of this part and with the goals and timetables for the appropriate area as listed in the notice required by 41 CFR 60-4.2 with regard to that trade. For the purposes of this part 60-4, a contractor is not participating in a Hometown Plan for a particular trade if it:

(1) Ceases to be signatory to a Hometown Plan covering that trade;

(2) Is signatory to a Hometown Plan for that trade but is not party to a collective bargaining agreement for that trade;

(3) Is signatory to a Hometown Plan for that trade but is party to a collective bargaining agreement with labor organizations which are not or cease to be signatories to the same Hometown Plan for that trade;

(4) Is signatory to a Hometown Plan for that trade but is Party to a collective bargaining agreement with a labor organization for that trade but the two have not jointly executed

a specific commitment to minority and female goals and timetables and incorporated the commitment in the Hometown Plan for that trade;

(5) Is participating in a Hometown Plan for that trade which is no longer acceptable to the Office of Federal Contract Compliance Programs;

(6) Is signatory to a Hometown Plan for that trade but is party to a collective bargaining agreement with a labor organization for that trade and the labor organization and the contractor have failed to make a good faith effort to comply with their obligations under the Hometown Plan for that trade.

(b) Contractors participating in Hometown Plans must be able to demonstrate their participation and document their compliance with the provision of the Hometown Plan.

60-4.6 Goals and timetables.

The Director, from time to time, shall issue goals and timetables for minority and female utilization which shall be based on appropriate workforce, demographic or other relevant data and which shall cover construction projects; or construction contracts performed in specific geographical areas. The goals shall be applicable to each construction trade in a covered contractor's or subcontractor's entire workforce which is working in the area covered by the goals and timetables, shall be published as notices in the FEDERAL REGISTER, and shall be inserted by the contracting officers and applicants, as applicable, in the notice required by 41 CFR 60-4.2.

60-4.7 Effect on other regulations.

The regulations in this part are in addition to the regulations contained in this chapter which apply to construction contractors and subcontractors generally. See particularly, 41 CFR 60-1.4 (a), (b), (c), (d), and (e); 60-1.5; 60-1.7; 60-1.8; 60-1.26; 60-1.29; 60-1.30; 60-1.32; 60-1.41; 60-1.42; 60-1.43; and 41 CFR part 60-3; part 60-20; part 60-30; part 60-40; and part 60-50.

60-4.8 Show cause notice.

If an investigation or compliance review reveals that a construction contractor or subcontractor has violated the Executive order, any contract clause, specifications or the regulations in this chapter and if administrative enforcement is contemplated, the Director shall issue to the contractor or subcontractor a notice to show cause which shall contain the items specified in (i)-(iv) of 41 CFR 60-2.2(c)(1). If the contractor does not show good cause within 30 days, or in the alternative, fails to enter an acceptable conciliation agreement which includes where appropriate, make up goals and timetables, back pay, and seniority relief for affected class members, the OFCCP shall follow the procedure in 41 CFR 60-1.26(b): Provided. That where a conciliation agreement has been violated, no show cause notice is required prior to the initiation of enforcement proceedings.

60-4.9 Incorporation by operation of the order.

By operation of the order, the equal opportunity clause contained in § 60-1.4, the Notice of Requirement for Affirmative Action to Ensure Equal Employment Opportunity (Executive Order 11246) contained in § 60-4.2, and the Standard Federal Equal Employment Opportunity Construction Contract Specifications (Executive Order 11246) contained in § 60-4.3 shall be deemed to be a part of every solicitation or of every contract and subcontract, as appropriate, required by the order and the regulations in this chapter to include such clauses whether or not they are physically incorporated in such solicitation or contract and whether or not the contract is written.

[Appendix A and Appendix B-80, establishing the goals for females and minority utilization in construction, are reproduced in 45 Fed. Reg. 65979, 85750 (1980), and 46 Fed. Reg. 7533 (1981).—Ed.]

Part 60-20. Sex Discrimination Guidelines

60-20.1 Title and purpose.

The purpose of the provisions in this part is to set forth the interpretations and guidelines of the Office of Federal Contract Compliance Programs regarding the implementation of Executive Order 11246, as amended for the promotion and insuring of equal opportunities for all persons employed or seeking employment with Government contractors and subcontractors or with contractors and subcontractors performing under federally assisted construction contracts, without regard to sex. Experience has indicated that special problems related to the implementation of the Executive Order require a definitive treatment beyond the terms of the order itself. These interpretations are to be read in connection with existing regulations, set forth in Part 60-1 of this chapter.

60-20.2 Recruitment and advertisement.

(a) Employers engaged in recruiting activity must recruit employees of both sexes for all jobs unless sex is a bona fide occupational qualification.

(b) Advertisement in newspapers and other media for employment must not express a sex preference unless sex is a bona fide occupational qualification for the job. The placement of an advertisement in columns headed "Male" or "Female" will be considered an expression of a preference, limitation, specification, or discrimination based on sex.

60-20.3 Job policies and practices.

(a) Written personnel policies relating to this subject area must expressly indicate that there shall be no discrimination against employees on account of sex. If the employer deals with a bargaining representative for his employees and there is a written agreement on conditions of employment, such agreement shall not be inconsistent with these guidelines.

(b) Employees of both sexes shall have an equal opportunity to any available job that he or she is qualified to perform, unless sex is a bona fide occupational qualification. NOTE: In most Government contract work there are only limited instances where valid reasons can be expected to exist which would justify the exclusion of all men or all women from any given job.

(c) The employer must not make any distinction based upon sex in employment opportunities, wages, hours, or other conditions of employment. In the area of employer contributions for insurance, pensions, welfare programs and other similar "fringe benefits" the employer will not be considered to have violated these guidelines if his contributions are the same for men and women or if the resulting benefits are equal.

(d) Any distinction between married and unmarried persons of one sex that is not made between married and unmarried persons of the opposite sex will be considered to be a distinction made on the basis of sex. Similarly, an employer must not deny employment to women with young children unless it has the same exclusionary policies for men; or terminate an employee of one sex in a particular job classification upon reaching a certain age unless the same rule is applicable to members of the opposite sex.

(e) The employer's policies and practices must assure appropriate physical facilities to both sexes. The employer may not refuse to hire men or women, or deny men or women a particular job because there are no restroom or associated facilities, unless the employer is able to show that the construction of the facilities would be unreasonable for such reasons as excessive expense or lack of space.

(f)(1) An employer must not deny a female employee the right to any job that she is qualified to perform in reliance upon a State "protective" law. For example, such laws include those which prohibit women from performing in certain types of occupations (e.g., a bartender or a core-maker); from working at jobs requiring more than a certain number of hours; and from working at jobs that require lifting or carrying more than designated weights.

(2) Such legislation was intended to be beneficial, but, instead, has been found to result in restricting employment opportunities for men and/or women. Accordingly, it cannot be used as a basis for denying employment or for establishing sex as a bona fide occupational qualification for the job.

(g)(1) Women shall not be penalized in their conditions of employment because they require time away from work on account of childbearing. When, under the employer's leave policy the female employee would qualify for leave, then childbearing must be considered by the employer to be a justification for leave of absence for female employees for a reasonable period of time. For example, if the female employee meets the equally applied minimum length of service requirements for leave time, she must be granted a reasonable leave on account of childbearing. The conditions applicable to her leave (other than the length thereof) and to her return to employment, shall be in accordance with the employer's leave policy.

(2) If the employer has no leave policy, childbearing must be considered by the employer to be a justification for a leave of absence for a female employee for a reasonable period of time. Following childbirth, and upon signifying her intent to return within a reasonable time, such female employee shall be reinstated to her original job or to a position of like status and pay, without loss of service credits.

(h) The employer must not specify any differences for male and female employees on the basis of sex in either mandatory or optional retirement age.

(i) Nothing in these guidelines shall be interpreted to mean that differences in capabilities for job assignments do not exist among individuals and that such distinctions may not be recognized by the employer in making specific assignments. The purpose of these guidelines is to insure that such distinctions are not based upon sex.

60-20.4 Seniority system.

Where they exist, seniority lines and lists must not be based solely upon sex. Where such a separation has existed, the employer must eliminate this distinction.

60-20.5 Discriminatory wages.

(a) The employer's wages schedules must not be related to or based on the sex of the employees.

NOTE: The more obvious cases of discrimination exist where employees of different sexes are paid different wages on jobs which require substantially equal skill, effort and responsibility and are performed under similar working conditions.

(b) The employer may not discriminatorily restrict one sex to certain job classifications. In such a situation, the employer must take steps to make jobs available to all qualified employees in all classifications without regard to sex. (Example: An electrical manufacturing company may have a production division with three functional units: One (assembly) all female; another (wiring), all male; and a third (circuit boards), also all male. The highest wage attainable in the assembly unit is considerably less than that in the circuit board and wiring units. In such a case the employer must take steps to provide qualified female employees opportunity for placement in job openings in the other two units.)

(c) To avoid overlapping and conflicting administration the Director will consult with the Administrator of the Wage and Hour Administration before issuing an opinion on any matter covered by both the Equal Pay Act and Executive Order 11246, as amended.

60-20.6 Affirmative action.

(a) The employer shall take affirmative action to recruit women to apply for those jobs where they have been previously excluded. NOTE: This can be done by various methods. Examples include: (1) Including in itineraries of recruiting trips women's colleges where graduates with skills desired by the employer can be found, and female students of co-educational institutions and (2) designing advertisements to indicate that women will be considered equally with men for jobs.

(b) Women have not been typically found in significant numbers in management. In many companies management trainee programs are one of the ladders to management positions. Traditionally, few, if any, women have been admitted into these programs. An important element of affirmative action shall be a commitment to include women candidates in such programs.

(c) Distinctions based on sex may not be made in other training programs. Both sexes should have equal access to all training programs and affirmative action programs should require a demonstration by the employer that such access has been provided.

Part 60-50. Guidelines on Discrimination Because of Religion or National Origin

60-50.1 Purpose and scope.

(a) The purpose of the provisions in this part is to set forth the interpretations and guidelines of the Office of Federal Contract Compliance Programs regarding the implementation of Executive Order 11246, as amended, for promoting and insuring equal employment opportunities for all persons employed or seeking employment with Government contractors and subcontractors or with contractors and subcontractors performing under federally assisted construction contracts, without regard to religion or national origin.

(b) Members of various religious and ethnic groups, primarily but not exclusively of Eastern, Middle, and Southern European ancestry, such as Jews, Catholics, Italians,

Greeks, and Slavic groups, continue to be excluded from executive, middle-management, and other job levels because of discrimination based upon their religion and/or national origin. These guidelines are intended to remedy such unfair treatment.

(c) These guidelines are also intended to clarify the obligations of employers with respect to accommodating to the religious observances and practices of employees and prospective employees.

(d) The employment problems of blacks, Spanish-surnamed Americans, Orientals, and American Indians are treated under Part 60-2 of this chapter and under other regulations and procedures implementing the requirements of Executive Order 11246, as amended. Accordingly, the remedial provisions of § 60-50.2(b) shall not be applicable to the employment problems of these groups.

(e) Nothing contained in this Part 60-50 is intended to supersede or otherwise limit the exemption set forth in § 60-1. 5(a)(5) of this chapter for contracts with certain educational institutions.

60-50.2 Equal employment policy.

(a) *General requirements.* Under the equal opportunity clause contained in section 202 of Executive Order 11246, as amended, employers are prohibited from discriminating against employees or applicants for employment because of religion or national origin, and must take affirmative action to insure that applicants are employed, and that employees are treated during employment, without regard to their religion or national origin. Such action includes, but is not limited to the following: Employment, upgrading, demotion, or transfer; Recruitment or recruitment advertising; layoff or termination; rates of pay or other forms of compensation; and selection for training, including apprenticeship.

(b) *Outreach and positive recruitment.* Employers shall review their employment practices to determine whether members of the various religious and/or ethnic groups are receiving fair consideration for job opportunities. Special attention shall be directed toward executive and middle-management levels, where employment problems relating to religion and national origin are most likely to occur. Based upon the findings of such reviews, employers shall undertake appropriate outreach and positive recruitment activities, such as those listed below, in order to remedy existing deficiencies. It is not contemplated that employers necessarily will undertake all of the listed activities. The scope of the employer's efforts shall depend upon all the circumstances, including the nature and extent of the employer's deficiencies and the employer's size and resources.

(1) Internal communication of the employer's obligation to provide equal employment opportunity without regard to religion or national origin in such a manner as to foster understanding, acceptance, and support among the employer's executive, management, supervisory, and all other employees and to encourage such persons to take the necessary action to aid the employer in meeting this obligation.

(2) Development of reasonable internal procedures to insure that the employer's obligation to provide equal employment opportunity without regard to religion or national origin is being fully implemented.

(3) Periodically informing all employees of the employer's commitment to equal employment opportunity for all persons, without regard to religion or national origin.

(4) Enlisting the assistance and support of all recruitment sources (including employment agencies, college placement directors, and business associates) for the employer's commitment to provide equal employment opportunity without regard to religion or national origin.

(5) Reviewing employment records to determine the availability of promotable and transferable members of various religious and ethnic groups.

(6) Establishment of meaningful contacts with religious and ethnic organizations and leaders for such purposes as advice, education, technical assistance, and referral of potential employees.

(7) Engaging in significant recruitment activities at educational institutions with substantial enrollments of students from various religious and ethnic groups.

(8) Use of the religious and ethnic media for institutional and employment advertising.

60-50.3 Accommodations to religious observance and practice.

An employer must accommodate to the religious observances and practices of an employee or prospective employee unless the employer demonstrates that it is unable to reasonably accommodate to an employee's or prospective employee's religious observance or practice without undue hardship on the conduct of the employer's business. As part of this obligation, an employer must make reasonable accommodations to the religious observances and practices of an employee or prospective employee who regularly observes Friday evening and Saturday, or some other day of the week, as his Sabbath and/or who observes certain religious holidays during the year and who is conscientiously opposed to performing work or engaging in similar activity on such days, when such accommodations can be made without undue hardship on the conduct of the employer's business. In determining the extent of an employer's obligations under this section, at least the following factors shall be considered: (a) Business necessity, (b) financial costs and expenses, and (c) resulting personnel problems.

60-50.4 Enforcement.

The provisions of this part are subject to the general enforcement, compliance review, and complaint procedures set forth in Subpart B of Part 60-1 of this chapter.

60-50.5 Nondiscrimination.

The provisions of this part are not intended and shall not be used to discriminate against any qualified employee or applicant for employment because of race, color, religion, sex, or national origin.

Nondiscrimination Provisions of the Immigration Reform and Control Act of 1986

P. L. 99-603 (1986), 100 Stat. 3374, as amended by P. L.100-525 (1988), 102 Stat. 2610, P. L. 101-649 (1990), 104 Stat. 4978, P.L. 103-416 (1994), 108 Stat. 4317, P.L. 104-208 (1996), 110 Stat. 1771-1772

8 U.S.C. § 1324b

1324b Unfair immigration-related employment practices

(a) **Prohibition of discrimination based on national origin or citizenship status**

(1) **General rule**

It is an unfair immigration-related employment practice for a person or other entity to discriminate against any individual (other than an unauthorized alien, as defined in section 1324a(h)(3) of this section) with respect to the hiring, or recruitment or referral for a fee, of the individual for employment or the discharging of the individual from employment—

(A) because of such individual's national origin, or

(B) in the case of a citizen or intending citizen (as defined in paragraph (3)), because of such individual's citizenship status.

(2) **Exceptions**

Paragraph (1) shall not apply to—

(A) a person or other entity that employs three or fewer employees,

(B) a person's or entity's discrimination because of an individual's national origin if the discrimination with respect to that person or entity and that individual is covered under section 2000e-2 of Title 42, or

(C) discrimination because of citizenship status which is otherwise required in order to comply with law, regulation, or executive order, or required by Federal, State, or local government contract, or which the Attorney General determines to be essential for an employer to do business with an agency or department of the Federal, State, or local government.

(3) **"Protected individual" defined**

As used in paragraph (1), the term <TERM>"protected individual"</TERM> means an individual who—

(A) is a citizen or national of the United States, or

(B) is an alien who is lawfully admitted for permanent residence, is granted the status of an alien lawfully admitted for temporary residence under section 1161(a) or 1255a (a)(1) of this title, is admitted as a refugee under section 1157 of this title, or is granted asylum under section 1158 of this title; but does not include—

(i) an alien who fails to apply for naturalization within six months of the date the alien first becomes eligible (by virtue of period of lawful permanent residence) to apply for naturalization or, if later, within six months after November 6,1986 and

(ii) an alien who has applied on a timely basis, but has not been naturalized as a citizen within 2 years after the date of the application, unless the alien can establish that the alien is actively pursuing naturalization, unless the alien can establish that the alien is actively pursuing naturalization, except that time consumed in the Service's processing the application shall not be counted toward the 2-year period.

(4) **Additional exception providing right to prefer equally qualified citizens**

Notwithstanding any other provision of this section, it is not an unfair immigration-related employment practice for a person or other entity to prefer to hire, recruit, or refer an individual who is a citizen or national of the United States over another individual who is an alien if the two individuals are equally qualified.

(5) **Prohibition of intimidation or retaliation**

It is also an unfair immigration-related employment practice for a person or other entity to intimidate, threaten, coerce, or retaliate against any individual for the purpose of interfering with any right or privilege secured under this section or because the individual intends to file or has filed a charge or a complaint, testified, assisted, or participated in any manner in an investigation, proceeding, or hearing under this section. An individual so intimidated, threatened, coerced, or retaliated against shall be considered, for purposes of subsections (d) and (g), to have been discriminated against.

(6) **Treatment of certain documentary practices as employment practices**

A person's or other entity's request, for purposes of satisfying the requirements of section 1324a(b) of this title, for more or different documents than are required under such section or refusing to honor documents tendered under such section or refusing to honor documents tendered that on their face reasonably appear to be genuine shall be treated as an unfair immigration-related employment practice if made for the purpose or with the intent of discriminating against an individual in violation of paragraph (1).

(b) **Charges of violations**

(1) **In general**

Except as provided in paragraph (2), any person alleging that the person is adversely affected directly by an unfair immigration-related employment practice (or a person on that person's behalf) or an officer of the Service alleging that an unfair immigration-related employment practice has occurred or is occurring may file a charge respecting such practice or violation with the Special Counsel (appointed under subsection (c) of this section). Charges shall be in writing under oath or affirmation and shall contain such information as the Attorney General requires. The Special Counsel by certified mail shall serve a notice of the charge (including the date, place, and circumstances of the alleged unfair immigration-related employment practice) on the person or entity involved within 10 days.

(2) **No overlap with EEOC complaints**

No charge may be filed respecting an unfair immigration-related employment practice described in subsection (a)(1)(A) of this section if a charge with respect to that practice based on the same set of facts has been filed with the Equal Employment Opportunity Commission under title VII of the Civil Rights Act of 1964 [42 U.S.C. 2000e *et seq.*], unless the charge is dismissed as being outside the scope of such title. No charge respecting an employment practice may be filed with the Equal Employment Opportunity Commission under such title if a charge with respect to such practice based on the same set of facts has been filed under this subsection, unless the charge is dismissed under this section as being outside the scope of this section.

(c) **Special Counsel**

(1) **Appointment**

The President shall appoint, by and with the advice and consent of the Senate, a Special Counsel for Immigration-Related Unfair Employment Practices (hereinafter in this section referred to as the "Special Counsel") within the Department of Justice to serve for a term of four years. In the case of a vacancy in the office of the Special Counsel the President may designate the officer or employee who shall act as Special Counsel during such vacancy.

(2) **Duties**

The Special Counsel shall be responsible for investigation of charges and issuance of complaints under this section and in respect of the prosecution of all such complaints before administrative law judges and the exercise of certain functions under subsection (i)(1) of this section.

(3) **Compensation**

The Special Counsel is entitled to receive compensation at a rate not to exceed the rate now or hereafter provided for grade GS-17 of the General Schedule, under section 5332 of Title 5.

(4) **Regional offices**

The Special Counsel, in accordance with regulations of the Attorney General, shall establish such regional offices as may be necessary to carry out his duties.

(d) **Investigation of charges**

(1) **By Special Counsel**

The Special Counsel shall investigate each charge received and, within 120 days of the date of the receipt of the charge, determine whether or not there is reasonable cause to believe that the charge is true and whether or not to bring a complaint with respect to the charge before an administrative law judge. The Special Counsel may, on his own initiative, conduct investigations respecting unfair immigration-related employment practices and, based on such an investigation and subject to paragraph (3), file a complaint before such a judge.

(2) **Private actions**

If the Special Counsel, after receiving such a charge respecting an unfair immigration-related employment practice which alleges knowing and intentional discriminatory activity or a pattern or practice of discriminatory activity, has not filed a complaint before an administrative law judge with respect to such charge within such 120-day period, the Special Counsel shall notify the person making the determination not to file such a complaint during such period and the person making the charge may (subject to paragraph (3)) file a complaint directly before such a judge within 90 days after the date of receipt of the notice. The Special Counsel's failure to file such a complaint within such 120-day period shall not affect the right of the Special Counsel to investigate the charge or to bring a complaint before an administrative law judge during such 90-day period.

(3) **Time limitations on complaints**

No complaint may be filed respecting any unfair immigration-related employment practice occurring more than 180 days prior to the date of the filing of the charge with the Special Counsel. This subparagraph shall not prevent the subsequent amending of a charge or complaint under subsection (e)(1) of this section.

(e) **Hearings**

(1) **Notice**

Whenever a complaint is made that a person or entity has engaged in or is engaging in any such unfair immigration-related employment practice, an administrative law judge shall have power to issue and cause to be served upon such person or entity a copy of the complaint and a notice of hearing before the judge at a place therein fixed, not less than five days after the serving of the complaint. Any such complaint may be amended by the judge conducting the hearing, upon the motion of the party filing the complaint, in the judge's discretion at any time prior to the issuance of an order based thereon. The person or entity so complained of shall have the right to file an answer to the original or amended complaint and to appear in person or otherwise and give testimony at the place and time fixed in the complaint.

(2) **Judges hearing cases**

Hearings on complaints under this subsection shall be considered before administrative law judges who are specially designated by the Attorney General as having special training respecting employment discrimination and, to the extent practicable, before such judges who only consider cases under this section.

(3) **Complainant as party**

Any person filing a charge with the Special Counsel respecting an unfair immigration-related employment practice shall be considered a party to any complaint before an administrative law judge respecting such practice and any subsequent appeal respecting that complaint. In the discretion of the judge conducting the hearing, any other person may be allowed to intervene in the proceeding and to present testimony.

(f) **Testimony and authority of hearing officers**

(1) **Testimony**

The testimony taken by the administrative law judge shall be reduced to writing. Thereafter, the judge, in his discretion, upon notice may provide for the taking of further testimony or hear argument.

(2) **Authority of administrative law judges**

In conducting investigations and hearings under this subsection and in accordance with regulations of the Attorney General, the Special Counsel and administrative law judges shall have reasonable access to examine evidence of any person or entity being investigated. The administrative law judges by subpoena may compel the attendance of witnesses and the production of evidence at any designated place or hearing. In case of contumacy or refusal to obey a subpoena lawfully issued under this paragraph and upon application of the administrative law judge, an appropriate district court of the United States may issue an order requiring compliance with such subpoena and any failure to obey such order may be punished by such court as a contempt thereof.

(g) **Determinations**

(1) **Order**

The administrative law judge shall issue and cause to be served on the parties to the proceeding an order, which shall be final unless appealed as provided under subsection (i) of this section.

(2) **Orders finding violations**

(A) **In general**

If, upon the preponderance of the evidence, an administrative law judge determines that any person or entity named in the complaint has engaged in or is engaging in any such unfair immigration-related employment practice, then the judge shall state his findings of fact and shall issue and cause to be served on such person or entity an order which requires such person or entity to cease and desist from such unfair immigration-related employment practice.

(B) **Contents of order**

Such an order also may require the person or entity—

(i) to comply with the requirements of section 1324a(b) of this title [70]

---

70. Editor's note: Section 1324a(b) states:

(b) **Employment verification system**

The requirements referred to in paragraphs (1)(B) and (3) of subsection (a) of this section are, in the case of a person or other entity hiring, recruiting, or referring an individual for employment in the United States, the requirements specified in the following three paragraphs:

(1) **Attestation after examination of documentation**

(A) **In general**

The person or entity must attest, under penalty of perjury and on a form designated or established by the Attorney General by regulation, that it has verified that the individual is not an unauthorized alien by examining—

(i) a document described in subparagraph (B), or

(ii) a document described in subparagraph (C) and a document described in subparagraph (D).

A person or entity has complied with the requirement of this paragraph with respect to examination of a document if the document reasonably appears on its face to be genuine. If an individual provides a document or combination of documents that reasonably appears on its face to be genuine and that is sufficient to meet the requirements of the first sentence of this paragraph, nothing in this paragraph shall be construed as requiring the person or entity to solicit the production of any other document or as requiring the individual to produce such another document.

(B) **Documents establishing both employment authorization and identity**

A document described in this subparagraph is an individual's—

(i) United States passport;

(ii) certificate of United States citizenship;

(iii) certificate of naturalization;

(iv) unexpired foreign passport, if the passport has an appropriate, unexpired endorsement of the Attorney General authorizing the individual's employment in the United States; or

(v) resident alien card or other alien registration card, if the card—

(I) contains a photograph of the individual or such other person identifying information relating to the individual as the Attorney General finds, by regulation, sufficient for purposes of this subsection, and

(II) is evidence of authorization of employment in the United States.

(C) **Documents evidencing employment authorization**

A document described in this subparagraph is an individual's—

(i) social security account number card (other than such a card which specifies on the face that the issuance of the card does not authorize employment in the United States);

(ii) certificate of birth in the United States or establishing United States nationality at birth, which certificate the Attorney General finds, by regulation, to be acceptable for purposes of this section; or

(iii) other documentation evidencing authorization of employment in the United States which the Attorney General finds, by regulation, to be acceptable for purposes of this section.

(D) **Documents establishing identity of individual**

A document described in this subparagraph is an individual's—

(i) driver's license or similar document issued for the purpose of identification by a State, if it contains a photo-

(ii) in the case of individuals under 16 years of age or in a State which does not provide for issuance of an identification document (other than a driver's license) referred to in clause (ii), documentation of personal identity of such other type as the Attorney General finds, by regulation, provides a reliable means of identification.

(2) **Individual attestation of employment authorization**

The individual must attest, under penalty of perjury on the form designated or established for purposes of paragraph (1), that the individual is a citizen or national of the United with respect to individuals hired (or recruited or referred for employment for a fee) during a period of up to three years;

(ii) to retain for the period referred to in clause (i) and only for purposes consistent with section 1324a(b)(5) of this title, the name and address of each individual who applies, in person or in writing, for hiring for an existing position, or for recruiting or referring for a fee, for employment in the United States;

(iii) to hire individuals directly and adversely affected, with or without back pay;

(iv)(I) except as provided in subclauses (II) through (IV), to pay a civil penalty of not less than $250 and not more than $2,000 for each individual discriminated against,

(II) except as provided in subclause (IV), in the case of a person or entity previously subject to a single order under this paragraph, to pay a civil penalty of not less than $2,000 and not more than $5,000 for each individual discriminated against,

(III) except as provided in subclause (IV), in the case of a person or entity previously subject to more than one order under this paragraph, to pay a civil penalty of not less than $3,000 and not more than $10,000 for each individual discriminated against, and

(IV) in the case of an unfair immigration-related employment practice described in subsection (a)(6), to pay a civil penalty of not less than $100 and not more than $1,000 for each individual discriminated against;

(v) to post notices to employees about their rights under this section and employers' obligations under section 274A,

(vi) to educate all personnel involved in hiring and complying with this section or section 274A about the requirements of this section or such section,

---

States, an alien lawfully admitted for permanent residence, or an alien who is authorized under this chapter or by the Attorney General to be hired, recruited, or referred for such employment.

(3) **Retention of verification form**

After completion of such form in accordance with paragraphs (1) and (2), the person or entity must retain the form and make it available for inspection by officers of the Service, the Special Counsel for Immigration-Related Unfair Employment Practices, or the Department of Labor during a period beginning on the date of the hiring, recruiting, or referral of the individual and ending—

(A) in the case of the recruiting or referral for a fee (without hiring) of an individual, three years after the date of the recruiting or referral, and

(B) in the case of the hiring of an individual—

(i) three years after the date of such hiring, or

(ii) one year after the date the individual's employment is terminated, whichever is later.

(4) **Copying of documentation permitted**

Notwithstanding any other provision of law, the person or entity may copy a document presented by an individual pursuant to this subsection and may retain the copy, but only (except as otherwise permitted under law) for the purpose of complying with the requirements of this subsection.

(5) **Limitation on use of attestation form**

A form designated or established by the Attorney General under this subsection and any information contained in or appended to such form, may not be used for purposes other than for enforcement of this chapter and sections 1001, 1028, 1546, and 1621 of Title 18.

(vii) to order (in an appropriate case) the removal of a false performance review or false warning from an employee's personnel file, and

(viii) to order (in an appropriate case) the lifting of any restrictions on an employee's assignments, work shifts, or movements.

(C) **Limitation on back pay remedy**

In providing a remedy under subparagraph (B)(iii), back pay liability shall not accrue from a date more than two years prior to the date of the filing of a charge with the Special Counsel. Interim earnings or amounts earnable with reasonable diligence by the individual or individuals discriminated against shall operate to reduce the back pay otherwise allowable under such subparagraph. No order shall require the hiring of an individual as an employee or the payment to an individual of any back pay, if the individual was refused employment for any reason other than discrimination on account of national origin or citizenship status.

(D) **Treatment of distinct entities**

In applying this subsection in the case of a person or entity composed of distinct, physically separate subdivisions each of which provides separately for the hiring, recruiting, or referring for employment, without reference to the practices of, and not under the control of or common control with, another subdivision, each such subdivision shall be considered a separate person or entity.

(3) **Orders not finding violations**

If upon the preponderance of the evidence an administrative law judge determines that the person or entity named in the complaint has not engaged and is not engaging in any such unfair immigration-related employment practice, then the judge shall state his findings of fact and shall issue an order dismissing the complaint.

(h) **Awarding of attorney's fees**

In any complaint respecting an unfair immigration-related employment practice, an administrative law judge, in the judge's discretion, may allow a prevailing party, other than the United States, a reasonable attorney's fee, if the losing party's argument is without reasonable foundation in law and fact.

(i) **Review of final orders**

(1) **In general**

Not later than 60 days after the entry of such final order, any person aggrieved by such final order may seek a review of such order in the United States court of appeals for the circuit in which the violation is alleged to have occurred or in which the employer resides or transacts business.

(2) **Further review**

Upon the filing of the record with the court, the jurisdiction of the court shall be exclusive and its judgment shall be final, except that the same shall be subject to review by the Supreme Court of the United States upon writ of certiorari or certification as provided in section 1254 of Title 28.

(j) **Court enforcement of administrative orders**

(1) **In general**

If an order of the agency is not appealed under subsection (i)(1) of this section, the Special Counsel (or, if the Special Counsel fails to act, the person filing the charge) may petition the United States district court for the district in which a violation of the order is alleged to have occurred, or in which the respondent resides or transacts business, for the enforcement of the order of the administrative law judge, by filing in such court a written petition praying that such order be enforced.

(2) **Court enforcement order**

Upon the filing of such petition, the court shall have jurisdiction to make and enter a decree enforcing the order of the administrative law judge. In such a proceeding, the order of the administrative law judge shall not be subject to review.

(3) **Enforcement decree in original review**

If, upon appeal of an order under subsection (i)(1) of this section, the United States court of appeals does not reverse such order, such court shall have the jurisdiction to make and enter a decree enforcing the order of the administrative law judge.

(4) **Awarding of attorney's fees**

In any judicial proceeding under subsection (i) of this section or this subsection, the court, in its discretion, may allow a prevailing party, other than the United States, a reasonable attorney's fee as part of costs but only if the losing party's argument is without reasonable foundation in law and fact.

(k) **Termination dates**

(1) This section shall not apply to discrimination in hiring, recruiting, referring, or discharging of individuals occurring after the date of any termination of the provisions of section 1324a of this title, under subsection (*l*) of that section.

(2) The provisions of this section shall terminate 30 calendar days after receipt of the last report required to be transmitted under section 1324a(i) of this title if—

(A) the Comptroller General determines, and so reports in such report that-

(i) no significant discrimination has resulted, against citizens or nationals of the United States or against any eligible workers seeking employment, from the implementation of section 1324a of this title, or

(ii) such section has created an unreasonable burden on employers hiring such workers; and

(B) there has been enacted, within such period of 30 calendar days, a joint resolution stating in substance that the Congress approves the findings of the Comptroller General contained in such report.

The provisions of subsections (in) and (n) of section 1324a of this title shall apply to any joint resolution under subparagraph (B) in the same manner as they apply to a joint resolution under subsection (1) of such section.

(l) **Dissemination of information concerning anti-discrimination provisions**

(1) Not later than 3 months after the date of the enactment of this subsection, the Special Counsel, in cooperation with the chairman of the Equal Employment Opportunity Commission, the Secretary of Labor, and the Administrator of the Small Business Administration, shall conduct a campaign to disseminate information respecting the rights and remedies prescribed under this section and under title VII of the Civil Rights Act of 1964 in connection with unfair immigration-related employment practices. Such campaign shall be aimed at increasing the knowledge of employers, employees, and the general public concerning employer and employee rights, responsibilities, and remedies under this section and such title.

(2) In order to carry out the campaign under this subsection, the Special Counsel—

(A) may, to the extent deemed appropriate and subject to the availability of appropriations, contract with public and private organizations for outreach activities under the campaign, and

(B) shall consult with the Secretary of Labor, the chairman of the Equal Employment Opportunity Commission, and the heads of such other agencies as may be appropriate.

(3) There are authorized to be appropriated to carry out this subsection $10,000,000 for each fiscal year (beginning with fiscal year 1991).

Section 102(b) of P.L. No. 99-603:

(b) *No Effect on EEOC Authority*—Except as may be specifically provided in this section, nothing in this section shall be construed to restrict the authority of the Equal Employment Opportunity Commission to investigate allegations, in writing and under oath or affirmation, of unlawful employment practices, as provided in section 706 of the Civil Rights Act of 1964 (42 U.S.C. 2000e-5), or any other authority provided therein.

Americans with Disabilities Act of 1990, as Amended

P.L. 101-336, 104 Stat. 327, amended by P.L. 102-166 (1991), 105 Stat. 1017,
P.L. 104-1 (1995), 109 Stat. 8, 16, 41, P.L. 110-325 (2008), 122 Stat. 3553
[deletions shown by lines through struck provisions and 2008 amendments in bold]

Sec. 2 [42 U.S.C. § 12101] Findings and Purpose

(a) Findings

The Congress finds that

~~some 43,000,000 Americans have one or more physical or mental disabilities, and this number is increasing as the population as a whole is growing older;~~

(1) physical or mental disabilities in no way diminish a person's right to fully participate in all aspects of society, yet many people with physical or mental disabilities have been precluded from doing so because of discrimination; others who have a record of a disability or are regarded as having a disability also have been subjected to discrimination;

(2) historically, society has tended to isolate and segregate individuals with disabilities, and, despite some improvements, such forms of discrimination against individuals with disabilities continue to be a serious and pervasive social problem;

(3) discrimination against individuals with disabilities persists in such critical areas as employment, housing, public accommodations, education, transportation, communication, recreation, institutionalization, health services, voting, and access to public services;

(4) unlike individuals who have experienced discrimination on the basis of race, color, sex, national origin, religion, or age, individuals who have experienced discrimination on the basis of disability have often had no legal recourse to redress such discrimination;

(5) individuals with disabilities continually encounter various forms of discrimination, including outright intentional exclusion, the discriminatory effects of architectural, transportation, and communication barriers, overprotective rules and policies, failure to make modifications to existing facilities and practices, exclusionary qualification standards and criteria, segregation, and relegation to lesser services, programs, activities, benefits, jobs, or other opportunities;

(6) census data, national polls, and other studies have documented that people with disabilities, as a group, occupy an inferior status in our society, and are severely disadvantaged socially, vocationally, economically, and educationally;

~~(7) individuals with disabilities are a discrete and insular minority who have been faced with restrictions and limitations, subjected to a history of purposeful unequal treatment, and relegated to a position of political powerlessness in our society, based on characteristics that are beyond the control of such individuals and resulting from stereotypic assumptions not truly indicative of the individual ability of such individuals to participate in, and contribute to, society;~~

(~~8~~**7**) the Nation's proper goals regarding individuals with disabilities are to assure equality of opportunity, full participation, independent living, and economic self-sufficiency for such individuals; and

(~~9~~**8**) the continuing existence of unfair and unnecessary discrimination and prejudice denies people with disabilities the opportunity to compete on an equal basis and to pursue those opportunities for which our free society is justifiably famous, and costs the United States billions of dollars in unnecessary expenses resulting from dependency and nonproductivity.

(b) Purpose

It is the purpose of this Act—

(1) to provide a clear and comprehensive national mandate for the elimination of discrimination against individuals with disabilities;

(2) to provide clear, strong, consistent, enforceable standards addressing discrimination against individuals with disabilities;

(3) to ensure that the Federal Government plays a central role in enforcing the standards established in this chapter on behalf of individuals with disabilities; and

(4) to invoke the sweep of congressional authority, including the power to enforce the fourteenth amendment and to regulate commerce, in order to address the major areas of discrimination faced day-to-day by people with disabilities.

Sec. 12102 ~~Definitions~~ Definition of disability

As used in this Act:

~~(1) Auxiliary aids and services~~

The term "auxiliary aids and services" includes

~~(A) qualified interpreters or other effective methods of making aurally delivered materials available to individuals with hearing impairments;~~

(B) qualified readers, taped texts, or other effective methods of making visually delivered materials available to individuals with visual impairments;

(C) acquisition or modification of equipment or devices; and

(D) other similar services and actions.

(~~2~~ 1) Disability

The term "disability" means, with respect to an individual

(~~i~~A) a physical or mental impairment that substantially limits one or more major life activities of such individual;

(~~ii~~ B) a record of such an impairment; or

(~~iii~~ C) being regarded as having such an impairment (as described in paragraph (3)).

~~(3) State~~

The term "State" means each of the several States, the District of Columbia, the Commonwealth of Puerto Rico, Guam, American Samoa, the Virgin Islands, the Trust Territory of the Pacific Islands, and the Commonwealth of the Northern Mariana Islands.

(2) Major Life Activities

(A) In general

For purposes of paragraph (1), major life activities include, but are not limited to, caring for oneself, performing manual tasks, seeing, hearing, eating, sleeping, walking, standing, lifting, bending, speaking, breathing, learning, reading, concentrating, thinking, communicating, and working.

(B) Major bodily functions

For purposes of paragraph (1), a major life activity also includes the operation of a major bodily function, including but not limited to, functions of the immune system, normal cell growth, digestive, bowel, bladder, neurological, brain, respiratory, circulatory, endocrine, and reproductive functions.

(3) Regarded as having such an impairment

For purposes of paragraph (1)(C):

(A) An individual meets the requirement of "being regarded as having such an impairment" if the individual establishes that he or she has been subjected to an action prohibited under this chapter because of an actual or perceived physical or mental impairment whether or not the impairment limits or is perceived to limit a major life activity.

(B) Paragraph (1)(C) shall not apply to impairments that are transitory and minor. A transitory impairment is an impairment with an actual or expected duration of 6 months or less.

(4) Rules of construction regarding the definition of disability

The definition of "disability" in paragraph (1) shall be construed in accordance with the following:

(A) The definition of disability in this chapter shall be construed in favor of broad coverage of individuals under this chapter, to the maximum extent permitted by the terms of this chapter.

(B) The term "substantially limits" shall be interpreted consistently with the findings and purposes of the ADA Amendments Act of 2008.

(C) An impairment that substantially limits one major life activity need not limit other major life activities in order to be considered a disability.

(D) An impairment that is episodic or in remission is a disability if it would substantially limit a major life activity when active.

(E)(i) The determination of whether an impairment substantially limits a major life activity shall be made without regard to the ameliorative effects of mitigating measures such as

(I) medication, medical supplies, equipment, or appliances, low-vision devices (which do not include ordinary eyeglasses or contact lenses), prosthetics including limbs and devices, hearing aids and cochlear implants or other implantable hearing devices, mobility devices, or oxygen therapy equipment and supplies;

(II) use of assistive technology;

(III) reasonable accommodations or auxiliary aids or services; or

(IV) learned behavioral or adaptive neurological modifications.

(ii) The ameliorative effects of the mitigating measures of ordinary eyeglasses or contact lenses shall be considered in determining whether an impairment substantially limits a major life activity.

(iii) As used in this subparagraph

(I) the term "ordinary eyeglasses or contact lenses" means lenses that are intended to fully correct visual acuity or eliminate refractive error; and

(II) the term "low-vision devices" means devices that magnify, enhance, or otherwise augment a visual image.

Sec. 12103. Additional definitions

As used in this chapter

(1) Auxiliary aids and services

The term "auxiliary aids and services" includes

(A) qualified interpreters or other effective methods of making aurally delivered materials available to individuals with hearing impairments;

(B) qualified readers, taped texts, or other effective methods of making visually delivered materials available to individuals with visual impairments;

(C) acquisition or modification of equipment or devices; and

(D) other similar services and actions.

(2) State

The term "State" means each of the several States, the District of Columbia, the Commonwealth of Puerto Rico, Guam, American Samoa, the Virgin Islands of the United States, the Trust Territory of the Pacific Islands, and the Commonwealth of the Northern Mariana Islands.

SUBCHAPTER I—EMPLOYMENT

Sec. 101 [42 U.S.C. § 12111] Definitions

As used in this subchapter:

(1) Commission

The term "Commission" means the Equal Employment Opportunity Commission established by section 2000e-4 of this title.

(2) Covered entity

The term "covered entity" means an employer, employment agency, labor organization, or joint labor-management committee.

(3) Direct threat

The term "direct threat" means a significant risk to the health or safety of others that cannot be eliminated by reasonable accommodation.

(4) Employee

The term "employee" means an individual employed by an employer. With respect to employment in a foreign country, such term includes an individual who is a citizen of the United States.

(5) Employer

(A) In general

The term "employer" means a person engaged in an industry affecting commerce who has 15 or more employees for each working day in each of 20 or more calendar weeks in the current or preceding calendar year, and any agent of such person, except that, for two years following the effective date of this subchapter, an employer means a person engaged in an industry affecting commerce who has 25 or more employees for each working day in each of 20 or more calendar weeks in the current or preceding year, and any agent of such person.

(B) Exceptions

The term "employer" does not include

(i) the United States, a corporation wholly owned by the government of the United States, or an Indian tribe; or

(ii) a bona fide private membership club (other than a labor organization) that is exempt from taxation under section 501(c) of title 26.

(6) Illegal use of drugs

(A) In general

The term "illegal use of drugs" means the use of drugs, the possession or distribution of which is unlawful under the Controlled Substances Act [21 U.S.C. 801 et seq.]. Such term does not include the use of a drug taken under supervision by a licensed health care professional, or other uses authorized by the Controlled Substances Act or other provisions of Federal law.

(B) Drugs

The term "drug" means a controlled substance, as defined in schedules I through V of section 202 of the Controlled Substances Act [21 U.S.C. 812].

(7) Person, etc.

The terms "person", "labor organization", "employment agency", "commerce", and "industry affecting commerce", shall have the same meaning given such terms in section 2000e of this title.

(8) Qualified individual ~~with a disability~~

The term "qualified individual ~~with a disability~~" means an individual ~~with a disability~~ who, with or without reasonable accommodation, can perform the essential functions of the employment position that such individual holds or desires. For the purposes of this subchapter, consideration shall be given to the employer's judgment as to what functions of a job are essential, and if an employer has prepared a written description before advertising or interviewing applicants for the job, this description shall be considered evidence of the essential functions of the job.

(9) Reasonable accommodation

The term "reasonable accommodation" may include

(A) making existing facilities used by employees readily accessible to and usable by individuals with disabilities; and

(B) job restructuring, part-time or modified work schedules, reassignment to a vacant position, acquisition or modification of equipment or devices, appropriate adjustment or modifications of examinations, training materials or policies, the provision of qualified readers or interpreters, and other similar accommodations for individuals with disabilities.

(10) Undue hardship

(A) In general

The term "undue hardship" means an action requiring significant difficulty or expense, when considered in light of the factors set forth in subparagraph (B).

(B) Factors to be considered

In determining whether an accommodation would impose an undue hardship on a covered entity, factors to be considered include

(i) the nature and cost of the accommodation needed under this chapter;

(ii) the overall financial resources of the facility or facilities involved in the provision of the reasonable accommodation; the number of persons employed at such facility; the effect on expenses and resources, or the impact otherwise of such accommodation upon the operation of the facility;

(iii) the overall financial resources of the covered entity; the overall size of the business of a covered entity with respect to the number of its employees; the number, type, and location of its facilities; and

(iv) the type of operation or operations of the covered entity, including the composition, structure, and functions of the workforce of such entity; the geographic separateness, administrative, or fiscal relationship of the facility or facilities in question to the covered entity.

Sec. 102 [42 U.S.C. § 12112] Discrimination

(a) General rule

No covered entity shall discriminate against a qualified individual ~~with a disability because of the disability of such individual~~ **on the basis of disability** in regard to job application procedures, the hiring, advancement, or discharge of employees, employee compensation, job training, and other terms, conditions, and privileges of employment.

(b) Construction

As used in subsection (a) of this section, the term ~~"discriminate"~~ **"discriminate against a qualified individual on the basis of disability"** includes

(1) limiting, segregating, or classifying a job applicant or employee in a way that adversely affects the opportunities or status of such applicant or employee because of the disability of such applicant or employee;

(2) participating in a contractual or other arrangement or relationship that has the effect of subjecting a covered entity's qualified applicant or employee with a disability to the discrimination prohibited by this subchapter (such relationship includes a relationship with an employment or referral agency, labor union, an organization providing fringe benefits to an employee of the covered entity, or an organization providing training and apprenticeship programs);

(3) utilizing standards, criteria, or methods of administration

(A) that have the effect of discrimination on the basis of disability;

(B) that perpetuates the discrimination of others who are subject to common administrative control;

(4) excluding or otherwise denying equal jobs or benefits to a qualified individual because of the known disability of an individual with whom the qualified individual is known to have a relationship or association;

(5) (A) not making reasonable accommodations to the known physical or mental limitations of an otherwise qualified individual with a disability who is an applicant or employee, unless such covered entity can demonstrate that the accommodation would impose an undue hardship on the operation of the business of such covered entity; or

(B) denying employment opportunities to a job applicant or employee who is an otherwise qualified individual with a disability, if such denial is based on the need of such covered entity to make reasonable accommodation to the physical or mental impairments of the employee or applicant;

(6) using qualification standards, employment tests or other selection criteria that screen out or tend to screen out an individual with a disability or a class of individuals with disabilities unless the standard, test or other selection criteria, as used by the covered entity, is shown to be job-related for the position in question and is consistent with business necessity; and

(7) failing to select and administer tests concerning employment in the most effective manner to ensure that, when such test is administered to a job applicant or employee who has a disability that impairs sensory, manual, or speaking skills, such test results accurately reflect the skills, aptitude, or whatever other factor of such applicant or employee that such test purports to measure, rather than reflecting the impaired sensory, manual, or speaking skills of such employee or applicant (except where such skills are the factors that the test purports to measure).

(c) Covered entities in foreign countries

(1) In general

It shall not be unlawful under this section for a covered entity to take any action that constitute discrimination under this section with respect to an employee in a workplace in a foreign country if compliance with this section would cause such covered entity to violate the law of the foreign country in which such workplace is located.

(2) Control of corporation

(A) Presumption

If an employer controls a corporation whose place of incorporation is a foreign country, any practice that constitutes discrimination under this section and is engaged in by such corporation shall be presumed to be engaged in by such employer.

(B) Exception

This section shall not apply with respect to the foreign operations of an employer that is a foreign person not controlled by an American employer.

(C) Determination

For purposes of this paragraph, the determination of whether an employer controls a corporation shall be based on

(i) the interrelation of operations;

(ii) the common management;

(iii) the centralized control of labor relations; and

(iv) the common ownership or financial control of the employer and the corporation.

(d) Medical examinations and inquiries

(1) In general

The prohibition against discrimination as referred to in subsection (a) of this section shall include medical examinations and inquiries.

(2) Preemployment

(A) Prohibited examination or inquiry

Except as provided in paragraph (3), a covered entity shall not conduct a medical examination or make inquiries of a job applicant as to whether such applicant is an individual with a disability or as to the nature or severity of such disability.

(B) Acceptable inquiry

A covered entity may make preemployment inquiries into the ability of an applicant to perform job-related functions.

(3) Employment entrance examination

A covered entity may require a medical examination after an offer of employment has been made to a job applicant and prior to the commencement of the employment duties of such applicant, and may condition an offer of employment on the results of such examination, if

(A) all entering employees are subjected to such an examination regardless of disability;

(B) information obtained regarding the medical condition or history of the applicant is collected and maintained on separate forms and in separate medical files and is treated as a confidential medical record, except that

(i) supervisors and managers may be informed regarding necessary restrictions on the work or duties of the employee and necessary accommodations;

(ii) first aid and safety personnel may be informed, when appropriate, if the disability might require emergency treatment; and

(iii) government officials investigating compliance with this chapter shall be provided relevant information on request; and

(C) the results of such examination are used only in accordance with this subchapter.

(4) Examination and inquiry

(A) Prohibited examinations and inquiries

A covered entity shall not require a medical examination and shall not make inquiries of an employee as to whether such employee is an individual with a disability or as to the nature or severity of the disability, unless such examination or inquiry is shown to be job-related and consistent with business necessity.

(B) Acceptable examinations and inquiries

A covered entity may conduct voluntary medical examinations, including voluntary medical histories, which are part of an employee health program available to employees at that work site. A covered entity may make inquiries into the ability of an employee to perform job-related functions.

(C) Requirement

Information obtained under subparagraph (B) regarding the medical condition or history of any employee are subject to the requirements of subparagraphs (B) and (C) of paragraph (3).

Sec. 103 [42 U.S.C § 12113] Defenses

(a) In general

It may be a defense to a charge of discrimination under this chapter that an alleged application of qualification standards, tests, or selection criteria that screen out or tend to screen out or otherwise deny a job or benefit to an individual with a disability has been shown to be job- related and consistent with business necessity, and such performance cannot be accomplished by reasonable accommodation, as required under this subchapter.

(b) **Qualification standards**

The term "qualification standards" may include a requirement that an individual shall not pose a direct threat to the health or safety of other individuals in the workplace.

(c) **Qualification standards and tests related to uncorrected vision**

Notwithstanding section 12102(4)(E)(ii), a covered entity shall not use qualification standards, employment tests, or other selection criteria based on an individual's uncorrected vision unless the standard, test, or other selection criteria, as used by the covered entity, is shown to be job-related for the position in question and consistent with business necessity.

(~~c~~ **d**) Religious entities

(1) **In general**

This subchapter shall not prohibit a religious corporation, association, educational institution, or society from giving preference in employment to individuals of a particular religion to perform work connected with the carrying on by such corporation, association, educational institution, or society of its activities.

(2) **Religious tenets requirement**

Under this subchapter, a religious organization may require that all applicants and employees conform to the religious tenets of such organization.

(~~d~~**e**) **List of infectious and communicable diseases**

(1) **In general**

The Secretary of Health and Human Services, not later than 6 months after July 26, 1990, shall

(A) review all infectious and communicable diseases which may be transmitted through handling the food supply;

(B) publish a list of infectious and communicable diseases which are transmitted through handling the food supply;

(C) publish the methods by which such diseases are transmitted; and

(D) widely disseminate such information regarding the list of diseases and their modes of transmissibility to the general public.

Such list shall be updated annually.

(2) **Applications**

In any case in which an individual has an infectious or communicable disease that is transmitted to others through the handling of food, that is included on the list developed by the Secretary of Health and Human Services under paragraph (1), and which cannot be eliminated by reasonable accommodation, a covered entity may refuse to assign or continue to assign such individual to a job involving food handling.

(3) **Construction**

Nothing in this chapter shall be construed to preempt, modify, or amend any State, county, or local law, ordinance, or regulation applicable to food handling which is designed to protect the public health from individuals who pose a significant risk to the health or safety of others, which cannot be eliminated by reasonable accommodation, pursuant to the list of infectious or communicable diseases and the modes of transmissibility published by the Secretary of Health and Human Services.

Sec. 104 [42 U.S.C. § 12114] Illegal Use of Drugs and Alcohol

(a) **Qualified individual with a disability**

For purposes of this subchapter, ~~the term "qualified individual with a disability" shall a~~ **qualified individual with a disability shall** not include any employee or applicant who is currently engaging in the illegal use of drugs, when the covered entity acts on the basis of such use.

(b) **Rules of construction**

Nothing in subsection (a) of this section shall be construed to exclude as a qualified individual with a disability an individual who

(1) has successfully completed a supervised drug rehabilitation program and is no longer engaging in the illegal use of drugs, or has otherwise been rehabilitated successfully and is no longer engaging in such use;

(2) is participating in a supervised rehabilitation program and is no longer engaging in such use; or

(3) is erroneously regarded as engaging in such use, but is not engaging in such use;

except that it shall not be a violation of this chapter for a covered entity to adopt or administer reasonable policies or procedures, including but not limited to drug testing, designed to ensure that an individual described in paragraph (1) or (2) is no longer engaging in the illegal use of drugs.

(c) **Authority of covered entity**

A covered entity

(1) may prohibit the illegal use of drugs and the use of alcohol at the workplace by all employees;

(2) may require that employees shall not be under the influence of alcohol or be engaging in the illegal use of drugs at the workplace;

(3) may require that employees behave in conformance with the requirements established under the Drug-Free Workplace Act of 1988 (41 U.S.C. 701 et seq.);

(4) may hold an employee who engages in the illegal use of drugs or who is an alcoholic to the same qualification standards for employment or job performance and behavior that such entity holds other employees, even if any unsatisfactory performance or behavior is related to the drug use or alcoholism of such employee; and

(5) may, with respect to Federal regulations regarding alcohol and the illegal use of drugs, require that

(A) employees comply with the standards established in such regulations of the Department of Defense, if the employees of the covered entity are employed in an industry subject to such regulations, including complying with regulations (if any) that apply to employment in sensitive positions in such an industry, in the case of employees of the covered entity who are employed in such positions (as defined in the regulations of the Department of Defense);

(B) employees comply with the standards established in such regulations of the Nuclear Regulatory Commission, if the employees of the covered entity are employed in an industry subject to such regulations, including complying with regulations (if any) that apply to employment in sensitive positions in such an industry, in the case of employees of the covered entity who are employed in such positions (as defined in the regulations of the Nuclear Regulatory Commission); and

(C) employees comply with the standards established in such regulations of the Department of Transportation, if the employees of the covered entity are employed in a transportation industry subject to such regulations, including complying with such regulations (if any) that apply to employment in sensitive positions in such an industry, in the case of employees of the covered entity who are employed in such positions (as defined in the regulations of the Department of Transportation).

(d) Drug testing

(1) In general

For purposes of this subchapter, a test to determine the illegal use of drugs shall not be considered a medical examination.

(2) Construction

Nothing in this subchapter shall be construed to encourage, prohibit, or authorize the conducting of drug testing for the illegal use of drugs by job applicants or employees or making employment decisions based on such test results.

(e) Transportation employees

Nothing in this subchapter shall be construed to encourage, prohibit, restrict, or authorize the otherwise lawful exercise by entities subject to the jurisdiction of the Department of Transportation of authority to

(1) test employees of such entities in, and applicants for, positions involving safety-sensitive duties for the illegal use of drugs and for on-duty impairment by alcohol; and

(2) remove such persons who test positive for illegal use of drugs and on-duty impairment by alcohol pursuant to paragraph (1) from safety-sensitive duties in implementing subsection (c) of this section.

Sec. 105 [42 U.S.C. § 12115. Posting Notices

Every employer, employment agency, labor organization, or joint labor-management committee covered under this subchapter shall post notices in an accessible format to applicants, employees, and members describing the applicable provisions of this chapter, in the manner prescribed by section 2000e-10 of this title.

Sec. 106 [42 U.S.C. § 12116] Regulations

Not later than 1 year after July 26, 1990, the Commission shall issue regulations in an accessible format to carry out this subchapter in accordance with subchapter II of chapter 5 of title 5.

Sec. 107 [42 U.S.C. § 12117] Enforcement

(a) Powers, remedies, and procedures

The powers, remedies, and procedures set forth in sections 2000e-4, 2000e-5, 2000e-6, 2000e-8, and 2000e-9 of this title shall be the powers, remedies, and procedures this subchapter provides to the Commission, to the Attorney General, or to any person alleging discrimination on the basis of disability in violation of any provision of this chapter, or regulations promulgated under section 12116 of this title, concerning employment.

(b) **Coordination**

The agencies with enforcement authority for actions which allege employment discrimination under this subchapter and under the Rehabilitation Act of 1973 [29 U.S.C. 701 et seq.] shall develop procedures to ensure that administrative complaints filed under this subchapter and under the Rehabilitation Act of 1973 are dealt with in a manner that avoids duplication of effort and prevents imposition of inconsistent or conflicting standards for the same requirements under this subchapter and the Rehabilitation Act of 1973. The Commission, the Attorney General, and the Office of Federal Contract Compliance Programs shall establish such coordinating mechanisms (similar to provisions contained in the joint regulations promulgated by the Commission and the Attorney General at part 42 of title 28 and part 1691 of title 29, Code of Federal Regulations, and the Memorandum of Understanding between the Commission and the Office of Federal Contract Compliance Programs dated January 16, 1981 (46 Fed. Reg. 7435, January 23, 1981)) in regulations implementing this subchapter and Rehabilitation Act of 1973 not later than 18 months after July 26, 1990.

TITLE V—MISCELLANEOUS PROVISIONS

Sec. 501 [42 U.S.C. § 12201] Construction

(a) **In general**

Except as otherwise provided in this chapter, nothing in this chapter shall be construed to apply a lesser standard than the standards applied under title V of the Rehabilitation Act of 1973 (29 U.S.C. 790 et seq.) or the regulations issued by Federal agencies pursuant to such title.

(b) **Relationship to other laws**

Nothing in this chapter shall be construed to invalidate or limit the remedies, rights, and procedures of any Federal law or law of any State or political subdivision of any State or jurisdiction that provides greater or equal protection for the rights of individuals with disabilities than are afforded by this chapter. Nothing in this chapter shall be construed to preclude the prohibition of, or the imposition of restrictions on, smoking in places of employment covered by subchapter I of this chapter, in transportation covered by subchapter II or III of this chapter, or in places of public accommodation covered by subchapter III of this chapter.

(c) **Insurance**

Subchapters I through III of this chapter and title IV of this Act shall not be construed to prohibit or restrict

(1) an insurer, hospital or medical service company, health maintenance organization, or any agent, or entity that administers benefit plans, or similar organizations from underwriting risks, classifying risks, or administering such risks that are based on or not inconsistent with State law; or

(2) a person or organization covered by this chapter from establishing, sponsoring, observing or administering the terms of a bona fide benefit plan that are based on underwriting risks, classifying risks, or administering such risks that are based on or not inconsistent with State law; or

(3) a person or organization covered by this chapter from establishing, sponsoring, observing or administering the terms of a bona fide benefit plan that is not subject to State laws that regulate insurance.

Paragraphs (1), (2), and (3) shall not be used as a subterfuge to evade the purposes of subchapter I and III of this chapter.

(d) Accommodations and services

Nothing in this chapter shall be construed to require an individual with a disability to accept an accommodation, aid, service, opportunity, or benefit which such individual chooses not to accept.

(e) Benefits under State worker's compensation laws

Nothing in this chapter alters the standards for determining eligibility for benefits under State worker's compensation laws or under State and Federal disability benefit programs.

(f) Fundamental alteration

Nothing in this chapter alters the provision of section 12182(b)(2)(A)(ii), specifying that reasonable modifications in policies, practices, or procedures shall be required, unless an entity can demonstrate that making such modifications in policies, practices, or procedures, including academic requirements in postsecondary education, would fundamentally alter the nature of the goods, services, facilities, privileges, advantages, or accommodations involved.

(g) Claims of no disability

Nothing in this chapter shall provide the basis for a claim by an individual without a disability that the individual was subject to discrimination because of the individual's lack of disability.

(h) Reasonable accommodations and modifications

A covered entity under subchapter I, a public entity under subchapter II, and any person who owns, leases (or leases to), or operates a place of public accommodation under subchapter III, need not provide a reasonable accommodation or a reasonable modification to policies, practices, or procedures to an individual who meets the definition of disability in section 12102(1) solely under subparagraph (C) of such section.

Sec. 502 [42 U.S.C. § 12202] State Immunity

A State shall not be immune under the eleventh amendment to the Constitution of the United States from an action in Federal or State court of competent jurisdiction for a violation of this chapter. In any action against a State for a violation of the requirements of this chapter, remedies (including remedies both at law and in equity) are available for such a violation to the same extent as such remedies are available for such a violation in an action against any public or private entity other than a State.

Sec. 503 [42 U.S.C. § 12203] Prohibition Against Retaliation and Coercion

(a) Retaliation

No person shall discriminate against any individual because such individual has opposed any act or practice made unlawful by this chapter or because such individual made a charge, testified, assisted, or participated in any manner in an investigation, proceeding, or hearing under this chapter.

(b) Interference, coercion, or intimidation

It shall be unlawful to coerce, intimidate, threaten, or interfere with any individual in the exercise or enjoyment of, or on account of his or her having exercised or enjoyed, or on account of his or her having aided or encouraged any other individual in the exercise or enjoyment of, any right granted or protected by this chapter.

(c) Remedies and procedures

The remedies and procedures available under sections 12117, 12133, and 12188 of this title shall be available to aggrieved persons for violations of subsections (a) and (b) of this section, with respect to subchapter I, subchapter II and subchapter III of this chapter, respectively.

Sec. 505 [42 U.S.C. § 12205] Attorney's Fees

In any action or administrative proceeding commenced pursuant to this chapter, the court or agency, in its discretion, may allow the prevailing party, other than the United States, a reasonable attorney's fee, including litigation expenses, and costs, and the United States shall be liable for the foregoing the same as a private individual.

Sec. 12205a. Rule of Construction Regarding Regulatory Authority

The authority to issue regulations granted to the Equal Employment Opportunity Commission, the Attorney General, and the Secretary of Transportation under this chapter includes the authority to issue regulations implementing the definitions of disability in section 12102 (including rules of construction) and the definitions in section 12103, consistent with the ADA Amendments Act of 2008.

Sec. 508 [42 U.S.C. § 12208] Transvestites

For the purposes of this chapter, the term "disabled" or "disability" shall not apply to an individual solely because that individual is a transvestite.

Sec. 509 [42 U.S.C. § 12209] Instrumentalities of Congress

The General Accounting Office, the Government Printing Office, and the Library of Congress shall be covered as follows:

(1) In general

The rights and protections under this chapter shall, subject to paragraph (2), apply with respect to the conduct of each instrumentality of the Congress.

(2) Establishment of remedies and procedures by instrumentalities

The chief official of each instrumentality of the Congress shall establish remedies and procedures to be utilized with respect to the rights and protections provided pursuant to paragraph (1).

(3) Report to Congress

The chief official of each instrumentality of the Congress shall, after establishing remedies and procedures for purposes of paragraph (2), submit to the Congress a report describing the remedies and procedures.

(4) Definition of instrumentalities

For purposes of this section, the term "instrumentality of the Congress" means the following: the General Accounting Office, the Government Printing Office, and the Library of Congress.

(5) Enforcement of employment rights

The remedies and procedures set forth in section 2000e -16 of this title shall be available to any employee of an instrumentality of the Congress who alleges a violation of the rights and protections under sections 12112 through 12114 of this title that are made applicable by this section, except that the authorities of the Equal Employment Opportunity Commission shall be exercised by the chief official of the instrumentality of the Congress.

(6) Enforcement of rights to public services and accommodations

The remedies and procedures set forth in section 2000e -16 of this title shall be available to any qualified person with a disability who is a visitor, guest, or patron of an instrumentality of Congress and who alleges a violation of the rights and protections under sections 12131 through 12150 of this title or section 12182 or 12183 of this title that are made applicable by this section, except that the authorities of the Equal Employment Opportunity Commission shall be exercised by the chief official of the instrumentality of the Congress.

(7) Construction

Nothing in this section shall alter the enforcement procedures for individuals with disabilities provided in the General Accounting Office Personnel Act of 1980 and regulations promulgated pursuant to that Act.

Sec. 510 [42 U.S.C. § 12210] Illegal Use of Drugs

(a) In general

For purposes of this chapter, the term "individual with a disability" does not include an individual who is currently engaging in the illegal use of drugs, when the covered entity acts on the basis of such use.

(b) Rules of construction

Nothing in subsection (a) of this section shall be construed to exclude as an individual with a disability an individual who

(1) has successfully completed a supervised drug rehabilitation program and is no longer engaging in the illegal use of drugs, or has otherwise been rehabilitated successfully and is no longer engaging in such use;

(2) is participating in a supervised rehabilitation program and is no longer engaging in such use; or

(3) is erroneously regarded as engaging in such use, but is not engaging in such use;

except that it shall not be a violation of this chapter for a covered entity to adopt or administer reasonable policies or procedures, including but not limited to drug testing, designed to ensure that an individual described in paragraph (1) or (2) is no longer engaging in the illegal use of drugs; however, nothing in this section shall be construed to encourage, prohibit, restrict, or authorize the conducting of testing for the illegal use of drugs.

(c) Health and other services

Notwithstanding subsection (a) of this section and section 12211(b)(3) of this subchapter, an individual shall not be denied health services, or services provided in connection with drug rehabilitation, on the basis of the current illegal use of drugs if the individual is otherwise entitled to such services.

(d) "Illegal use of drugs" defined

(1) In general

The term "illegal use of drugs" means the use of drugs, the possession or distribution of which is unlawful under the Controlled Substances Act (21 U.S.C. 801 et seq.). Such term does not include the use of a drug taken under supervision by a licensed health care professional, or other uses authorized by the Controlled Substances Act or other provisions of Federal law.

(2) Drugs

The term "drug" means a controlled substance, as defined in schedules I through V of section 202 of the Controlled Substances Act (21 U.S.C. 812).

Sec. 511 [42 U.S.C. § 12211] Definitions

(a) Homosexuality and bisexuality

For purposes of the definition of "disability" in section 12102(2) of this title, homosexuality and bisexuality are not impairments and as such are not disabilities under this chapter.

(b) Certain conditions

Under this chapter, the term "disability" shall not include

(1) transvestism, transsexualism, pedophilia, exhibitionism, voyeurism, gender identity disorders not resulting from physical impairments, or other sexual behavior disorders;

(2) compulsive gambling, kleptomania, or pyromania; or

(3) psychoactive substance use disorders resulting from current illegal use of drugs.

Sec. 513 [42 U.S.C. § 12212] Alternative Means of Dispute Resolution

Where appropriate and to the extent authorized by law, the use of alternative means of dispute resolution, including settlement negotiations, conciliation, facilitation, mediation, fact-finding, minitrials, and arbitration, is encouraged to resolve disputes arising under this chapter.

Sec. 514 [42 U.S.C. § 12213] Severability

Should any provision in this chapter be found to be unconstitutional by a court of law, such provision shall be severed from the remainder of the chapter, and such action shall not affect the enforceability of the remaining provisions of the chapter.

ADA Amendments Act of 2008

Footnotes begin here: Pub. Law 110–325 (2008)

Sec 1. Short Title.

This Act may be cited as the "ADA Amendments Act of 2008".

SEC. 2. FINDINGS AND PURPOSES.

(a) **Findings.**

Congress finds that—

(1) in enacting the Americans with Disabilities Act of 1990 (ADA), Congress intended that the Act "provide a clear and comprehensive national mandate for the elimination of discrimination against individuals with disabilities" and provide broad coverage;

(2) in enacting the ADA, Congress recognized that physical and mental disabilities in no way diminish a person's right to fully participate in all aspects of society, but that people with physical or mental disabilities are frequently precluded from doing so because of prejudice, antiquated attitudes, or the failure to remove societal and institutional barriers;

(3) while Congress expected that the definition of disability under the ADA would be interpreted consistently with how courts had applied the definition of a handicapped individual under the Rehabilitation Act of 1973, that expectation has not been fulfilled;

(4) the holdings of the Supreme Court in Sutton v. United Air Lines, Inc., 527 U.S. 471 (1999) and its companion cases have narrowed the broad scope of protection intended to be afforded by the ADA, thus eliminating protection for many individuals whom Congress intended to protect;

(5) the holding of the Supreme Court in Toyota Motor Manufacturing, Kentucky, Inc. v. Williams, 534 U.S. 184 (2002) further narrowed the broad scope of protection intended to be afforded by the ADA;

(6) as a result of these Supreme Court cases, lower courts have incorrectly found in individual cases that people with a range of substantially limiting impairments are not people with disabilities;

(7) in particular, the Supreme Court, in the case of Toyota Motor Manufacturing, Kentucky, Inc. v. Williams, 534 U.S. 184 (2002), interpreted the term "substantially limits" to require a greater degree of limitation than was intended by Congress; and

(8) Congress finds that the current Equal Employment Opportunity Commission ADA regulations defining the term "substantially limits" as "significantly restricted" are inconsistent with congressional intent, by expressing too high a standard.

(b) **Purposes.**

The purposes of this Act are—

(1) to carry out the ADA's objectives of providing "a clear and comprehensive national mandate for the elimination of discrimination" and "clear, strong, consistent, enforceable standards addressing discrimination" by reinstating a broad scope of protection to be available under the ADA;

(2) to reject the requirement enunciated by the Supreme Court in Sutton v. United Air Lines, Inc., 527 U.S. 471 (1999) and its companion cases that whether an impairment substantially limits a major life activity is to be determined with reference to the ameliorative effects of mitigating measures;

(3) to reject the Supreme Court's reasoning in Sutton v. United Air Lines, Inc., 527 U.S. 471 (1999) with regard to coverage under the third prong of the definition of disability and to reinstate the reasoning of the Supreme Court in School Board of Nassau County v. Arline, 480 U.S. 273 (1987) which set forth a broad view of the third prong of the definition of handicap under the Rehabilitation Act of 1973;

(4) to reject the standards enunciated by the Supreme Court in Toyota Motor Manufacturing, Kentucky, Inc. v. Williams, 534 U.S. 184 (2002), that the terms "substantially" and "major" in the definition of disability under the ADA "need to be interpreted strictly to create a demanding standard for qualifying as disabled," and that to be substantially limited in performing a major life activity under the ADA "an individual must have an impairment that prevents or severely restricts the individual from doing activities that are of central importance to most people's daily lives";

(5) to convey congressional intent that the standard created by the Supreme Court in the case of Toyota Motor Manufacturing, Kentucky, Inc. v. Williams, 534 U.S. 184 (2002) for "substantially limits", and applied by lower courts in numerous decisions, has created an inappropriately high level of limitation necessary to obtain coverage under the ADA, to convey that it is the intent of Congress that the primary object of attention in cases brought under the ADA should be whether entities covered under the ADA have complied with their obligations, and to convey that the question of whether an individual's impairment is a disability under the ADA should not demand extensive analysis; and

(6) to express Congress' expectation that the Equal Employment Opportunity Commission will revise that portion of its current regulations that defines the term "substantially limits" as "significantly restricted" to be consistent with this Act, including the amendments made by this Act.

* * *

Sec. 8. Effective Date

This Act and the amendments made by this Act shall become effective on January 1, 2009.

Genetic Information Nondiscrimination Act of 2008

42 U.S.C. §§ 2000ff Note; Pub. L. No. 110-233, 122 Stat. 881 (2008)

Sec. 2 [42 U.S.C. § 2000ff Note] Findings

Congress makes the following findings:

(1) Deciphering the sequence of the human genome and other advances in genetics open major new opportunities for medical progress. New knowledge about the genetic basis of illness will allow for earlier detection of illnesses, often before symptoms have begun. Genetic testing can allow individuals to take steps to reduce the likelihood that they will contract a particular disorder. New knowledge about genetics may allow for the development of better therapies that are more effective against disease or have fewer side effects than current treatments. These advances give rise to the potential misuse of genetic information to discriminate in health insurance and employment.

(2) The early science of genetics became the basis of State laws that provided for the sterilization of persons having presumed genetic "defects" such as intellectual disabilities, mental disease, epilepsy, blindness, and hearing loss, among other conditions. The first sterilization law was enacted in the State of Indiana in 1907. By 1981, a majority of States adopted sterilization laws to "correct" apparent genetic traits or tendencies. Many of these State laws have since been repealed, and many have been modified to include essential constitutional requirements of due process and equal protection. However, the current explosion in the science of genetics, and the history of sterilization laws by the States based on early genetic science, compels Congressional action in this area.

(3) Although genes are facially neutral markers, many genetic conditions and disorders are associated with particular racial and ethnic groups and gender. Because some genetic traits are most prevalent in particular groups, members of a particular group may be stigmatized or discriminated against as a result of that genetic information. This form of discrimination was evident in the 1970s, which saw the advent of programs to screen and identify carriers of sickle cell anemia, a disease which afflicts African-Americans. Once again, State legislatures began to enact discriminatory laws in the area, and in the early 1970s began mandating genetic screening of all African Americans for sickle cell anemia, leading to discrimination and unnecessary fear. To alleviate some of this stigma, Congress in 1972 passed the National Sickle Cell Anemia Control Act, which withholds Federal funding from States unless sickle cell testing is voluntary.

(4) Congress has been informed of examples of genetic discrimination in the workplace. These include the use of pre-employment genetic screening at Lawrence Berkeley Laboratory, which led to a court decision in favor of the employees in that case *Norman-Bloodsaw v. Lawrence Berkeley Laboratory (135 F.3d 1260, 1269* (9th Cir. 1998)). Congress clearly has a compelling public interest in relieving the fear of discrimination and in prohibiting its actual practice in employment and health insurance.

(5) Federal law addressing genetic discrimination in health insurance and employment is incomplete in both the scope and depth of its protections. Moreover, while many States have enacted some type of genetic non-discrimination law, these laws vary widely with respect to their approach, application, and level of protection. Congress has collected substantial evidence that the American public and the medical community find the existing patchwork of State and Federal laws to be confusing and inadequate to protect them from discrimination. Therefore Federal legislation establishing a national and uniform basic standard is necessary to fully protect the public from discrimination and allay their

concerns about the potential for discrimination, thereby allowing individuals to take advantage of genetic testing, technologies, research, and new therapies.

Title II—Prohibiting Employment Discrimination on the Basis of Genetic Information

Sec. 201 [42 U.S.C. § 2000ff] Definitions

In this Chapter:

(1) Commission. The term "Commission" means the Equal Employment Opportunity Commission as created by section 705 of the Civil Rights Act of 1964 (42 U.S.C. 2000e-4).

(2) Employee; employer; employment agency; labor organization; member.

(A) In general. The term "employee" means—

(i) an employee (including an applicant), as defined in section 701(f) of the Civil Rights Act of 1964 (42 U.S.C. 2000e(f));

(ii) a State employee (including an applicant) described in section 304(a) of the Government Employee Rights Act of 1991 (42 U.S.C. 2000e-16c(a));

(iii) a covered employee (including an applicant), as defined in section 101 of the Congressional Accountability Act of 1995 (2 U.S.C. 1301);

(iv) a covered employee (including an applicant), as defined in *section* 411(c) of title 3, United States Code; or

(v) an employee or applicant to which section 717(a) of the Civil Rights Act of 1964 (42 U.S.C. 2000e-16(a)) applies.

(B) Employer. The term "employer" means—

(i) an employer (as defined in section 701(b) of the Civil Rights Act of 1964 (42 U.S.C. 2000e(b)));

(ii) an entity employing a State employee described in section 304(a) of the Government Employee Rights Act of 1991 [42 USCS § 2000e-16c(a)];

(iii) an employing office, as defined in section 101 of the Congressional Accountability Act of 1995 [2 USCS § 1301];

(iv) an employing office, as defined in section 411(c) of title 3, United States Code; or

(v) an entity to which section 717(a) of the Civil Rights Act of 1964 [42 USCS § 2000e-16(a)] applies.

(C) Employment agency; labor organization. The terms "employment agency" and "labor organization" have the meanings given the terms in section 701 of the Civil Rights Act of 1964 (42 U.S.C. 2000e).

(D) Member. The term "member", with respect to a labor organization, includes an applicant for membership in a labor organization.

(3) Family member. The term "family member" means, with respect to an individual—

(A) a dependent (as such term is used for purposes of section 701(f)(2) of the Employee Retirement Income Security Act of 1974 [29 USCS § 1181(f)(2)]) of such individual, and

(B) any other individual who is a first-degree, second-degree, third-degree, or fourth-degree relative of such individual or of an individual described in subparagraph (A).

(4) Genetic information.

(A) In general. The term "genetic information" means, with respect to any individual, information about—

(i) such individual's genetic tests,

(ii) the genetic tests of family members of such individual, and

(iii) the manifestation of a disease or disorder in family members of such individual.

(B) Inclusion of genetic services and participation in genetic research. Such term includes, with respect to any individual, any request for, or receipt of, genetic services, or participation in clinical research which includes genetic services, by such individual or any family member of such individual.

(C) Exclusions. The term "genetic information" shall not include information about the sex or age of any individual.

(5) Genetic monitoring. The term "genetic monitoring" means the periodic examination of employees to evaluate acquired modifications to their genetic material, such as chromosomal damage or evidence of increased occurrence of mutations, that may have developed in the course of employment due to exposure to toxic substances in the workplace, in order to identify, evaluate, and respond to the effects of or control adverse environmental exposures in the workplace.

(6) Genetic services. The term "genetic services" means—

(A) a genetic test;

(B) genetic counseling (including obtaining, interpreting, or assessing genetic information); or

(C) genetic education.

(7) Genetic test.

(A) In general. The term "genetic test" means an analysis of human DNA, RNA, chromosomes, proteins, or metabolites, that detects genotypes, mutations, or chromosomal changes.

(B) Exceptions. The term "genetic test" does not mean an analysis of proteins or metabolites that does not detect genotypes, mutations, or chromosomal changes.

Sec. 2 [42 U.S.C. § 2000ff-1] Employer Practices

(a) Discrimination based on genetic information. It shall be an unlawful employment practice for an employer—

(1) to fail or refuse to hire, or to discharge, any employee, or otherwise to discriminate against any employee with respect to the compensation, terms, conditions, or privileges of employment of the employee, because of genetic information with respect to the employee; or

(2) to limit, segregate, or classify the employees of the employer in any way that would deprive or tend to deprive any employee of employment opportunities or otherwise adversely affect the status of the employee as an employee, because of genetic information with respect to the employee.

(b) Acquisition of genetic information. It shall be an unlawful employment practice for an employer to request, require, or purchase genetic information with respect to an employee or a family member of the employee except—

(1) where an employer inadvertently requests or requires family medical history of the employee or family member of the employee;

(2) where—

(A) health or genetic services are offered by the employer, including such services offered as part of a wellness program;

(B) the employee provides prior, knowing, voluntary, and written authorization;

(C) only the employee (or family member if the family member is receiving genetic services) and the licensed health care professional or board certified genetic counselor involved in providing such services receive individually identifiable information concerning the results of such services; and

(D) any individually identifiable genetic information provided under subparagraph (C) in connection with the services provided under subparagraph (A) is only available for purposes of such services and shall not be disclosed to the employer except in aggregate terms that do not disclose the identity of specific employees;

(3) where an employer requests or requires family medical history from the employee to comply with the certification provisions of section 103 of the Family and Medical Leave Act of 1993 (29 U.S.C. 2613) or such requirements under State family and medical leave laws;

(4) where an employer purchases documents that are commercially and publicly available (including newspapers, magazines, periodicals, and books, but not including medical databases or court records) that include family medical history;

(5) where the information involved is to be used for genetic monitoring of the biological effects of toxic substances in the workplace, but only if—

(A) the employer provides written notice of the genetic monitoring to the employee;

(B) (i) the employee provides prior, knowing, voluntary, and written authorization; or

(ii) the genetic monitoring is required by Federal or State law;

(C) the employee is informed of individual monitoring results;

(D) the monitoring is in compliance with—

(i) any Federal genetic monitoring regulations, including any such regulations that may be promulgated by the Secretary of Labor pursuant to the Occupational Safety and Health Act of 1970 (29 U.S.C. 651 et seq.), the Federal Mine Safety and Health Act of 1977 (30 U.S.C. 801 et seq.), or the Atomic Energy Act of 1954 (42 U.S.C. 2011 et seq.); or

(ii) State genetic monitoring regulations, in the case of a State that is implementing genetic monitoring regulations under the authority of the Occupational Safety and Health Act of 1970 (29 U.S.C. 651 et seq.); and

(E) the employer, excluding any licensed health care professional or board certified genetic counselor that is involved in the genetic monitoring program, receives the results of the monitoring only in aggregate terms that do not disclose the identity of specific employees; or

(6) where the employer conducts DNA analysis for law enforcement purposes as a forensic laboratory or for purposes of human remains identification, and requests or requires genetic information of such employer's employees, but only to the extent that such genetic information is used for analysis of DNA identification markers for quality control to detect sample contamination.

(c) **Preservation of protections.** In the case of information to which any of paragraphs (1) through (6) of subsection (b) applies, such information may not be used in violation of paragraph (1) or (2) of subsection (a) or treated or disclosed in a manner that violates section 206 [42 USCS § 2000ff-5].

Sec. 3 [2000ff-2] Employment Agency Practices

(a) **Discrimination based on genetic information.** It shall be an unlawful employment practice for an employment agency—

(1) to fail or refuse to refer for employment, or otherwise to discriminate against, any individual because of genetic information with respect to the individual;

(2) to limit, segregate, or classify individuals or fail or refuse to refer for employment any individual in any way that would deprive or tend to deprive any individual of employment opportunities, or otherwise adversely affect the status of the individual as an employee, because of genetic information with respect to the individual; or

(3) to cause or attempt to cause an employer to discriminate against an individual in violation of this title [42 USCS §§ 2000ff et seq.].

(b) **Acquisition of genetic information.** It shall be an unlawful employment practice for an employment agency to request, require, or purchase genetic information with respect to an individual or a family member of the individual except—

(1) where an employment agency inadvertently requests or requires family medical history of the individual or family member of the individual;

(2) where—

(A) health or genetic services are offered by the employment agency, including such services offered as part of a wellness program;

(B) the individual provides prior, knowing, voluntary, and written authorization;

(C) only the individual (or family member if the family member is receiving genetic services) and the licensed health care professional or board certified genetic counselor involved in providing such services receive individually identifiable information concerning the results of such services; and

(D) any individually identifiable genetic information provided under subparagraph (C) in connection with the services provided under subparagraph (A) is only available for purposes of such services and shall not be disclosed to the employment agency except in aggregate terms that do not disclose the identity of specific individuals;

(3) where an employment agency requests or requires family medical history from the individual to comply with the certification provisions of section 103 of the Family and Medical Leave Act of 1993 (29 U.S.C. 2613) or such requirements under State family and medical leave laws;

(4) where an employment agency purchases documents that are commercially and publicly available (including newspapers, magazines, periodicals, and books, but not including medical databases or court records) that include family medical history; or

(5) where the information involved is to be used for genetic monitoring of the biological effects of toxic substances in the workplace, but only if—

(A) the employment agency provides written notice of the genetic monitoring to the individual;

(B) (i) the individual provides prior, knowing, voluntary, and written authorization; or

(ii) the genetic monitoring is required by Federal or State law;

(C) the individual is informed of individual monitoring results;

(D) the monitoring is in compliance with—

(i) any Federal genetic monitoring regulations, including any such regulations that may be promulgated by the Secretary of Labor pursuant to the Occupational Safety and Health Act of 1970 (29 U.S.C. 651 et seq.), the Federal Mine Safety and Health Act of 1977 (30 U.S.C. 801 et seq.), or the Atomic Energy Act of 1954 (42 U.S.C. 2011 et seq.); or

(ii) State genetic monitoring regulations, in the case of a State that is implementing genetic monitoring regulations under the authority of the Occupational Safety and Health Act of 1970 (29 U.S.C. 651 et seq.); and

(E) the employment agency, excluding any licensed health care professional or board certified genetic counselor that is involved in the genetic monitoring program, receives the results of the monitoring only in aggregate terms that do not disclose the identity of specific individuals.

(c) **Preservation of protections.** In the case of information to which any of paragraphs (1) through (5) of subsection (b) applies, such information may not be used in violation of paragraph (1), (2), or (3) of subsection (a) or treated or disclosed in a manner that violates section 206 [42 USCS § 2000ff-5].

Section 4 [§ 2000ff-3] Labor Organization Practices

(a) **Discrimination based on genetic information.** It shall be an unlawful employment practice for a labor organization—

(1) to exclude or to expel from the membership of the organization, or otherwise to discriminate against, any member because of genetic information with respect to the member;

(2) to limit, segregate, or classify the members of the organization, or fail or refuse to refer for employment any member, in any way that would deprive or tend to deprive any member of employment opportunities, or otherwise adversely affect the status of the member as an employee, because of genetic information with respect to the member; or

(3) to cause or attempt to cause an employer to discriminate against a member in violation of this title [42 USCS §§ 2000ff et seq.].

(b) **Acquisition of genetic information.** It shall be an unlawful employment practice for a labor organization to request, require, or purchase genetic information with respect to a member or a family member of the member except—

(1) where a labor organization inadvertently requests or requires family medical history of the member or family member of the member;

(2) where—

(A) health or genetic services are offered by the labor organization, including such services offered as part of a wellness program;

(B) the member provides prior, knowing, voluntary, and written authorization;

(C) only the member (or family member if the family member is receiving genetic services) and the licensed health care professional or board certified genetic counselor involved in providing such services receive individually identifiable information concerning the results of such services; and

(D) any individually identifiable genetic information provided under subparagraph (C) in connection with the services provided under subparagraph (A) is only available for purposes of such services and shall not be disclosed to the labor organization except in aggregate terms that do not disclose the identity of specific members;

(3) where a labor organization requests or requires family medical history from the members to comply with the certification provisions of section 103 of the Family and Medical Leave Act of 1993 (29 U.S.C. 2613) or such requirements under State family and medical leave laws;

(4) where a labor organization purchases documents that are commercially and publicly available (including newspapers, magazines, periodicals, and books, but not including medical databases or court records) that include family medical history; or

(5) where the information involved is to be used for genetic monitoring of the biological effects of toxic substances in the workplace, but only if—

(A) the labor organization provides written notice of the genetic monitoring to the member;

(B) (i) the member provides prior, knowing, voluntary, and written authorization; or

(ii) the genetic monitoring is required by Federal or State law;

(C) the member is informed of individual monitoring results;

(D) the monitoring is in compliance with—

(i) any Federal genetic monitoring regulations, including any such regulations that may be promulgated by the Secretary of Labor pursuant to the Occupational Safety and Health Act of 1970 (29 U.S.C. 651 et seq.), the Federal Mine Safety and Health Act of 1977 (30 U.S.C. 801 et seq.), or the Atomic Energy Act of 1954 (42 U.S.C. 2011 et seq.); or

(ii) State genetic monitoring regulations, in the case of a State that is implementing genetic monitoring regulations under the authority of the Occupational Safety and Health Act of 1970 (29 U.S.C. 651 et seq.); and

(E) the labor organization, excluding any licensed health care professional or board certified genetic counselor that is involved in the genetic monitoring program, receives the results of the monitoring only in aggregate terms that do not disclose the identity of specific members.

(c) **Preservation of protections.** In the case of information to which any of paragraphs (1) through (5) of subsection (b) applies, such information may not be used in violation of paragraph (1), (2), or (3) of subsection (a) or treated or disclosed in a manner that violates section 206 [42 USCS § 2000ff-5].

* * *

Sec. 206 [§ 2000ff-5] Confidentiality of Genetic Information

(a) **Treatment of information as part of confidential medical record.** If an employer, employment agency, labor organization, or joint labor-management committee possesses genetic information about an employee or member, such information shall be maintained on separate forms and in separate medical files and be treated as a confidential medical record of the employee or member. An employer, employment agency, labor organization, or joint labor-management committee shall be considered to be in compliance with the maintenance of information requirements of this subsection with respect to genetic information subject to this subsection that is maintained with and treated as a confidential medical record under section 102(d)(3)(B) of the Americans With Disabilities Act (42 U.S.C. 12112(d)(3)(B)).

(b) Limitation on disclosure. An employer, employment agency, labor organization, or joint labor-management committee shall not disclose genetic information concerning an employee or member except—

(1) to the employee or member of a labor organization (or family member if the family member is receiving the genetic services) at the written request of the employee or member of such organization;

(2) to an occupational or other health researcher if the research is conducted in compliance with the regulations and protections provided for under part 46 of title 45, Code of Federal Regulations;

(3) in response to an order of a court, except that—

(A) the employer, employment agency, labor organization, or joint labor-management committee may disclose only the genetic information expressly authorized by such order; and

(B) if the court order was secured without the knowledge of the employee or member to whom the information refers, the employer, employment agency, labor organization, or joint labor-management committee shall inform the employee or member of the court order and any genetic information that was disclosed pursuant to such order;

(4) to government officials who are investigating compliance with this *title* [42 USCS §§ 2000ff et seq.] if the information is relevant to the investigation;

(5) to the extent that such disclosure is made in connection with the employee's compliance with the certification provisions of section 103 of the Family and Medical Leave Act of 1993 (29 U.S.C. 2613) or such requirements under State family and medical leave laws; or

(6) to a Federal, State, or local public health agency only with regard to information that is described in section 201(4)(A)(iii) [42 USCS § 2000ff(4)(A)(iii)] and that concerns a contagious disease that presents an imminent hazard of death or life-threatening illness, and that the employee whose family member or family members is or are the subject of a disclosure under this paragraph is notified of such disclosure.

* * *

Sec. 7 [§ 2000ff-6] Remedies and Enforcement

(a) Employees covered by title VII of the Civil Rights Act of 1964.

(1) In general. The powers, procedures, and remedies provided in sections 705, 706, 707, 709, 710, and 711 of the Civil Rights Act of 1964 (42 U.S.C. 2000e-4 et seq.) to the Commission, the Attorney General, or any person, alleging a violation of title VII of that Act (42 U.S.C. 2000e et seq.) shall be the powers, procedures, and remedies this title [42 USCS §§ 2000ff et seq.] provides to the Commission, the Attorney General, or any person, respectively, alleging an unlawful employment practice in violation of this title [42 USCS §§ 2000ff et seq.] against an employee described in section 201(2)(A)(i) [42 USCS § 2000ff(2)(A)(i)], except as provided in paragraphs (2) and (3).

(2) Costs and fees. The powers, remedies, and procedures provided in subsections (b) and (c) of section 722 of the Revised Statutes of the United States (42 U.S.C. 1988),

shall be powers, remedies, and procedures this title [42 USCS §§ 2000ff et seq.] provides to the Commission, the Attorney General, or any person, alleging such a practice.

(3) Damages. The powers, remedies, and procedures provided in section 1977A of the Revised Statutes of the United States (42 U.S.C. 1981a), including the limitations contained in subsection (b)(3) of such section 1977A, shall be powers, remedies, and procedures this title [42 USCS §§ 2000ff et seq.] provides to the Commission, the Attorney General, or any person, alleging such a practice (not an employment practice specifically excluded from coverage under section 1977A(a)(1) of the Revised Statutes of the United States).

* * *

Sec. 8 [§ 2000ff-7] Disparate Impact

(a) **General rule.** Notwithstanding any other provision of this Act, "disparate impact", as that term is used in section 703(k) of the Civil Rights Act of 1964 (42 U.S.C. 2000e-2(k)), on the basis of genetic information does not establish a cause of action under this Act.

* * *

Sec. 10 [§ 2000ff-9] Medical Information That Is Not Genetic Information

An employer, employment agency, labor organization, or joint labor-management committee shall not be considered to be in violation of this *title [42 USCS §§ 2000ff* et seq.] based on the use, acquisition, or disclosure of medical information that is not genetic information about a manifested disease, disorder, or pathological condition of an employee or member, including a manifested disease, disorder, or pathological condition that has or may have a genetic basis.